CW00684083

MATTHEW

BELIEF

A Theological Commentary
on the Bible

GENERAL EDITORS

Amy Plantinga Pauw
William C. Placher[†]

MATTHEW

ANNA CASE-WINTERS

WESTMINSTER
JOHN KNOX PRESS
LOUISVILLE • KENTUCKY

© 2015 Anna Case-Winters

2015 paperback edition
Originally published in hardback in the United States
by Westminster John Knox Press in 2015
Louisville, Kentucky

15 16 17 18 19 20 21 22 23 24—10 9 8 7 6 5 4 3 2 1

All rights reserved. No part of this book may be reproduced or transmitted in any form
or by any means, electronic or mechanical, including photocopying, recording,
or by any information storage or retrieval system, without permission in writing
from the publisher. For information, address Westminster John Knox Press,
100 Witherspoon Street, Louisville, Kentucky 40202-1396.
Or contact us online at www.wjkbooks.com.

Scripture quotations are from the New Revised Standard Version of the Bible are
copyright © 1989 by the Division of Christian Education of the National Council
of the Churches of Christ in the U.S.A. and are used by permission.

Scripture quotations marked NIV are from *The Holy Bible, New International Version.* Copyright
© 1973, 1978, 1984, 2011 by Biblica, Inc.® Used by permission. All rights reserved worldwide.

Scripture quotations marked RSV are from the Revised Standard Version of the Bible, copyright
© 1946, 1952, 1971, and 1973 by the Division of Christian Education of the National Council of the
Churches of Christ in the U.S.A., and are used by permission.

Book design by Drew Stevens
Cover design by Lisa Buckley
Cover illustration: © David Chapman/Design Pics/Corbis

Library of Congress Cataloging-in-Publication Data

Case-Winters, Anna, 1953-
Matthew / Anna Case-Winters. -- First edition.
pages cm. -- (Belief: a theological commentary on the Bible)
Includes bibliographical references and index.
ISBN 978-0-664-23267-2 (hbk. : alk. paper) -- ISBN 978-0-664-26113-9 (pbk. : alk. paper) 1.
Bible. Matthew--Commentaries. I. Title.
BS2575.53.C37 2014
226.2'07--dc23

2014029790

♾ The paper used in this publication meets the minimum requirements
of the American National Standard for Information Sciences—
Permanence of Paper for Printed Library Materials, ANSI Z39.48-1992.

Contents

Publisher's Note   vii

Series Introduction by William C. Placher
and Amy Plantinga Pauw   ix

Preface   xiii

Acknowledgments   xv

Abbreviations   xvii

Introduction: Why Matthew? Why Now?   1

COMMENTARY

PART 1: THE BIRTH OF THE MESSIAH   **21**

1:1–2:23   *Jesus the Messiah, King of the Jews*   23
Further Reflections: "God Is with Us"   32
Further Reflections: Slaughter of the Innocents   38

PART 2: THE LIFE AND MINISTRY OF JESUS   **41**

3:1–4:25   *Narrative: Called and Calling*   43
Further Reflections: Baptism as Calling to Ministry   59
Further Reflections: Encounter with Evil   66

5:1–7:29   *Teaching: The Sermon on the Mount*   70
Further Reflections: Blessed Are the
   Peacemakers/Love Your Enemies   99
Further Reflections: Why Do We Pray?   101
Further Reflections: How Shall We Pray? Ethical
   Implications of the Lord's Prayer   106

8:1–9:38   *Narrative: "As One Having Authority"*   122
Further Reflections: Miracle Stories in
    an Age of Science   138

10:1–11:1   *Teaching: In Mission Together*   146
Further Reflections: The Church in the World Today
156

11:2–12:50   *Narrative: Facing Opposition*   164
Further Reflections: The Threefold Work of
    Prophet, Priest, and King   172

13:1–5   *Teaching: Parables of God's Reign*   175
Further Reflections: Jesus and the Reign of God   186

14:1–17:27   *Narrative: Preparing the Disciples for Ministry* 188

18:1–35   *Teaching: The New Community*   219
Further Reflection: On Being the Church   229

19:1–22:46   *Narrative: On the Way to Jerusalem Where
    the Conflict Intensifies*   236

23:1 –25:46   *Teaching: The Coming Judgment*   261
Further Reflections: Jesus and Judgment   281

PART 3: THE CROSS OF CHRIST   **287**

26:1–27:31   *On the Way to the Cross*   289

27:32–61   *The Crucified Savior*   308
Further Reflections: The Lord's Supper   314
Further Reflections: On the Meaning of the Cross   322

PART 4: THE RESURRECTION OF THE LORD   **333**

27:62–28:10   *At the Tomb*   335

28:11–20   *The Risen Lord*   337
Further Reflections: On the Meaning of
    the Resurrection   340

Final Thoughts   349

For Further Reading   355

Index of Ancient Sources   365

Index of Subjects   375

Publisher's Note

William C. Placher worked with Amy Plantinga Pauw as a general editor for this series until his untimely death in November 2008. Bill brought great energy and vision to the series, and was instrumental in defining and articulating its distinctive approach and in securing theologians to write for it. Bill's own commentary for the series was the last thing he wrote, and Westminster John Knox Press dedicates the entire series to his memory with affection and gratitude.

William C. Placher, LaFollette Distinguished Professor in Humanities at Wabash College, spent thirty-four years as one of Wabash College's most popular teachers. A summa cum laude graduate of Wabash in 1970, he earned his master's degree in philosophy in 1974 and his PhD in 1975, both from Yale University. In 2002 the American Academy of Religion honored him with the Excellence in Teaching Award. Placher was also the author of thirteen books, including *A History of Christian Theology, The Triune God, The Domestication of Transcendence, Jesus the Savior, Narratives of a Vulnerable God,* and *Unapologetic Theology.* He also edited the volume *Essentials of Christian Theology,* which was named as one of 2004's most outstanding books by both *The Christian Century* and *Christianity Today* magazines.

Series Introduction

Belief: A Theological Commentary on the Bible is a series from Westminster John Knox Press featuring biblical commentaries written by theologians. The writers of this series share Karl Barth's concern that, insofar as their usefulness to pastors goes, most modern commentaries are "no commentary at all, but merely the first step toward a commentary." Historical-critical approaches to Scripture rule out some readings and commend others, but such methods only begin to help theological reflection and the preaching of the Word. By themselves, they do not convey the powerful sense of God's merciful presence that calls Christians to repentance and praise; they do not bring the church fully forward in the life of discipleship. It is to such tasks that theologians are called.

For several generations, however, professional theologians in North America and Europe have not been writing commentaries on the Christian Scriptures. The specialization of professional disciplines and the expectations of theological academies about the kind of writing that theologians should do, as well as many of the directions in which contemporary theology itself has gone, have contributed to this dearth of theological commentaries. This is a relatively new phenomenon; until the last century or two, the church's great theologians also routinely saw themselves as biblical interpreters. The gap between the fields is a loss for both the church and the discipline of theology itself. By inviting forty contemporary theologians to wrestle deeply with particular texts of Scripture, the editors of this series hope not only to provide new theological resources for the church but also to encourage all theologians to pay more attention to Scripture and the life of the church in their writings.

We are grateful to the Louisville Institute, which provided funding for a consultation in June 2007. We invited theologians, pastors, and biblical scholars to join us in a conversation about what this series could contribute to the life of the church. The time was provocative and the results were rich. Much of the series' shape owes to the insights of these skilled and faithful interpreters, who sought to describe a way to write a commentary that served the theological needs of the church and its pastors with relevance, historical accuracy, and theological depth. The passion of these participants guided us in creating this series and lives on in the volumes.

As theologians, the authors will be interested much less in the matters of form, authorship, historical setting, social context, and philology—the very issues that are often of primary concern to critical biblical scholars. Instead, this series' authors will seek to explain the theological importance of the texts for the church today, using biblical scholarship as needed for such explication but without any attempt to cover all of the topics of the usual modern biblical commentary. This thirty-six-volume series will provide passage-by-passage commentary on all the books of the Protestant biblical canon, with more extensive attention given to passages of particular theological significance.

The authors' chief dialogue will be with the church's creeds, practices, and hymns; with the history of faithful interpretation and use of the Scriptures; with the categories and concepts of theology; and with contemporary culture in both "high" and popular forms. Each volume will begin with a discussion of *why* the church needs this book and why we need it *now*, in order to ground all of the commentary in contemporary relevance. Throughout each volume, text boxes will highlight the voices of ancient and modern interpreters from the global communities of faith, and occasional essays will allow deeper reflection on the key theological concepts of these biblical books.

The authors of this commentary series are theologians of the church who embrace a variety of confessional and theological perspectives. The group of authors assembled for this series represents more diversity of race, ethnicity, and gender than any other commentary series. They approach the larger Christian tradition with a critical respect, seeking to reclaim its riches and at the same time to acknowledge its shortcomings. The authors also aim to make available to readers a wide range of contemporary theological voices from many parts of the world. While it does recover an older genre of writing, this series is not an attempt to retrieve some idealized past. These commentaries have learned from tradition, but they are most importantly commentaries for today. The authors share the conviction that their work will be more contemporary, more faithful, and more radical, to the extent that it is more biblical, honestly wrestling with the texts of the Scriptures.

William C. Placher
Amy Plantinga Pauw

Preface

However good a Gospel commentary may be, the Gospel is better! I urge a close reading and rereading of the text of Matthew's Gospel, passage by passage. Hopefully, this commentary will illumine the reading in some small way, but the text itself will yield riches beyond anything a commentary may uncover.

This commentary meanders among layers of meaning. One layer is the initiating events in the life and ministry of Jesus. To these we have no direct access but rely upon the testimonies of those in the community of faith that followed him. Another layer of meaning is Matthew's own context in his community of faith with its particular struggles. These give shape to his particular portrait of the life and ministry of Jesus. Beyond these layers there is always the horizon of meaning contemporary readers bring to the text as we interpret it (and it interprets us). When we engage these texts they continue to surprise and seize us as we seek to live faithfully today.

The lens of interpretation that I bring as a minister/theologian/commentator has its own distinctive contours. I work from a position of privilege as an academic theologian in a North American context. I am grateful to have been conscientized by exposure to a wider world through work in the church that has taken me outside my comfort zone in global and ecumenical endeavors. I am grateful to McCormick Seminary, the Presbyterian Church (U.S.A.), and the World Communion of Reformed Churches for the opportunities to learn and grow and serve.

Conversation partners with whom I have been steadily engaged through the years shape my orientation, my questions, and my constructive thinking. In particular, I have come under the influence of Reformed theology and tradition, ecumenical dialogues, process philosophy and theology, feminist/liberationist commitments, eco-justice concerns, and the current "religion and science" dialogues. These resources continue to form and inform me as a theologian and will likely be apparent in my comments.

Acknowledgments

There are many to whom I owe a great debt of gratitude for their part in this endeavor. First of all I want to express appreciation to colleagues at McCormick Theological Seminary. I am grateful to the board of trustees for granting the yearlong sabbatical that made it possible to undertake and complete a project of this scope. The seminary has been generous in granting me time and resources for continuing in research, writing, and reflection. Faculty colleagues lightened the way daily in our shared commitments and camaraderie. Their support and kind interest in this work has been a steady source of encouragement for me. I thank the students at McCormick. More than once a student question or comment has helpfully redirected me; they "keep it real" and keep it interesting. Special thanks to my colleagues Reggie Williams, Robert Cathey, and Linda Eastwood, who stepped in to help with research when I needed it most. The staff at Jesuit-Kraus-McCormick library have been good partners in my research, especially Barry Hopkins, who exceeded all reasonable expectations in tracking down essential texts for me. The extended family of McCormick Seminary includes many churches who have kindly engaged and tested my thinking in adult education settings. Surrounded by a great cloud of witnesses, I am grateful.

Acknowledgments are also due to Westminster John Knox Press for embracing the vision of "theological commentaries" and inviting theologians across a broad spectrum to thoughtfully engage the biblical texts. It is a bold endeavor that challenges us to transgress the boundaries that separate biblical studies and theology into academic specializations. Bill Placher, who helped conceive this undertaking, would be gratified to see the fruits of these endeavors. Amy Plantinga Pauw and Don McKim have been patient, encouraging, and helpful editors for this volume and have shown themselves able leaders in guiding the Belief series as a whole. I was fortunate in the selection of a reader from the field of New Testament to take a critical look at my first draft. Princeton's Professor of Biblical Theology, Clifton Black, gave this text a careful and thoughtful reading and made a number of on-target suggestions that have sharpened and improved this text. Julie Tonini and Daniel Braden did a superb job on the copyediting of the manuscript, for which I am very grateful.

My children, Jenny, Michael, and Danny, continue to be a source of delight and refreshment along the way. They keep me grounded. As their adult lives unfold with engaging work all their own, they have nevertheless taken interest in this work of mine and celebrated each small advance in this project. My life is blessed by them.

My husband of forty years, R. Michael Winters III, is my foremost partner in this and every good endeavor. He has offered not only support and encouragement but also guidance and skillful editing. His many years in pastoral ministry as an able and inspired preacher brought an invaluable perspective to this work. For his eager partnership in all things and his love that upholds my life, I am more grateful than words can express.

Abbreviations

KJV	King James Version
NIV	New International Version
NRSV	New Revised Standard Version
RSV	Revised Standard Version

Introduction:
Why Matthew? Why now?

Beloved from the beginning, the Gospel of Matthew continues to speak with eloquence and power. The portrait it paints of the life of Jesus is compelling. Matthew's distinctive interpretation is shaped by the challenges of the church in his own time and yet resonates remarkably with challenges we face today. This Gospel was written in a time

> when there was conflict and division in the community of faith;
>
> when some were insiders and others were outsiders;
>
> when political and religious leaders were coopted, mistrusted, and discredited;
>
> when the great majority of the common people were without power;
>
> when cultures clashed.

Matthew has a word for us that we urgently need to hear. It is a message about who Jesus is and what he did and taught. In these texts we see Jesus facing up to conflict and controversy, ministering at the margins, overturning presuppositions about insiders and outsiders, privileging the powerless, demonstrating the authority of ethical leadership, challenging allegiance to empire, and pointing the way to a wider, divine embrace than many dared imagine. After a basic orientation to the Gospel of Matthew, this introduction will sketch its content in relation to these five issues. In doing so we will begin to trace an outline of the distinctive portrait of Jesus this Gospel offers.

The Gospel of Matthew

Matthew was perhaps the favorite among the Gospels in the early church. Writers in the early church quoted Matthew extensively. In listings of the Gospels it is given the prominence of first place. A closer look at the Gospel of Matthew makes it easy to see why it was so heavily favored. Matthew, who was an able teacher, presented the gospel in a form that lends itself to teaching and preaching. It is organized into five major teaching blocks; each one has a narrative segment followed by a discourse or teaching. These are bookended by the birth of Jesus and the passion of Jesus. The worship life of the church drew heavily on Matthew's Gospel and usually chose his rendering of such elements as the Lord's Prayer and the Beatitudes. Matthew is the only Gospel to address directly matters of church authority and discipline. It is especially attentive to the teaching and preaching task of interpreting Scripture (the Hebrew Scriptures of his community) in Matthew's context. Another appeal of this Gospel is that in comparison with the other Gospels it offers a fuller picture of the life, ministry, and teachings of Jesus. There are some elements included in Matthew—such as the visit of the wise men and Peter's walking on water—that are not found in the other Gospels. Beyond this, Matthew is a blatantly theological book. It is about God's saving work in Jesus Christ. It is addressed to a church community to help it better understand and communicate its faith.

The date of the writing of this Gospel is somewhat uncertain, but scholars are able to identify a range of time within which it was likely written. Since it includes reference to the burning of Jerusalem and the desecration/destruction of the Temple, then it must be dated after that event in 70 CE. Since Ignatius, bishop of Antioch, makes use of the Gospel of Matthew, then it must have been available before 107 CE. The writing shows familiarity with and reliance upon the book of Mark: about 90 percent of what is in Mark is included in Matthew. In addition to drawing from Mark, Matthew apparently drew from another source from which Luke also drew. Scholars name this the "Q" source. There may also have been a source (termed the "M" source) that is unique to Matthew's community. Additional sources available only to the author of Matthew may also have been employed. The community that the author of the Gospel of Matthew was most immediately addressing is not known with certainty. Evidence points to a prosperous, Greek-speaking, urban area with a large Jewish population. Some speculate that it may have been Antioch, the capital of Syria, which would fit this description.[1] It is clear that Matthew's congregation is Jewish and is beginning to incorporate Gentile members.

Conflict and Division in the Community of Faith: Is Jesus really the Messiah?

Conflict and division within communities of faith is a very familiar picture for us today. "There is no fight like a church fight," we say. Matthew's community of faith had its own conflicts, and a closer look at one in particular has important implications for us. A closer study will show us that the main conflict in this Gospel is not, as some interpreters have cast it, a conflict between Christians and Jews; it is conflict *within* Judaism. The texts show that it was not the intent (of Jesus or Matthew) to "start a new religion." The Jesus movement was rather a "renewal movement within Judaism."[2] Correcting our reading of Matthew accordingly may help us to rediscover the root-edness of Christian faith within Judaism. We may also find support in countering the rhetoric and practices of anti-Judaism that have yielded tragedy and atrocity in our history.[3] We may find more ways of aligning rather than alienating in our interreligious encounters.

The Gospel of Matthew is written in a context in which Jewish leaders are seeking to preserve their faith and traditions after the destruction of the Temple. They are expressing their commitment to the Torah. Matthew's Jewish community is at odds with the Jewish

---

1. B. H. Streeter, *The Four Gospels* (London: Macmillan & Co., 1924).
2. Gerd Theissen, *Sociology of Early Palestinian Christianity* (Philadelphia: Fortress, 1977), 30.
3. Although there is some dispute about how anti-Judaism is related to the race-based anti-Semitism of the Nazi era, the historical research of Susannah Heschel makes a strong case for connection. The theological anti-Judaism of the time apparently fed into "virulent racial denigration regarding the nature and danger of the Jews." James E. McNutt, "A Very Damning Truth: Walter Grundmann, Adolf Schlatter, and Susannah Heschel's *The Aryan Jesus*," *Harvard Theological Review* 105:280–301.

community under the leadership of the Pharisees. Both groups see themselves as people of God and faithful followers of the Torah.

The Pharisees were actually also a reform movement within Judaism; the scribes are the leaders among them. Their good intent was to breathe new life into the practice of Judaism by extending into the life of the ordinary Jew the laws of purity usually reserved to the priests."[4] This signified that Israel was a "nation of priests" and that every aspect of life is to be lived in service to God. The "tradition of the elders," which the Pharisees took care to defend, was a whole set of "regulations and customs that had developed in interpretation of the law in order to apply it to everyday life."[5] In particular these had to do with issues of cultic purity, tithing, and Sabbath observance.

The reforms of the Pharisees "were intended to renew Jewish piety and to provide a stronger sense of Jewish identity in the face of incursions by Hellenistic culture."[6] Jesus shared the concerns of the Pharisees. In many ways, he was closer to their thinking than to that of the Sadducees or the Essenes. However, he differed from Pharisees in his understanding of the importance of ritual purity, tithing, and Sabbath observance in relation to the "weightier matters of the law" (Matt. 23:23).

For Matthew's community these differences came to be intensified further by historical circumstances. The preface to Matthew in *The Jewish Annotated New Testament* suggests that the timing of Matthew's writing is important for understanding the rhetoric. The failed rebellion against Rome resulted in the burning of Jerusalem and the destruction of the Temple in 70 CE. Thousands of Jews had been killed or exiled and the survival of Judaism was in doubt. The strength of the polemic may reflect a competition for survival between Jewish Christians and traditional Jews at that time.[7]

There followed very turbulent times within Judaism. Jewish religious identity that had centered on the Temple was disrupted and was in the process of being reconstructed with Torah as its center. It

4. Donald Senior, *The Gospel of Matthew*, Interpreting Biblical Texts (Nashvilie: Abingdon Press,1997), 258.

5. Ibid., 176.

6. Ibid., 258.

7. Aaron M. Gale, "The Gospel according to Matthew," in *The Jewish Annotated New Testament*, ed. Amy-Jill Levine and Marc Zvi Brettler (Oxford: Oxford University Press, 2011), 2.

is probable that the Pharisees sought to consolidate their influence in the synagogues and were in an adversarial relation to minority groups, such as those who believed that Jesus was the Messiah. Jewish Christian missionaries likely faced opposition from the Pharisees comparable to that described in 23:34. The "woes" that conclude chapter 23 climax in a bitter denunciation of their persecution. In this life-and death struggle, Jerusalem's demise is cast as divine judgment on these religious leaders who rejected Jesus. The Pharisees' leadership is being delegitimized in these accounts.

The polemical language of several texts in Matthew are extreme to our ears. Pharisees are definitely presented as the "bad guys." Matthew emphasizes their opposition and records Jesus' bitter diatribes against them. We are taken aback by accounts of such invective from one who is "gentle and lowly" and loves his enemies. This writing, however, reflects the polemics of the day. Its language is like that employed by both Gentile and Jewish groups in situations of conflict. The name-calling is actually very much like the invective employed by the minority Jewish group at Qumran (which produced the Dead Sea Scrolls). There the leader of the majority group is called a "wicked priest" and "the Liar."[8]

In some circles, the harsh criticism of this polemic against one group of Jewish leaders has been generalized to a "verdict on all Jews and Jewish religious leaders for all time."[9] In point of fact, however, there is no wholesale condemnation of Jews or Judaism in these texts. They cannot even be read as a wholesale condemnation of the Pharisees, because not all Pharisees were guilty of the abuses to which Jesus alludes in Matthew. In early rabbinic writings, Pharisees themselves engage in pointed criticism of those who manifest the flaws that Jesus notes here.

The Gospel of Matthew as a whole is not anti-Jewish or anti-Judaism. It does not tell a story of "God's rejection of Israel or Israel's rejection of God."[10] Matthew has been rightly termed "the Jewish Gospel." The five major discourses follow the fivefold form of the

8. Michael G. Reddish, *An Introduction to the Gospels*. (Nashville: Abingdon Press, 1997), 119.
9. Warren Carter, *Matthew and the Margins: A Socio-Political and Religious Reading* (Sheffield, England: Sheffield Academic Press, 2000), 449.
10. Ibid.

Pentateuch. Jesus is presented as an authoritative interpreter of the law. The Hebrew Scriptures are of central importance in Matthew, which is full of quotations and allusions to the prophets, especially Isaiah and Jeremiah. For Matthew, Jesus is the fulfillment of both the law and the prophets. This Gospel takes pains to show Jesus' parallels with Moses and his reception as "son of David." Jesus and Matthew speak as pious Jews.

As we read these sharp-edged texts today we are tempted to let them rest in the past as a condemnation of a particular subset of the Pharisees. We locate ourselves among the righteous and know that Jesus is talking not about "us" but about "them." What if, instead, we took the texts as an occasion to examine our own religious life and practice to see if the things Jesus speaks so heatedly against are to be found there? Those who are religious leaders might look particularly closely at what is condemned. Where are the places that we as leaders fall into hypocrisy, status seeking, self-importance, and self-delusion? These texts are surely a cautionary tale instructive for religious leaders and all "would-be" followers of Jesus.

The anti-Pharisee texts are the polemics of a fight within the family; there is no repudiation of Judaism. Unfortunately these texts have been used as "pre-texts" for anti-Judaism. This use misunderstands and misapplies the texts. What we have here is the rhetoric of a minority group (the Christian community) that is alienated from the majority group (mainstream) in Judaism. Matthew's community of faith is a sect within Judaism. The conflict is a conflict within Judaism, with each group claiming that they are the true heirs of Judaism and that the other group is in error. The argument is not with "the Jews" or Judaism as such but with certain Pharisees who are being accused of misleading the people.

The claim that Jesus is the Messiah and the authoritative teacher of the law is the major point of difference. The extension of the promises of God to Gentiles is a second contentious point. Matthew's way of arguing these points is thoroughly grounded in the Scriptures and traditions of Judaism. There are a number of elements in this Gospel that have led interpreters to refer to Matthew as "the Jewish Gospel."

The members of Matthew's community are mostly Jewish. For them it is important to show the continuity of following Jesus with their Jewish faith. The claim being advanced is that Jesus is the long-awaited Messiah and that the promise of Emmanuel "God with us" (Matt. 1:23) is fulfilled in him. Jesus' genealogy (Matt 1:1–16) is given to establish that he is the Son of David. When Matthew presents important events in the life of Jesus they are often introduced with a formulaic saying, "This was to fulfill what had been spoken by the Lord through the prophet . . . " There are about fifty scriptural references in the Gospel. These texts (taken out of their original context) function to show how Jesus fulfills the prophets and how the promises of God to the people of Israel are met in him. Jesus takes the role of teacher and shows himself to be an authoritative interpreter of the law. There are parallels between Jesus and Moses throughout Matthew. The focus of attention in Matthew's Gospel is more on Jesus' teaching than on the miracles stories. The Gospel shows an awareness of Jewish observances such as the Sabbath laws (12:1–14). Many small indicators signal Jewish sensibilities. For example, Luke uses "kingdom of God," but Matthew uses "kingdom of heaven," thus aligning with the Jewish custom of not saying the divine name (which is too holy to speak). As Matthew's community admits Gentiles, he interprets this inclusion as a fulfillment of the eschatological hope that one day "the nations" would come to know the God of Israel (Isaiah 2:1–4). These elements constitute a basis for thinking of Matthew as "the Jewish Gospel."

A reading of the Gospel of Matthew with a better understanding of the context of its writing allows us to see Christian faith as dependent on and fully in continuity with Judaism. Calvin's theology has carried this insight particularly well, and the theological statements of the Presbyterian Church (U.S.A.) align with this understanding. The relationship between Christians and Jews "is not merely one instance among many interfaith relations."[11] The statement affirms that in Christ, "we who were far off have been brought near" to the covenant promise of God with Israel and have been "engrafted" into the people of God. The Presbyterian Church (U.S.A.) explicitly opposes supersessionism (the view that Christianity has replaced

11. "Christians and Jews: People of God," Presbyterian Church (U.S.A.), Office of Theology and Worship, Church Issues Series 7:2.

Judaism) and emphasizes instead "the continuity and trustworthi-
ness of God's commitments and God's grace."[12]

Many Christians today are committed to putting an end to "the
teaching of contempt" for the Jews. We cannot forget the history of
persecution of Jews by Christians and must acknowledge that the
Holocaust was perpetrated by baptized Christians. These realities
call us to renewed determination to overcome anti-Judaism and
anti-Semitism. The Gospel of Matthew can help, if we read it rightly.
Those polemical texts directed against the Pharisees are misunderstood when taken as anti-Jewish and misused when they become
pre-texts for anti-Judaism.

Ministry at the Margins

The ministry of Jesus and the disciples was a ministry at the margins. This is the case in two fundamental ways. The community of
disciples was marginal in its "standpoint" at the political margins of
empire and at the religious majority group in the synagogue. Furthermore, their ministry was focused on those who were marginalized in one way or another: people who were tax collectors and
sinners, sick and unclean, Gentiles and foreigners, women and
children.

Reevaluating the Arrangements: Insiders and Outsiders

Matthew's community is located on the margins of the empire and
on the margins of mainstream religious life in the synagogue.[13]
Theologian Jung Young Lee draws on sociological meanings for
marginality as living in two societies or cultures that are different
and often conflicted. This situation is more complicated if one of the
two societies or cultures is dominant and has the power to define the
normative center and to exclude the other. This is the situation of
Matthew's community and of the persons with whom Jesus engages
in ministry. They are "in-between," marginal by virtue of their

12. Ibid., 13.
13. Warren Carter, *Matthew and the Margins*, 43–49.

situation. However, a different kind of marginality is open to them: they can define themselves and *choose* to be an alternative community—no longer just "in-between" but now "in-both."[14] There may even be a sense of "over-against" in this relation if the alternative community has values and vision that are in tension with the values and vision of the dominant group. This is the case for Matthew's community in relation to empire. Choosing the reign of God over imperial reign will mean forming a community with very different power arrangements. "Great ones" serve (20:20–28). Hierarchical and patriarchal patterns are challenged (18:1–4; 19:3–9). The way of non-retaliation and nonviolence is honored (5:43–48). Carter proposes that Matthew's Gospel is in fact challenging the community of disciples to embrace a "more consistent and faithful marginal identity and alternative way of life in anticipation of the completion of God's salvific purposes"[15] To adopt intentionally the standpoint of marginal identity constitutes a reevaluation of relationships, arrangements, and allegiances in the dominant culture.

The margins are not only the standpoint for ministry but also the focus of ministry for Jesus and his disciples. It is a ministry that overturns expectations about "insiders" and "outsiders." The socially, religiously, and politically marginalized are at the center of Jesus' ministry. The very first of Jesus' healings was of a man with leprosy (8:1–4), which could signify any one of a number of disfiguring or contagious diseases and entailed not only physical suffering but also social exclusion. The man would live outside the city, could not attend community worship, and had to call out "unclean" in order to warn people as he moved about . It was forbidden and shocking that Jesus touched him.

The categories of "the sick" and "the sinful" blur in Jesus' ministry (9:12–13), since it was assumed that sickness was God's judgment on sin. When Jesus forgave the sins of the man who was paralyzed (9:1–7), he faced the charge of blasphemy; forgiveness was God's prerogative. That the man could walk was a kind of confirmation that he was forgiven. Jesus came under attack for his association with

14. Jung Young Lee, *Marginality: The Key to Multicultural Theology* (Minneapolis: Fortress, 1995), 47–53.
15. Carter, *Matthew and the Margins*, 49.

sinners and tax collectors. Jesus is charged with eating with them and even befriending them (9:9–13; 11:19).

Jesus risked reproach in ministry when he extended care to Gentiles and foreigners. In that day the world was divided into Jews and non-Jews (goyim). The term goyim carried with it indications of non-Jewish ancestry and worship of idols rather than the true and living God, YHWH. Not all Gentiles were foreigners, and there were in fact sometimes good relations among Jews and Gentiles, especially in the diaspora (dispersion of Jews away from Palestine). However, there remained constraints on socializing with goyim and a taboo on intermarriage.[16] Jesus transgresses these boundaries. The centurion whose servant he heals (8:5–13) is an outsider on three counts: he is a Gentile, a foreigner, and an enforcer of Roman imperial rule.

In Jesus' ministry at the margins rules of exclusion are ignored, socially constructed boundaries are transgressed, and shocking inclusions occur. Those who would follow him will presumably do likewise. This puts some uncomfortable questions before the "would be" followers of Jesus today. Who are the "outsiders" in our context? Where are people being excluded from power and privilege? Who are the "untouchables"? The various contemporary exclusions and "isms" that marginalize people because of race, class, gender, sexual orientation, or immigration status become all the more suspect. Perhaps our arrangements regarding insiders and outsiders need reevaluation.

Privileging the Powerless: Ministry as if Women and Children Counted

There is no question that the Gospel of Matthew is written in a patriarchal context and reflects patriarchal views of the secondary status of women and children. That such views are sometimes incorporated into the text carries no surprises for us. One example is "who counts" in feeding stories (14:21; 15:38). That men are counted and women and children are "besides" is just as would be expected in a

---

16. N. T. Wright, *Matthew for Everyone, Part 1* (Louisville, KY: Westminster John Knox, 2004), 211.

patriarchal society. However, this social reality makes all the more remarkable the texts where patriarchal assumptions are transcended or even negated. There are many such instances in Matthew. Women and children, powerless in their culture, are privileged in the ministry and teaching of Jesus.

Children in patriarchal culture had no power and no voice in their larger social world. Yet, in the Gospel of Matthew, Jesus privileges children. It is they and not "the wise and the intelligent" who are the privileged recipients of revelation (11:25–26). When asked in 18:3–7, "Who is the greatest in the kingdom of heaven?" Jesus brings a child to center stage. Children are put forward as exemplars of the humility that is needful for greatness under God's reign. Jesus takes the matter further when he says, "whoever welcomes one such child in my name welcomes me" (v. 5). There follow dire warnings of judgment on any who would put a stumbling block before one of these "little ones." When people began bringing their children to Jesus and when the disciples would refuse them Jesus was clear, "Let the little children come to me, and do not stop them; for it is to such as these that the kingdom of heaven belongs" (19:13–15). It is the children who announce Jesus as he rides into Jerusalem: they cry out "Hosanna to the Son of David" (21:15). When the chief priests object, Jesus reminds them of what it says in Psalm 8:2, "Out of the mouths of infants and nursing babies you have prepared praise for yourself." Children are the privileged sources of God's praise. In all these ways, children are elevated above all expectation as Jesus privileges the powerless.

In ancient societies of the Mediterranean not only was there a basic differentiation into upper and lower strata (the elite and the masses), there was also differentiation according to gender.[17] It was a patriarchal society in which women were of inferior status and had limited rights. Their domain was restricted to the sphere of home and family. Their rights of inheritance, opportunities for education, and freedom of movement or choice in relationships are severely curtailed. In the Palestinian Jewish culture of Matthew's writing, it was the practice of Jewish men to pray three benedictions each

---

17. Ekkehard W. Stegemann and Wolfgang Stegemann, *The Jesus Movement: A Social History of its First Century,* trans. O. C. Dean (Edinburgh: T&T Clark, 1999), 361.

day, one of which thanked God that he was not made a woman.[18] The portrayal of women in the Gospel of Matthew and the account-ings of Jesus' interactions with women are extraordinary given these social realities.

In contrast to the society in which women were largely invisible, in the Gospel of Matthew, women have high visibility both in Jesus' life and in the ministry of Jesus. A few examples include the geneal-ogy of Jesus, stories of healing, Jesus' teachings in the parables and apocalyptic materials, Jesus' anointing at Bethany, the women fol-lowing him from Galilee to Jerusalem, those present at the cross, and those bearing witness to the resurrection. In many cases the women in the Gospel become exemplars, often in contrast to men in the same story.

The genealogy, though patrilineal, breaks the traditional patriar-chal pattern of "was the father of" with the inclusion of five women in the line. Raymond Brown reviews the history of interpretations of this surprising inclusion. Two traditional proposals were that (1) four of these women were "sinners," thus foreshadowing the salva-tion of sinners in Christ, and (2) four of the women were foreigners, thus foreshadowing the inclusion of the Gentiles. Brown seems to lean toward a third proposal that includes all five of the women. They all share "irregularities" in their unions with men, which though scandalous to outsiders, were embraced in the lineage of Jesus. All of them also showed initiative and had a role in God's saving work.[19]

Among the healing stories there are two in particular that dem-onstrate the faith and initiative of women: the woman with the hem-orrhage (9:20–22) and the Canaanite woman (15:21–28). These two women are not identified in relation to "an embedded status in a patriarchal family."[20] Each is doubly marginalized. Not only are they both women, but also one is unclean and the other is a Gentile. With each healing Jesus praises the faith of each woman and responds

18. T. Johnson Chakkuvarackal, "Woman-Power in the Canonical Gospels: A Paradigm for Modern Patriarchal Societies," *Bangalore Theological Forum* 24:58.

19. Raymond E. Brown, *The Birth of the Messiah: A Commentary on the Infancy Narratives in Matthew and Luke* (Garden City, NY: Doubleday, 1977), 22.

20. Janice Capel Anderson, "Matthew: Gender and Reading" in *A Feminist Companion to Matthew*, ed. Amy-Jill Levine (Sheffield, England: Sheffield Academic Press, 2001), 34.

with healing. "Jesus treatment of both explodes the boundaries of acceptable association."[21]

The parables of the reign of God (chaps. 13 and 25) include the image of "leaven" that a woman mixed into flour until it was all leavened. Interestingly, the history of interpretation of the parables in Matthew 13 makes a ready connection between God and "the (male) sower who went out to sow" but not between God and the woman who leavened the mix. Yet the parallel is there. In chapter 25 the parable of the wise and foolish bridesmaids is among the "Wisdom" teachings that Jesus employs. In Proverbs 7–9 "Wisdom" is a female representative of the divine.[22] In the apocalyptic segments of Matthew, women are not forgotten. From the two women grinding (24:41) to the expressed concern for women who are pregnant or nursing infants, women are remembered and made visible.

The unnamed woman anoints Jesus at Bethany and in doing so enacts his messianic destiny; "messiah" means anointed one. The disciples, by contrast, complain of the extravagance of her gift. In the passion narrative, Matthew names not only the three women at the cross (Mary Magdalene, Mary the mother of James and Joseph, and the mother of the sons of Zebedee) but also "many women" who "followed Jesus from Galilee and had provided for him" (27:55–56). They were also at the crucifixion "looking on from a distance." These women "stand with Jesus in the hour of his passion when the disciples have forsaken him and fled."[23] Mary Magdalene's prominence among the disciples is notable. In fact, she expresses the quality of "true discipleship" in contrast to Peter, who denies Jesus, and in contrast to Judas, who betrays him.[24] It is not the disciples but the women who watch over the burial and visit the tomb. Two of them (Mary Magdalene and the other Mary, 28:1) share the distinction of being the first to see the risen Jesus and the first commissioned

---

21. Ibid., 35.
22. Mary Rose D'Angelo, "(Re) Presentations of Women in the Gospel of Matthew and Luke–Acts" in *Women and Christian Origins*, ed. Ross Shepard Kraemer and Mary Rose D'Angelo (New York: Oxford University Press, 1999), 177.
23. Anderson, "Matthew: Gender and Reading," 41.
24. Chakkuvarackal, "Woman-Power," 63.

to proclaim the resurrection. These women, "last at the cross, first at the tomb,"[25] become exemplars of faith and discipleship.

In the Gospel of Matthew, women have an unexpected prominence in the life and ministry of Jesus. Jesus appears to be privileging the powerless and overturning assumptions about who "counts." The "surprises" in this challenge traditional habits of assigning women a secondary status in the life of the church.

The Authority of Ethical Leadership

The news in our day, whether it is about political or religious leaders, is fraught with stories of scandal, corruption, and abuse of power. Beyond the extreme reports are the criticisms of leaders who do not lead or who lead in ways that protect the wealthy and powerful while neglecting "the 99 percent." It is as true today as it was in Matthew's time that the people are "harassed and helpless, like sheep without a shepherd" (9:36). Compared with the other Gospel accounts, Matthew's Gospel is particularly attentive to the common people and gentle with the disciples. Conversely, Matthew's Gospel is particularly harsh with its portrayal of political and religious leaders. Their interactions with Jesus only serve to underscore that he (in contrast to Herod and Pilate) is the true King of the Jews and (in contrast to the Pharisees) is the true interpreter of the law.

"The crowd" receives a largely positive presentation. The common people follow Jesus around; they are hungry for his teaching, confident of his healing power, ready to proclaim him the Son of David, the Messiah (4:25; 5:1; 7:28; 8:1). They crowds respond eagerly to Jesus; they are amazed, filled with awe, and they glorify God because of him (7:28; 9:8). Jesus receives the crowd warmly, teaching them, feeding them, healing them. He has "compassion" on them because they are "harassed and helpless, like sheep without a shepherd" (9:36).

Even though the disciples misunderstand, betray, desert, and deny Jesus in Matthew's Gospel, just as they do in the other Gospels,

25. Anderson, "Matthew: Gender and Reading," 41.

in Matthew they receive a kinder assessment. For example, in the storm at sea story in Mark they are criticized as having "no faith," (4:40) but in the same story in Matthew they are said to have "little faith." (8:26). The disciples stand in need of teaching and nurturing—a task Jesus undertakes. At the end of Matthew's account, they are commissioned to continue the teaching and ministry of Jesus "in all the world" (chap. 28). Mark, by contrast closes with the disciples fleeing from the tomb in fear and amazement and telling no one (Mark 16:8).

Herod and Pilate, as political leaders, get a very negative assessment; they are weighed and found wanting in Matthew's Gospel. They fail to be "shepherds of the people." Herod and Pilate both act to destroy God's Messiah, yet God's overrules them and they prove not to be the great powers they think they are. From his place at the seat of power, Herod plots the destruction of God's Messiah from the time the wise men come seeking the King of the Jews. Unsuccessful, frightened, and scheming, he slaughters innocent children in a mad rage to protect his power and place. Even so, God protects the infant Jesus. Pilate, a coopted instrument of the empire, is a leader without the courage of his convictions. Even though he believes Jesus to be innocent, he washes his hands of the matter and hands Jesus over to be crucified, because of his fear of a riot. Through Pilate the empire does the worst that it can do. The empire appears to have the power of life and death, but God raises Jesus from the dead. In contrast to these failed political leaders, Jesus is the true "King of the Jews."

Religious leaders fare no better in the Gospel of Matthew. It is important to remember that religious leaders in that context were really part of the power system of the empire's ruling elite. Separation of church and state was not an operative principle. Their power is significant. These leaders, who are charged with the guidance of the people, mislead and misguide. He charges the Pharisees with being "blind guides," "hypocrites," and "a brood of vipers." (Matt. 23) They do not understand the law, and they will not do what they teach. Jesus, by contrast, understands the law; he teaches it, and he obeys it. He is the authoritative teacher of the law.

Preaching Good News to the Poor: Jesus and Empire

Issues of empire are very much to the fore in Matthew, written as it is in the context of Roman rule. The relevance and urgency of this Gospel's message on the matter becomes all the more apparent when we realize that imperialism is not confined to New Testament times. It is very much a part of life in our world today wherever people in power seek to exercise control over other people (their lands, their resources) and pursue their own interests at the expense of others. "Control" can be economic, political, or military.

A case in point, many believe, is the current global economic system. It dominates and exploits weaker parties, puts profits before people, allows unlimited growth regardless of ecological consequences, and encourages unrestrained competition and consumerism. The system is unjust because it protects the interests of the powerful to the neglect of social obligation to the poor and the weak—"the least of these" (25:40). The "few" benefit at the expense of the "many." The World Communion of Reformed Churches has committed itself to fullness of life or all. In Covenanting for Justice in the Economy and the Earth, the Accra Confession declares, "We are challenged by the cries of the people who suffer and by the woundedness of creation itself . . . We believe the economy exists to serve the dignity and well-being of people in community, within bounds of the sustainability of Creation."[26]

> This community of disciples of Jesus is marked by its commitment to him and by an alternative set of practices and lifestyles that challenge practices and values of the imperial world.
>
> Carter, *Matthew and Empire,* 170.

Warren Carter has done extensive study of resistance to the Roman Empire in Matthew's writings and shows how this Gospel offers both a theological and a social challenge to empire.[27] In the context of the book of Matthew, the common people were on the outside looking in. They were victims of Rome and the elite who

---

26. "Accra Confession," World Communion of Reformed Churches, #5; #22.
27. Warren Carter, *Matthew and Empire: Initial Explorations* (Harrisburg, PA: Trinity Press International, 2001).

colluded with Rome. They formed a circle of power that oppressed and dispossessed the common people. There are a number of examples of the Gospel's oppositional stance to the empire's sovereignty.

The citations from Isaiah, which are so frequent in Matthew, invoke an eighth-century BCE situation of oppression by a foreign power (the Assyrian Empire) that is similar to the situation of Matthew's community under Roman rule. The particular texts selected from Isaiah make clear God's opposition to the Assyrian empire and God's power to deliver the people from it.

Another aspect of the Gospel of Matthew's "narrative of resistance" is the extremely negative portrayal of Rome's representatives, Herod and Pilate. When God protects the infant Jesus against Herod's devices, the implied question is, "Who is sovereign here?" Pilate, who (apparently) has the power of Jesus' life and death in his hands, washes his hands and yields to those clamoring to have Jesus crucified. The resurrection shows that God alone is sovereign over life and death. However things may appear, the reality is that the power of Rome and Roman justice is "all washed up."[28]

Taxes exacted in tribute to Rome were a costly enactment of Roman oppression. The practice siphoned off much needed resources from the people. Carter proposes that much of the sickness Jesus was curing could be attributed to the conditions under which people lived as subjects of the empire with its acquisitive and exploitative practices.[29] Although Jesus instructs Simon to pay the tax; the shekel for payment is taken from a fish's mouth. This is an interesting twist in that it was customary to assume the emperor had sovereignty over the fishes of the sea.[30] The story demonstrates where true sovereignty lies.

The invitation "take my yoke upon you" (11:28–30) may be yet another subversion. On the one hand, "yoke" was a symbol of the law and Jesus may be offering an alternative to the "yoke of the Pharisees" whose interpretation of the law was burdensome to the people; Jesus' teaching concerning the law, however, was life-giving and restorative. On the other hand, it may be possible that "yoke"

28. Carter, *Matthew and Empire*, 145.
29. Ibid., 5.
30. Ibid.

was used here as a metaphor for imperial control. This was a more common usage in the context. In this case the text could be read as an invitation to those bowed down under Rome's rule to accept Jesus' yoke instead and "so live for God's salvation or 'rest' from that rule."[31] They are invited to offer allegiance and obedience to God rather than to Rome; take on God's yoke—not Rome's.

Each of these elements (and more besides) can be read as a challenge to Rome's authority. The reign of God contrasts with and contradicts imperial reign. Those living under God's reign form an alternative community that is inclusive and egalitarian and both theologically and socially resistant to the empire. The theological challenge is in the conviction that the world belongs to God—not to Rome; and God's saving purposes and blessings are to be found in Israel and in Jesus—not Rome.[32] The new community and its practices provide an alternative vision and way of living that challenges empire.

> We reject any claim of economic, political and military empire which subverts God's sovereignty over life and acts contrary to God's just rule.
>
> "Accra Confession" World Communion of Reformed Churches, #19.

Exclusive or Inclusive: How Wide Is the Divine Embrace?

Matthew's faith community struggles over issues around Jews and Gentiles in the purposes of God. There was considerable controversy over this as we know from other New Testament texts (Acts 1–15; Gal. 1–2). Can the Gentiles be included among the people of God? How wide is the divine embrace? This is another question that resonates between our context and Matthew's. Although the particulars of our contexts are very different, we share with Matthew's community the challenges and opportunities of a multicultural and religiously pluralistic reality.

31. Ibid., 170.
32. Ibid., 171.

For Christians today the question is sometimes put this way: How may we affirm that "Jesus is Lord" in a religiously pluralistic context? What does that claim mean for us today? Responses differ. Some are comfortable with language of "uniqueness" or "singularity" and Jesus as the "only savior." Others are concerned to keep a certain reserve about the extent to which we may know the mind of God and the ways of God with other people.

Reformed confessions collectively express the full range of perspectives, and sometimes this full range is even expressed within a single confession. For example, the Second Helvetic Confession says, "we teach and believe that this Jesus Christ our Lord is the unique and eternal Savior of the human race" (5.077). It goes on (in the very same section) to say that this is the one "in whom by faith are saved all who before the law, under the law, and under the Gospel were saved, and however many will be saved at the end of the world" (5.077). This seems to extend God's salvific work rather broadly to include those who never knew Jesus; even people who never knew Moses. This confession cautions, "We must not judge rashly or prematurely . . . nor undertake to exclude, reject, or cut off those whom the Lord does not want to have excluded" (5.140).

This confession seems to say yes to two differing intuitions. It invites us to affirm our central faith convictions about Jesus with the full wealth of conviction. At the same time, it acknowledges the sovereign freedom of God to transgress our boundaries of culture and religion. "God can illumine whom and where he will . . . ." (5.007).

In Matthew's day the issue of real concern was whether the Gentiles could be included among the people of God as more than just "God-fearers." The prospect of the promises of God being extended to the Gentiles was a point of contention that separated Matthew's Jewish community from the majority view. It is a question of some urgency for them. Matthew's community is set within a Greek-speaking urban area, and Gentiles are beginning to join the community.

Matthew's Gospel takes great care in handling this delicate question. At various points it makes clear the priority of God's covenant with Israel in salvation history. Jesus himself says that he is "sent only to the lost sheep of the house of Israel" (15:24). When the disciples are sent out in mission they are instructed to "go nowhere among the Gentiles"

(10:5). However, alongside this apparent limitation in mission, there is a counter-narrative. Gentiles keep coming to Jesus. The three wise men (2:1–23), the Roman centurion (8: 5–18), and the Canaanite woman (15:21–28) all figure prominently in the story. They are Gentiles; yet they are not turned away. In fact, they show themselves to be exemplars of humility and faith to which all God's people are called. As the story proceeds, it becomes clear that there is no exclusion; the whole world is in view (5:13, 16; 24:1; 26:13; 28:19). It seems that in these texts there is a dawning realization that from beginnings in particularity (the people of God in Israel) there is an opening out to a wider reach of divine grace to all God's people.

Matthew is intent on interpreting this as a fulfillment of the promises of God made in the covenant with Israel rather than an abrogation of it. He draws on texts in Isaiah (e.g., Isa. 2:2–4; 60:1–6) as explication for what is occurring. These texts prophesy the universalizing of God's blessing to Israel. The promise of blessing given in the covenant is for all nations (Gen. 22:18). Israel is "blessed" in order to be a blessing, a light to the nations. This is no diminishment of the heritage of Judaism but is rather consistent with its most profound insights. The divine embrace is wide indeed.

Conclusion

These five themes are prominent in Matthew, and they make clear the powerful connections between the world of the Gospel and our world today. Yet they are but a first installment on the riches of this Gospel. Already we may see meaning unfolding on three levels. At the base there is the compelling story of the life and ministry of Jesus. At a second level this story intersects with the world of Matthew's faith community. Their issues and struggles give shape to Matthew's narrative and his distinctive interpretation of the story of Jesus. Then there is the world of the contemporary readers like us who are seeking insight and inspiration for the life of faith today amid our own issues and struggles. The back and forth between the "then" of the story of Jesus and the "now" of our own stories is an interaction of great power and promise.

PART 1

THE BIRTH OF THE MESSIAH

1:1–2:23

1:1–2:23
Jesus the Messiah, King of the Jews

1:1–25
Jesus the Messiah, the Son of David, the Son of Abraham, Emmanuel

The opening words of the Gospel of Matthew begin, "the genealogy of Jesus the Messiah . . ." "Messiah" (*mashiach*) is a Hebrew word meaning "anointed one."[1] When translated into Greek it is rendered as *"Christos"* from which we get the title "Christ." In our everyday usage we forget that "Christ" is not Jesus' last name. It is a rather audacious faith affirmation that Jesus is *the Christ*—the Messiah— God's anointed one.

As it goes forward, the genealogy proceeds as a mind-numbing list of names. But the author is up to something here. He is making yet another audacious messianic claim. One vision of the coming Messiah was as one who would be a great and powerful king like King David. The genealogy shows that Jesus is of David's royal lineage, a true "son of David."

We are meant to see the contrast between Jesus and King Herod, whom we meet in chapter 2. Herod has no royal blood. He is not even fully Jewish. He is just an opportunistic military commander that the Romans have coopted for their own political agenda.[2] He is a puppet king. Jesus, as Matthew means us to understand, is the true King of the Jews. This designation, present here at the beginning, will appear again at the end of the story (Matt. 27:11, 29, 37, 42)

---

1. This reflects the ritual practice of pouring oil on the head of someone who was being inaugurated into the office of prophet (Isa. 61:1), priest (Exod. 40:15), or king (1 Sam. 10:1). Classic expositions thus refer to the "threefold office" of the Messiah, and the work of Christ has been interpreted as fulfilling all three roles. Ordinary usage makes the royal connection most prevalent. Eugene Boring, *The New Interpreter's Bible: New Testament Articles, Matthew, Mark* (Nashville: Abingdon Press, 1995), 8:357.
2. N. T. Wright, *Matthew for Everyone, Part 1* (Louisville, KY: Westminster John Knox, 2004), 3.

when the charge placed over his head reads, "This is Jesus, King of the Jews."

After the designation "son of David" there follows the designation "son of Abraham." The lineage is traced all the way back to Abraham, the great patriarch who received God's covenant promise. Jesus is the one in whom the promise of blessing given in the covenant (Gen. 22:18) comes to full fruition. In this listing, there are fourteen generations from Abraham to David and fourteen more from David to Jesus. The names can also be divided into six groups of seven names. The number seven was considered the "perfect" number. The symbolic power of locating Jesus in the auspicious place as the first of the seventh seven would not have been lost on the early audience.

> The Messiah does not wander onto the stage of history as an impressive newcomer to the drama, but in continuity with God's saving history in the past.
>
> Boring, *The New Interpreters Bible*, 8:131.

There are other extraordinary things about this genealogy. One of the most striking is the inclusion of the names of women. Luke's genealogy does not include any women, not even Mary. Including women, as Matthew does, in a genealogy that is traced down through the male line is uncommon. It concludes with Joseph "the husband of Mary" even though Matthew intends us to understand that Joseph was not the father. This is strange and so is the inclusion of four other women along the way. Much has been made of issues around sexuality for these women: Tamar seduced her father-in-law; Rahab was a prostitute; Ruth seduced her kinsman Boaz; Bathsheba committed adultery, and so on. However, this really does not distinguish them from the men in the list(!)—Judah was seeking a prostitute when he came upon Tamar, and David committed adultery with Bathsheba. That God works with ordinary people in the midst of the irregularities and scandals of their lives could be part of Matthew's point. He does, in fact, have to counter the scandal around Mary and the charge of Jesus' illegitimacy. Perhaps a more notable distinction than the issues around sexuality, however, is the fact that these women are Gentiles: Tamar is a Canaanite, Rahab is from Jericho,

Ruth is a Moabite, Bathsheba a Hittite. These women are "outsiders," and yet they stand in the messianic line. The inclusion of these Gentile women in the unfolding of God's promise underscores from the beginning of Matthew's Gospel, a theme that will run throughout. God's promise to Abraham has universal dimensions; through him all the nations would be blessed (Gen. 12:3).[3] Note that all four of these women were "socioeconomically, politically, or cultically powerless, and all fulfilled their role in Israel's salvation history by overcoming obstacles created by people in authority unwilling to fulfill their responsibilities."[4]

More about the identity of Jesus unfolds when Joseph, in a dream, is instructed to "name him Jesus, for he will save his people from their sins" (1:21). Only Matthew offers an explanation of this name. The name Jesus, like the name Joshua, (both common in that time) is an affirmation of faith as the Hebrew root Yeshua or Jeshu means "YHWH saves." There is in this naming an explicit reminder of the many ways God has saved God's people along the way. Echoes of the Exodus ring through. As Joshua brought the Israelites into the promised land after the death of Moses, Jesus will now fulfill what the law of Moses intended. As God through Moses delivered the people of Israel out of the house of bondage in Egypt, so now God in Jesus will save them—and people of all nations—from their sin.

Jesus' identity is illumined further by his miraculous conception. Matthew draws on Isaiah 7, "Look the virgin shall conceive and bear a son . . . ." The reference to a virgin conceiving is not found in the original Hebrew. There it is simply a "young woman" who will conceive. However, the Greek translation (the Septuagint) of the Hebrew Scriptures uses the Greek word for "virgin." Matthew follows this reading.[5] In doing so he heightens the sense that in

---

3. Raymond Brown proposes that "It is the combination of the scandalous or irregular union and of divine intervention through the woman that explains best Matthew's choice in the genealogy." *The Birth of the Messiah* (Garden City, NY: Doubleday, 1977), 74.

4. Amy-Jill Levine, *The Social and Ethnic Dimensions of Matthean Social History: "Go Nowhere among the Gentiles"* (Lewiston, NY: Edwin Mellen Press, 1988), 277.

5. "Jewish communities of the diaspora considered the Greek text of the Septuagint (LXX) rather than the Hebrew text to be authoritative Scripture. By the middle of the first century CE, large segments of the Christian church employed this Greek translation as their Bible, as writings like Matthew, the epistles of Paul, ... and the epistle to the Hebrews attests." George Nickelsburg, "The Jewish Context of the New Testament" in *The New Interpreter's Bible: New Testament Articles, Matthew, Mark* (Nashville: Abingdon Press, 1995), 8:27.

this birth there is a special working of God. It echoes the extraordinary conceptions of central figures in the history of Israel such as Isaac and Samuel, who were born to women thought to be barren (Gen. 20:15–21:7 and 1 Sam. 1:15–25). Their extraordinary conceptions were taken to be signs that God had a special purpose for them in God's saving work. God is involved and the unsuspecting are expecting.

It is interesting that Matthew does not give Mary center stage the way Luke (1–2) does. Joseph is the actor featured here. He becomes an exemplar in his obedience to God (1:20–25; 2:13–14, 19–21). The theme of "higher righteousness" that is drawn out in the larger Gospel of Matthew is first illustrated in Joseph. A central problem in Matthew's community was the tension between keeping the letter of the law and being "righteous."[6] Joseph faced that tension. He was prepared to "do the right thing," which in the cultural context was to dismiss Mary, and he was even planning to do so compassionately, "quietly," rather than expose her to pubic disgrace. Then the angel appeared to Joseph in a dream and called him to follow the divine leading rather than doing what was expected. Joseph, in obeying, becomes the model for all disciples who confront the tension of "you have heard that it was said . . . but I say to you." This tension, set forth more fully in the Sermon on the Mount, is between what is commonly understood to be commanded by God and the new thing God is doing in Jesus.[7]

In this first chapter the double direction of Matthew's proclamation is already manifest. Jesus is "embedded in the history and hopes of Israel and yet inaugurating a breakthrough to the nations."[8] When the final naming (v. 23) is introduced we learn what matters most is not necessarily the genealogy—God can "raise up children to Abraham" from stones (3:9)—nor is it the fulfillment of promise. It is not even the special circumstances of Jesus' birth. What matters most is this is Emmanuel—"God with us." This is the message that frames the book of Matthew. It is a promise reiterated at the end of

6. Boring, *The New Interpreter's Bible*, 8:138.
7. Ibid., 136.
8. Donald Senior, *The Gospel of Matthew*, Interpreting Biblical Texts (Nashville: Abingdon Press, 1997), 45.

the Gospel when Jesus says, "I am with you always, to the end of the age" (28:20).

2:1–23
King of the Jews: A Threat to Herod

At the opening of the second chapter, wise men come from the east seeking "the child who has been born King of the Jews." They have seen his star "at its rising." What we translate here as "wise men" is the Greek word *magos,* which often means astrologer. It makes sense that astrologers might follow an extraordinary sign in the heavens. Scholars have speculated about what might have been going on in the night sky at this time that could provide some historical setting for this account of the natal star. One of the more interesting proposals is that Jupiter and Saturn were in conjunction with each other three times in 7 BCE. Jupiter was known as the "royal," or kingly, planet, and Saturn was thought to represent the Jews.[9]

In this chapter there is a sharp contrast in the receptions the newly born Jesus receives. On the one hand, there are these wise men, nameless strangers and aliens who have come a great distance following that "star of wonder." They come in an attitude of seeking. They are prepared to do homage, bringing gifts[10] fit for a king. On the other hand, there is King Herod, who is no stranger or alien but one who sits in the seat of power. What he seeks is to secure his power and his place. He is frightened and scheming, killing innocent babes in his rage.

There is another sharp contrast in this chapter between Jerusalem and Bethlehem. Jerusalem is the place the wise men expect to find this auspicious event occurring, the birth of the King of the Jews. Jerusalem, after all, is the center of power politically and religiously. Bethlehem, by contrast, is a seemingly inconsequential place inhabited by people at the margins—peasants, like Mary and Joseph.

---

9. Wright, *Matthew for Everyone, Part 1,*10.
10. Matthew does not give an interpretation to the three gifts of the magi. Nevertheless, interpretations have grown up around them all the same. Gold has been associated with his kingship, frankincense (used in anointing oil) with his priestly office, and myrrh (sometimes used in embalming) with his humanity and death.

Yet Bethlehem is the place where God is at work in ways that will threaten the imperial power entrenched in Jerusalem. When King Herod was frightened, the text says "all Jerusalem" was frightened with him (2:3). Likely this "all" would mean the elite and powerful centered at Jerusalem, those who had something to lose if there were changes afoot. Herod calls together "the chief priests and scribes of the people, his advisory council the Sanhedrin."[11] They, along with the Pharisees and Sadducees (3:7), would be members of the governing classes, who are in alliance with Rome and Rome's representatives (i.e., Herod and Pilate). This first appearance of the religious leaders who will be major players in the Gospel story does not bode well, for they are linked with Jerusalem's fear, and they are allied with Herod's scheming (2:3).[12]

One commentator titles this chapter in Matthew, "The Empire Strikes Back."[13] Why is the great King Herod threatened by this little baby? Matthew means for us to know that the threat is real. The announcement from the wise men is political dynamite for Herod. Jesus is the true King of the Jews in the line of David. Herod is an imposter, a usurper.[14] Matthew carefully drew out the genealogy that established Jesus' royal lineage, and now even Gentiles from far parts seem already to know that this newborn is the King of the Jews. Herod reacts with haste and deploys the wise men in his plot of destruction, enjoining them to "go and search diligently for the child" (2:8)—indeed, track him down! The sense of threat is so strong that when Herod's plot is unsuccessful, he is so infuriated that he orders all children in the whole region of Bethlehem who are age two and under to be put to death.[15]

It is not only King Herod and the religious leaders at Jerusalem who will recognize Jesus as a threat to the present order. As the

11. Warren Carter, *Matthew and the Margins: A Socio-Political and Religious Reading* (Sheffield England: Sheffield Academic Press, 2000), 77.
12. Ibid.
13. Ibid., 73.
14. Wright, *Matthew for Everyone, Part 1*, 11.
15. This is not Herod's first massacre nor would it be his last. When he came to the throne, he had members of the Sanhedrin executed and kept its influence to a minimum thereafter. David E. Garland, *A Literary and Theological Commentary on the First Gospel* (New York: Crossroad, 1993), 27. He gave orders when he was dying for the leading citizens of Jericho to be slaughtered when he died so that there would be weeping at the time of his funeral. Wright, *Matthew for Everyone, Part 1*, 14.

story unfolds, Jesus will face opposition and conflict with elites and authorities all along the way. The problem is that he overturns tables (21:12) and expectations, violates religious and cultural rules, privileges the powerless, questions the agreed arrangements regarding insiders and outsiders. The opposition that attends his ministry culminates in the Jerusalem establishment confirming that Jesus must be crucified. Within a generation even Rome will feel the threat and will persecute his followers as a danger to good order.[16]

With the aid of divine warning, King Herod's threat is made known to the wise men and to Joseph, and Herod's attempt to impede God's saving work is itself impeded. The wise men do not return and report to Herod, warned in a dream they go home by another way. Joseph and Mary take the baby and flee to Egypt.

With his family's flight into Egypt, Jesus joins the company of all those who are hunted or homeless, migrants or refugees. In our own day this company is a staggering number. The United Nations estimates that 43.7 million people worldwide are now migrants. The causes include war, natural disasters, civil unrest, human rights abuses, and lack of economic opportunity.[17] Matthew's telling of the desperate flight of Jesus and family does not lend itself to sweet, sentimentalized renderings we are more accustomed to seeing on Christmas cards. What if our Christmas cards featured the faces of some of these 43.7 million? If we are paying attention to the story as Matthew tells it, we can no longer think of the hunted, the homeless, migrants, or refugees without seeing in them the face of Jesus. The Gospel of Matthew calls us to see Jesus in "the least of these" (25:45) and will charge us rather directly to do so when we come near to the end of the story, (25:45) "Lord when did we see you hungry or thirsty, or a stranger or naked or sick or in prison . . . ?" When indeed?

This child who is Emmanuel—God with us—does not enter the world in ease and comfort; he is not born into privilege and power. Already, in his infancy, oppression and violence and terror have

---

16. Wright, *Matthew for Everyone, Part 1,* 14.
17. "Who Is My Neighbor—Churches Seek Faithful Response to Migration," *Reformed Communiqué* (December 2011).

touched his life. But then, if he is really to be "God with us," he will be with us where the pain is.[18]

When King Herod dies and Jesus and family are at last free to return to Israel, even then they remain under threat, for Herod's son Archelaus—more of the same—now rules in his stead. There is no safe place in Judea. So the family settles in Galilee in the city of Nazareth (2:23). This again is an inauspicious place, one that was scorned by the Jerusalem elite. Situated in a secluded valley in lower Galilee (disparaged as "Galilee of the Gentiles"), it was a "backwater" town. In the words of Nathaniel (John 1:46), "Can anything good come out of Nazareth?"

The three other place names in this chapter that appear in the quotations from Hebrew Scriptures revisit decisive moments in the history of Israel. It is as if Jesus recapitulates the history of his people. Bethlehem (2:6) is the city of David, Egypt (2:13) is the land of slavery and the Exodus, and Ramah (2:18) is the place of mourning for the exile. Only Matthew tells the story of the family's flight from Bethlehem into Egypt and their later return to Israel. We are meant to see the direct parallels with Israel's story. Even the slaughter of the innocents that occurs in this chapter resonates with Pharaoh's orders to the Hebrew midwives at the time of Moses' birth to kill all the male newborns. Like Moses, Jesus is miraculously delivered, and like Moses, he in turn will deliver his people. As God through Moses delivered them from slavery in Egypt, so now God through Jesus will save them from their sin. Matthew's quotation from Jeremiah (31:15) is an allusion to the exile. In the time when Jesus is born things are so bleak for Israel that they are reminiscent of the exile. Even in these times, God's deliverance is at hand.

Conclusion

The birth and infancy narratives in Matthew's Gospel prefigure the full story of the life of Jesus. Several central themes have already emerged in these first two chapters. Among them are a privileging of

---

18. Wright, *Matthew for Everyone, Part 1*, 15.

the powerless, conflict with the elite authorities, an openness to the Gentiles, and Jesus as the fulfillment of the law and prophets.

As it was with the wise men and the obedient Mary and Joseph, so it will be in the rest of the story, faithful people who stand at the margins—strangers, foreigners, common folk—will be the ones who follow Jesus and receive God's blessing. The wise men—strangers and foreigners—receive divine guidance when they are warned in a dream about Herod's scheme and they leave for their own country by another way.[19] Joseph and Mary—common people from the margins of the empire—receive divine protection when they are warned in a dream to flee to Egypt.

There is a foreshadowing of both the opposition Jesus will encounter from religious and political leaders and the recognition and homage he will receive from Gentiles. The passion at the hands of the authorities is prefigured. Just as Herod seeks the aid of these Gentile wise men in locating the King of the Jews with a view to killing him, so also will the Jerusalem establishment in the final chapters of the Gospel seek the aid of Gentiles to crucify Jesus. The charge placed over his head will be what the wise men knew: this is the "King of the Jews." Not only is he King of the Jews, he is also the hope of all the nations—the dividing walls between races and cultures are breaking down.[20]

The coming of these Gentiles from the East looks both backward and forward. It looks back to the Hebrew Scriptures that prophesy the universalizing of God's blessing to Israel. In that time, as Isaiah 2:2–4 anticipates, "all the nations shall stream" to the house of the Lord. The promise is reiterated in Isaiah 60:1–6, which declares, "Nations shall come to your light." The wise men come following the "light" of Jesus' star on the rise. The story of the wise men also looks forward to the point where the disciples are sent forth to "all

---

19. Songwriter James Taylor wrote a song titled, "Home by Another Way" that draws counsel from the experience of the wise men, warned in a dream of Herod's evil intent. Among other things he counsels to "steer clear of royal welcomes." He urges that we should "keep an eye to the charts on high" and "go home by another way." *Never Die Young Album* (1988), Sony Music Entertainment, Inc.

20. Boring, *The New Interpreter's Bible*, 8:145.

nations" (20:19)[21] and even to his own day when Gentiles are entering the community of faith.

These early chapters are full of dreams and angels and prophecies.
Joseph receives divine guidance in dreams (1:20; 2:13, 20) and so
do the wise men (2:12). The words of the prophets interpret what
is happening. In these first two chapters there are no less than five
references to Hebrew Scripture (1:22–23; 2:5–6, 15, 17–18, 23).
In each case the reference is prefaced by something to the effect,
"this was to fulfill what was spoken by the prophet . . ." Some have
noted that Matthew takes these texts out of context, because what he
makes of them is not what they meant in their original setting. For
Matthew, new meanings break forth from these texts as God is doing
a new thing. Matthew reimagines these texts, if you will, to make a
theological claim that God is at work in all these happenings and is
bringing to fulfillment what was promised from of old. Throughout
the rest of the Gospel there will be more references[22] like these as
Matthew seeks to demonstrate that Jesus is the fulfillment of the law
and the prophets.

FURTHER REFLECTIONS
"God Is with Us"

"Who do you say that I am?" This is the comprehensive question
Jesus will put to the disciples later in the Gospel (15:16). In this
first chapter, Matthew already provides some clues as the name
Jesus (God saves), the title Messiah (the anointed one), and the
designations of son of David and son of Abraham are offered. In
1:23 the name Emmanuel (God is with us) is added. The church has
reflected much on the question Jesus posed to the disciples. This
reflection (developed in the doctrine of the incarnation) concluded
that in Jesus of Nazareth, it is God with whom we have to do. The

---

21. Frederick Murphy, *An Introduction to Jesus and the Gospels* (Nashville: Abingdon Press, 2005), 146.
22. Forty-two explicit references occur in this Gospel as compared with nineteen in Mark, nineteen in Luke, and fourteen in John. Garland, *Reading Matthew*, 28.

Chalcedonian Formula (451), "truly God and truly human," came to express what we believe.

While Matthew does not have the more fully developed incarnational Christology that we find in John, he seems to move further in that direction than Mark or Luke. Later in the Gospel, at Jesus' Baptism, Matthew adds the designation "Son of God" to the names already ascribed in chapter 1. It is not agreed whether for Matthew this identification necessarily entails divinity. In the context it would likely have been heard as a reference to kingship more than referring to divinity. Psalm 2, a royal psalm composed for a coronation, in verse 7 uses the words, "You are my son; today I have begotten you." Some have argued that "sonship" in Matthew's Christology is functional rather than ontological—that Jesus is God's Son because he is obedient to God rather than because he is divine. This seems to be the understanding in the Gospel of Mark. Matthew does, however, move further in the direction of ascribing divinity. He uses the term Son of God with more frequency and variety than Mark does (14:33; 16:16; 27:40, 43). Matthew's focus on the virginal conception of Jesus moves further in this direction also,[23] though it is not put forward as a "proof" of divinity.[24] Matthew's birth narrative, which presents Jesus as a baby who is passive and vulnerable (as he will be again in the passion narrative) works to convey the full humanity of Jesus.

> Matthew begins and ends his story with the fragile human life of Jesus surrounded by God, who is the hidden actor throughout.
>
> Boring, *The Interpreter's Bible*, 137.

Truly God and Truly Human?

What does it mean to affirm "truly God and truly human . . . two natures . . . in one person" as the Council of Chalcedon (451 CE) affirmed? This claim has seemed to be at best paradoxical, at worst contradictory. There is an assumed polar opposition between God and all else (the eternal vs. the temporal, the unchanging vs. the

23. Mitchell G. Reddish, *An Introduction to the Gospels* (Nashville: Abingdon Press, 1997), 117.
24. In Matthew's context there were stories of heroes and special persons who were "sons" or "daughters" of God through miraculous conception. Boring, *The Interpreter's Bible*, 137.

changing). This framework of philosophical dualism sets up a mutual exclusion that makes any joining of divine and human unthinkable. In face of this incoherence, many Christians have settled either for a "Christology from above" emphasizing the divine or a "Christology from below" emphasizing the human. These views lose the balance of the two natures. The first risks Docetism—the view that God only "appeared" to be human. The second risks Adoptionism—the view that Jesus was not divine in nature but only a human who was the adopted "son of God." Another way Christians have dealt with the apparent contradiction of "truly God and truly human" has been to "parcel out" different attributes to the two natures (e.g., only the human nature could suffer).

Serious theological problems are posed by these sorts of distortions. If Jesus is not truly human, then he cannot serve as an exemplar for human beings. We cannot seriously be expected to follow him—to walk in the way he walked—for we are only human beings and not God. Nor can we discern in him who we, as human beings, are called to be. At the same time, if he is not truly God, then he cannot manifest to us what God is like. More to the point for the Christian tradition, he cannot accomplish our salvation. Only God can save us. Theologians through the centuries have approached these claims and reinforced them in distinctive ways. Gregory of Nazianzus, fourth-century Archbishop of Constantinople, articulated a view that it is precisely by assuming human flesh that God's healing (saving) work is accomplished for human beings. As he said, "what has not been assumed is not healed." Anselm, eleventh-century Archbishop of Canterbury, argued the same point from another direction. In his book *Cur Deus Homo* (usually translated "Why God Became Man") he used the metaphor of debt as describing the human predicament. Human sin creates a debt that is owed to God. The debt must, of course, be paid by the one who owes it—thus the one who redeems must be a human being. However, since the debt is infinite, only God can pay it. Consequently, the redeemer must be both fully human and fully God.

The claim of "fully human, fully God" is fundamental to the Christian soteriology (understanding of how God saves us). How may we make a more coherent and religiously viable articulation of these central claims of our faith? How may we better answer the question, "Who do you say that I am?" Perhaps it would help if we took more seriously the affirmation made in this first chapter of Matthew— "God is with us." If God is truly with us as the One "in whom we live and move and have our being" (Acts 17:28), then we are in God and God is in us. The framework of philosophical dualism has misrepresented our fundamental relation with God. If God is really already "in" the world, and "in" all things, then the whole creation is, in a sense, co-constituted by the divine. Divine reality includes and does not exclude created reality. God is genuinely "all in all." Perhaps this can help us understand that it is not contradictory to say that God was "in" Christ. We see divine presence and activity in him distinctly and decisively, but this does not mean that God is ordinarily absent from the world. As it says in Colossians, "For in him all the fullness of God was pleased to dwell, and through him God was pleased to reconcile to himself all things . . . ." (1:19). What we see in God's incarnation in Jesus Christ is the truth about divine presence and reconciling work in all things. "God's incarnation reaches into the very depths of material existence."[25] Perhaps the deepest implication of the incarnation is that God is in, with, and for the world. The whole world then becomes "a place of grace."

> Once we have encountered God in Christ we must encounter God in all things.
>
> Alan Galloway, *The Cosmic Christ,* (New York: Harper Brothers, 1951), 250.

Cosmic Christology

"God with us" is a divine way of being even before the foundation of the world. God is a God in relation and not a God who is content in splendid isolation. In the work of creation God makes room for a genuine other. Jürgen Moltmann uses the Jewish kabbalistic notion of *zimzum* to puzzle through how it can be that there can be anything other than God if God is really "all in all." *Zimzum* means "concentration and contraction, and signifies a withdrawing of oneself

---

25. Niels Henrik Gregersen, "Deep Incarnation: Why Evolutionary Continuity Matters in Christology, *Toronto Journal of Theology* 26/2 (2010): 174.

into oneself."[26] In the work of creation there is a sense in which God "makes room" in Godself for an "other." An important conceptual parallel in Christian theology is the divine self-emptying (Greek *kenōsis*, Phil. 2) that takes place in the incarnation.

Creation is a work of love. The divine embrace includes the whole of creation. The world is in God and God is in the world. Sometimes the meaning of the Christ event is reduced to redeeming human beings' souls from sin. Christians then become preoccupied with "saving souls" and getting to a better world.[27] This is a narrowing of the traditional and biblical understanding that sees a cosmic dimension to God's creative/redemptive work.[28] Colossians 1:15–20 is representative:

> He is the image of the invisible God, the firstborn of all cre-
> ation; for in him all things in heaven and on earth were created,
> things visible and invisible, whether thrones or dominions or
> rulers or powers—all things have been created through him
> and for him. He himself is before all things, and in him all things
> hold together. He is the head of the body, the church; he is
> the beginning, the firstborn from the dead, so that he might
> come to have first place in everything. For in him all the full-
> ness of God was pleased to dwell, and through him God was
> pleased to reconcile to himself all things, whether on earth or
> in heaven, by making peace through the blood of his cross.

In this way of seeing things, the incarnation is no "emergency measure" on God's part for dealing with human sin. It lies rather in the primordial creative intent of God. The Christ event pertains to the fundamental structure of the universe.[29] The goal of all creation is union with God. The redemption that is ours in Christ is, in its

---

26. Jürgen Moltmann, *The Way of Jesus Christ: Christology in Messianic Dimensions* (London: SMC Press, 1990), 136.

27. Zachary Hayes, "Christ and the Cosmos," in *The Epic of Creation: Scientific, Biblical, and Theological Perspectives on Our Origins* (Unpublished paper, Zygon Center of Religion and Science, 2004), 25.

28. Notable theologians of the early church (Justin Martyr, Irenaeus, Clement of Alexandria), twelfth- and thirteenth-century theologians (especially Bonaventure), and most all Greek Orthodox theologians emphasize this approach. Key texts for consideration include John 1:1–14; 1 Cor. 8:6; Eph. 1:13–14; Phil. 2:6–11; Heb. 1:1–4.

29. Hayes, "Christ and the Cosmos," 25.

fullness, a cosmic transformation, a new heaven and a new earth—when God will be all in all (1 Corinthians 15:28).

There is a sense in which the work of Christ is redemptive precisely because the union with God—that is intended for all—is manifest in him. Thus, when the Symbol of Chalcedon articulates how we are to understand Jesus, the Christ—truly God and truly human—it expresses the destiny for which God intends us all.

God's self-revelation in Jesus Christ is a decisive revelation of who God is and what God is doing

> **He became as we are, that we might become as he is.**
>
> Irenaeus, *Against Heresies*, Book 5, preface.

everywhere and always. God's intentions and actions become "transparent" in Jesus, the Christ. The incarnation is an instance of transparency to ultimate reality—not an exception to it.

What we see in the incarnation is echoed in the sacrament of the Lord's Supper. In Matthew 26:26, 28, when Jesus takes the bread, he says, "Take, eat: this is my body," and takes the cup saying, "Drink from it, all of you; for this is my blood"; he has identified common elements with his body and blood. As Arthur Peacocke observes, "Jesus identified the mode of his incarnation and reconciliation of God and humanity ('his body and his blood') with the very stuff of the universe when he took the bread, blessed, broke and gave it to his disciples . . . "[30] Taken seriously a notion of divine *real presence* in the incarnation and reiterated in sacrament must entail a revaluation of all material reality as open to and indwelt by the divine.

What we see in God's incarnation in Jesus, the Christ is the truth about divine presence and activity in the world as "real presence"—as cosmic incarnation. The divine purposes are here revealed as "worldly" in nature and universal in scope. In Jesus, the Christ, divine primordial purposes to be *in, with,* and *for* creation become transparent. The Christ event signals divine creative love and redemptive transformation that seeks the reconciliation, reunification, and reconstitution of all things. At the heart of created reality there is an openness to the God who "unfolds" and "enfolds" it.

---

30. Arthur Peacocke, *Paths from Science towards God: The End of All Our Exploring* (Oxford: One World, 2001), 149.

We need a better understanding of our central faith affirmation of "truly God, truly human." Of course, God's nature is mystery through and through. We should not presume to think we know what it is to be divine. There is some question whether we can even agree on what it means to be human. Even as we acknowledge this great mystery, we should not "misplace the mystery" by using the term "mystery" to cover over contradictions that we ourselves have created. It may be time to jettison the picture of God drawn by philosophical dualism that makes our christological affirmations into contradictions. We might replace it with the vision of God we have come to see in the incarnation—a God who exists in loving relation with all things. In Jesus Christ we see God's "real presence" in this world that God loves. We are then pointing toward the mystery of "God with us."

> Divine purposes are worldly in their direction and cosmic in their scope.

FURTHER REFLECTIONS
Slaughter of the Innocents

The story of King Herod's slaughter of the innocents is deeply troubling for us on so many levels. The situation of state sponsored violence at the point of Jesus' birth is seen again at the point of his death on the cross, an instrument of state execution. This text tells a story that unfortunately is a recurring reality in the world we know: human history is a slaughter of the innocents. At the time of this writing the news is full of disruption, violence, and war around the world. Many victims are innocent children. Theologian Johann Baptist Metz, reflecting on the "interruptive experience" of the Holocaust, proposed that the whole of Christian theology needs to be rethought from the ground up in light of the suffering of the innocents. The "slaughter of the innocents" presents a momentous challenge requiring direct address in the human community. We seek ways of resisting this recurrent reality where we have the power to do so and frustrating it when we do not. This is what Moses' mother Jochebed did with the basket floated among the bulrushes and what Mary and Joseph do here in their flight to Egypt.

It also poses theological challenges for those who are believers in a God who is all powerful and completely good. Why is there so much suffering and evil in the world? Some of the usual answers do not satisfy. The stock answer of retributive justice—that suffering is the result of sin—does not fly, because we are here facing the suffering of the innocent. Nor does the response that suffering and evil build character satisfy. It may well be that we often learn and grow from what we endure, and the world is a "vale of soul-making"; but in this situation the persons are destroyed (they are slaughtered): there can be no growth or learning for them in this suffering. Even the promise that in the end all will be well rings hollow, because a good ending does not undo the damage. That Jesus receives special deliverance does not help with the question of all the others. The slaughter of the innocents is irredeemably unjust, and we ask with the psalmist, "How long, O LORD?" (89:46). We direct our protest to God.

But is this "slaughter of the innocents" God's doing? In Matthew 2, it is Herod's doing. We have the situation of horrendous suffering caused by human decision and action (moral evil). We may still ask, Why does God not prevent it? God's power, however we understand it, is apparently sufficiently subtle and self-limiting to permit genuine freedom—even at the risk of allowing evil. Freedom is the risk that divine love takes. It may be that God's perfect power is best displayed as vulnerability and suffering love, such as we see expressed in the cross of Jesus and the resistance to evil that we see in the life and ministry of Jesus. There we see a saving solidarity in the face of suffering and a redemptive resistance in the face of evil. That God is active in both the solidarity and the resistance is a confession of faith we make.

God's interaction with creation is not the coercive exercise of controlling power, but love and the vulnerability love entails. This vision is beautifully articulated in the hymn by W. H. Vanstone, "Love's Endeavor, Love's Expense." In the hymn, Vanstone rejects the picture of God as a monarch who sits easy and distant from the world and its suffering. God is rather pictured as One who embraces the world with arms of love that "Aching, Spent, the world sustain."[31]

The real question about evil is not where does it come from, but what are we going to do about it.

---

31. W. H. Vanstone, "Love's Endeavor, Love's Expense" in *Love's Endeavor, Love's Expense,* (Edward Marks Music Corp, 1924).

PART 2

THE LIFE AND MINISTRY OF JESUS

3:1–25:46

3:1–4:25
Narrative: Called and Calling

3:1–12
"Repent, for the kingdom of heaven has come near:" John the Baptist

John the Baptist comes on the scene with a startling message and a startling appearance. A strange and somewhat frightening figure, he does not dress in the clothing of more civilized society. He is dressed like a wild man in camel's hair and a leather belt.[1] His mode of dress not only sets him apart but has the effect of identifying him with Elijah, "a hairy man with a leather belt around his waist" (2 Kings 1:8). Jesus makes this identification explicit in 11:14, "He is Elijah who is to come." The return of Elijah as a messenger of the end time was a prominent eschatological expectation that signaled the advent of the day of the Lord (Mal. 3:1 and 4:5–6).[2] Just as John's message and his appearance set him apart, his odd diet signals that he is a man at the margins. He does not eat the food of civilized society but lives on locusts and wild honey. This was ritually clean food (according to Lev. 11:22) and the main diet of the poorer people of the desert from then until now.[3]

John the Baptist occupies a liminal space.[4] Although he lives on the edge, in the wilderness of Judea, he comes with a message for the whole society, even to those at the very center religiously and politically. As he traverses from the margin to the center, his word, like that of the prophets before him, is "over-against" that society. He

---

1. His appearance identifies him with Elijah, "a hairy man with a leather belt around his waist" (2 Kgs. 1:8), an identity Jesus makes explicit in 11:14. John is the Elijah who is to Come.
2. "Lo, I will send you the prophet Elijah before the great and terrible day of the Lord comes" (Malachi 4:5).
3. Eugene Boring, *The New Interpreter's Bible: New Testament Articles, Matthew, Mark* (Nashville: Abingdon Press, 1995), 8:156.
4. Warren Carter, *Matthew and the Margins: A Socio-Political and Religious Reading* (Sheffield, England: Sheffield Academic Press, 2000), 90.

advocates a full reorientation because "the kingdom of heaven has come near," and he threatens that judgment is coming.

Only two of the Gospels begin with the birth of Jesus, but all four preface Jesus' ministry with the story of John the Baptist. He is a pivotal figure as herald of the Messiah. For Matthew, both John's preaching and his special role call to mind the words of Isaiah the prophet (40:3) about one who is "crying out in the wilderness, 'Prepare the way of the LORD, make his paths straight.'" John the Baptist is not only herald to the Messiah; he is also a religious leader in his own right. The multitudes come out to hear his message and receive his baptism. The historian Josephus praises John's piety and leadership and speculates that Herod had him killed because of his growing popularity and the threat of political upheaval he posed.[5]

John's message is a call to repentance in face of the proximity of the reign of heaven. This is, in fact, the very same message that Jesus himself will take up in the next chapter as he begins his ministry (4:17). The forewarning that judgment is coming is central to the message both John and Jesus proclaim.

Repentance (Greek *metanoia*) has the connotation of "changing one's mind" and "turning around." It is a term not new with John the Baptist or Jesus; it was the standard Jewish prophetic call to reconciliation with God, "turn" or "return" (Hebrew *sub*).[6] John is calling people to turn (or return) to God. It is a word from the prophets who preceded him as they again and again proclaimed that God's people have gone astray to their own destruction through wayward wandering and following after idols of their own making. They should turn around and return to God, not only because they are on a path that leads to destruction, but because a loving and merciful God beckons them home.

It is the call expressed in Isaiah, "Return to me, for I have redeemed you" (44:22), and again in Joel, "Rend your hearts and not your clothing. Return to the LORD, your God, for he is gracious and merciful, slow to anger, and abounding in steadfast love . . ." (2:13).

5. Josephus, *Antiquities*, 18.5.2 as referenced in Douglas R. A. Hare, *Matthew, Interpretation: A Bible Commentary for Teaching and Preaching* (Louisville, KY: Westminster John Knox Press, 1993), 18.
6. Boring, *The New Interpreters Bible*, 8:167.

In Ezekiel the calling comes again, "Cast away from you all the transgressions that you have committed against me, and get yourselves a new heart and a new spirit! Why will you die, O house of Israel? For I have no pleasure in the death of anyone, says the Lord GOD. Turn, then, and live" (18:31–32).

To "turn" or "return" to God is to find grace and steadfast love, life, and liberation. God's people need deliverance from all that is destructive and death dealing. There are not only personal but also social-political dimensions to answering the call to return and live. We hear echoes of the return from slavery in Egypt and the return from exile in Babylon. There is a promise entailed in this. The God who set people free from oppressive powers in Egypt and Babylon is the same God who still delivers—even in the face of Rome's Empire.

Part of the urgency in John's call to repent and return to God is the nearness of the kingdom of heaven. In the other Gospels "kingdom of God" is the language used, but Matthew's choice here is "kingdom of heaven." In Jewish tradition the name of God is a name too holy to be spoken. Perhaps it is in keeping with this sensibility that Matthew speaks indirectly, referring to the place of God's abode. Heaven is God's "throne" as the earth is God's footstool (5:34–35). Matthew's further elaboration on the "kingdom of heaven" makes clear that "kingdom" does not refer to a place or realm but rather a new reality—the reign of God. It is the advent of God's reign in our midst that John is announcing.[7] The rest of Matthew's Gospel will unfold the meaning of this mysterious, disturbing, liberative, and transformative power of God's reign in our midst.[8]

> God's reign, as presented in Psalm 72, for example, liberates and protects people from oppressive allegiances, structures, relationships, and powers which usurp God's role and claim. It establishes God's life-giving and just empire in their place.
>
> Carter, *Matthew and the Margins*, 93.

The call to repentance and the announcement of God's reign

---

7. With this meaning in view, where I am not quoting the text from the NRSV, I will use the phrase "reign of God" to express the underlying meaning more clearly.
8. Carter, *Matthew and the Margins*, 93.

coming near is accompanied by a warning of coming judgment. The Pharisees and Sadducees are the first to hear about the "wrath to come" (3:7), and it is they who receive the full force of the threat. Pharisees[9] and Sadducees[10] were two very different groups within Judaism and would not ordinarily be lumped together as they are here. What unites them is their opposition to Jesus.[11] Both John (v. 7) and Jesus (12:34; 23:33) give them a scathing address, "You brood of vipers!" "Vipers" is not simply an insulting term; it is a very particular accusation. They are charged with being "predatory, poisonous, false teachers who pervert the people."[12] The image evoked by John when he talks about their attempt to "flee from the wrath to come" (v. 7) is that of snakes slithering away from a fire.

Were the Pharisees and Sadducees there to be baptized by John? It seems unlikely. These two groups stood in opposition to John and his baptism, as we find out later in the story (21:23–27). Commentators note that the Greek text says they were coming "upon (Greek *epi*) the baptism of John" not coming "to be baptized" by John. The NIV may have a more accurate translation saying that they came "to the place where he was baptizing." They were perhaps coming to observe what John was doing rather than to be baptized by him (21:23–27).[13]

All the same, John takes this occasion to chastise them. Washing with waters of baptism is an empty ritual if it is devoid of true repentance. He cautions that they should "bear fruit worthy of repentance" (v. 8). If they "change their minds" it will change their lives. Where is the evidence of this? Ritual purity without righteousness counts for nothing. This message is strong in the ethical tradition of Judaism. It shows up in the critique of false piety found

---

9. Pharisees were the legal experts who aimed to purify Israel through intensified observation of the law, Torah. They developed "their own traditions about the precise meaning and application of scripture, their own patterns of prayer and other devotion, and their own calculations of the national hope." N. T. Wright, *Matthew for Everyone, Part 1* (Louisville, KY: Westminster John Knox Press, 2004), 217.

10. The Sadducees were the aristocracy of Judaism. They were based in Jerusalem and included most of the priestly families. They did not survive the destruction of the Temple in 70 CE (Ibid., 220).

11. Hare, *Matthew*, p. 19

12. Boring, *New Interpreter's Bible*, 8:157.

13. Ibid.

in so many writings of the prophets. The unrepentant are like the people of whom the prophet Isaiah speaks, "these people draw near with their mouths and honor me with their lips while their hearts are far from me . . . "(Isa. 29:13). The prophet Amos gives voice to divine displeasure in worship that is not accompanied by justice and righteousness: "I hate, I despise your festivals, and I take no delight in your solemn assemblies . . . but let justice roll down like waters, and righteousness like an ever-flowing stream" (Amos 5:21–24).

It seems that these leaders whom John accuses presume upon their ancestry and ethnicity as immunity from the wrath to come. They say to themselves, "We have Abraham as our ancestor" (v. 9). John knocks this prop out from under them. "God is able from these stones to raise up children to Abraham" (v. 9). The reference to stones evokes Isaiah's account of how God has already raised up a whole people from a "rock": "Look to the rock from which you were hewn, and to the quarry from which you were dug. Look to Abraham your father and to Sarah who bore you; for he was but one when I called him, but I blessed him and made him many" (Isa. 51:1–2). What God has done before, God can do again.

What matters in one's standing before God is not ritual purity or ethnicity but rather faith in God, obedience to God, and doing God's will. Such a message opens the doors to a wider company of persons who cannot make claims based upon ritual purity or ethnicity. Throughout the Gospel of Matthew this message will recur. The Gentile centurion's faith is greater than any Jesus found in Israel (8:10). It is the second son in the parable of the Two Sons (21:28–32) who does the will of his father and not the firstborn son who at first says he will but then does not.[14] One's place in the family of God is determined by doing the will of God. This is a principle that is axiomatic in Jewish ethical tradition.[15] Whether one has faith in God and does God's will is what counts in the judgment.

---

14. Donald Senior, *The Gospel of Matthew*, Interpreting Biblical Texts (Nashville: Abingdon Press, 1997), 92–93.
15. Donald Senior, *Abingdon New Testament Commentaries: Matthew* (Nashville: Abingdon Press, 1998), 53.

John announces that the one who is coming will baptize with the Holy Spirit and with fire (v. 11). This continues the theme of judgment coming. He follows with the warning that "his winnowing fork is in his hand (v. 12). In the process of winnowing, the fork raises wheat and chaff together into the wind. The chaff is carried off by the wind, and the edible grain falls to the threshing floor. The wheat can then be gathered, and the chaff can be collected and burned. The combination of these two verses is all the more powerful when we remember that the word we translate here as "Spirit" is from the Greek word (*pneuma*) that can also mean "wind." The baptism with "wind" and fire implies a judgment like unto the harvesting of wheat to which wind and fire are essential.

These first twelve verses of chapter 3 are full of the matter of judgment. Interestingly, Matthew 3:1–12 is a text scheduled in the lectionary for the second Sunday of Advent (Year A). Churches today tend to focus primarily on preparation for Christmas in this season, but it was not always so. The focus of the four Sundays of Advent historically was on preparation for the second coming—Christ's coming in judgment. Attention to the matter of judgment has mostly fallen by the way in the church's progress toward the tableau of the holy family. Center stage is the baby Jesus, meek and mild.[16] This uncompromising text calls us back to the recognition that Christ's coming is not as harmless as all that. Already the "ax is laid to the root." The hypocrisy and presumption and self-deception such as that displayed by the Pharisees and Sadducees who hold the center place of power stands under judgment. We are called to come like those crowds from the margins to repent and be baptized, to come in authentic faith in God and obedience to the will of God.

Looking at judgment in another light, there is a sense in which it is not to be dreaded but rather to be hoped for. Divine judgment when it comes will be a "setting right." It has been said that without judgment there is no justice. People who are the victims of injustice long for their day in court. The reader of these texts cannot help calling to mind the innocents who were slaughtered by Herod's decree in chapter 2. Their unavenged tears cry out for justice. That a just

16. Hare, *Matthew,* 18–20.

judge is coming is good news for those unjustly treated. The image of judgment in Psalm 96:11–13 is a very positive image:

> Let the heavens be glad, and let the earth rejoice;
> let the sea roar, and all that fills it;
> let the field exult, and everything in it.
> Then shall all the trees of the forest sing for joy
> before the LORD; for he is coming,
> for he is coming to judge the earth.
> He will judge the world with righteousness,
> and the peoples with his truth.

Surely the news that the reign of God is coming near is good news for those who long for justice. It is no threat to those who align themselves with God's purposes. Finally! God is coming to judge; the reign of God comes near!

The images in this text are images of tending and harvesting: cutting out the dead wood that bears no fruit and taking up a winnowing fork that separates the wheat from the chaff. These are ordinary practices of tending and harvesting that any careful grower/farmer would use. The metaphor need not be strained into an analogy—some of us are wheat, others of us are chaff. Perhaps there is a bit of both in each of us. Elsewhere in Scripture the image of refining is employed. "For he is like a refiner's fire . . . and he will purify the descendants of Levi and refine them like gold and silver, until they present offerings to the Lord in righteousness" (Mal. 3:2–3). In all these images, the result is positive, what is good is preserved. God does what any good grower, farmer, refiner would do. It is the preserving, perfecting work of a loving God.

Alfred North Whitehead in talking about God's way of judging in a world in which there is both good and evil speaks of "the judgment of a tenderness which loses nothing that can be saved. It is also the judgment of wisdom which uses what in the temporal world is mere wreckage . . . He is the poet of the world, with tender patience leading it by his vision of truth, beauty and goodness."[17]

---

17. Alfred North Whitehead, *Process and Reality* (New York: Macmillan Co., 1978), 346.

3:13–17
"This is my Son, the Beloved,
with whom I am well pleased": Jesus' Baptism

To John's surprise and apparent discomfiture, Jesus presents himself to be baptized by him. Perhaps we are as puzzled as John. John has been preaching a baptism that signifies repentance. Why would Jesus need to be baptized? What does he need to repent? Our theological tradition has insisted that Jesus is without sin. The text in Hebrews 4:15 makes the affirmation that "we do not have a high priest who is unable to sympathize with our weaknesses, but we have one who in every respect has been tested as we are, *yet without sin*." How are we to understand Jesus presenting himself for the baptism of repentance?

One way we might understand Jesus' presenting himself for baptism is as a sign of his solidarity with sinners. In this context, "to fulfill all righteousness" is to be with God's people, stand in their place, share in their penitence, live their life, die their death.[18] We might also inquire into the meaning of "righteousness." In the Hebrew Scriptures the term (*tsedaqah*) is not so much about sinless perfection as it is about right relationship and the fulfilling of covenant obligations. It is about the establishment of God's will that justice should everywhere prevail. God's righteousness is connected with "vindication," "deliverance," and "salvation" (tsedaqah is alternately translated by these terms). God's righteousness is seen in God's special regard for those who are powerless or oppressed and stand in need of justice. Warren Carter points out that "righteousness" gets elaborated in Psalm 72. There the king is "righteousness" because he "delivers the needy when they call, the poor and those who have no helper. He has pity on the weak and the needy, and saves the lives of the needy. From oppression and violence he redeems their life . . . " (vv. 12–14). Thus righteousness is not conceived as a static quality that one possesses (what one is) but rather a matter of what one does in living life before God.

For readers of the Hebrew Scriptures, the report of Jesus' baptism has many resonances. That he is baptized in the Jordan (v. 13) recalls

---

18. Wright, *Matthew for Everyone, Part 1*, 22.

the crossing of the Jordan into the promised land. That when he comes up from the water, the Spirit descends like a "dove" reminds us of the links between water and Spirit in Genesis, as "a wind from God swept over the waters" (Gen. 1:2). After the flood Noah sends out a dove. Themes of creation and new creation are reverberating here.[19]

Regular ritual washing with water was widely practiced within Judaism and its symbolism of cleansing from sin was understood. This singular experience of "baptism" that John was practicing is more reminiscent of the practice of "proselyte baptism." When Gentiles converted they were baptized. In extending this practice to everyone, John is in effect declaring that everyone stands in need of conversion, signaling their repentance and turning to God. Even the religious leaders stood in need of baptism.

Interestingly, only Matthew's Gospel makes the divine affirmation of Jesus a public declaration. In Mark, the address is to Jesus himself, "You are my son" (Mark 1:11). Matthew's version (v. 13) reads, "This is my son." Here again there are resonances with key Scriptures. Psalm 2, a royal Psalm that celebrates King David's coronation, resonates with this divine announcement. "You are my son, today I have begotten you" (v. 7). That Jesus is the true king, and the one promised from the lineage of David, is clear in this parallel. The words also evoke Isaiah 42:1: "Here is my servant whom I uphold, my chosen, in whom my soul delights; I have put my spirit upon him; he will bring forth justice to the nations." As the Spirit descends on Jesus, John's announcement that the one who is coming will baptize with the Holy Spirit is realized. Just as God's Spirit was at work in Jesus' conception (Matt. 1:18) and now in his baptism (3:16), so the Spirit will lead him throughout his ministry. The first stop is the wilderness into which Jesus is "led up by the Spirit."

This chapter of inaugural events in the ministry of Jesus advances the central emphases of the Gospel of Matthew: the coming of the reign of God, the need to prepare through true repentance and transformed life, the calling to righteousness and justice, and the threat (or promise) of the coming judgment. The chapter takes the affirmation of Jesus as the Son of God to a new level. It is not only a matter

19. Carter, *Matthew and the Margins*, 103.

of his mysterious origin through God's Spirit as we read about in the birth narratives; it is also a matter of his obedience to God, "fulfilling all righteousness." The chapter culminates in the divine declaration, "This is my Son, the Beloved, with whom I am well pleased" (v. 17).

4:1–11

"If you are the Son of God ...": The Temptation

The Spirit that alighted on Jesus now leads him into the wilderness where he will be "tempted by the devil." The affirmation that Jesus is "the Son of God" needs to be worked out as to its meaning. In each of the temptations, the tempter begins, "If you are the son of God ..." Eugene Boring points out that the word translated "if" (Greek *ei*) could equally well be translated "since." The question at issue is not whether Jesus is the Son of God, but *since* he is the Son of God, what will that mean, how will he live out his relationship to God? The temptations he faces will each in turn urge him to take his relationship to God as a position of privilege, using it to meet his own needs, receive protection from the vulnerability of his humanity, and gain power over all the kingdoms of the world. Is this what it means to be "the Son of God"? Or will Jesus understand his calling in terms of God's redemptive work and take up a role of serving God and God's people toward that end—even if the end was suffering and death for him?

In the infancy narrative Jesus recapitulated Israel's experiences of exodus and exile. Now, having come through the waters of baptism as Israel came through the Red Sea, he enters into forty days of fasting like Israel's forty years in the wilderness, and he will be tested as Israel was tested. Jesus' faithfulness in his time of testing will contrast sharply with the points of compromise that attended those historic wilderness wanderings. Once again, Jesus is revealed as the one who "fulfills all righteousness." God's word and calling guide his responses to all that would distract him from his vocation or co-opt his mission.

In Israel's experience, the wilderness was not only a place of testing; it was also a place of divine guidance (the cloud by day and pillar of fire by night), providential care (feeding on the manna from heaven), revelation (the giving of the Law on Mt. Sinai). Jesus relies on texts that illumined Israel's wilderness experience to guide him in his own wilderness experience. The recurring phrase, "It is written," frames all three of his responses. The parallel to Deuteronomy 6–8, the text that follows the giving of the Ten Commandments, is unmistakable as Jesus takes each of the temptations in turn.

"If you are the Son of God, command these stones to become loaves of bread" (4:3). One of the Messianic expectations was that the Messiah would reproduce the miracle of the Manna, and there would be a lavish supply of food in the messianic age. Jesus does not perform this miracle to prove himself or to assuage his hunger. He is clear in his teaching about the importance of providing food for hungry people, and he twice feeds the hungry (14:15–21; 15:32–38). But he does not use the power he has to his own advantage. He looks to the wilderness experience and quotes from Deuteronomy 8:2–3. There Moses reminds the people how God tested them in the wilderness, allowing them to hunger and only then providing manna in order to make them understand that "one does not live by bread alone, but by every word that comes from the mouth of God" (4:4). The readers of this text would surely also remember that in the wilderness the people's faith in God wavered until the coming of the manna. Jesus, by contrast—though hungry and with no miraculous divine provision to sustain him—remains faithful.

In the second temptation the devil urges that Jesus make a sensational demonstration. He should throw himself from the pinnacle of the Temple and count on God's special protection. The spectacle will surely confirm that he is the Son of God. The tempter even backs up the suggestion with Scripture about how angels would bear him up. This is an extraordinary example of how even Scripture (in the wrong hands) can become the vehicle of a demonic alternative to the path of obedience and suffering that is the path of the Messiah.[20] The path of obedience will one day lead Jesus to the cross without benefit of deliverance by angels (26:53). Though a miraculous display would confirm for all to see, it is not the path he chooses. Again

20. Boring, *The New Interpreter's Bible*, 8:164.

Jesus looks to Deuteronomy for an answer, and he finds it in the injunction that one should not "put God to the test" (Deut. 6:16).

The third temptation is to possess kingdoms and power and glory. The setting of this temptation is a high mountain looking down on "all the kingdoms of the world and their splendor" (v. 8). It is the view from above, looking down. It is a vantage point and life orientation that Jesus will resolutely refuse. Jesus could rule over all the kingdoms of the world—much as the Roman emperor actually did. All that would be required in exchange is to "fall down and worship" the devil. We might speculate with interest whether Matthew means to imply that these kingdoms and empires are in the devil's hands to give. Israel's great creedal affirmation as recorded in Deuteronomy 6:4–5 shapes Jesus' final answer to the invitation of the tempter to serve another as god. "Hear, (*Shema*) O Israel: The LORD is our God, the LORD alone. You shall love the LORD your God with all your heart and with all your soul, and with all your might."[21] This is an affirmation and calling that Jesus, as a faithful Jew, would have learned from his earliest instruction. God alone is God. So he answers, "It is written, "Worship the LORD your God, and serve only him." With this he dismisses the devil.

> Jesus refuses the lure of evil by proclaiming the abiding commitment of his life and mission: "Worship the LORD your God, and serve only him."

In Matthew's writing, mountaintops figure prominently as places of important events and revelations. Here we see the first "mountaintop experience" in the form of the temptation. Perhaps it could even be cast as the temptation of the "view from above." There are other mountaintop moments. The first of

> Jesus and the disciples will continue to struggle against demonic powers throughout the Gospel, but it is a defeated enemy they face.
>
> Boring, *The New Interpreter's Bible*, 8:164.

---

21. The text goes on, "Keep these words that I am commanding you today in your heart. Recite them to your children and talk about them when you are at home and when you are away, when you lie down and when you rise. Bind them as a sign on your hand, fix them as an emblem on your forehead, and write them on the doorposts of your house and on your gates" (Deut. 6:6–8).

the five teaching discourses will be the Sermon on the Mount. In 15:29–30, Jesus goes up the mountain near the Sea of Galilee. There he sits down and crowds of people follow him up the mountain seeking healing. As the mute, the lame, the blind and the maimed come down the mountain cured, the amazed crowds praise the God of Israel. The transfiguration occurs on a mountaintop (17:1–2). Jesus and the disciples, after the Last Supper, go out to the Mount of Olives where Jesus reveals that all will desert him but that he will be raised and go before them to Galilee (26:30–32). The Gospel's story will culminate on a mountaintop with the giving of the Great Commission (28:16–20).

These tempter's words will be thrown at Jesus yet again at the moment of his death as the chief priests, scribes, and passers-by taunt him, (27:40): "If you are the Son of God, come down from the cross." Even Peter, who was so clear that Jesus was "the Messiah, the Son of the living God," urged him to turn back from the way of the cross. Jesus heard the echo of the tempter in Peter's words and responded, "Get behind me, Satan" (16:22–23). Peter the "rock" in verse 18 became the "stumbling block" in verse 23. In this first encounter with the tempter, however, Jesus has already shown what it means for him that he is the Son of God. It means that he will live from the word of God—trusting rather than testing God—and he will worship God alone.

4:12–17

Galilee of the Gentiles

The text that follows is an important transition text. It is the beginning of Jesus' ministry, and Matthew provides four brief scenes: Jesus preaching the reign of God, his return to Galilee, the calling of the disciples, and his demonstration of God's transforming reign in their midst through Jesus' teaching, preaching, and healing.[22]

John has been arrested. His work as forerunner of the Messiah is complete, and Jesus' own ministry begins in earnest. Remarkably Jesus dares to take up the very same message that got John arrested,

---

22. Senior, *Abingdon New Testament Commentaries*, 61.

"Repent, for the kingdom of heaven has come near." The word translated "arrest" in the NRSV literally means "handed over" (Greek
paradidomi). It will appear at several junctures where Jesus is to be
"handed over" (17:22; 20:18; 26:2) leading up to the point where
he is to be "handed over to be crucified" (26:2).

When Jesus heard that John had been arrested, it says that he
"withdrew" to Galilee. This is the same word used when Mary and
Joseph must flee with the baby Jesus, under Herod's threat. The
reader may be given to understand that Jesus is once again under
threat. The word translated "withdrew" (Greek *anachoreo*) is only used
twice in the other Gospels, but Matthew uses it ten times—as describing Jesus' response to threats. It presents Jesus as one who responds in
nonviolent and nonretaliatory ways to aggression against him.[23]

Going to Galilee is doubly significant. Galilee is in the very heart of
Israel. This location keeps faith with a priority of Jesus' mission, which
is first to Israel (10:5). At the same time, it is a place referred to as
"Galilee of the Gentiles," which signals the coming breakthrough of
the mission to the "nations."[24] Matthew quotes Isaiah 9:1, 2, "the people who walked in darkness have seen a great light" (v. 16). It is a text
rich with messianic associations and expectation of a light that would
enlighten the Gentiles in the messianic age. In its original context, this
text refers to the situation of oppression after 722 BCE when Assyria
occupied Zebulun and Naphtali (in the region of Galilee) and exiled
the leadership. Here Matthew transposes the text from one situation
of imperial aggression to another as Israel now suffers under Rome's
imperial control. The promise of the passages that follow (e.g., Isa.
11:4–7) is that the "rod of the oppressor" will be broken "through one
who will embody God's reign of justice, righteousness, and peace."[25]

4:18–22
"Follow Me"

One of the first things Jesus does at this beginning of his ministry is
to call disciples. He forms an alternative community to share in the

23. Boring, *The New Interpreters Bible*, 8:167.
24. Senior, *Abingdon New Testament Commentaries*, 1998, 99.
25. Carter, *Matthew and the Margins*, 115.

work of preaching and showing forth the reign of God. Most rabbis did not seek out their students but rather were sought by them. Here, by contrast, all the initiative rests with Jesus. He comes to them, he sees them, and he calls them to *follow*. It is worth noting that the calling is not a calling to worship Jesus and form a "cult of Jesus." It is not even a calling to "accept him as their personal Lord and savior." They are called to follow him; to walk in the way that he is walking as he proclaims and makes manifest the reign of heaven.

The passage follows a call and response and transition to new identity format. We get a first glimpse of the dynamics of discipleship: in Peter, Andrew, James, and John we see a prototype of all future followers who will respond to Jesus' call.[26] Jesus calls them and they drop everything and follow him "immediately" (4:20). They do not ask where he is going, and he does not tell them. There is no mention of their being "apostles" to hint at their future importance. Nor is there mention of what this calling will cost them. Did Peter and Andrew have any inkling that they would both end up crucified?

The call is unexpected, disruptive, and intrusive. The disciples are called from other good and important things—from work that sustains them and from families that love them. This new commitment may not break these relationships and obligations, but it will now take precedence.

An old hymn titled "They Cast Their Nets in Galilee" captures the ambiguous blessing that is this calling. It pictures the disciples before their encounter with Jesus—peaceful and contented—living the lives of simple fisherfolk. But then, upon encountering Jesus, they find "the peace of God that filled their hearts brimful and broke them too."[27]

It is notable that Jesus is here calling disciples from among the lower social ranks. Warren Carter, describing their status, notes that in Cicero's ranking of occupations, owners of cultivated land rank first and fishermen last.[28] In Athenaeus's writings they are placed on a par with moneylenders and are socially despised as greedy thieves.

---

26. Hare, *Matthew*, 30.
27. William Alexander Percy, "They Cast Their Nets in Galilee," in *The Hymnbook* (New York: Edward B. Marks Music Corp, 1924), 420.
28. Carter, *Matthew and the Margins*, 121.

Furthermore, they are obligated to the empire, which has an economic monopoly. As Juvenal records, "Every rare and beautiful
thing in the wide ocean . . . belongs to the imperial treasury." Not
only must they supply enough fish for themselves and the empire,
they must pay tax upon what they retain and tax upon any transport
of fish. Indeed, Peter, Andrew, James, and John lead an economically
and socially precarious existence.

Jesus' calling comes first to some of the most vulnerable of
people. They are called out of their ordinary lives and customary service to Rome and into God's service. They do receive an
odd sort of promise—they will now "fish for people." They join
God's great and gracious "dragnet" that takes in all kinds of fish
(13:47).

4:23–25
"And great crowds followed him"

The disciples have been called to follow. They will know the commitment and the cost of discipleship. Then there are the crowds
that "follow" Jesus in the sense of following him seeking to hear
the "good news" and receive the "healing" that he offers. Through
his ministry of teaching and healing Jesus not only announces but
actualizes the reality of God's reign.[29] He is God's saving presence in
their midst. Already the circle of influence is enlarging as Jesus, the
itinerant preacher and healer, goes throughout Galilee, and his fame
spreads even into Syria.

While Matthew does not detail the stories of healing here, we
have a summary preview. There are general terms, "the sick, those
who were afflicted with various diseases and pains" (4:24) and there
are particular illnesses named, "demoniacs, epileptics, and paralyt-
ics." Each word designates personal, social, and economic misery for
each victim. In the midst of all this suffering Jesus extends compassion and engages in God's saving work.

29. Senior, *Abingdon New Testament Commentaries*, 63.

FURTHER REFLECTIONS
Baptism as Calling to Ministry

Matthew's account of the baptism of Jesus (in Matthew 3:1–17) adds a significant dimension to the theology and practice of baptism. Jesus' baptism is accompanied by divine blessing, spiritual testing (4:1–11), and the inauguration of his ministry (4:17). If his life and ministry are the "pattern" for ours, what are the implications to be drawn from Matthew's accounting of his baptism? At the end of Matthew's Gospel will come the commission to make disciples, "baptizing them in the name of the Father and of the son and of the Holy Spirit" (Matt. 28:20). This Trinitarian formula has been preserved almost universally in the historic practice of Christian baptism. What does it signify? This brief reflection will first make some general observations regarding sacraments and then turn to consider theology and practice of baptism. Then it will turn to the particular insights drawn from Jesus' baptism as presented in Matthew and the commission to baptize in the name of the Trinity.

A sacrament is sometimes spoken of as a visible sign of an invisible grace. In the wider church there is a continuum of understandings from more symbolic (sacraments stand for something—Huldrych Zwingli) to more instrumental (sacraments do something—Roman Catholic theology) understandings. There is also a range of views as to the place of faith in the reception of the sacrament. For Roman Catholic theology the sacrament in itself is efficacious, received with or without the response of faith. For Zwingli sacraments are primarily an exercise of faith. Somewhere between is Calvin, for whom the sacraments are not "bare signs" and do convey God's grace; however, if not received by faith they do not have their true effect. It would be like pouring water over a stone, which cannot absorb what it is receiving.

In the administration of the sacraments it is customary that there be prayer, invocation of the Spirit, and interpretation through proclamation of the Word. There is also a range of perspectives on how closely the "sign" is related to the "thing signified." At the Roman Catholic end of the spectrum these are very much identified; at the

Zwinglian end of the spectrum they are not to be identified. Luther and Calvin navigate between these extremes, seeing the sign and the thing signified as, in a sense, neither to be confused nor to be separated, with Luther's view closer to the Roman Catholic view and Calvin's closer to Zwingli's view. Generally, the validity of the sacrament does not depend so much upon the celebrant or the recipient as on God's acting or prior acting signified in the sacrament. God's initiative of grace is at the center.

Theology of Baptism

There are multiple dimensions of meaning in the sacrament of baptism. A brief note on some of the dimensions must suffice:

1. Baptism is a sacrament of incorporation into the one body of Christ. It is the rite of Christian initiation (1 Cor. 12:12–13; Gal. 3:27–28) in which God claims us as God's own and we are joined to all who belong to God in Christ.
2. Baptism signifies a washing away of sin (Eph: 5:26). Perhaps this is our most basic symbol in baptism. One of our most basic sensibilities of sin is stain or uncleanness. The prophet Isaiah expresses it this way: "Woe is me! I am lost, for I am a man of unclean lips, and I live among a people of unclean lips" (Isa. 6:5). The psalmist prays, "Purge me with hyssop and I shall be clean, wash me and I shall be whiter than snow" (Ps. 51:7). Baptism is a time for repentance, renunciation of evil, and washing away of sin that signifies forgiveness of sins (Acts 2:38).
3. In baptism there is a dying and rising with Christ. "So if anyone is in Christ, there is a new creation: everything old has passed away; see, everything has become new!" (2 Cor. 15:17)
4. Passing through the waters of baptism is likened to the crossing of the Red Sea in the Exodus, marking a transition from slavery to freedom. Or the crossing of the Jordan, entering into the land of promise. (Rom. 6:1–4; Titus 3:5)
5. In baptism there is an anointing with the Spirit that consecrates setting one apart for service. Prophets, priests, and kings were all anointed. We are incorporated into the threefold work of Christ's ministry as prophet, priest, and king by this anointing (Rev. 1:5–6).

Practice of Baptism

Denominations differ as to their practice around the timing of Baptism. Some baptize infants and adults while others baptize only adults or those who have reached what is referred to as the age of discretion and are able to make their own testimony of faith. The matter cannot be settled by appeal to Scripture. Both sides claim biblical warrants. All the explicitly mentioned baptisms in the New Testament were baptism of adults. However, entire families were baptized that probably included children (Acts 16:15). While there is no explicit mention of the baptism of a child, neither was there explicit mention of baptism of someone who had grown up in the church. It is unclear what the practice in the second generation came to be.

Two important faith convictions are carried by both of these forms of practice, though carried differently by each. The convictions are that God's grace has priority and that our response matters.

Those who welcome infants of members in the faith community for baptism affirm that these are already "children of the covenant," God's own beloved children. God's grace is extended to all of us (adults too) before we are able to respond to God—while we are yet sinners. Baptism is not about what we do but about what God has done. Communities who follow this practice still carry the conviction that our response matters. The parents and congregation promise to raise their children in the nurture and admonition of the Lord so that they may mature in the faith. When they reach the age of discretion they are "confirmed" and "commissioned." At this point they claim for themselves the promises that were claimed for them in their baptism.

Those traditions that baptize only adults are emphasizing the importance of a faith commitment made in baptism. Our response to God matters. Communities that follow this practice still carry the conviction of the priority of God's grace and usually have some form of welcoming practice of dedication or christening for infants. In this way they are acknowledging that indeed these children are already received and beloved by God.

Each practice offers helpful admonitions to the other. It is important to maintain the priority of God's grace in baptism. This sacrament is not about us but about God's grace to us. At the same time, it is important for those who baptize infants to be sure that this does not become something automatic—a kind of rite of passage or social nicety. The radical demands of discipleship must be kept before the whole community of faith. The balance of divine gift and human response is a delicate one.

Denominations also practice various methods of baptism. Immersion, pouring, and sprinkling are all commonly practiced. There are different understandings of the historic practice of baptism. However, each of these three common practices conveys a deep symbol central to the meanings we attach to baptism. Visually and symbolically, immersion seems to lend itself to themes of dying and rising; pouring conveys cleansing from sin; and sprinkling is linked to anointing. Most denominations share in a mutual recognition of baptism and do not "rebaptize" someone who has been baptized by another method in another denomination.

Historical Controversies

Historic controversies around the meaning and practice of baptism may further illumine our theology of the sacrament. One controversy arose around whether the one who administers the sacrament must be pure in the faith in order for the sacrament to be efficacious. In North Africa in the fourth century, during the Diocletian persecution, many of the faithful—including priests—fell away. The Donatists insisted that the weakness in faith of these priests invalidated their sacramental ministries. They formed a separate sect around those priests who had remained faithful. They were encouraging others to join them because only they could offer valid sacramental ministry. Augustine countered this movement. He argued that when the sacraments are administered the true minister is Christ. He is present and, in a sense, presiding at every table. The priest might be a sinner, a heretic, or even a schismatic, but the validity of the sacrament does not depend on the minister but on Christ alone.

Another controversy centered on the person being baptized. Baptism should signify regeneration, but what if, after baptism, one is not truly transformed? Did it mean that baptism did not "take"? Concern over post-baptismal sin led to two odd practices: people seeking rebaptism or people delaying baptism until their death-bed. The conclusion of the church was that this was not necessary. No one needed to be rebaptized nor should baptism be unduly delayed. God's grace granted in baptism has priority and is sufficient. God is faithful to God's promises. Ritual practices such as confession/absolution and extreme unction (last rites) developed as means of addressing pastorally the reality of ongoing struggles of the baptized with faithful living.

Another controversy arose around the place of the community of faith in baptism. The practice of "private baptism" arose, leaving the congregation out of the picture altogether. It has been important for the church to recover the communal dimension of baptism as incorporation into the body of Christ. The community makes a commitment to the one being baptized. Baptism is not an individual matter. "Private baptism" is an oxymoron. If there are extreme circumstances that prevent coming to community worship for baptism (or communion), then most denominations make provision that representatives from the community be present with the one administering the sacrament.

Jesus' Baptism

Jesus' baptism as presented in Matthew 3:1–17 illumines the meaning of baptism still further. In Jesus' context, the baptism John was practicing was a bit of a scandal. It was customary for those who converted to Judaism to undergo "proselyte baptism" indicating their conversion. John, however, came preaching a message of repentance calling everyone—even practicing Jews—to conversion and the baptism that signaled conversion. This was what was at issue in Jesus' dispute with the Pharisees regarding whether the baptism of John was "from heaven" (Matt. 21:25).

Jesus presents himself to John for baptism. With this act, several things happen that are crucial to our understanding of the meaning of Jesus' baptism. John, recognizing Jesus as righteous, is reluctant to baptize him and thinks it would be better if Jesus baptized John instead. Baptism is for those who are repenting. Jesus insists, and in this act Jesus identifies himself with sinners, standing in solidarity with them. The Spirit descends on Jesus and a voice from heaven

says, "This is my Son, the Beloved." Three of the dimensions of baptism that were listed above are present here: the symbol of repentance and washing from sin, the descent of the Spirit (anointing),
and God's "naming and claiming" of Jesus.

An element of Jesus' baptism that the church has not fully recognized is also here. Baptism for Jesus came at the commencing
of his vocation; he responds to God's calling into ministry. What is
the connection between baptism and calling? Karl Barth makes the
radical proposal that these are inextricably connected. In fact, *baptism is ordination for ministry.* His claim is that "all those baptised as
Christians are *eo ipso* concecrated, ordained, and dedicated to the
ministry of the church."[30] This is a provocative insight that recognizes
God's claim upon the lives of all believers in the sacrament of baptism.

It is interesting that in the early church those who had not been
brought up in the church spent three years in catechesis prior to
baptism. Ordination, for those who were baptized, required nothing
further than the service of the laying on of hands, recognizing their
calling to a particular role of leadership and service in the church.
Practices today, for many denominations, are just the reverse. Baptism is readily granted to persons not nurtured in the church, but
ordination—even for those nurtured in the church—requires three
years of concentrated study. Perhaps the church would do well to
reclaim the full force of what it means to be baptized—including
more explicitly the calling to ministry that baptism entails.

In the struggle around ordination for women in the Roman Catholic Church, those who favor the ordination of women have made
a related observation. They argue that in order to be theologically
consistent, the church should either start ordaining women or
should stop baptizing them.

Jesus' own baptism is fundamentally connected with his calling
into ministry and is a kind of commencement of his vocation. This
dimension might profitably be reclaimed by the church today. The
provocative idea of baptism as ordination to ministry might help
the church to live out its conviction of the priesthood of all believers
more fully and faithfully.

---

30. Karl Barth, *Church Dogmatics,* IV/4, *The Christian Life,* ed. G. W. Bromiley and T. F. Torrance,
trans. G. W. Bromiley (Edinburgh: T. & T. Clark, 1981), 201.

Commissioned to Baptize

Not only does Jesus submit himself to baptism; he also commissions the disciples to baptize. He says, "Go therefore and make disciples of all nations, baptizing them in the name of the Father and of the Son and of the Holy Spirit, and teaching them to obey everything that I have commanded you. And remember, I am with you always, to the end of the age" (Matt. 28:20).

As they "make disciples" they are charged to teach them all that Jesus has commanded. With this charge is the assurance of Jesus' ongoing presence. The Trinitarian formula is commended for use in baptism. The new community, by the time of Matthew's writing, would likely be employing this formula in the practice of baptism. It has been carried forward through the history of the church.

As early as Hippolytus, the Trinitarian formula was used around 215 CE in interrogatory form in the service of baptism. Instructions remain from that day and reveal what may have been a rudimentary form of the Apostles' Creed:

> When the person being baptized goes down into the water, he who baptizes him, putting his hand on him, shall say, "Do you believe in God, the Father Almighty?" And the person being baptized shall say, "I believe." Then holding his hand on his head, he shall baptize him once. And then he shall say, "Do you believe in Christ Jesus, the Son of God, who was born of the Virgin Mary, and was crucified under Pontius Pilate, and was dead and buried, and rose again the third day, alive from the dead, and ascended into heaven, and sat at the right hand of the Father, and will come to judge the living and the dead?" And when he says: "I believe," he is baptized again. And again he shall say, "Do you believe in the Holy Spirit, in the holy church, and the resurrection of the body?" The person being baptized shall say, "I believe," and then he is baptized a third time.[31]

Baptism in the name of "the Father, and of the Son, and of the Holy Spirit" is "not a magical incantation. It is a witness to the love of the triune God whose own life is in community and who welcomes

---

31. Hippolytus, "Iterrogatory Creed," *The Apostolic Tradition*, 21, 215 C.E.

all into the new human community founded on grace alone."[32]
From Matthew's faith community to our own today, we baptize in
this name.

FURTHER REFLECTIONS
Encounter with Evil

The temptation text makes reference to "the devil" or "the tempter."
There will be similar references such as "Satan" or "the evil one" at
several points in Matthew as, for example, in the accounts of exorcisms. This is not a way of thinking or speaking that is common in
our day and time—at least at this end of the theological spectrum—
apart from works of fiction and fantasy. Such language is trivialized
in expressions like, "The devil made me do it!" Even ordinary speech
takes on overtones of an evil outside us when we say things like,
"whatever *possessed* you?" Nevertheless, this is the language and
imagery of Jesus' day and the thought-world from which Matthew
writes. What do we make of such references? Do we have to receive
these as literal accounts in order to be faithful to the text?

In the Hebrew Bible "the Satan" (literally "the accuser") is a member of the divine court, a kind of prosecuting attorney who puts
suspected offenders to the test (Job 1–2). With the development
of apocalyptic thought between the Testaments, "Satan" becomes
a proper name for one sometimes thought of as a fallen angel who
rebels against God and resist's God's will.[33] Reference to Satan and
demons as a personal force of evil were part of the social world that
Jesus and Matthew inhabited. Many illnesses were thought of in
terms of demon possession.

In the New Testament healing stories, we have accounts of people
who were "beside themselves" and not in their "right mind." They
come to themselves and regain their sanity through Jesus' healing
powers. Whatever "possessed them" is exorcised; they are set free.
In his prescientific day, when belief in demons was widespread,

32. Daniel Migliore, *Faith Seeking Understanding: An Introduction to Christian Theology* (Grand
Rapids: Eerdmans, 1991), 219.
33. Boring, *The New Interpreter's Bible*, 8:163.

this was the preferred mode of accounting for negative phenomena that had no known explanation. The understanding of disease and mental illness that prevailed in that day assumed evil spirits or demons at work. It makes sense that the healing they found in Jesus would be understood as an exorcising of demons.

Perhaps today, having medical explanations, we do not think of mental illness or disease in terms of demon possession. Robert Cathey has pointed out that talk of demons is "a way of naming evil" that we inherited from an ancient social world; it is a world that many modern Christians simply "no longer inhabit." To go back to this way of speaking would be "like trying to believe the earth is flat and at the center of the universe." Our cosmology is different from the cosmology of the Bible. It does not make sense "to bind the minds and consciences of Christians today to believe in an ancient symbolism of evil as literally true."[34]

The story of the temptation has been variously interpreted in this regard. Some have "demythologized" the text by presenting it in terms of an internal conflict that Jesus experiences as he seeks to understand the meaning of his baptism and his particular calling. How will he live out his role as Messiah? Will he presume upon his special relationship with God for special provision and protection and power? Another approach has been to take a moralistic turn with this text. Jesus serves as a moral example of how to face and fight temptations that come our way. His reliance upon Scripture is lifted up as the best defense.

Yet another approach is to read this story in the wider context of Matthew's presentation of who Jesus, the Messiah, is. The messianic expectations envisioned someone with wonder-working power who would overthrow Israel's oppressors and restore the Davidic monarchy. Matthew presents instead a more humble and more human figure. Instead of the "bread, circuses, and political power" that Matthew's community would have identified with the Roman Empire, Jesus presents an alternative vision of what the kingdom of God might be.[35] Jesus is a trusting and obedient child of God who

---

34. Robert Cathey, "Introduction to Theology" (lecture, McCormick Theological Seminary, Chicago, IL, Spring 2010).

35. Boring, *The New Interpreter's Bible*, 8:166.

does not seek to be an exception to the human condition through special provision, protection, and power. This passage, for Matthew, is definitive as a revelation of what kind of messiah this Jesus will be.

Reflecting theologically on this personification of evil, there is still much more that can be said. This personification is a way of imaging or symbolizing a phenomenon that is very real in our lives. It names a reality that does not go away simply because we demythologize it. We know something of what it is to be possessed as individuals and as entire societies with such things as insatiable greed, unmitigated anxiety, unexamined prejudice, and lust for power. Ordinary people can be turned into "brutal, bloodthirsty mobs or simply into people who are coldly indifferent to injustice and the needs and suffering of others."[36]

Evil is something bigger than our own intentions and actions. It is embedded in systems and structures that have shaped our lives and have us in their thrall. Even today people use the word "demonic" when they make reference to such things as genocide, torture, ethnic cleansing, and human trafficking. It is beyond our comprehension how ordinary people can do such things to other people. It pushes us beyond ordinary language to name this reality.

In relation to evil we are not only responsible agents (guilty, sinners) but also tragic victims. Our misuse of freedom only tells part of the story. We are also deceived, seduced, and ensnared. We have a sense of being overpowered by something larger than ourselves that comes to us from outside ourselves and from which we cannot extricate ourselves. As Paul expresses it in Romans 7:19, "I do not do the good I want, but the evil I do not want is what I do." Scripture has named this experience in many ways—slavery, a struggle with "principalities and powers" (Eph. 6:12 RSV), or the work of "the evil one" (Matt. 13:19). In relation to this reality we need to be "delivered," "set free" by the action of God who saves us and breaks the power of evil in our lives.

This reality should not be lost sight of in our modern reservations about its personification. Nevertheless, some cautionary notes might be sounded, as we acknowledge this phenomenon and its reality. Hendrikus Berkhof, who wrote extensively on sin, cautioned against the temptation to appeal to things outside ourselves—whether an

---

36. Shirley Guthrie, *Christian Doctrine*, rev. ed. (Louisville, KY: Westminster John Knox Press, 1994), 181.

"evil one" or systemic evil or our environment or our heredity—as the reason for what we do. To do so is to abdicate responsibility and have "a coward's excuse for sin."[37]

Another caution is to beware of preoccupation with "the powers of darkness" so that they become a centerpiece for our life of faith. There is some risk of this in the "spiritual warfare" movement in its preoccupation with "battles" and methods of protection from the onslaughts of the evil one. Most scriptural accounts of the devil or the demonic are accounts of *God's* opposition and defeat of them. While we take the power of evil in our lives seriously, we take God more seriously.[38]

> It is the power of God over sin and evil, not sin and evil as such that interests us and is the most important thing we have to talk about.
>
> Guthrie, *Christian Doctrine*, 180.

Following the wisdom already here in Matthew, we also should beware of a tendency to go looking for evil in all the wrong places. We should look not so much to the culturally and religiously "designated" unrighteous (prostitutes and tax collectors in Matthew). We should look to ourselves ("Surely not I, Lord?" 26:22) and to the "designated righteous" (Scribes and Pharisees in Matthew), leaders who mislead the people or are coopted by oppressive powers or use God-language to further their own interests. There are places where evil masquerades as good and deceives us with most beguiling forms. There are other places where powers and influences that are not necessarily evil in themselves come to be diverted from their proper end and become destructive of human life and its possibilities. Then there are the mundane forms of evil in all our petty compromises, self-deceptive rationalizations, and self-serving actions—all those things that diminish our lives.

37. Hendrikus Berkhof, *The Christian Faith: An Introduction to the Study of the Faith*, rev. ed. (Grand Rapids: Eerdmans, 1986), 112.
38. Guthrie, *Christian Doctrine*, 179–82.

5:1–7:29

Teaching: The Sermon on the Mount

Introduction

The Sermon on the Mount is the best known passage in all of Matthew's Gospel. This is the "first and defining moment of Jesus' teaching."[1] It goes to the heart of what it means to live life toward God. New ways of relating to others (5:21–48) and to God (6:1–18) open up in these verses. Exhortations to discernment and warnings of judgment follow (7:1–27).

There are three recurring questions about the Sermon on the Mount: Is the Sermon on the Mount a realistic expectation of how Christians should live? What is the relationship between future (eschatological) hope and pre-sent reality in these teachings? Is there a bit too much emphasis on "works righteousness"? I will elaborate these questions and suggest some ways of thinking about them as we take the Sermon on the Mount to heart.

> The Sermon on the Mount has become a central text ... even today it kindles a longing and hope for a new breed of humanity and a better world.
>
> Ulrich Luz, *The Theology of the Gospel of Matthew*, New Testament Theology (Cambridge, UK: Cambridge University Press, 1995), 42.

(1) What is really expected? Does the Sermon on the Mount offer a realistic ethic?

---

1. Donald Senior, *The Gospel of Matthew*, Interpreting Biblical Texts (Nashville: Abingdon Press, 1997), 102.

Many approaches, as outlined by Joachim Jeremias,[2] seek to narrow the applicability of the Sermon on the Mount and thereby undermine its power to call us to a radically different way of living. Here are some of those proposals:

— This is just an "interim ethic." The second coming was thought to be imminent in the context of the writing of this Gospel. These extreme requirements were only for the brief interim. They were "emergency measures" that are no longer in force in our context. The delay of the second coming calls for a different kind of ethic.

— This is in fact a perfectionist code, and it is required but only for the inner circle of followers. It is not intended for ordinary people who have to live in the real world of economics and politics and must therefore compromise the ethic of love. So this is just for the disciples, or, as was the view in the High Middle Ages, just for those who enter the priesthood or religious orders.

— This is an impossible ethic. Its real function is to show that it is impossible to be righteous. It moves us to cast ourselves on God's mercy and grace. It functions as what we call the "second use of the law;" it convicts us of our sin.

There are valid insights in each of these perspectives, but any one of these taken as the whole story seems designed to deliver us from the demands of discipleship. I would propose that the ethic of the Sermon on the Mount is a fitting ethic not just for "the interim" and not just for an inner circle, but for followers of Jesus in all times and places. It has been pointed out that a new way of life is at the heart of the gospel call.

> The church does not have a social ethic; the church is a social ethic.
>
> Stanley Hauerwas, *The Peaceable Kingdom: A Primer in Christian Ethics* (Notre Dame, IN: University of Notre Dame Press, 1983), 99.

The Sermon on the Mount, in its clarion call to a radically different way of life, does unmask the sinfulness of the life we now

2. Joachim Jeremias, *New Testament Theology: The Proclamation of Jesus.* (New York: Charles Scribner's Sons, 1971).

live—turned in on ourselves as we are. Indeed, it makes our need for God's grace very clear, but the message also moves and motivates us toward the higher righteousness to which Jesus calls us. It does so not by giving a set of prescriptions to be followed in a legalistic manner but rather examples of life oriented by the love of God and neighbor. The living of the law of love is illumined by its application to a few "focal instances." In every case, the disciple is urged to follow in God's way by doing as God does: loving without limits (5:44–45), doing justice, and being merciful (5:7) and forgiving (6:12).

Lisa Sowle Cahill sees this ethic as grounded in the "converted relationship"[3] in which one has indeed turned (or returned) to God as both Jesus and John the Baptist urged. This new relationship is exemplified and made possible in Jesus. It so transforms us in all our other relations that we begin to look upon all—even enemies—with love, just as God does. The calling of the Sermon on the Mount is a calling to behavior "commensurate with whole relationships rather than broken relationships" She notes that this radical reorientation is begun in us though not yet experienced in all its fullness.[4]

(2) What is the relation of future hope (futuristic eschatology) and present reality (realized eschatology) in relation to these teachings?

The "dialectical eschatology"[5] in Matthew is neither simply realized eschatology nor strictly a futuristic eschatology. For Matthew there is a nearness of the reign of God that resists collapsing into futuristic eschatology on the one hand or realized eschatology on the other. The Sermon is full of eschatological themes of warning and the coming future judgment. At the same time, one is called to repent now, because the reign of God has come near. Though the reign of God is not yet present in all its fullness, it has been inaugurated in Jesus Christ. We live now in the tension between the "already" and the "not yet." The reality of God's reign that one day will come in all its fullness already impinges on our present reality. It casts an illuminating light from the future that God intends into the present context. The reign of God is—even now—a "substantive

---

3. Lisa Sowle Cahill, "The Ethical Implications of the Sermon on the Mount," *Interpretation* 41, no. 2 (1987):148.
4. Ibid.
5. Thomas Ogletree, *The Use of the Bible in Christian Ethics* (Philadelphia: Fortress, 1983), 177.

reality" that encourages faithful living oriented by love. It shapes a new and different reality "which maintains standards and perceptions different from the dominant society"[6] So the vision of these teachings in Matthew sees God's reign not only as a future hope but also something that we work for and live into even now.

There is a tendency in reflection on Christian eschatology to collapse into either a realized eschatology on the one hand or a futurized eschatology on the other. Painting with broad strokes, these are liberal and conservative tendencies respectively. Realized eschatology thinks of God's ends as having to do primarily with a new quality of life in the here and how. Taken to an extreme this may reduce the complexity of eschatological symbols to "ciphers of inner self-consciousness." Futuristic eschatology, by contrast, locates fulfillment of God's ends in a radically different reality beyond history. At the extreme, it may divest itself of hope for the historical realization of God's purposes. The former view thinks in terms of continuity while the latter view thinks in terms of discontinuity.

The Gospel of Matthew (and Scripture generally) resists reduction to either of these extremes. The language of "a new creation" or "a new heaven and a new earth" signal both continuity and discontinuity that, held together, represent the "strange logic of eschatology."[7] Future dimensions are expressed in hope for the establishment of peace and justice on earth, the renewal of nature, and the inclusion of the nations. An exclusively futuristic orientation, however, is destabilized by teachings elsewhere that indicate the reign of God as already present in our midst. In Matthew we hear how the reign of God is like a "mustard seed" or like "yeast" leavening the dough. It is something inconspicuous, growing quietly and hiddenly (13:31–33). The transformations it is working

> Redemption beyond history is a basis for hope within history, affecting what is possible within history.
>
> Marjorie Hewitt Suchocki, *The End of Evil: Process Eschatology in Historical Context* (Albany, NY: State University of New York Press, 1988), 82.

6. Ibid.
7. John Polkinghorne and Michael Welker, *The End of the World and the Ends of God: Science and Theology on Eschatology* (Harrisburg, PA: Trinity Press International, 2000), 2.

will become more evident, but may be seen even now in dramatic reversals occurring. Religious values are reevaluated, as in the story of the Pharisee and the publican where, remarkably, it is the publican (the presumed sinner) and not the Pharisee (the presumed righteous one) who is justified.

The balance between futuristic and realized eschatology is maintained in Matthew and is best observed when we see that God's judgment, transformation, and redemption are both future hope and present reality. The reign of God has come near!

(3) Is there not a bit too much emphasis on "works righteousness" in these teachings?

Perhaps the Sermon on the Mount strikes a better balance between God's grace and human action than this question suggests. It is true that it is full of commands to do God's will and "bear fruit," but right alongside these are promises of divine mercy and blessing along the way. These are intertwined throughout. A case in point is the place in the Lord's Prayer where we are enjoined to pray that God will "forgive us our debts as we forgive our debtors." Both grace and responsibility are joined to one another in this text. There is a text later in Matthew that explicates further. In 18:23–35 the "unforgiving debtor" whose debt gets called in serves as a cautionary tale.

Theologically, it seems that Matthew is aligned with the book of James, which insists, "Faith by itself, if it has no works, is dead" (Jas. 2:17). It seems less friendly to Pauline theology where it sometimes seems to disparage works, "we know that a person is justified not by the works of the law but through faith in Jesus Christ" (Gal. 2:16). Martin Luther, out of a conviction that the book of James was unclear on the matter of justification by grace through faith, declared it "an epistle of straw." Lutheran voices to this day place a strong emphasis on justification as the *forgiveness of sins* that is ours in Christ. Roman Catholic voices have focused more on sanctification and *the renewal of life* that is ours in Christ.

John Calvin falls somewhere between these emphases, holding justification and sanctification together as a *duplex gratia*, a "twofold grace." Calvin judged the book of James more favorably and commented approvingly, "faith, without the evidence of good works, is vainly pretended."[8] The balance is struck when we affirm that what we do is "the fruit and not the root" of our salvation. As Calvin went on to say in his commentary on James 2:17, "fruit ever comes from the living root of a good tree." The Second Helvetic Confession makes a clarifying comment that good works have nothing to do with "earning eternal life;" rather they are "for the glory of God, to adorn our calling, to show gratitude to God, and for the profit of the neighbor."[9] The statement has a double impact of rejecting any merit that might be attached to good works while at the same time insisting on the importance of good works.

There is, even to this day, much discussion of the relation of faith and works. The Joint Declaration on the Doctrine of Justification[10] handles the matter very evenhandedly in a consensus statement (Roman Catholics and Lutherans affirming together!): "good works—a Christian life lived in faith, hope, and love—follow from justification and are its fruits" (par. 37). Such a view has no quarrel with the book of James or with Matthew's viewpoint. Put more simply, it has been said that God, as loving parent, will love us no matter what we do, but precisely because God loves us, what we do matters to God.

In the Sermon on the Mount, this twofold grace is exemplified. Grace and calling to obedience intertwine. They are not a before and after. The law is not primarily a judge that convicts us of sin; it is primarily a guide for life in relation to God and neighbor. It is already an expression of God's grace to us. In Matthew's view of the law one hears tones of Psalm 19 where the law is experienced as reviving the soul, making wise the simple,

> The Sermon elaborates the contours of a way of life commensurate with God's gift and reign.
>
> Warren Carter, *Matthew and the Margins: A Socio-Political and Religious Reading* (Sheffield, England: Sheffield Academic Press, 2000), 105.

---

8. John Calvin, *Commentary on the Epistle of James*, trans. John Owen (Grand Rapids: Wm. B. Eerdmans, 1966), 2:17–18.

9. *The Constitution of the Presbyterian Church (U.S.A.)* Part I, *Book of Confessions* (Louisville, KY: Office of the General Assembly, Presbyterian Church (U.S.A.), 1999), 5.117.

10. Anna Case-Winters, "Joint Declaration on the Doctrine of Justification: Reformed Comments," (88–98), in *Concord Makes Strength: Essays in Reformed Ecumenism*, ed. John Coakley (Grand Rapids: Eerdmans, 2002).

rejoicing the heart, and enlightening the eyes. The law is a good gift of God in its role as a guide for living.[11] To live in this way is to already experience the hoped for reign of God. The new relationship with God that Jesus exemplifies is open now for all who would follow him.

Another note needs to be sounded here. The "righteousness" to which the Sermon on the Mount calls people is not a sinless perfection but a calling to do justice and love mercy (*tsedaqah*). Matthew is the only synoptic Gospel that uses the word *dikaiosynē*, or justice. Five of his seven uses are here in the Sermon on the Mount. Clearly it is an important theme for him in understanding Jesus' central message. To "know God" is to do justice (Jer. 22:15–16).

5:3–12

Blessed . . .

When Jesus goes up the mountain and sits down he is surrounded by his disciples and he begins to teach them (5:1–2). These are persons who have "encountered God's saving initiative, call and demand in Jesus and have responded positively to it."[12] The crowds are overhearing and given to know that this transformed life lived under the reign of God is possible for them as well—with all its blessing and all its risks.

The orientation and experience reflected in the beatitudes are commensurate with this commitment. Their new relationship with God transforms life in such a way that hard circumstances (mourning, persecution) and committed service (peacemaking, hungering and thirsting for righteousness/justice) are transformed into blessing. The first four beatitudes declare blessing for those who were traditionally understood as being defended by God: the poor, those who mourn, the meek, and those who hunger and thirst for righteousness/justice. The second set blesses those who do what is right by being merciful and pure in heart, making peace and enduring

---

11. This is the traditional "third use of the law." The first use is to convict of sin. The second is for regulation of the society. The third use of the law, in Reformed theology, is its primary use.
12. Warren Carter, *What Are They Saying about Matthew?* (New York: Paulist Press, 1994), 83.

the persecution[13] that attends following in the way of Jesus Christ. When one's life is characterized by the attributes highlighted in the beatitudes, two things are assured: blessedness on the one hand and persecution on the other.

Matthew's rendering of the beatitudes differs from Luke's in a couple of ways. Luke says "Blessed are the poor," where Matthew says, "Blessed are the poor in spirit." Luke says, "Blessed are you who hunger now" where Matthew says, "Blessed are those who hunger and thirst for righteousness." Many commentators treat this as a "spiritualizing" that waters down the prophetic impact of Luke's version.[14] Senior has pointed out that Matthew's approach is to emphasize human response to the Gospel through authentic virtue and doing God's will. The blessings are directed toward those who have a certain disposition and inclination to act in ways consistent with God's will rather than toward those who have a particular circumstance or status. Matthew is taking an ethical perspective.[15]

In a way the beatitudes are "more description than instruction;" they are a kind of report from the other side of radical commitment for those who have entered into life within God's community of love and justice.[16] For those who have "crossed over" there is genuine blessedness. They are living—even now—in the reign of God. Patricia Farris speaks of how the Beatitudes "turn the world upside down with their shocking promise that is full of dramatic reversals—comfort for the mourning, inheritance for the meek, satisfaction that comes from hungering and thirsting for righteousness/justice. The beatitudes, she says, are a welcome "antidote to the contrived happiness of consumerism and mindless entertainment of our day, they are good news to God's people, the humble of the earth . . . "[17] Those

---

13. At the time of Matthew's writing, persecution was used against those holding religious beliefs that were different. It could include social and economic reprisals (boycotting goods, refusal to hire, imposition of fines), exclusion from the synagogue, imprisonment, flogging, and even death. Michael Crosby, *House of Disciples: Church Economics and Justice in Matthew.* (Maryknoll, NY: Orbis, 1988), 169.
14. Senior, 104.
15. Ibid.
16. Patricia Farris, "Be Happy (Micah 6:1–8; Matthew 5:1–12)" *Christian Century* (January 26, 2005): 18.
17. Ibid., 18.

who have "crossed over" to radical commitment do not find a life of ease and luxury; they find a life of blessedness instead.

The phrases of the beatitudes may well have reference not only to discipleship attitudes but to minority social position (those who are meek, poor in spirit, hungering and thirsting for righteousness/justice).[18] That would be consistent with the warnings elsewhere in Matthew (6:19-21) concerning the danger that wealth and power present to the higher righteousness to which the disciples are called.

For those of us who mean to be in that company of the blessed the question necessarily arises concerning how we may live this alternative reality in the face of the powers that oppress the poor, crush the meek, persecute the righteous, and promulgate violence around the world and in our streets? What gestures will we offer that accompany these words? What commitments will we make? What risks will we take? What dreams will we dream?"[19] If we would—even now—live under the reign of God, there are implications. The alternative reality will chaff against the present reality. To love as God loves is to be discontented with the present reality. "Until the eschatological reversal takes place, it is not possible to be content with the status quo."[20] In our discontent, we may pray with William Sloane Coffin, "Because we love the world . . . we pray now . . . for grace to quarrel with it, O Thou Whose lover's quarrel with the world is the history of the world . . ."[21]

5:13-16
Salt and Light

Next comes a transition from the beatitudes to the instruction portion of the Sermon on the Mount. It is prefaced with "salt and light" sayings addressed to the disciples in a way that points them toward their mission in the world. Neither salt nor light exists for its own sake. The salt needs to stay salty to fulfill its function and the light

18. Cahill, "The Ethical Implications of the Sermon on the Mount," 151.
19. Farris, "Be Happy," 18.
20. W. D. Davies and D. C. Allison, "Matthew 1-7," in *The Gospel according to St. Matthew.* 3 vols., International Critical Commentary (Edinburgh: T & T Clark, 1988-97), 448.
21. Commencement Prayer, Yale, 1962.

needs to be lifted up to give light. These metaphors imply a turning outward toward mission in the world. The impact of the followers of Jesus upon others is part of the message here. Something good and desirable is given that will cause them to give glory to God (v. 16). The scope of this blessing is the widest possible—"salt of *the earth*," "light of *the world*."

The universal scope of divine blessing through the people of God is consistent with the theme in Hebrew Scriptures of "blessed in order to be a blessing" (Gen. 12:2; 22:18) and called to be a "light to the nations" (Isa. 2:2–5, 42:6; 49:6). Particular blessings are for the sake of the universal blessing. The gifts/functions of salt and light are not self-contained; they are meant to be shaken out and shining forth. Followers of Jesus need to be salty and we have to shine. Are we "salt of the earth" kind of people? Are we "shining examples" of God's light in the world? Do people have cause to praise God (v. 16) because of us? In passing, the illustration of a city set on a hill is also employed. The community of disciples cannot be a closed community, an "introverted secret society shielding itself from the world."[22] Its witness is public.

5:17–20
Fulfilling the Law and the Prophets

Jesus' fulfilling the law and the prophets can have several dimensions of meaning:

1. That Jesus brings into being what the law and prophets promised. Reference to the fulfilling of the law is often made just before Matthew quotes something from the Hebrew Bible.
2. That Jesus himself does what the law and prophets in fact require of us. His life is molded by the law, and it defines his vocation and the conduct of his life.[23]

22. Eugene Boring, *The New Interpreters Bible: New Testament Articles, Matthew, Mark* (Nashville: Abingdon Press, 1995), 8:182.
23. Warren Carter, *What Are They Saying about Matthew's Sermon on the Mount?* (New York: Paulist Press, 1994), 95.

3. That Jesus teaches and lives the deeper meaning of the law,
which is best understood in terms of the love command on
which "hang all the law and the prophets" (22:40). All the
laws concerning tithing, ritual purity, and Sabbath observance remain in place, but they are subordinate to the love
command. Love exceeds these. It requires more and not
less than the law.

All three of these dimensions seem to be involved in Jesus' relation to the law and the prophets as variously presented in the Sermon on the Mount. There is a balance of Jesus' obligation to the
law and the prophets and his authority to interpret their weightier
matters. The commandments of the Torah are not all of the same
weight. Jesus argues later that love and compassion for the neighbor
outweighs matters such as cultic observance (12:1–14; 22:40). He
chides the scribes and Pharisees because they "tithe the mint, dill
and cumin, and have neglected the weightier matters of the law: justice, mercy and faith." Jesus' own life is an exemplar of attending to
the weightier matters.

The disciples are warned that their righteousness must exceed
that of the scribes and Pharisees. There follow six vignettes that
exemplify the higher righteousness Jesus is talking about.

5:21–48
Calling to a Higher Righteousness

The six vignettes in the next section are each introduced by "you
have heard that it was said, . . . But I say to you . . ." Some have called
these the six "antitheses," but this makes it sound as if Jesus contradicts the teaching given. He does not. Quite the contrary, he insists
that "not one letter, not one stroke of a letter" (5:18) will pass away.
He rather employs a method from "rabbinic rhetoric" where the second statement clarifies a previous statement. His purpose seems to
be to "deepen, intensify and radicalize" the teachings that have been
given.[24] Taking each focal instance in turn, it can be seen that the

24. Pinchas Lapide, *The Sermon on the Mount: Utopia or Program for Action?* (Maryknoll, NY:
Orbis, 1986), 45–46.

love command, when placed at the heart and center of these pro-
nouncements, extends their meaning.

1. Love goes further than "not murdering." It curtails even
   anger and insults that would alienate us from one another.
   Reconciliation with an offended brother or sister takes
   precedence even over acts of worship, as we see in the
   injunction concerning offerings (5:23–24). One is first to
   be reconciled with one's brother or sister and only then to
   come and offer one's gift.
2. Love goes further than "not committing adultery. Faithfulness of the heart (v. 28) and of the whole self is enjoined.
   Here, as in the preceding example, Jesus intensifies and
   "internalizes" the law. It is not only murder but anger, not
   only adultery, but also lust that is ruled out. It is not just
   what can be seen but what goes on in the heart that counts.
   One is reminded of the promise in Jeremiah 31:33: "I will
   put my law within them, and I will write it on their hearts;
   and I will be their God, and they shall be my people."
3. Love does not presume upon technical/legal permissions
   such as the provision for divorce. By custom in that day,
   divorce was technically permitted. It was even made easy
   as long as a proper certificate was given. Notably, in the
   patriarchal context of this vignette, the question only pertains to a man who "divorces his wife" (5:13) and never
   to a woman divorcing her husband. Women were always
   disadvantaged by divorce due to their complete economic dependency on their husbands. Unlike the situation of women today, a divorced woman in that context
   was socially and economically marginalized, being left
   without means of support for herself and her children. In
   19:3–9, Jesus elaborates that divorce is not God's intention but an accommodation to reprehensible hard-heartedness. In the present passage, the rule of love limits the
   exercise of this option to the extremes where the relationship is already broken.
4. The traditional injunction not to swear falsely but to fulfill
   what one swears to is further intensified to insist on full
   truthfulness quite apart from the swearing of oaths. Love
   already entails truthfulness. One's "yes" means "yes," and
   "no" means "no;" so that one need not swear at all.

5. "An eye for an eye and a tooth for a tooth" was a law that kept vengeance from running rampant. Where vengeance is without such restraints in some cultures entire villages may be destroyed in retaliation for a wrong done or an offense given. The "eye for an eye" that seems extreme to us served to maintain a norm of proportionality in retaliation. Love requires more than measured, proportional retaliation. There follow (6:29–30) five instances in which one person acts in disregard for another: striking, robbery, begging, confiscation, and conscription. In every case, Jesus proposes an unexpected counteraction such as turning the other check. Each response exemplifies a practice of "nonretaliation" that Jesus commends. The response to these impositions is not that of a passive victim but as an agent who asserts power in a way that is positive and unconventional. What might have been a humiliation is met with a "dignity asserting" act of giving.[25] For example, at that time representatives of Rome had the legal right to conscript civilians into service to carry their gear for up to a mile. Rather than begrudging this imposition, Jesus invites his followers to a generosity that does more than what is asked—to go the second mile.[26] Although these responses are counterintuitive and countercultural, they reflect a generosity that is a more fitting response for people living under God's reign of love.

6. Love for members of one's own household was to be expected. "Love your neighbor" (following the command from Leviticus 19:18) already extended this to an unexpectedly wide circle. Jesus draws the circle wider still in this final injunction. It is hard enough in many instances to love your neighbor, but "love your enemies"? Really? Reconciliation and love rather than retribution and enmity are befitting life under the reign of God.

These six "focal instances" provide examples of what it would look like to live out the "higher righteousness" to which the people of God are called. As the people of God, the love we manifest should be more like God's love, illustrated by letting the sun rise and the

---

25. Warren Carter, "Love Your Enemies," *Word and World* 28, no. 1 (2008): 18.
26. Crosby, *House of Disciples*, 184.

rain fall on both righteous and unrighteous (v. 45). This is love without limits and exclusions. If we love and act lovingly only toward those who love us, what do we do more than others? In what way are we showing ourselves to be the children of a God whose love is "perfect"? We are enjoined to be perfect as God is perfect (v. 48). For this, reciprocity is not good enough; a greater (divinely demonstrated) generosity is required. In the Septuagint the word translated "perfect" is *teleios*. It has the connotation of being complete or whole. To be perfect in this sense is to be wholehearted[27] in our love. Living in this way, we imitate God's perfection in love.

The higher righteousness demonstrated in these vignettes does not constitute a set of prescriptions (legalism) on the one hand nor does it imply an abrogation of the law (antinomianism) on the other.[28] For Jesus, as for the Pharisees, the law is God's good gift and guide for living. What Jesus offers here might be termed an "interpretive key" for understanding what the law, at its heart, requires. "It is a radical gift of self to God and neighbor in both inner thought and outward action. It pursues the Law to its ultimate intention . . ."[29]

As Ulrich Luz has pointed out, "The Sermon on the Mount contains examples, pictorial hyperboles (e.g., 7:2–4) and metaphorical imperatives (e.g., 5:29–30) to goad its readers into motion. But it does not set down 'laws.'"[30] These examples do not provide a comprehensive set of explicit instructions for living life in the service of love. They rather suggest a "pattern" that is open-ended and could be extended to many very different situations. The axioms of "love your enemies" and "do unto others" have to be worked out as they are lived out. The pattern stimulates moral imagination and calls people to responsible living. As Lisa Cahill has observed, the ethics of the Sermon on the Mount are "ethics as imitation of God."[31] Living life in this way is a foretaste of the Reign of God.

---

27. Warren Carter, *Matthew and Empire: Initial Explorations* (Harrisburg, PA: Trinity Press International, 1994), 95.
28. This view held that with the advent of the Gospel, obedience to the law is not necessary. Christ is the end of the law, and salvation is by grace through faith. Paul contended with this view in Romans 6:1ff. "Shall we continue in sin in order that grace may abound? By no means!"
29. Crosby, *House of Disciples*, 182.
30. Luz, *Theology of the Gospel of Matthew*, 56.
31. Cahill, "Ethical Implications of the Sermon on the Mount," 149.

In the face of various aggressions and impositions (being struck on the cheek, having one's coat taken, being forced to go one mile, being importuned by beggars), completely unconventional counter actions are urged. Warren Carter notes that with these counterintuitive and countercultural responses, each, in its own way, is not only a loving response but also an assertion of dignity and power and an implicit invitation to the enemy, aggressor, or importuner to a different kind of interaction.[32] Turning the other cheek, for example, "does not betoken passivity, weakness, resigned indifference, or submission, and it will not change the system. Rather it is an act of self-assertion that counters the intent to humiliate and invites the striker to interactions other than violence."[33]

One feature of these particular instances is that they are all in tension with our ordinary ways of thinking and acting. They shock and provoke; they unsettle and destabilize. The crowds were "astounded at his teaching" (7:28). Robert Tannehill suggests the hearer's "mouth falls open." The first response might be defensive, immediately moving to justify and protect our ordinary ways of being. All the same, the provocation of these powerful "focal instances" arouses our moral imagination[34] and invites a reorientation. A new disposition and intentionality accompanies this reorientation to God's reign of love, and these changes issue in new habits of thought and action.

> Ordinary religious and moral expectations are shaken to their roots and one is transfixed by Jesus' transparency to the reign of God.
>
> Cahill, "Ethical Implications of the Sermon on the Mount," 153.

6:1–35

True Piety

Even one's practices of piety receive a reorientation. Here follows a discussion of the practices of authentic piety as they may be seen

---

32. Carter, "Love Your Enemies," 17.
33. Ibid., 18.
34. Robert Tannehill, "The 'Focal Instance' as a Form of New Testament Speech: A Study of Matthew 5:39–42," *Journal of Religion* 50 (1970): 372–85.

in relation to almsgiving, praying, fasting, and putting possessions in their place. The word here translated as "piety" (6:1) is actually the Greek word *dikaiosynē*, which is translated "righteousness" in the chapter before. This chapter is a continuation of the discussion of "a higher righteousness," and the use of the same term for both "piety" and "righteousness" underscores that there is "no distinction between devotion to God, expressed in acts of worship (6:1–18), and acts of personal integrity, justice, and love directed to human beings, *all* of which are called *dikaiosynē*."[35]

The term usually translated "righteousness" can equally well be translated "justice." It appears five times in the Sermon on the Mount alone (5:5, 10, 20; 6:1, 33). This theme is so prominent in the Gospel of Matthew that it has been called the "Gospel of Justice."[36] Justice includes a (re)ordering of relationships with God, with one another, and in the social/political arena. A right ordering will adjust toward equality and reciprocity and a general sharing of resources. Patriarchy, hierarchy, and inequitable distribution will be overturned. The emphasis is on creating a new kind of community where justice prevails. The Sermon on the Mount proclaims God's opposition to the ordinary practices of violence, oppression of the meek, and greed for material goods. Michael Crosby draws out the implications of righteousness/justice in the book of Matthew for ecclesiology (church house order) and economics (world house order). This central theme of the concern for justice shapes the way Jesus' teaching about explicitly religious practices such as almsgiving, prayer, and fasting might best be understood. The chapter will conclude with the calling to serve God alone and to seek God's reign above all else.

A central point in what follows is a recurring caution that true piety is not for show. Contrasts run through the discussion of almsgiving, fasting, and prayer. On the one hand are ostentatious practices done publicly to be seen by people and resulting in their immediate approbation. On the other hand are practices of genuine piety that are done inconspicuously and directed toward God (who knows the heart and will reward accordingly). These reflect

35. Boring, *The New Interpreter's Bible*, 8:200.
36. Crosby, *House of Disciples*, 146.

higher righteousness, which Jesus represents and to which he calls his followers.

In this section of the Sermon on the Mount, the problem of hypocrisy receives more considered attention. The Greek term *hupokritai* is used in 6:2, 6:5, and 6:16. In classical Greek culture *hupokritai* referred to persons reciting poetry or performing drama. In that context it did not necessarily have a negative connotation. However, it could take on a negative connotation just as when "acting" (a term not negative in its own right) may come to be negative when it conveys "pretense" or "deception." In the Septuagint and Hellenistic Jewish literature *hupokritēs* generally had the pejorative connotation of intentional deception.[37] Dan Via has argued that in Matthew, hypocrisy is not only a matter of deception of others but also a matter of self-deception. The "hypocrites" in these verses make a show of righteousness. They are motivated by desire for the praise of others (6:2). This show, along with the praise they receive, allows them to deceive themselves that they are righteous. Via draws upon Bruce Wilshire's observation of the phenomenon of "mimetic engulfment" in this connection. We may succeed in "hiding ourselves from ourselves by believing that we are what others believe us to be, by becoming engulfed in their opinions about us. We convince others by pious acts that we are righteous, and their belief about us reinforces our belief that we are righteous."[38]

In this passage, "hypocrites" believe that they are deserving of divine reward, but this is delusion—they already have their reward in the praise of others. Only those whose piety is "wholehearted"—arising from integrity between internal being and external action—will be rewarded. The concern for "wholeness" expressed in 5:48 is reinforced in the discussion of "true piety," which now follows in 6:1–19.

6:2–4 *Giving Alms*

The passage begins with the cautions around hypocrisy which makes a show, sounding a trumpet to call attention to giving alms.

37. Dan Via, *Self-Deception and Wholeness in Paul and Matthew* (Philadelphia: Fortress, 1990), 92.
38. Ibid, 93.

This recasts the action as not being rightly motivated by love of God or neighbor (true piety) but ordered toward making a spectacle for a play for public approbation.

The word translated "alms" here (Greek *eleemosune*) means "gifts of mercy." It is a word which, in the Septuagint, is one of the two Greek terms used to translate the Hebrew concept *tsedaqah*. The other term (Greek *dikaiosunē*) means "justice." Thus, in place of the more comprehensive integrated term *tsedaqah*, we have justice on the one hand and mercy on the other. These two belong together for Matthew. The gifts of mercy are given in compassion so that people may have their basic needs met. This is a central concern of justice. Hebrew Scriptures used *tsedaqah* to reference the responsibility of the upper classes to meet the needs of the under classes. It was not charity, but simple justice for those with greater resources to use them on behalf of those who were poor. It did not go without notice that in many cases it was the poor, in fact, who helped create those greater resources.[39]

In our day, when the gap between rich and poor is great and growing, these texts stand out with particular relevance and urgency. In Matthew's day, among households and house churches of his community "there existed a huge gap between the powerful and the powerless, the rich and the poor,"[40] those with status and those at the margins. Almsgiving was a kind of voluntary redistribution of resources. It was consonant with the religious heritage of Judaism in which Sabbath days and Sabbath years protected the poor and the land from overworking or unrelieved exploitation.

> Almsgiving was not so much a matter of charity as an essential demand of justice.
>
> Crosby, *House of Disciples*, 187.

For Matthew there is also a connection between this mercy/compassion and feeding hungry people. This is reiterated in several texts (9:13; 12:7; 14:14; 15:32). There is a connection to breaking bread together and table fellowship in the house churches. "Table companionship should be celebrated by those who have compassion; who invite the stranger, who do not betray each other, who have

39. Crosby, *House of Disciples*, 187.
40. Ibid.

been reconciled, and who share their resources with those in need
. . . In the eucharist, those who are full of this mercy will receive it."[41]
Sharing bread at table is a fundamental practice of communion and
justice.

6:5-15 Giving Alms

As with almsgiving, true piety in prayer is not for show. In making
the contrast Matthew draws out some negative examples, some are
from the Jewish synagogue and some are from Gentiles practices.
It is a mistake to assume from these singular negative examples
that this entails a wholesale renunciation of the worship practices
of Jews or Gentiles. Matthew's worship community includes both
Jews and Gentiles. The concern is for authenticity.

Jesus criticizes hypocrites (Greek *hupokritai*, "stage actors")
who make a public spectacle in the synagogue and street corners
in order to be seen praying. This is not a critique of public community prayer as such; else "he would called for the abolition of
the whole institution of Temple and synagogue."[42] The phrases of
the Lord's Prayer are plural indicating communal corporate prayer.
The point is that the prayer should be directed to God alone.
Furthermore, one does not have to be in a "holy place" in order to
pray—God can hear prayers offered from an inner room or closet
or shed (Greek *tameion*). Jesus' warnings against hypocrisy are
consistent with Jewish teachings in his own time against ostentation in prayer.[43]

Nor is it necessary to "heap up empty phrases" in order for
God to hear prayer (v. 7). Heaping up empty praises may refer
to the practice of praying to many gods, repetition of prayer
formulas, or *glossolalia*. The fault here could again be misdi-
rection, praying in a way that calls attention to oneself so that
observers may hear and judge approvingly. It might be from a
theological misunderstanding, that God—otherwise inatten-
tive, uncaring, and reluctant to respond to human need—will
be moved to listen by many words. Jesus claims the contrary

41. Ibid., 165.
42. Boring, *The New Interpreter's Bible*, 8:201.
43. Ibid.

when he insists that God "already knows" what we need and knows even before we ask. This is a God who is paying attention and cares and provides (7:25–33). This is the same God who, in the story of the Exodus, saw and heard and responded to the need of the people (Exod. 3:7–8).

Given that this is the kind of God to whom we pray, Jesus commends a brief and simple prayer that has ever since been offered up by his followers all around the world and down the years. No New Testament text is better known or has had more influence on Christian piety than the Lord's Prayer.[44] The Lord's Prayer sits squarely in the middle of the Sermon on the Mount as its "structural and theological center."[45] Matthew's form of the Lord's Prayer "breathes the spirit of Jewish piety found in such synagogue prayers as the Kaddish."[46] It was customary for Jewish prayers of the first century to address God as "Our Father," to pray for the hallowing of God's name and the coming of God's reign.[47] The transformation of thought and life reflected in the Sermon on the Mount is not feasible apart from the life of prayer. The practice of prayer reflects the reality of God's reign in our lives here and now. To pray this prayer has ethical implications. (See "Further Reflections: How Shall We Pray? Ethical Implications of Praying the Lord's Prayer," pp. 106–22.)

6:16–18 *Fasting*

As with almsgiving and prayer, fasting that reflects true piety precludes making a public display of it. The custom of covering the face with a cloth or ashes (Greek *aphanizo*, "to disfigure or render unrecognizable") and not washing turns an act of worship into theater.[48] This is hypocrisy and not true fasting. To wash and put oil on the head as Jesus urges would render the fasting inconspicuous to others but visible and acceptable to God.

Fasting is, in its own way, a countercultural act. In a setting of the

---

44. Donald Senior, *Abingdon New Testament Commentaries: Matthew* (Nashville: Abingdon Press, 1998), 84.
45. Boring, *The New Interpreter's Bible*, 8:202.
46. Senior, *Abingdon New Testament Commentaries*, 1998, 84.
47. Boring, *The New Interpreter's Bible*, 8:202.
48. Carter, *Matthew and the Margins*, 170.

Roman Empire (a setting not unlike our own) economic structures serve the rich elite and the powerful. They do not serve the 99 percent. The poorest of the poor in particular are in desperate situations. The norm is greedy accumulation and a self-indulgent consumption. The self-denial entailed in fasting is not only a spiritual discipline but a countercultural act.

As Crosby notes, Matthew, more than any other Gospel, relies on Second Isaiah (Isa. 40–55). Jesus is the fulfillment of the righteousness/justice that Second Isaiah proclaims. It is fitting, then, to draw a connection between this text in Matthew on the practice of fasting and Isaiah 58 on fasting. One should not fast "like the hypocrites" (v. 16) for whom this is a mere show of piety, but rather one should seek a "true fast." Isaiah 58:3–5 rails against people who go through the ritual of fasting while practicing injustice. The people complain that God is not responsive to their fasting, and their complaint receives an answer.

> "Why do we fast, but you do not see?
>   Why humble ourselves, but you do not notice?"
> Look, you serve your own interest on your fast-day,
>   and oppress all your workers.
> Look, you fast only to quarrel and to fight
>   and to strike with a wicked fist.
> Such fasting as you do today
>   will not make your voice heard on high.
> Is such the fast that I choose,
>   a day to humble oneself?
> Is it to bow down the head like a bulrush,
>   and to lie in sackcloth and ashes?
> Will you call this a fast,
>   a day acceptable to the LORD?

Verses 6–7 follow, describing the fast that God chooses.

> Is not this the fast that I choose:
>   to loose the bonds of injustice,
>   to undo the thongs of the yoke,
> to let the oppressed go free,
>   and to break every yoke?

Is it not to share your bread with the hungry,
and bring the homeless poor into your house;
when you see the naked, to cover them,
and not to hide yourself from your own kin?

An implied participation in economic reordering toward justice is here connected with fasting. This is a fasting born of a true piety.

6:19–35 *Putting Possessions in Their Place*

Another measure of true piety is in putting possessions in their place. God and God's reign take center stage. Possessions should not be the focus of the heart's devotion, inordinate valuation, or anxious striving. Jesus drives home the point with sayings regarding two treasures, two eyes, and two masters.

Storing up treasures on earth is a fruitless enterprise, for these possessions are vulnerable to decay and loss,[49] and one risks one's heart in the bargain. "For where your treasure is, there will your heart be also" (v. 21). Storing up treasures on earth is contrasted here with storing up treasures in heaven. In Judaism "treasure in heaven" was connected with charitable giving to those in need.[50] People who have put possessions in their place are less likely to be in a state of anxious striving to accumulate and protect possessions with a callous disregard of the demands of justice or the needs of others. Consequently, they are free to be generous with others. Again the higher righteousness/justice is invoked. It is the real "treasure" (vv. 19, 20; Greek *thēsaurous*) to be "treasured." The sayings about the healthy and the unhealthy eye may be more difficult to interpret, but in the context of this discussion on possessions they may be best understood as another metaphor making the same point. Senior points out that the common assumption that the eye is the window to the soul was carried further in Jewish thought where "the healthy eye" was a

---

49. Senior, *Abingdon New Testament Commentaries*, 87.
50. Charles H. Talbert, *Reading the Sermon on the Mount: Character Formation and Decision Making in Matthew 5–7* (Grand Rapids: Baker Books, 2008), 121.

metaphor for one who is generous whereas "the unhealthy eye" signaled one who was covetous and possessive.[51] "A greedy man's eye is not satisfied with a portion" (Sir. 14:9). "A stingy man's eye begrudges bread" (Sir. 14:10).

Jesus warns very directly that, "You cannot serve God and wealth" (Matt. 6:24). To attempt this divided service is to have a divided heart. Only a wholehearted commitment to God will do. There is an either/or decision implied here, with the caution that to be devoted to one is to despise the other. To serve wealth is to "despise" God. Wealth can, and often does, become a functional deity to whom we give dedicated service. In our materialist/consumerist society, where we "live to shop," this is perhaps the chief competitor for our heart's allegiance. It was also the case in the time of Matthew's writing. Carter has pointed out Juvenal's comment in the Satires that "*Pecunia* (wealth), even without its own altar, is the most honored god among the Romans."[52] One must reject this "god" in order to worship the true and living God.

> Being a disciple has always required Christians to be cultural atheists, publically disavowing . . . the myriad . . . gods of popular life.
>
> Frederick Dale Bruner, *The Christbook: Matthew 1–12* (Grand Rapids: Eerdmans, 2004), 182.

The theme of "putting possessions in their place" continues in three "Do not worry about . . ." passages (vv. 25, 31, 34) in which Jesus urges his followers to seek the reign of God first and trust that what is needed will be provided. Of course, it is not enough to say, "Do not worry." Capacity to trust in God's providence enough not to worry requires seeing the world altogether differently. With illustrations from the natural world, Jesus leads toward a new way of seeing. God's care is so apparent in the natural world. More than once in Matthew's Gospel Jesus looks to the world of nature when he wants to talk about God's providence—a personal and particular care (10:29). Everywhere we turn our eyes there is evidence of God's provision. Birds of the air that "neither sow nor reap nor gather into barns" receive their food. The lilies of the field are gloriously clothed

51. Senior, *Abingdon New Testament Commentaries*, 87.
52. Juvenal, *Satires* (1.112.14; 3.162.3), referenced in Carter, *Matthew and the Margins*, 175.

even though they do not toil or spin. He makes his case with an *a minore ad maius* argument (from the lesser to the greater). If God cares for birds and lilies, will God not also care for us? So why should we worry so much, obsessing over, "What will we eat?" or "What will we drink?" or "What will we wear?"

The direction of Jesus' comments does not signal disregard of the struggle for survival that many people face. Other texts make clear his concern and calling to care for the poor (19:21). Neither does this text evidence naiveté concerning the importance of being attentive to basic needs. "Do not worry" is not a license for irresponsibility but an occasion for reorienting ourselves. It urges us to place our needs within the larger horizon of God's reign to which we are whole-heartedly committed and to trust in God's continual care and provision for all creation.

What is excluded is "a debilitating anxiety that is antithetical to trust in God."[53] The cognate noun of the verb used here ("anxiety, worry:" Greek *merimna*) is used elsewhere in association with sleeplessness (1 Macc. 6:10 and Sir. 42:9). What is being prohibited is the energy draining, chronic, paralyzing anxiety that is futile and even self-destructive. Not only does it not "add a single hour to your span of life" (Matt. 6:27), it sucks the life right out of you. It shortens lives and makes what life we do have a fretful misery. Instead of expending ourselves in needless, unproductive, debilitating anxiety we are invited to trust in God and seek first God's reign and righteousness (v. 33).

The problem of anxiety was perhaps exacerbated for persons in Matthew's time by the prevailing philosophical views that asserted that people were in the hands of either fate (*necessitas*), the Stoics' position, or fortune (*fortuna*), the Epicurean position. John Calvin opposed both positions and insists that Christians should be delivered from such anxieties, because we understand ourselves to be "in the hands of a loving Father."

The matter of "true piety" is explored through various lenses in chapter 6: in almsgiving, prayer, fasting, and putting possessions in their place. Throughout there is embedded a central concern for

---

53. Senior, *Abingdon New Testament Commentaries*, 88.

justice and a recurring caution of the risk of hypocrisy. To do what is good only for the sake of show and self-promotion is not true piety. God knows the heart. True piety evinces a higher righteousness that reflects God's own just and generous ways.

7:1–6
Not Judging

The themes of seeking justice, imitating divine generosity, and avoiding hypocrisy continue in the opening verses of the next chapter. We are cautioned against ungenerously condemning others and enjoined to be merciful in judgments. "For with the judgment you make you will be judged, and the measure you give will be the measure you get" (v. 2). There is a commonsense logic to this given the way things actually turn out in human social life, but this is also pertinent in the relationship to God. God has been gracious with us and we, in an ethic of imitation, should show that same graciousness to others. The injunction "judge not, so that you may not be judged" resonates with earlier passages in the Sermon on the Mount such as "blessed are the merciful for they shall obtain mercy" or "forgive us our debts as we have forgiven our debtors."

There is hypocrisy involved in being judgmental and demanding a strict accounting from others. This attitude evidences a failure to see one's own need for mercy and forgiveness. Self-righteousness can only be a self-deception. "Hypocrisy in Matthew is self-deception, the intentional not-knowing the truth about oneself."[54] The self-deception of the hypocrite in these verses is a kind of selective "blindness" that can see the speck in one's neighbor's eye without ever noticing the log in one's own (7:1–5). The metaphor of "blindness" in connection with hypocrisy will figure prominently in the diatribe in chapter 23 (vv. 16, 17, 19, 24, 26) where the Pharisees are accused of being "blind guides." A chief complaint against them is hypocrisy.[55]

Matthew uses the term hypocrites thirteen times in his Gospel as compared to Mark's single use and Luke's three uses. Matthew sees

---

54. Via, *Self Deception and Wholeness in Paul and Matthew*, 92.
55. Ibid., 92–95.

what a serious problem it may be. This is partly because of the way it stands opposed to "true piety." It is also a significant problem by virtue of its contrast to justice/mercy, which would yield fair and more generous judgments of others.[56]

Matthew seems to assume that in the Christian community there will be mutual admonition and correction. Nevertheless, a gentleness and humility should characterize these interactions. Verses 3–5 in the Sermon on the Mount set parameters. "First take the log out of your own eye, and then you will see clearly to take the speck out of your neighbor's eye." Condemnation is ruled out. Perhaps the risk of "mutual assured destruction" applies? There is also our complete incapacity to see as God sees. God alone can judge rightly. When we condemn another we are "playing God." Discernment and gentle, humble correction completed by forgiving one another is what is called for in community discipline—not condemnation,

Carter interprets the next verse, about not throwing pearls before swine, in the context of what has just been said. Not only is it wrong to judge others, our judgments and intentions to offer helpful correction are not likely to be welcomed but rather disvalued, even trampled underfoot. The recipient may "turn and maul you."[57]

7:7–11
Asking, Searching, Knocking

"Ask, and it shall be given you; search, and you will find; knock and the door shall be opened . . ." (v. 7). There is a "call and response" format to each of these pairs. A confident anticipation of God's gracious response pervades. The strong verbs "ask," "search," "knock" invite a boldness in our approach to God. It is an attitude consistent with the promise held out in chapter 6, assuring us that God already knows what we need before we ask and will give us "all these things." From this insight, it becomes clear that prayer is not aimed at informing God of our needs or persuading God to meet them. It is more about our relationship with God as God's own children, living our lives in

56. Crosby, *House of Disciples*, 193.
57. Carter, *Matthew and the Margins*, 182.

humble dependence upon divine grace. The verb tense used here is the imperfect. It implies ongoing action, perhaps indicating a "tenacity in prayer" and a "faithful disposition and way of life focused on God."[58]

Again Jesus employs the *a minore ad maius* form of argument. If we as human parents are responsive to our children, would not God be responsive to God's children? We would not give our children a stone in place of bread or a snake in place of a fish. This would be a cruel joke since there is a visible resemblance between flat cakes of bread and Palestinian stones and between the eel-like fishes commonly served and snakes.[59] Can we not trust that God, who is immeasurably greater, will give us good things? (v. 9–10) Can we not trust the graciousness of God?

John Calvin associated trust in the graciousness of God with "true piety":

> We may learn to await and seek all these things from him, and thankfully to ascribe them, once received, to him. For this sense of the powers of God is for us a fit teacher of piety, from which religion is born. I call "piety" that reverence joined with love of God which the knowledge of his benefits induces.
>
> Thus we may learn to await and seek all these things from him, and thankfully to ascribe them, once received, to him. For this sense of the powers of God is for us a fit teacher of piety, from which religion is born. I call "piety" that reverence joined with love of God which the knowledge of his benefits induces.[60]

7:12

Following the Golden Rule

Next we come to what has been termed the "Golden Rule," and this is the conclusion and summation of the teaching of the Sermon on the Mount: "Do to others as you would have them do to you." It is a classic ethical principle. It sometimes appears in the negative, "do

58. Ibid., 183.
59. Boring, *The New Interpreter's Bible*, 8:213.
60. John Calvin, *Institutes of the Christian Religion* 1.1.1; ed. John T. McNeill, trans. Ford Lewis Battles, LCC (Philadelphia: Westminster Press, 1960), 1:41.

not do to others what you do not want them to do to you." Jesus
chooses the (also common) positive phrasing of the principle and
adds the comment "this is the law and the prophets." His conclusion
parallels that of Hillel, "What is hateful to you do not do to your
neighbor; that is the whole Torah, while the rest is commentary
thereon; go and learn it."[61] Reference to the "law and the prophets"
recalls 5:17, where Jesus expounds on the binding nature of the law
and the prophets and makes clear that he comes not to abolish but to
fulfill it. This axiom that concludes
the sermon may guide response to
a whole host of different circumstances. Its meaning is further
fleshed out for Matthew in the
Great Commandment (22:40) on
which hangs "all the law and the
prophet."

> Actions that spring from love
> of God and love of neighbor
> fulfill the "law and the
> prophets" for Matthew.
>
> Talbert, *Reading the Sermon on the Mount,* 89.

7:13–28
Warnings

If the Sermon on the Mount began with blessings, it ends with
warnings. In fact, all four of the major teaching segments in Matthew finish with reference to the judgment (10:40–42; 13:47–50;
18:23–35; 25:31–46). The closing verses bring a set of cautions in
the form of "the admonition of the two ways:" two gates/roads, two
trees (and two kinds of prophets), two builders. The rhetorical form
would be familiar to both Jews and Greeks.

The "two ways" is an ancient and conventional image. Another
instance appears in Jeremiah, "Thus says the LORD: See I am setting
before you the way of life and the way of death" (21:8). Those who
would follow in the way of Jesus must forgo the wide gate with the
easy road that leads to destruction and choose instead the narrow
gate with the hard road that leads to life. This statement reminds the
audience once again that to follow in this way is to take a difficult

---

61. Babylonian Talmud, tractate *Shabbat,* 31a.

path. They will be out of step with the wider society and will likely come under persecution. The warnings make it clear that those who seek life under the reign of God have difficult choices to make. It is not possible to have this life on one's own terms—going through the wide gate and along the easy way. This is a self-deception that ends in disaster.[62]

Jesus' followers must also distinguish between true prophets and false ones (wolves in sheep's clothing) (7:15); they will know them by their fruit—just as with good trees and bad trees. Two kinds of concerns are mixed in this segment. First is a concern that appearance and reality do not necessarily correspond. There are false prophets who appear in "sheep's clothing" but are wolves underneath the disguise. The second is a concern that followers evaluate according to real effects. False prophets do not bear good fruit.

True followers must not be like those who give lip service to God (saying "Lord, Lord" v. 21). Even doing great deeds of power guarantees nothing (vv. 22–23). What matters is hearing and acting upon the message Jesus proclaims ("these words of mine"); anything less is foolish—building a house on shifting sand. This image of the house built on sand still speaks to us, but it was all the more powerful in Jesus' context. Homes in Palestine were not built with foundations. Their stability depended entirely upon the ground on which they were built. A house built on sand might look fine in the dry season, but when the rains come and the dry wadis fill, floods might sweep away a house not built on rock.[63] Followers of Jesus must be doers of the will of God—like a wise man building a house on rock (vv. 24–26). Matthew's image of wisdom and foolishness in building a house echoes a theme in Proverbs, "The wise woman builds her house, but the foolish tears it down with her own hands" (Prov. 14:1).

The reference to "these words of mine" is likely a reference to the whole of the Sermon on the Mount as it comes at the conclusion. In this Sermon on the Mount we have the essentials of Jesus' message according to Matthew. Central elements include the reign of God and the calling to live a life congruent with God's reign. It is a life that

62. Via, *Self Deception and Wholeness in Paul and Matthew*, 92–95.
63. Boring, *The New Interpreter's Bible*, 8:218.

will be modeled after God's own righteousness/justice and unlimited love. This rule of love that Jesus proclaims is the fulfillment of the law and the prophets.

7:29
As One Having Authority

The scene shifts now back to the crowds with which the account of the Sermon on the Mount opened. They are "astounded." One pictures mouths dropped open. There is something different about this teacher. He teaches "as one having authority" and not as the scribes and Pharisees—those who officially held religious and political power. This notation transitions into the next chapter where Jesus performs deeds of power.

FURTHER REFLECTIONS
Blessed Are the Peacemakers/Love Your Enemies

"Blessed are the peacemakers, . . ."

The translation "peacemakers" recognizes that peace is not passive; it is more than an absence of violence. One has to "make" peace; one has to set the conditions of the possibility for peace. Justice and reconciliation lay the groundwork for any real and lasting peace. Peacemaking includes addressing the "underlying issues contributing to the hostility."[64]

To lay the foundations for peace is to create a new reality. The new reality results from "reordering relationships and resources . . . in a manner that reflected that eschatological condition where justice and peace would meet (Psalm 85:11)."[65]

". . . for they shall be called children of God."

There is no promise of reward for the work of peacemaking, rather this work is simply an expression of our identity as children of God;

---

64. Carter, *Matthew and the Margins*, 13.
65. Crosby, *House of Disicples*, 66.

it is a result of being in an "intimate and imitative relationship with God."[66] Children of God are those who act like God acts. The God whom we have come to know in Jesus Christ is One who is reconciling the world (2 Cor. 5:19). There should be something of a recognizable "family resemblance" among the children of God, just as we might say of someone, "He has his father's eyes." How would it be if we looked with God's eyes upon those with whom we differ—looked with loving regard, compassion, as one who is "slow to anger and abounding in steadfast love" (Exod. 34:6)? Perhaps then we could dare to say, "The hostilities stop here."[67]

"Love your enemies . . . ."

Later in the Sermon on the Mount Jesus takes the matter even further when he says, "You have heard that it was said, 'You shall love your neighbor and hate your enemy' But I say to you, Love your enemies . . . ." Most of us find it hard enough to love our neighbors. But love our enemies? Really?

In the spring of 2010, we in the United States had occasion to think again about enemies. Osama bin Laden was found and killed. There was wild rejoicing and much flag waving in the streets. At one level it was understandable, because it seemed to signal the ending to a horrific time. Some of those who lost loved ones and were the most hurt by the events of 9/11 all spoke of a "sense of closure." What had begun with 9/11 spread across the years and around the world as hurt turned to hate, and violence was met with violence. A seemingly permanent state of conflict, heightened security, and color coded threats of terror prevailed. So much had been lost, so many had been lost, so many others were drawn in and placed in harm's way in the aftermath. Even so, as we watched the wild celebrations many of us had uneasy feelings inside reminding us that there is something not right in celebrating someone's (anyone's) death like this—even your worst enemy. Jesus' calling to "love your enemies" may be the most difficult words we have to hear in the whole of the Sermon on the Mount.

There is an open-endedness about the command, "love your enemy." The passage does not give a detailed prescription

---

66. Carter, "Love Your Enemies," 21.
67. William Sloane Coffin, *Credo* (Louisville, KY: Westminster John Knox Press, 2004), 12.

concerning what "enemy-love" will look like in every circumstance. In the circumstances of the Gospel of Matthew the particular enemies were probably those who opposed Jesus and his message. Reference to "persecutors" follows close on both the blessing of peacemakers (5:9–11) and the calling to love your enemies (5:44). The command itself is indeterminate and may be widely applicable. The scholarly consensus is that the command includes personal, national, and religious enemies. As Warren Carter has suggested, "It is a command in search of elaboration, dialogue, discernment. It provides direction but leaves the itinerary to the travelers."[68]

Responding in kind to aggression and violence is simply ruled out. An eye for an eye and a tooth for a tooth has been laid aside already in the preceding verses. Reciprocal retaliatory violence is not the way for followers of Jesus. The way for us is rather the indiscriminate love that imitates God's love. Just as God grants the benefits of creation to all, making the sun shine and the rain fall on both the good and the evil, so also disciples should love without discrimination.

One personal story illumines my understanding of "enemy love." I was traveling for the World Communion of Reformed Churches for the Gospel and Cultures conference. We were in Torajaland in the heart of Sulawesi, Indonesia, an area not reached by Christian missionaries until around 1917. The practice of cannibalism was accepted in the culture historically. It was believed that by eating the flesh of enemies you would gain their power. One of our number asked why this group of Indonesian Christians no longer practiced cannibalism. We expected to hear that the missionaries had taught them that cannibalism was wrong. What they said instead was striking. "Jesus taught that we should love our enemies and do good to them. Because of Jesus we cannot really have enemies anymore."

This is an intimation (and an imitation) of the extravagant love of God that loves would-be enemies into an altogether different relationship. No more enemies. The hostilities stop here.

---

68. Carter, "Love Your Enemies," 13, 15.

FURTHER REFLECTIONS
Why Do We Pray?

This is a question asked by people of faith through the centuries. It takes many forms as people struggle with the place of prayer in the life of faith.

— Is there anyone out there or are we just talking to ourselves, just "whistling in the dark"?

— If there is a God, does God not already know what we need?

— Why would we have to persuade God to give us what we need?

— Is a God who is manipulated by prayer worthy of worship?

— Does it make sense to think of the God of the universe caring about the particulars of our personal lives?

— Does prayer really change things?

— What about unanswered prayer?

This exploration will engage some of these questions and offer a few insights and proposals but does not presume to answer these hard questions. Believers will continue to ask and faithfully struggle with such questions. Many have considered them and offered wisdom.

John Calvin grapples with the question of whether prayer might be superfluous: "Someone will say, does God not know, even without being reminded, both in what respect we are troubled and what is expedient for us, so that it may seem in a sense superfluous that he should be stirred up by our prayers—as if he were drowsily blinking or even sleeping until he is aroused by our voice?"[69]

Calvin's response is something to the effect "pray nevertheless!" He elaborates reasons[70] and concludes finally that "God's command" and "God's promise" are what ground our prayers. He references Matthew 7:7 for both as each phrase is a dialectic of command and promise, "Ask, and it will be given you; search, and you will find; knock, and the door shall be opened for you."

A side benefit, Calvin notes, is the effect of prayer upon those who pray. Continual prayer keeps our minds fixed upon God, keeps our lives honest before God, reminds us of our complete dependence

---

69. Calvin, *Institutes* 3.20.3.
70. Ibid., 3.20.1–52.

on God, and cultivates gratitude in us as we recognize that all good things come from God.

Calvin also offers some wisdom on the practice of prayer and goes on (for fifty-two sections!) to describe the dynamics of that dialogue with God, which is prayer. He says that prayer should be done in a spirit of reverence, with a mind that is not divided but completely devoted to God. Reverence is not fear; we may pray in the confidence of the beloved children of God. We should always pray from the heart[71] in complete honesty—with ourselves and God—about our need and our insufficiency and our sin. Since we do not "know how to pray as we ought," we must rely upon the Spirit to "intercede for us with sighs too deep for words" (Rom. 7:28).

Eugene Boring has offered the helpful insight that not all language is of the same kind. Prayer language is a peculiar kind of language; it is "confessional language." It is not primarily about giving information or about self-expression.[72] Implications may be drawn out further from this initial insight. Prayer is not informational language. If it were strictly informational, a kind of laundry list of things we want or want done, then indeed prayer would be superfluous. God already knows what we need (6:8). Furthermore, if we do not get what we wanted it could be said that our prayers were "unanswered." Prayer is not merely expressive language either—a venting of emotions. When we pray we are not just talking to ourselves. Prayer is grounded, however tenuously, in a belief that God is there and even hears and responds to our prayers. When we pray we are not talking to those around us. Jesus cautions against prayer as a show for the spectators (6:5–7). Prayer is indeed confessional language. When we pray for daily bread, for example, it is not in order to inform God that we are hungry or to persuade God (who is otherwise reluctant) to give us what we need. Rather we pray to confess our need before God and our dependence on God.

Prayer is also "relational" language. On the analogy of human relationships, we know that the bonds between us are formed and nurtured by communication. If we only speak with those whom we love when we want something or want them to do something, what

---

71. Ibid., 3.20.31.
72. Boring, *The New Interpreter's Bible*, 8:207.

kind of relationship is that? Sometimes we simply talk, sharing our lives with their joys and their sorrows, saying "thank you;" saying "I love you." Communication cultivates relationship.

To ask why the God of the universe should care about our small lives makes certain assumptions about the nature of God that may need reconsideration. The question assumes, for example, that God is at a distance—above and beyond the creation in such a way that we are but tiny insignificant specks in the vastness of it all. If, however, we were to take seriously divine omnipresence, then this is a misunderstanding. If God is *really present* in world process as the "one in whom we live and move and have our being" (Acts 17:28) then a different understanding is indicated. This is no distant God, but one who fills and enfolds the universe. Marjorie Suchocki suggests that the metaphor of water that fills all spaces might help us imagine how "God is pervasively present throughout all the universe, filling all its vast and small spaces, its greatest galaxies and its tiniest motes of stardust."[73] Such a God is in communion with all creation, closer to us than breathing, able to exercise personal and particular care (Matt. 6:25–33). Such a God is near at hand when we turn to God in prayer.

At its best, prayer is not an attempt to manipulate God—it is not magic. Neither is it monologue. People of faith believe that God is there and will hear and respond in ways appropriate. God is, in fact, already at work for good not idly waiting for our persuasion. When we speak of "unanswered prayer" (meaning that what we asked for did not happen in the way we wanted it to happen) we may be working from a misunderstanding of the nature of prayer and the nature of divine omnipotence. Prayer is not magic or manipulation. Omnipotence does not mean that God dominates and controls what happens in world process, divinely determining all the details. If divine power works like that, then all the evil we see is also God's doing. If, on the other hand, freedom is real (for us and for the semiautonomous unfolding of creation) then God's working in our midst does not override that freedom, but works in and through natural processes. We do not presume to know the shape which the

---

73. Marjorie Suchocki, *God's Presence: Theological Reflections on Prayer* (St. Louis: Chalice, 1996), 5.

"answer" to our prayers should take, but in faith we believe that God is working for good in all things.

Prayer changes things. It changes us, and as we open ourselves to divine leading, it even, in a sense, changes what God can do in and through us. Prayer is not only communication and communion with God, but also collaboration. There is a reciprocity and open-endedness in relational communication; we are listening as well as speaking. There is a posture of receptivity and an attitude of openness to God in prayer. "Speak, for your servant is listening" (1 Sam. 3:10). In prayer it sometimes happens that we discover how we may be active vehicles of God's response to our prayers. We pray for peace. How may we become "instruments" of God's peace (as St. Francis prayed)? We pray for God to change the world. How can we "be the change" we wish to see in the world?

> **Prayer is part of and not removed from nor a substitute for, the lived faithfulness of the disciples.**
>
> Carter, *Matthew and the Margins*, 169.

In the section that follows we will consider the Lord's Prayer and the ethical implications of praying this extraordinary prayer. On the way there, it is helpful to consider models for prayer found elsewhere in Scripture. In the book of Psalms we find prayers of intercession, petition, and protest as well as prayers of praise and thanksgiving. This double aspect of prayer is fundamental. Anne Lamott, in her book *Traveling Mercies,* says that the two best prayers she knows are "Help me, help me, help me" and "Thank you, thank you, thank you."

The models for prayer we find in Scripture surprise us with their specificity and boldness. We do not find bland or "wimpy" prayers. The prayer of Miriam after the crossing of the Red Sea (Exod. 15:21) thanks God for "horses and riders thrown into the sea." Most of us would have preferred to read a cleaned-up version that thanks God in a more general way for deliverance. In the psalms of petition there is often a bold outcry and even protest or accusation that lays the plight of the people at God's feet. The psalmist does not courteously and cautiously beg deliverance but demands it, saying, "Rouse yourself! Why do you sleep, O Lord? Awake, do not cast us off forever! Why do you hide your face? (Ps. 44:23–24). Walter Brueggemann, in *The Message of the Psalms,* sees this bold manner of praying as an act of faith. The world is presented to God as it is and not in some pretended way. This way of praying assumes that all our experience is proper subject matter for discourse with God. There is nothing out of bounds; everything belongs in this conversation of the heart. If we withhold parts of life from prayer, it is as if we are saying that God has nothing to do with that part but only has to do with the parts that can be sanitized.

There is a "world-creating" power in prayer. It can build an insular sheltered world that is neat and tidy or it can articulate an alternative world where the cries of the oppressed are heard and the vision of suffering is allowed to penetrate to the core of our being. Prayer can lead us into dangerous acknowledgment of how life really is. Brueggemann observes that in prayer we are led into the presence of a God where everything is not "polite and civil," where we can think unthinkable thoughts and utter unutterable words.[74]

FURTHER REFLECTIONS
How Shall We Pray?
Ethical Implications of the Lord's Prayer

The Lord's Prayer is a prayer on the lips of every Christian—across the theological spectrum, across all the divides of denomination, and across the disagreements of our current debates. It has been prayed by Christians for two millennia and is offered up most every Sunday in almost every church. Do we know what it is we are saying as we speak these words? Do we fully accept the claim laid on our lives by praying in this way?

A risk of this widespread, longstanding, and very frequent use is that we may pray this prayer

> We do well not to pray the prayer lightly . . . We can pray it in the unthinking and perfunctory way we usually do only by disregarding what we are saying.
>
> Frederick Buechner, *Listening to Your Life* (San Francisco: HarperSanFrancisco, 1992), 78.

---

74. Walter Brueggemann, *Praying the Psalms* (Winnona, MN: St. Mary's Press, 1982), 53.

mindlessly, by habit and by rote. We may fail to consider carefully what it is we are saying and what praying in this way might actually imply for how we live our lives. How may we come to a place where we not only "know it by heart" but pray it *"from the heart"* so that it has real impact on our lives? How may we come to live as we pray?

For this exploration I will be following the form of the prayer commonly used liturgically rather than the particular translation of the NRSV. Structurally there are two sets of three petitions each. Three center on God—God's holiness, God's reign, and God's will. Three focus upon us and our need for bread, forgiveness, and deliverance from temptation and evil. The prayer has a double frame of reference. On the one hand, it looks to God and petitions God's response; on the other hand, it assumes that human beings have an active part in all this. A case in point would be the petition that God "forgive us our debts as we forgive our debtors."

"Our Father who art in heaven"

In teaching us to pray "our" Father, the life of prayer is given its communitarian cast. We are all in this together. The prayer is not about me and mine, you and yours. We are tempted to privatize this prayer, praying it as we do in a context that stresses individualism and independence. The very language of the prayer with its plural pronouns throughout draws us into a larger circle of concern that is not only personal, but also communal and even global in its full reach. This

> [The Lord's Prayer] constructs a worldview and shapes the community which prays it to live accordingly.
>
> Carter, *Matthew and the Margins*, 169.

prayer is so very central to our communal life in the church. It should form us in our faith and guide our social/ethical practice, sustaining a new identity and lifestyle.[75]

Cyprian has an interesting reflection in this regard,

> The Teacher of peace and Master of unity did not wish prayer to be offered individually . . . as one would pray only for himself when he prays. We do not pray: "*My* Father who art in heaven" nor "give *me* this day my bread," nor does each one

---

75. Carter, *Matthew and the Margins*, 164.

ask that only his debt be forgiven him and that he be led not into temptation and that he be delivered from evil for himself alone. Our prayer is public and common, and when we pray we pray not for one but for the whole people, because we the whole people are one.[76]

There has been much discussion about calling God "Father." Feminists[77] have observed that the exclusive use of masculine images and pronouns for God may mislead us so that we come to imagine that God is *literally* male. Most people would quickly say that God is beyond gender. Yet "Father" language is so much used that we may forget that "Father" (like "rock" and "fortress") is a metaphor for God. We begin to treat it as if it were God's proper name. A whole range of difficulties arise. Most theologically problematic is the risk of idolatry, in which we take what is properly only a pointer to God and worship it in place of God. There are also ethical considerations due to the social consequences for the elevated status of men over women in society. Mary Daly put it succinctly, "If God is male, male is God."[78] There is a troubling practical outworking in church order, where, in some contexts, women cannot be ordained into ministry because they are not men. Issues regarding the religious viability of the metaphor arise for those who have had an absent or abusive father. How hard it is to redeem this name for God in the face of such obstacles.

All this invites a fuller discussion, and these few notes will only make a beginning. The metaphors for God in Scripture are much more rich and varied than what we commonly use. There are masculine, feminine, and gender neutral metaphors.[79] If we make use of this wider range of images in addition to father language we may avoid literalizing and thereby domesticating this particular metaphor. The variety would help us to remember the metaphorical character of all our speaking about God.

76. Cyprian, *The Lord's Prayer*, Treatise 4, chap. 8 in Roy Deferari, *The Fathers of the Church*, 36 (New York: The Fathers of the Church, Inc., 1958), 132.
77. For a very fine exploration of the matter of God-language, see Sallie McFague's *Metaphorical Theology*.
78. Mary Daly, *Beyond God the Father* (Boston: Beacon Press, 1973), 9.
79. Virginia Ramey Mollenkott offers fifteen images of God as female in the Bible. *The Divine Feminine: The Biblical Imagery of God as Female* (New York: Crossroad, 1983).

I would propose that this is too powerful and meaningful a metaphor to simply be retired. For those with good experiences of our fathers this image has the positive associations that called it into play in the first place—love, guidance, provision, protection. It remains religiously viable as a pointer toward God. For those with negative experiences, the "fatherhood" of God is the measure by which all fatherhood is judged. The metaphor also has the promise of offering an alternative; here is a loving and reliable father for those who have known none.[80]

If we look at Jesus' own use of the metaphor, especially here in the Lord's Prayer we may see a bit of a reimagining of the image. It is no surprise that in a patriarchal society that is the context of the writings in Scripture, masculine images and pronouns predominate. The surprises are when we see something other than that or when an image presumably patriarchal gets turned on its head, as Jesus does in the Lord's prayer. Jesus' practice here, as elsewhere, seems more a subversion of patriarchy than a reinforcement of it.

Jesus and his disciples spoke Aramaic rather than the formal Hebrew of the official synagogue liturgy. Aramaic was the common language of the people. Jesus' address of God has been preserved in several texts as the Aramaic *abba* transliterated into the Greek. An example would be Mark 14:36, where Jesus addresses God as "Abba, Father." This is the personal and intimate address of children for their fathers, the appellation they would likely have learned first. Some have proposed that *"abba"* is more like our term "Daddy" than the more formal address of "Father." Current NT scholarship questions whether "Daddy" is really an equivalent term to the Aramaic *"abba,"* which preserves dignity and respect even as it conveys intimacy. The intimacy of the term may have been scandalous to those who heard him. Even Matthew, who follows Mark's text at many points, does not take up Mark's usage of this term but stays with the more formal Greek term for father, *pater*. Jesus use of the term *abba* was, in its own way, a jarring reimagining of God language, reflecting a greater intimacy than was acceptable.

The appellation *"Our* Father" undermined patriarchy in another,

---

80. See Diane Tennis, *Is God the Only Reliable Father?* (Louisville, KY: Westminster/John Knox Press, 1985).

not so subtle way. Class and social standing in patriarchal cultures is determined by who your father is. The children of the highborn are given a higher place. Here all are God's children. It is a fundamental equalizing of status. The "our" is not possessive or exclusive as if we have made God our own, rather we have been adopted as *God's own* children.

The first phrase of the prayer moves from the language of intimacy to the language of ultimacy; "Our Father, *who art in heaven*." From divine immanence likened to the presence and care of a human Father, we shift to divine transcendence, an essential point theologically for Judaism and Christianity. This is no tribal deity, but the God above all gods, the creator of heaven and earth. This God to whom we pray is ever larger than our metaphors and our best theological concepts. This God is no idol made by human hands; neither can God be contained in a Temple made by human hands. Heaven is, at best, "the throne of God" and the whole of the earth God's "footstool" (Matthew 5:34–35). As King Solomon in his wisdom declares, at the dedication of the great Temple, "Even heaven and the highest heaven cannot contain you, much less this house that I have built!" (1 Kings 8:27) The allusion to heaven lifts our minds to the God beyond our highest and best constructs and constructions. This opening of the Lord's Prayer spans the theological paradox of immanence and transcendence. God is, on the one hand, really in the world. God is, on the other hand, always more than the world.

Hallowed be thy name

The prayer is God-centered and begins with three petitions that pertain to God as God—the hallowing of God's name, the coming of God's reign, and the fulfillment of God's will on earth. The question posed here will be what "hallows" God's name?

To "hallow" is to honor as holy.[81] Ezekiel 36:22–36 provides an interesting glimpse into the meaning of "hallowing God's name." The passage, set in the situation of the exile, begins "I will sanctify my great name," and then describes God's liberation from captors in the exile, a restoration and transformation of God's people. This is a hallowing of God's name.

81. Boring, *The New Interpreter's Bible*, 8:203

Another way of thinking about the ethical implications is to ask how may *we* hallow God's name, becoming participants in the hallowing for which we pray?[82] Suchocki suggests that the prophet Micah put it succinctly when he said, "What does the LORD require of you but to do justice, and to love kindness, and to walk humbly with your God?" (6:8).

One could ask the question in the contrary, "What profanes God's name?" The question calls to mind the commandment not to take God's name in vain. To think of this commandment merely as a caution against speaking God's name among assorted expletives is to trivialize the meaning. It may be much more of a profanation when we say, "God is on our side" as we go off to war. When we invoke the name of God as a patron of our causes we take God's name in vain... "dragging God into our crusades and cruelties."[83]

When we worship and praise and adore God we live lives in imitation of God's ways. As Augustine is attributed as saying, "We imitate whom we adore." In this way we are led to seek God's reign above all else, thus the prayer for God's name to be hallowed flows logically into prayer for God's reign to come and God's will to be done on earth as it is in heaven.

Thy kingdom come

God's "kingdom" for which we pray does not refer to a place or realm but rather a new reality—the reign of God. Matthew's Gospel unfolds the meaning of this mysterious, disturbing, liberative, and transformative power of God's reign in our midst.[84] Crosby suggests that praying the Lord's Prayer is a subversive activity. We are in fact praying for the overturning of the present order and the coming of God's reign on earth in its place.

If we pray this way, we must live

> To pray this prayer is to seek nothing less than the total transformation of life on earth. It is to reject the status quo and pray for its complete realignment in terms of God's will.
>
> Carter, *Matthew and the Margins,* 169.

---

82. Suchocki, *God's Presence,* 108.
83. William Willimon and Stanley Hauerwas, *Lord Teach Us: The Lord's Prayer and the Christian Life* (Nashville: Abingdon Press, 1996), 48.
84. Carter, *Matthew and the Margins,* 93.

this way. To pray these words is to align our hearts and our lives with the coming of God's reign, to lean into it even now, to live proleptically (as if it is already here) as we strain toward that which is coming. The coming of the reign of God is God's doing and not our own. Even so, we cannot pray these words and resist the coming transformation at the one and the same time.

Thy will be done on earth as it is in heaven.

The reign of God is large enough to embrace not only things in heaven but even things on earth. When we pray "thy will be done *on earth*" we commit ourselves to seeking God's will in an earthly, worldly context. With these words we implicitly affirm that God cares about worldly matters. This flies in the face of some alternative understandings that envision a very "otherworldly" God who cares only about "spiritual" matters and whose purpose is complete in the saving of souls.

Theologically this insight is carried in our most fundamental theological affirmations concerning creation, revelation, providence, redemption, and consummation. We affirm that God is the creator of all things. God calls it all into being (Gen. 1) and declares it all "good" (even before human beings come on the scene). The creation is a source of divine revelation as God's goodness shines forth everywhere we turn our eyes. Calvin spoke of the creation as a "theater of God's glory."[85] If we lack the capacity through weakness of vision to see what is right before our eyes, then the "spectacles" of Scripture can help us see God's revelation in the natural world.[86] God's providential care is not restricted to souls nor even to human beings. It is all encompassing in its scope and particular in its exercise. When talking about God's providence, Calvin is fond of referring to Matthew 10:29 (God's care for even the sparrow that falls). The incarnation is probably the place where we see most clearly that our God is a "down-to-earth" God. In Jesus Christ, God takes on material existence—even flesh—for the work of redemption. Our eschatological hope, expressed as "new creation," includes the renewal of all things. An ethical implication entailed in these central

---

85. John Calvin, *Consensus Gevevensis* CO, 8:294.
86. Calvin, *Institutes*, 1.4.1.

convictions is the calling to love the world as God loves the world. Can we be as "down-to-earth" as God is?

What will it look like for God's will to be done on earth as it is in heaven? The well-being of the whole of God's creation—the flourishing of each and all—would seem to be included. The Sermon on the Mount makes explicit an appeal for mercy and justice/righteousness. Ethical implications entailed in this petition of the Lord's Prayer go to the heart of the matter. When we pray for God's will to be done on earth, we are signing on to see this hope through insofar as it is possible for us.

Give us this day our daily bread

With this petition we shift into petitions to human need: bread, forgiveness, deliverance from temptation and evil. The first of these petitions addresses the most basic of economic needs.

Some have focused on the eschatological dimensions of the petition for bread interpreting *epiousian* (commonly translated as "daily") in terms of future provision ("bread for tomorrow"). This would be in continuity with the previous petitions that look to the future establishment of God's reign and God's will on earth. One of the hopes for the messianic age was that there would once again be manna from heaven. The early church, both Eastern and Western, also understood this petition as a prayer for the "blessing of the messianic banquet, when all God's people will sit down together, with enough food for all."[87]

Given the context of Jesus' ministry with the poor, it may be that the natural meaning of the petition, a prayer for the bread "necessary for survival" (*epi ousia*), is the primary meaning. The poor need this-worldly bread (daily). In praying this petition, we join in solidarity with people who are poor and hungry the world over.

According to the World Food Programme, one person in seven goes to bed hungry every night and will not have enough food to be healthy. One in four children in developing countries is underweight. Hunger is the number one health risk in the world today, killing more people than AIDS, malaria, and tuberculosis combined. The statistics are not improving; in fact hunger has been on the rise

---

87. Boring, *The New Interpreter's Bible*, 8:204.

for the last decade. Yet statistics reveal that there is sufficient food. "There is enough food in the world today for everyone to have the nourishment necessary for a healthy and productive life."[88] It is not possible to pray this prayer with this petition and withhold bread from the hungry. A commitment to sharing bread is implicit in the act of praying this prayer.

To pray in this way is to acknowledge our own need as well. Anguish and expectation infuses the prayer. It challenges our self-sufficiency and arrogance. In a sense, we all petition as needy, hungry, vulnerable people. We did not bring ourselves into this world. Neither can we sustain ourselves. All of us are born into a state of complete dependence on others for care and provision. We are "born needy" and have nothing that we have not received. This petition recognizes that this is how it is with us. In our relationship with God, it is all the more so. It is God who has made us and *not we ourselves* (Ps. 100:3 KJV). "Absolute dependence" (Schleiermacher) is the way it is in our relationship with God whether we see that or not. We approach God with our hands open to receive. In this regard, we are all on the same footing before God when we offer this prayer— regardless of social, political, or economic status.[89]

The meaning of the prayer is, however, significantly shaped by our situations. For those praying from situations of poverty this is clearly a prayer about survival. Prayed in situations of prosperity, the petition may have additional implications. When we who have more than we need pray for *daily* bread, this becomes a disruptive prayer. We constrain our ordinary expectations for "more than enough" if we pray this prayer from the heart. As Calvin cautioned, "those who, not content with daily bread but panting after countless things with unbridled desire, or sated with their abundance, or carefree in their piled-up riches, supplicate God with this prayer are but mocking him."[90]

In this petition there is an implicit critique of habits of greedy hoarding. We no longer ask to have more than we need. As with the

88. World Food Programme, "Frequently Asked Questions (FAQ), http://www.wfp.org/ hunger/faqs.
89. Carter, *Matthew and the Margins*, 164.
90. Calvin, *Institutes*, 3.20.44

manna in the wilderness, we are called to trust that God will provide on a *daily* basis—"morning by morning" (Exod. 16).

Another decisive element of this petition is that it does not say "give me," but "give us." How may we take the "us" in this petition more seriously? Bread is a *universal* need. Bread for "me" is not good enough. What we have stored up for ourselves for our future may be the bread intended for the neighbor today. Gregory of Nyssa pointed out the irrationality of praying this petition while seeking our bread at the expense of others. We cannot pray this prayer when we are "wedded to our own security or prosperity."[91] It may be that the unjust distribution of resources means that some do not have daily bread while others hoard it. The wealthy may eat of the bread of injustice acquired through "loans, interest, debt, high prices, limiting supply, taxes or tariffs" shortchanging workers and pursuing profit while depriving persons.[92] We may get our daily bread in ways that defraud others of theirs.[93] "All that we acquire through harming another belongs to another."[94] The traditional allusion to manna in the wilderness (Exod. 16) is apt. The instruction there was "gather as much of it as each of you needs," and as it happened, "those who gathered much had nothing over, and those who gathered little had no shortage; they gathered as much as each of them needed" (Exod. 16:18) There were some, however, who, even in the face of God's gracious provision, took more than they needed for the day, and hoarding it overnight, found that it was spoiled and became inedible.

Perhaps it is no accident that the petition for forgiveness and deliverance from evil follows close upon the prayer for daily bread. The hunger of masses of people in a world of abundance is a sin. The shortage of food is not due to any shortage of God's generosity and gracious provision for our need. It does not have anything to do with any failing in the fecundity of the earth. It has to do with structures of injustice and temptations of greed and patterns of

---

91. Rowan Williams, "Give Us Today Our Daily Bread" (keynote address, Eleventh Assembly of the Lutheran World Federation, Stuttgart, Germany, July 20–27, 2010), paragraph 4.
92. Carter, *Matthew and the Margins*, 167.
93. Suchocki, *God's Presence*, 109.
94. Calvin, *Insittutes*, 3.20.44.

consumption that destroy rich and poor alike. These are evils from which we all need to be delivered.

Disciples are called to a ministry of feeding hungry people. Jesus said to them, "They need not go away; you give them something to eat" (Matt. 14:16). To pray "give us this day our daily bread" is to commit ourselves to ensure that *all of us* have bread.

And forgive us our debts as we forgive our debtors.

Of all the petitions in the Lord's Prayer, this is the one that gets elaborated in the verses that follow. Perhaps this needed more explanation or emphasis. It underlines our need and responsibility in the matter of forgiveness. God's graciousness and generosity with us must be the model for all our relating to others. Again we glimpse a vision of ethics as imitation of God. The elaboration reminds us that it makes no sense for us to ask God's forgiveness if we do not even forgive one another. One cannot authentically pray this prayer unless one is willing to forgive. God's forgiveness comes first and makes it possible (and necessary) for us to forgive others. The cautions in vv. 14–15 do not mean that God's grace is conditional; rather they remind us not to *presume* upon God's grace. God's grace is free but it is not "cheap."

The matter of forgiveness can be elaborated in its personal, social, and global dimensions. In terms of the personal, we may consider the situation of the person asking forgiveness. Asking for forgiveness and acknowledging debt are difficult things in our culture. We spend much of our time trying to prove ourselves to be in the right, not needing forgiveness. Furthermore, can we pray, "forgive us our debts" while taking such care to establish that we do not really owe anyone anything—that we are "self-made" people? When we ask for forgiveness, we have given up all claim to being right or self-sufficient. We have acknowledged a debt to God and to others, admitting that we stand in need of reconciliation and restoration in our relationships. We need what can only come from another's acceptance of us. Praying for God's forgiveness does not take the place of asking those whom we have offended to forgive us. Indeed our readiness to come before God is connected to our readiness to ask forgiveness. In the Sermon on the Mount we are charged,

"When you are offering your gift at the altar, if you remember that your brother or sister has something against you, leave your gift there before the altar and go; first be reconciled to your brother or sister, and then come and offer your gift." (Matt. 5:23–24).

There are other considerations for the one offering forgiveness. Again the Gospel of Matthew offers guidance. Later in the Gospel Peter will ask how often he should forgive a member of the church who sins against him (18:21). He generously proposes to forgive seven times (after which he can presumably harden his heart). Jesus counters, "Not seven times, but, I tell you seventy-seven times" (18:22). This is, in effect, unconditional forgiveness—another intimation of the calling to love without limits.

Rowan Williams, in discussing this petition, talks about how forgiving is a participation in the "helplessness of God." He references Hosea 11:8–9, "How can I give you up, O Ephraim? For I am God and not a mortal." We are tempted to say, "You are God; you can do anything!" This text contradicts that view. It is precisely because God is God that "giving up" is impossible. We may give our love and take it back. God is not like that. We may be able to cut people off or give up on people, but God cannot. God's nature is love.[95] As we are more rooted in Christ, we come to share in God's loving nature and are less and less able to withhold forgiveness—that is a "power" we give up. Forgiveness is, in a way, a giving up of power. We come to recognize that we really cannot live without the other and the word of mercy and the healing of what has been wounded.[96]

Neither the forgiver nor the forgiven acquires the power that simply cuts off the past and leaves us alone to face the future: both have discovered that their past, with all its shadows and injuries, is now what makes it imperative to be reconciled so that they may live more fully from and with each other.[97]

One does not have to wait to be asked in order to extend forgiveness, though more healing comes when there is mutual acknowledgment of what has happened.

The Truth and Reconciliation Commission in South Africa, under

95. Williams, Paragraph 7.
96. Ibid.
97. Ibid.

the leadership of Desmond Tutu, dealt with the aftermath of apartheid. Atrocities were committed that were "unforgivable." People who had suffered much came to power; many had been imprisoned and tortured. Family members had been killed. Family lands had been stolen. A path of counterviolence and retaliation opened before them, but they did not take it. The commission counseled amnesty, requiring only that people tell the truth about what they had done. One participant observed, "Punishment will not bring back my brother. I just want to know who killed him. I want that person to look me in the eye and tell the truth about what happened." Reconciliation in that setting was grounded in truth telling. Desmond Tutu declared "Without forgiveness, there is no future."[98]

With this circumstance in view, it is important to reflect on what forgiveness does and does not mean. It does not mean that what happened was "OK" or that it does not matter. It does not require that people foolishly put themselves in harm's way to be hurt again. It means no longer bearing ill will and desiring the good for the offender. "The good" can certainly include hope for their healing and transformation as well as one's own. To forgive heals some of the damage as it releases the one forgiving from imprisonment in malice and resentment and desire for retaliation. Anne Lamott quipped that, "Not forgiving is like drinking rat poison and then waiting for the rat to die."[99]

The petition, "forgive us our debts, as we forgive our debtors" has global dimensions as well as personal and communal dimensions. The Greek word here translated as "debts" (*opheilēma*) signifies precisely a monetary debt in the material sense of the term. This petition, like the story of the unforgiving debtor (18:21–35), makes a clear demand for debt forgiveness. The word translated "forgive" (*aphesis*) is the same word used in the Septuagint for the jubilee year, which called for a forgiveness of debts (Lev. 25:23ff) and restoration of the land to families who had, through debt, become dispossessed. This was to be a protection for those who fell on hard times. The practice allowed for a restoration that put things right and also limited the aggrandizement of the rich and powerful in

98. Desmond Tutu, *No Future Without Forgiveness* (New York: Doubleday, 1999), 255.
99. Anne Lamott, *Traveling Mercies: Some Thoughts on Faith* (New York: Anchor Books, 1999), 134.

accumulating the rightful inheritances of others. There was an economic "reset" button that allowed respite and a restoration for the poor of the land.

Jesus seemed to employ a Jubilee economic when he responded to the inquiry, "Teacher, what good deed must I do to have eternal life?" He answered, "If you wish to be perfect, go, sell your possessions and give the money to the poor . . ." (19:21). The test of discipleship is in the willingness to reorder possessions toward the dispossessed.

"The problem of debt increased the tensions between the propertied class and the tenants and laborers of Jesus' and Matthew's day."[100] It was one of the mechanisms by which the rich became richer and the poor poorer. The rich had the power to set the terms of these transactions and were able, in fact, to profit from another's poverty.

In our day, the problem of economic debt has reached global crisis proportions. The poorest countries face the problem of "revolving debt." That is, they cannot even repay the interest on their debt year by year and fall ever deeper into debt. The most heavily indebted countries have paid $550 billion in principle and interest on a debt of $540 billion, yet there is still a $523 billion debt burden. Severely impoverished countries are paying 30 to 40 percent of their GNP just to service the debt. This results in inability to meet the basic needs of their people for health, education, and social services. Quality of life is diminished; a future of poverty for generations to come waits on the horizon.[101]

There are no simple answers to this enormous and complex problem. Nevertheless, "the necessity and urgency of an active response" is laid on our hearts[102] if we continue to pray the Lord's Prayer.

Lead us not into temptation but deliver us from evil

What might temptation mean here? Two chapters ago in Matthew's Gospel we read the account of Jesus' temptation. The Spirit led Jesus

---

100. Crosby, *House of Disciples*, 189.
101. Anup Shah, "The Scale of the Debt Crisis," Global Issues, last updated July 2, 2005, www .globalissues.org/article/30/scale-of-the-debt-crisis.
102. Accra Confession, World Communion of Reformed Churches, #15.

into the wilderness to be tempted; perhaps we cherish a hope that the Spirit will not lead us along a similar path. Perhaps we doubt our capacity to resist the temptations Jesus resisted.

There were three kinds of temptation that he faced: to use his power to gratify his own needs (turning stones into bread), to gain public acclaim through spectacle (surviving a leap from the pinnacle of the Temple through divine intervention), and gaining kingdoms and power and glory (worshiping the devil instead of God). Jesus' clarity concerning his vocation as well as his uncompromising devotion to God were proven in the testing. He demonstrated that his "way" would be to live from the word of God, trusting rather than testing God, and worshiping God alone.

So how may we follow in the "way" of Jesus Christ? The principalities and powers may tempt us to follow an easier path than he chose. Might we be tempted to betray our vocation by choosing the easier path that allows for self-serving, self-promotion, and power grabbing? Might we agree to worship other gods if the benefits were better?

Jesus remained firm in his resistance even to the point of death on a cross. What Jesus began in the desert he finished on the cross.[103] They could not take his life from him, for he gave it up. In a paradox of power, by laying down his life and giving up his power, "he disarmed the rulers and authorities and made a public example of them, triumphing over them in it" (Col. 2:15).

Another approach to discerning what temptation might mean in this context is to consider the petition in the context of the prayer itself and its earlier petitions. There is temptation to doubt whether God's reign will come and God's will be done on earth. When will that be? What is the delay? Where is God? What is God waiting for? There is temptation to doubt whether we may really receive the grace of God's forgiveness. There is temptation to withhold forgiveness from others even though it is incumbent upon us as forgiven sinners. It is a temptation to doubt the presence and power of God to "deliver us from evil." There is the temptation, in the face of these doubts, to succumb to the present order, to be coopted by it.

---

103. Michael Crosby, *Thy Will Be Done: Praying the Our Father as Subversive Activity* (Maryknoll, NY: Orbis Books, 1977), 166.

This petition includes a plea that we be delivered from evil. There are two "evils" from which we need deliverance: the evil we experience and the evil we do. Prayer does not ask that we never *experience* evil; that would be praying to live in some other world than this world we live in. The prayer is rather that we may be *delivered*. We pray that we may be upheld by God's presence and power in such a way that those things that would undo us cannot undo us. "Yea, though I walk through the valley of the shadow of death, I will fear no evil: for thou art with me . . ." (Ps. 23:4 KJV).

Miroslav Volf, in considering the evil we *do*, refers us back to the Sermon on the Mount itself and proposes that we discern what is sinful (evil) by its opposite, that is, by what Jesus' teaching in this sermon calls us to do instead. Volf does not claim that this is a full discussion of Jesus' implicit theology of sin, but he notes that two things stand out here as prominent foci of his message. "Jesus says, 'You cannot serve God and wealth,' and 'Love your enemies . . .' (6:24 and 5:44)."[104] Greed and violence are evils that are destructive in our lives, our communities, and our world. Devotion to wealth and hatred of enemies are evils from which the followers of Jesus must pray to be delivered.

Among the many temptations we face, there remains a temptation to privatize and personalize the petitions of this prayer. When we do this, the prayer does not impinge upon us with its ethical implications or its wider horizon (i.e., global problems of hunger and the debt crisis). There is the temptation to pray this prayer mindlessly, as an empty religious ritual, without feeling its world-shaking power and its implicit requirement to realign our lives for the work of overcoming all that stands in the way of God's just and life-giving reign.

For Thine is the kingdom and the power and the glory forever.

This ending, which we commonly append, is not in the original. The earliest manuscripts do not show it. It is clearly a much later addition. What do we make of this? Why would it be added? Can it be that we are much more preoccupied with kingdoms and power and

---

104. Miroslav Volf, *Exclusion and Embrace: A Theological Exploration of Identity, Otherness, and Reconciliation* (Nashville: Abingdon Press, 1996), 115.

glory than Jesus was? That may well be. Nevertheless, this addition makes an affirmation consistent with the message of the book of Matthew. Jesus teaches that the kingdom, the power, and the glory belong to God and not to some other.

8:1–9:38

Narrative: "As One Having Authority"

Authority

Jesus has shown his authority as a teacher in chapters 5–7; now he will show his authority as a healer in chapters 8–9—thus revealing his authority in word and in deed. It is the crowds and the people at the margins who recognize his authority and receive his teaching and healing.

Social scientists observe that for authority to be effective it demands legitimation by those over whom it is exercised. The context of Jesus and Matthew was a very stratified society, patriarchal and hierarchical to the core. There were designated authorities who received their power by virtue of office or appointment. Key among them were the chief priests, the Sadducees, the Pharisees, the scribes, and the elders. The Sanhedrin, which was the highest local governing body, had representatives from all these groups. At the apex of the structures of all authorities was Roman imperial rule. In varying ways these "authorities" reinforced Roman rule. Chief priests, for example, served at the behest of Rome's authority and tended not to be critical of Roman authority.[1] The "designated" leaders lost their legitimacy with the people as they were coopted by and directed by Roman imperial rule that had been established by military conquest. Kingsbury notes that the religious leaders "rightly perceive that he (Jesus) stands as a moral threat to their authority and therefore to

1. Michael Crosby, *House of Disciples: Church Economics and Justice in Matthew* (Maryknoll, NY: Orbis, 1988), 77–79.

the religion and society based on that authority (15:13; 21:43)."[2] Much of the Gospel of Matthew revolves around this conflict of authorities.

"Into that world Jesus came as a charismatic figure teaching with authority (7:29), healing with authority (9:6; 10:1) and even forgiving sins with authority (9:6)."[3] Jesus distinguishes himself from those who were given social, religious, and political authority over the people. It is not by virtue of office or special appointment that Jesus receives his legitimation, but from the people whom he teaches, heals, and forgives. They are people at the margins, "harassed and helpless" (9:36); they care more about basic survival than proper lines of authority.

While those with the least power readily recognize Jesus' authority, those with the most power resolutely resist it. "They took offense at him" (13:57). Jesus undermines the authority of the religious leaders in four ways in particular, according to Crosby: (1) reordering table fellowship, (2) reordering Torah and Temple, (3) reordering Sabbath to meet human needs, and (4) forming a new kind of collegial community for doing God's will.[4] The leaders will ask, "By what authority are you doing these things, and who gave you this authority?" (21:23). They judge that Jesus does not have a "legitimate" basis for his authority within the structures of power that are in place.[5] Consequently, they seek to discredit him, casting aspersions on his deeds of power. They accuse him of blasphemy in presuming to forgive sins—that is God's prerogative (8:3). They accuse him, "He cast out demons "by the ruler of the demons" (9:34).

For these authorities, Jesus is at one and the same time "too high" and "too low." He is overreaching when he presumes to forgive sins. He is sinking low when he aligns himself with the ruler of the demons.

In many contexts today there is suspicion of "authorities." There are places where "the authorities" means "the people who have the power to do what they want" or "people who have an army to back them up." Authority is associated with power and power with

2. Ibid., 80.
3. Ibid., 79.
4. Ibid., 80.
5. Ibid., 79.

violence.[6] Oppression, exploitation, and human rights violations are all over the news. Corrupt politicians supported by system of "law and order" that are without transparency or accountability constitute authority in many locations. Suspicion of such authorities is well justified. But what if there was a different kind of authority, a different kind of power? Jesus demonstrates an altogether different kind of authority. It has nothing to do with violence and violations. It is the power to help and to heal, to show mercy and justice/righteousness.

Structure of 8:1–9:38

Jesus coming down from the Sermon on the Mount (8:1) is reminiscent of Moses coming down from Mount Sinai. Ten miracles follow. This number may be intended as another parallel to Moses and the ten "deeds of power" Moses did in the Exodus story. Ten plagues lead to deliverance might be contrasted with Jesus' ten acts of mercy and healing that lead to deliverance.

These miracle stories are in three groups (of three, three, and four). There is a decided focus on healing of people at the margins (lepers, Gentiles, women, demoniacs, tax collectors, the cultically impure, and even the dead). (See Introduction, "Ministry at the Margins" section.) In this way Matthew's account demonstrates the inclusiveness of the new community.[7]

Interspersed among the healings are notations on the mixed response to Jesus—amazement from the crowds, rejection from the authorities. In addition there are examples of faith and teachings concerning faith (little faith, 8:26; great faith, 9:22; healing faith, 9:29). There are texts of Scripture referenced that illumine the events and the questions posed (Isa. 53; Hos. 6:6; Ezek. 34). There is steady emphasis on the power Jesus exercises as he performs healings and

6. N. T. Wright, *Matthew for Everyone, Part 1* (Louisville, KY: Westminster John Knox Press, 2004), 96.
7. Amy-Jill Levine, "Matthew," in *The Women's Bible Commentary*, ed. Carol Newsom and Sharon Ringe (Louisville, KY: Westminster/John Knox Press, 1992), 256.

exorcisms "with a word." Each of the three sections ends with teachings on discipleship.

Another strong theme is opening the way to the Gentiles. As the book began with the wise men from the east bringing homage, so now we see a Roman centurion, and even demon possessed Gadarenes bear witness. This is a sign of the great in-gathering of the nations that God is bringing about (Isa. 2).

As the story unfolds it seems that Jesus is not much concerned with matters of insiders and outsiders, clean and unclean. He goes about touching lepers, healing Gentiles, and eating with sinners and tax collectors. Any one of these could be seen as a violation of expectations and codes concerning purity. Jesus is concerned rather with the weightier matters of the law which have mostly to do with mercy and compassion. He quotes Hosea 6:6, "I desire mercy, not sacrifice." Something new is going on here that calls for "fresh wineskins" (9:17).

In this set of miracles, the titles "Son of God" (8:29), "Son of Man" (9:6), and "Son of David" (9:27) all appear. In comparison with the other synoptic Gospels' treatment of these stories, Matthew particularly highlights Jesus' title as "Son of David" and associates that title with healing. He also gives more attention to the faith of the petitioners who come to Jesus and draws out their dialogue with him more fully.[8]

8:1–17

Deeds of Power: For People at the Margins

8:1–4 *"Lord, if you choose, you can make me clean."*

The healing stories which follow in chapter 8 and 9 show Jesus interacting with and healing a number of people who, for one reason or another, live at the margins of community and cultic life or are even excluded from these circles: a leper, a centurion (not only a Gentile, but a representative of Roman oppression), a servant, persons possessed by demons, a little girl, and a woman with a flow of blood

---

8. Frederick J. Murphy, *An Introduction to Jesus and the Gospels* (Nashville: Abingdon Press, 2005), 151.

(unclean). The overlooked and the excluded are included in his ministry of healing.

The very first healing is the healing of a man with leprosy. Leprosy here may refer to any number of skin diseases and disfigurements of varying degrees of contagion. For the victims it meant not only dealing with the physical suffering of the disease but also with exclusion from the community (Lev. 13–14). It was prescribed that lepers live outside the city or in their own separate houses. If they went out they had to call out "unclean" as a warning to any who might encounter them. Lepers could not attend worship. There was a general assumption that such an awful affliction must surely be punishment for a grievous sin.

In an act that must have shocked the bystanders, Jesus "stretched out his hand and touched him." (8:2). This was unthinkable, a violation of purity laws. To touch a person with leprosy would make Jesus "unclean." In a dramatic reversal, Jesus' touch makes the man with leprosy clean. Jesus then counsels that the healed man must now show himself to the priest. This was in keeping with what the law prescribed. Only in this way could the man with leprosy be officially declared clean and reintegrated into life in the community. Thus, in this encounter Jesus both upholds the law on the one hand, and—for mercy's sake—transcends it on the other.

8:5–13 *"Such faith"*

The next supplicant is a centurion. This man is an outsider on three counts: he is a foreigner, an enforcer of Roman imperial rule,[9] and a Gentile. The story takes surprising turns. Even though as a centurion, this man is an officer with up to one hundred soldiers to command, he subordinates himself to one who is under his authority.

The healing of the centurion's servant makes a point of Jesus' authority. This is a man who understands authority. When he gives an order, things happen. Surely Jesus has authority like this. He does not need to go into the centurion's home. All he need do is "speak the word."

There is some debate among the scholars concerning the translation

9. Warren Carter, *Matthew and the Margins: A Socio-Political and Religious Reading* (Sheffield, England: Sheffield Academic Press, 2000), 201.

of Jesus' response in v. 7. It reads in the NRSV, "I will come and cure him." However, the Greek sentence structure indicates a question, "Am I to go and cure him?"[10] This expression of hesitation may be the more likely reading. Translating it in this way would make it a close parallel to Jesus' encounter with the Canaanite woman in 15:21–31 where he at first protests that he has been sent to the house of Israel, and then is so moved by the humility and faith of this Gentile supplicant that he responds. In the centurion's story there is an issue of cultic purity in that the man is "at home paralyzed" and healing him would entail both entering the house of a Gentile and touching a Gentile who is sick. Furthermore there is the issue of Jesus' mission, which he interprets as being "to the lost sheep of the house of Israel" (10:6; 15:24). The centurion responds to Jesus in humility: "I am not worthy to have you come under my roof" (8:8), and expresses great faith in Jesus' power to heal even at a distance as if giving an order that it be so (8:8–9). Jesus praises his remarkable faith: "Truly I tell you, in no one in Israel have a found such faith" (8:10). This overturns common expectations in a context where "Gentile" and "unbeliever" were synonymous. The exceptional character of this Gentile man's faith will stand out all the more later in the chapter as Jesus' own disciples will show themselves to be of "little faith" (8:26).

If we lay the centurion's story alongside that of the Canaanite woman's in chapter 15, the pattern is the same: Jesus' seeming resistance, a humble request evidencing great faith, Jesus' wonder at finding a Gentile with such faith, and a response of healing. This pattern in these encounters further supports the mission to the Gentiles. Jesus' messianic authority extends beyond the boundaries of Israel.[11] They have first place in this mission, but not an exclusive place. Jesus next references the prophetic hope that the nations and the scattered faithful Israelites (of the Diaspora) will come from east and west to the messianic banquet with Abraham and Jacob (Isa. 2:2–4; 25:6; 43:5–6). He also warns that some who by rights should be there—meaning the scribes and Pharisees—will instead be cast

---

10. Eugene Boring, *The New Interpreter's Bible: New Testament Articles, Matthew, Mark* (Nashville: Abingdon Press, 1995), 8:226.
11. Donald Senior, *The Gospel of Matthew*, Interpreting Biblical Texts (Nashville: Abingdon Press, 1997), 113.

out. Birthright is no guarantee; faith and justice/righteousness are what matter.

8:14–17 *"She got up and began to serve him."*

This is the first healing of a woman in the book of Matthew. In the patriarchal context of Jesus and Matthew, women were very much at the margins socially and religiously. Yet, in these two chapters, three of the healings are done for women. It is also notable that new descriptions attach to them that are very central in Jesus' life and ministry—serving (*diēkonei*), being saved or made well (*esōthē*), and being raised (*ēgerthē*) (8:15; 9:22; 9:25).

An unusual thing about this particular healing of Peter's mother-in-law is that here we have the only example of Jesus taking the initiative to heal. In all other cases, he was petitioned by the persons needing healing or by some other persons on their behalf. Jesus "sees" her, just as in the account of the calling of the first disciples (4:18, 21).[12] Levine proposes that in this accounting, there is an implicit interest in moving toward a more egalitarian social structure. "The woman literally rises to this occasion:"[13] she gets up from her bed and serves Jesus. In Matthew 20:26–28, Jesus describes his own role as that of serving and enjoins the disciples to serve as well. The use of the same term *diēkonei* for this woman's service is interesting as this is the term from which we derive the name for the ecclesiastical office of "deacon." Feminist readings propose that women should indeed rise up to serve Jesus.

There is a summative comment at the end of this first set of healings indicating there were many more than what is presented here, and that Jesus healed "all" (8:16). The formula phrase used in connection with Jesus birth (1:22–23), ministry (4:14–16), and teachings (5:17–20) appears again in reference to his healing work. "This was to fulfill what had been spoken . . ." (8:17). A text from Isaiah 53 (the suffering servant psalm) provides the interpretive lens for understanding what is going on. Jesus fulfills what the prophet spoke about the suffering servant of God who "took our weaknesses and

---

12. Carter, *Matthew and the Margins*, 204.
13. Levine, "Matthew," 256.

bore our diseases" (8:17).[14] Jesus' authority is seen in his healing power; his healing power is connected with his serving and his suffering.

8:18-22
"Follow me."

At the close of this first set of three deeds of power, there is a teaching on discipleship and the commitments and costs it entails. It is drawn from encounters with two would-be disciples. The first is a scribe who volunteers, boldly asserting, "Teacher, I will follow you wherever you go." Jesus cautions him about the sacrifice of a settled existence that accompanying Jesus—who is truly homeless—will entail (8:20). Another, who is already a disciple, seems to be wavering in his commitment. He asks for reprieve to bury his father. All the hearers would recognize the obligation to bury one's father as a sacred obligation. Jesus' refusal would be disturbing. The commentaries have tried to soften this effect by speculating that his father is not yet dead and this is really a postponement of discipleship that amounts to a refusal. However, there is scant evidence for this speculation. Left to stand as it is, the story lays bare the radical demands of discipleship. These two would-be disciples "underestimate the cost of discipleship."[15] This commitment overrides all other allegiances and all claims to ease. One must be willing to give up "home and security and even family obligations"[16]—to leave it all behind and cross over to the other side.

8:23-9:17
Deeds of Power: Beyond All Expectations

8:23-27 *Crossing over "to the Other Side"*

As if to underscore the insecurities and uncertainties and costs of following, Jesus gets into a boat and heads for the "other side," which

14. Wright, *Matthew for Everyone, Part 1*, 88.
15. Donald Senior, *Abingdon New Testament Commentaries: Matthew* (Nashville: Abingdon Press, 1998), 111.
16. Mitchell G. Reddish, *An Introduction to the Gospels* (Nashville: Abingdon Press, 1997), 127.

is Gentile territory. The disciples go with him to this dubious destination in a perilous passage. Storms assail them. For the people of Israel, who were not a seafaring people, the sea was "a symbol of wild, untamable power," a place where darkness and evil threatened.[17] The sea as such is not much discussed in the Hebrew Scriptures except in the places where God overcomes it. In the work of creation when "a wind from God, moved over the face of the waters," chaos becomes cosmos. In the Exodus story, when the sea was blocking the path to freedom, the power of God again overcame the waters. "The Israelites walked on dry ground through the sea, the waters forming a wall for them on their right and on their left" (Exod. 14:29). So now, on this storm tossed sea, Jesus displays a power like God's power and the waters were calmed. The disciples remark in amazement, "What sort of man is this, that even the winds and the sea obey him?" (Matt. 8:27).

It is the epitome of authority to command the winds and the sea as Jesus does. For Matthew this story may also be an allegory for the church and the storms that assailed his community as they extended the church's mission to the Gentiles. This perilous crossing is a harbinger of things to come. The way will be stormy, but Jesus will be with them. The promise of Jesus' presence and authority over storms was a needed word. "Why are you afraid, you of little faith?" (8:26)

8:28–34 *"What have you to do with us, Son of God?"*

Having crossed over the sea, the disciples are now in Gentile territory. This is vividly apparent in the presence of a herd of swine (animals unclean in Jewish law and associated with Gentiles).[18] The answer to the disciples' query ("What sort of man is this ... ?") receives its answer unexpectedly from the lips of Gentile demoniacs when they address Jesus as "Son of God" (8:29). There follows an odd interchange between Jesus and the demoniacs. They ask whether he has come to torment them "before the time." Among the eschatological hopes was the expectation that the advent of God's reign would mean the overcoming of evil powers. The demons negotiate their fate with Jesus and he shows mercy (even to the demons!).

17. Wright, *Matthew for Everyone, Part 1,* 89.
18. Senior, *Abingdon New Testament Commentaries,* 102.

Here Jesus is seen to practice the mercy God desires (9:13) to the extreme. Jesus accedes to their request to be sent into the swine who then rush headlong down a steep bank and into the sea. It is no surprise, under the circumstances, that the townspeople begged Jesus to leave. One can imagine them saying "Thanks, but no thanks, this kind of healing is bad for business."

9:1–17 *"Take heart, your sins are forgiven."*

Returning to his own town, Jesus is met with a paralyzed man whose friends have brought him to Jesus for healing. Jesus first tells him that his sins are forgiven. In the context of this writing diseases and even death were widely viewed as punishment for sin. As there was a connection between sin and disease, so also there was a connection between forgiveness and healing. Insofar as body and spirit are a psychosomatic unit, it is reasonable to think that a troubling in one's soul could have physical effects. It we take this too far we risk a "blaming the victim" mentality. Even Augustine, who assumed all suffering was the result of sin, agreed that there is no perfect proportionality between sin and suffering on an individual basis, as many people suffer from the sins of others. "Sin" is more than individual culpable acts; "it is a moral condition that holds all human beings in its grip, and only the power of God can overcome it."[19] Sin, in this more comprehensive meaning, is indeed destructive to human well-being. The healing Jesus offers is for whole persons, not for bodies or souls in isolation from one another. The text has already prepared the reader for the fuller dimension of Jesus' healing work as the name "Jesus" is given because he will "save his people from their sins" (1:21)

When Jesus speaks these words of forgiveness to the paralyzed man there is once again a mixed response: The scribes say "This man is blaspheming." Forgiveness of sins, in their view, is God's prerogative. Who is this man to speak for God? There may be another reason for their complaint. Matters concerning God's forgiveness and expiation of sin were handled through the Temple system administered by priests. To make such an offer "outside the system" is to

19. Ibid., 104.

abrogate their authority and assume their prerogative. This constitutes another kind of threat.

In contrast to the scribes' response, the crowds respond with wonder, "filled with awe, and they glorified God who had given such authority to human beings" (9:8). Note that it is "human beings" (not just Jesus) who are authorized. This foreshadows the events of chapter 16 where Peter and the disciples are given power "to bind" and "to "loose." This understanding was congruent with the practice of forgiveness in the church of Matthew's community.

9:9–17 *"Why does your teacher eat with sinners and tax collectors?"* Another discussion of the meaning of discipleship closes this second set of deeds of power. It hinges on the question of who can be included. Who can be called to be a disciple? The case in point is Matthew the tax collector. As a tax collector he is an unlikely choice. To be a tax collector for Rome was to be a collaborator with the oppressor. Tax collectors were assumed to be thieves as well as collaborators, collecting more than was required and profiting from the power of their positions. On top of all this, tax collectors were "unclean" by virtue of their continual dealings with Gentiles and Gentile goods. Yet here is Jesus calling Matthew the tax-collector to follow him. Jesus is calling sinners to be disciples (9:13).

With this action, the ammunition against Jesus is accumulating. He forgives sins—as if he were God or an agent of God like a priest (9:3). He eats with sinners and tax collectors, which implies friendship with them and makes him as unclean as they are. Now he calls a tax collector to be among his followers. This is unheard of. As shocking as his healings are, even more shocking to the authorities is his forgiving sinners, associating with them, and calling them to follow. Jesus is a man with friends in low places.

The Pharisees' questions read like accusations. Jesus makes his defense (9:12–13). "While other religious leaders of the day saw their task as being to keep themselves in quarantine, away from possible sources of moral and spiritual infection, Jesus saw himself as a doctor who'd come to heal the sick."[20] A text from Hosea is the centerpiece of his understanding of what God desires, "I desire mercy,

20. Wright, *Matthew for Everyone, Part 1*, 101.

not sacrifice" (6:6). So Jesus has come not to call the righteous, but sinners.

The Pharisees don't get it. Even the disciples of John have some questions. Why are Jesus and his disciples not fasting? This is unexpected behavior. John's disciples (like the Pharisees) "fast often" (9:14). Jesus has no objection to fasting, in fact he upholds the practice as we saw in the Sermon on Mount (6:16–18). It is a question of timing. This is not the time for it—the bridegroom is here and this is the time of the wedding banquet. "The eschatological banquet was a biblical metaphor for the fulfillment of Israel's hopes."[21] This amounts to an announcement that the long awaited banquet is on. Something really new and extraordinary is happening that justifies their unexpected behavior. New wine calls for new wineskins. Nevertheless, the "new thing" God is doing does not abrogate the old things that went before or bring an end to Torah or supersede Judaism[22]—the goal is that "both are preserved" (9:17).

9:18–38

Deeds of Power: "Never has anything like this been seen in Israel."

9:18–26 *"Take heart, daughter"*

The healing of the synagogue leader's daughter and the woman with a flow of blood (whom Jesus addresses as "daughter") are here intertwined—a healing within a healing. On the way to restoration of one, Jesus restores the other.

In both healing stories Jesus will violate ritual purity customs. These are not meaningless regulations; they are a matter of protecting personal and communal health. Washing hands before eating, avoiding contact with what could be contaminated or disease-bearing; these were deeply ingrained and wise practices. Nevertheless, in the space of these few verses (9:18–26), Jesus will be touched by

---

21. Senior, *Abingdon New Testament Commentaries*, 107.
22. Murphy, *An Introduction to Jesus and the Gospels*, 150.

a hemorrhaging woman and will touch a dead body. He does not protect himself, but extends himself for those in need of healing. It is not because ritual purity is unimportant but because ritual purity is secondary to the demands of mercy and compassion.

A leader ("of the synagogue" is not there in the Greek) comes and kneels before Jesus. His approach is humble, as Jesus teaches that leaders should be (20:26). His daughter has died. Commentators treat this as a resurrection story and the leader's faith that Jesus can restore her to life is very much to the point. The girl was surely already dead; else the funeral proceedings would not be so far advanced. This is not a case of mistaking sleep for death or treating death as only "sleep" and nothing final. The story is about Jesus' power to raise the dead. A general resurrection was another sign in the hope for the messianic age. The story is, of course, written after the resurrection and interpreted accordingly. "Jesus is pictured as the one for whom death is already vanquished, and he raises the young woman from the "sleep" of death as he will raise all at the eschaton."[23] This presentation is a statement of faith in the power of the risen Lord to raise the dead.

Undeterred by the laughter of those gathered for the funeral, "He took her by the hand, and the girl got up." It is interesting that the verb used in this restoration to life (Greek *ēgerthē*) is the same verb used in multiple references to Jesus' resurrection (14:2; 26:32; 28:6–7). The term appears with some frequency in the healing stories of these two chapters. The paralyzed man "stood up" (*egeire* 9:5); Peter's mother-in-law "got up" (*egeirthe* 8:15)." The term is even used of Matthew the tax collector who, when called to be a disciple Matthew "got up" and followed Jesus (*eigeire* 9:9)." All these others were, in a sense, given back their lives through Jesus' healing power. Healing power is resurrection power.

The English term "resurrection" is not so clearly equivalent in its association, but other languages carry the meaning. The German term for resurrection is *auferstehung*, literally "upstanding." The African American Spiritual makes the connection when it speaks of resurrection as "that great 'getting up' morning."

Along the way to restore this girl to life, Jesus encounters a hemorrhaging woman. She approaches him discreetly and timidly from

23. Boring, *The New Interpreter's Bible*, 8:238.

behind. Unlike the leader (9:18) who makes a public appeal, she does not even call for Jesus' attention to her need. Her approach is consistent with her status—doubly marginalized by her gender and her ritual impurity.[24] Matthew underscores the Jewishness of Jesus even more than other Gospel writers, and mentioning the detail of the "fringe" of his cloak identifies him as a pious Jew.

The woman has faith that she will be healed if she can only touch the fringe. Jesus turns to her, recognizing her need, and says, "Take heart daughter, your faith has made you well" (9:22). This woman becomes yet another example of faith of people at the margins, in contrast with the disciples who have "little faith" (8:26).

As was the case for the man with leprosy, this woman with hemorrhages is doubly afflicted: not only is she physically ill, she is also excluded from social and ritual life in her community. Because she has an abnormal bodily discharge, she is unclean and everything she touches is unclean (Lev. 15).[25] No one was supposed to touch her or any of her things. Persons who touch even her bedclothes or her chair become unclean and must undergo ritual purification. She has lived this way for twelve years.

9:27–31 *"Their eyes were opened."*

Matthew regards the deeds of power done by Jesus in chapters 8 and 9 as fulfilling the eschatological promise of salvation as given by the prophet Isaiah (35:4–6; 58:6; 61:1–2). For the eyes of the blind to be opened was an essential sign. Matthew alludes to this promise in 11:5 when Jesus answers John's question of whether Jesus is the one who is to come. "Go and tell John what you hear and see; the blind receive their sight, the lame walk, the lepers are cleansed, the deaf hear, the dead are raised, and the poor have good news brought to them."

With these blind men the cast of marginalized characters continues.[26] As with other sicknesses, people thought blindness was a

24. Levine, "Matthew," 256.
25. Boring, *The New Interpreter's Bible*, 8:238.
26. Carter, *Matthew and the Margins*, 227.

divine punishment. We see this attitude reflected in the question, 'Rabbi, who sinned, this man or his parents, that he was born blind?' (John 9:2) Blind persons were disqualified from service as priests (Lev. 21:16–20). They were often victims of cruelty. They were economically vulnerable as they were dependent on their families and/ or begging for their support. Matthew understands their healing to be a sign of God's promised salvation.

When the blind men are healed they are charged to "See that no one knows of this." (9:30) Similar injunctions are found elsewhere. It is called the "messianic secret." However, this is a secret that just won't keep. The men went away "and spread the news about him throughout that district" (9:31).

9:32–34 *"The crowds were amazed."*

In the healing of the man possessed by demons and mute, there is yet another essential sign of the in-breaking of God's salvation and promised reign (Isa. 35:6). His healing meets with mixed reaction. For the third time in this section we have a contrast between the responses of the people and the responses of the leadership. While the crowds are amazed, the Pharisees are affronted. The people remark, "Never has anything like this been seen in Israel" (9:33). The Pharisees judge that Jesus is casting out demons by "the ruler of the demons" (9:34). Complaints are piling up: Jesus "blasphemes" when he takes it upon himself to forgive sins. Jesus eats with sinners and tax collectors. He and his disciples do not fast as they should. Yes, he casts out demons, but by what authority? Perhaps he has his power to exorcise from the one in charge of demons. This last is the worst accusation yet. Opposition is strengthening.

9:35–38 *Conclusion*

There follows a transitional summary. "Jesus went about all the cities and villages, teaching in their synagogues, and proclaiming the good news of the kingdom, and curing every disease and every sickness" (9:35). This is almost verbatim from 4:23 and shows that this section is a literary unit.[27] Jesus' authority as a teacher is established in chapters 5–7 with the Sermon on the Mount. His authority as a healer is demonstrated in the healings in chapters 8–9.

His work is a work of compassion. "When he saw the crowds, he had compassion for them, because they were harassed and helpless, like sheep without a shepherd" (9:36). The reference evokes Ezekiel 34 as a criticism of the current leadership,

> Ah, you shepherds of Israel who have been feeding yourselves! Should not shepherds feed the sheep? You eat the fat, you clothe yourselves with the wool, you slaughter the fatlings; but you do not feed the sheep. You have not strengthened the weak, you have not healed the sick, you have not bound up the injured, you have not brought back the strayed, you have not sought the lost, but with force and harshness you have ruled them. So they were scattered, because there was no shepherd; and scattered, they became food for all the wild animals. (2–5)

The compassion of Jesus for these "harassed and helpless" people echoes God's compassionate response in Ezekiel 34. "I myself will be the shepherd of my sheep, and I will make them lie down, says the Lord GOD. I will seek the lost, and I will bring back the strayed, and I will bind up the injured, and I will strengthen the weak" (15–16).

This section closes with a compelling call to discipleship, "The harvest is plentiful, but he laborers are few; therefore ask the Lord of the harvest to send out laborers into his harvest" (Matt. 9:37–38). What Jesus has done in teaching and healing (chaps. 5–9) the disciples will now be charged to do in chapter 10, which has been termed the "Missionary Discourse." This transfer of calling and authority from Jesus to the disciples is parallel to the transfer from Moses to Joshua in Numbers 27:17. There Moses uses the same phrase, "sheep without a shepherd," as he prepares for death and expresses concern about who will take up the care and leading of the people.[28] Matthew 10:10 makes explicit the calling, authorizing, and sending of the disciples to continue and extend the ministry of Jesus.

27. Boring, *The New Interpreter's Bible*, 8:241.
28. Ibid., 252.

FURTHER REFLECTIONS
Miracle Stories in an Age of Science

How may we understand these miracle stories in an age of science? In our day, the regime of truth is scientific; science sets the parameters of what can and cannot happen. Is there really room for "miracle" in what science teaches about the way the world works (laws of nature, cause and effect relations)? If "miracle" means divine intervention from outside this (apparently) closed system and an overriding of the laws of nature, there is an unavoidable conflict. People of faith ask whether and in what sense God "acts" in the world at all, if we accept the scientific worldview. Faced with this difficulty, two responses are typical: either adopt the biblical account and ignore issues science would raise, or adopt the scientific account and exclude the possibility of miracles. After discussing Matthew's handling of the miracle stories, I will contrast these two options and then offer an alternative approach.

Miracle Stories in Matthew

Miracle stories were common in the Hellenistic world. That miracles can happen was a part of the mental furniture of that context. What is distinctive about Jesus is not that he works miracles but the meanings attached to the miracles he works and the salvific orientation of the miracles. "Unlike writings of the Hellenistic world generally . . . the canonical Gospels contain no stories in which miraculous power is used punitively against human beings."[29] The miracles are always saving/healing acts that demonstrate the mercy and compassion of God as Jesus teaches and enacts it.

Matthew generally abbreviates the narrative element in the miracle tradition he inherits and emphasizes instead the conversations within them and the conclusions to be drawn from them. The relationship between faith and miracle is important in Matthew's Gospel. Miracles are never used as a proof to generate faith; rather it is persons who already have faith that approach Jesus for help or healing.[30]

29. Ibid., 244.
30. Ibid., 245.

There is an interesting "anti-miraculous" theme that runs along-side these stories in Matthew. In the temptation Jesus refuses to do miracles for self-gratification or as public spectacle (4:1–11). He also refuses to "perform" for the Pharisees and Sadducees when they ask him for a sign (12:38–43; 16:1-4). Jesus forgoes the option of miracu-lous intervention as a way out at the point of his arrest and execu-tion (26:53–56; 27:39–44).

Common Approaches:

The Gospel of Matthew is full of miracles stories. Understanding the nature and meaning of these stories is particularly difficult in an age of scientific explanations. Broadly speaking, the discussion has yielded two points of view, each with variations.

One point of view affirms that miracles can and do occur. God breaks into history and overturns natural processes now and then. Persons who hold this view are not all of one mind regarding whether miracles were only "then" or whether they may also occur "now." Protestant reformers generally advanced the view of "then, but not now." The miracles appearing in the Bible serve the func-tion of confirming revelation. In the New Testament, they confirm who Jesus is as the Son of God and provide evidence of the truth of Christianity. They have served their purpose, and now the "age of miracles" has passed. Roman Catholic teaching, on the other hand, affirms both "then and now." Miracles continue in the life of the church. In the polemic of the Reformation era it was said that if there is an absence of miracles in the life of the Protestant churches, then that is just more evidence of the lack of fullness in those churches. Today there continue to be those who associate the "age of miracles" with the early church and those who main-tain that what God has done God can still do, but these view-points are a difference within denominations and not between them.

A second point of view is that miracles do not occur—not then and not now. The causal nexus is tightly knit, and the God who cre-ated the natural world with its lawfulness does not occasionally come down and unravel it. Persons who hold this view approach it differently. For some, the best way forward is to view the miracles as primitive understandings of what are in fact very natural occurrences. Eugene Boring offers several examples of rationalistic explanations of the miracles: Demon possession is a primitive way of understanding mental disturbance. Blindness and paralysis can be psychosomatic. Jesus' healing is a thing of the mind and spirit for these persons. The feeding of the five thousand (14:21) is a miracle of sharing. Accounts of raising the dead are in reality cases of "(almost) premature burial." Walking on water is either an optical illusion or a mistranslation of "on" (the Greek word *epi* can also mean "at the edge of.")[31] To call these events miracles is a misunderstanding.

For others within the second framework (no miracles occur) a "mythological" approach seems best. The miracles are not so much events as vehicles for communicating profound truths of faith through story and image. From this perspective, whether miracles are events "is not only doubtful, but also beside the point."[32] The miracles are more than events. The question is not so much "did it happen?" as "what does it communicate?" Perhaps miracles, like parables, tell about things that never happened but are "always happening." The power of the story of the prodigal son, for example, goes well beyond any single historical happening. It is a story that transcends itself in illuminating how it is between us and God. Rudolf Bultmann states the present challenge in this way, "It is impossible to use electric light and the wireless and to avail ourselves of modern medical and surgical discoveries and at the same time to believe in the New Testament world of demons and spirits."[33] He proposes that the Gospels are not so much historical documents as theological documents. Bultmann was deeply skeptical regarding the historical/factual reliability of these texts, but continued to believe the essential message of the Gospels. He thought we should take the myths as they stand and restate them in terms of our existence (existentially)—we should "demythologize."

31. Ibid., 248.
32. Ibid.
33. Rudolf Bultmann, "New Testament and Mythology," in *Kerygma and Myth*, ed. H. W. Bartsch (New York: Harper, 1961), 5.

Exploring an Alternative Approach

Each of these points of view is an effort at coherence with an assumption that one has to choose between miracle and science. Each option has its difficulties. The first view takes the miracles at face value, disregarding what we know from science about the way the world works. It amounts to a *sacrificium intellectus* (sacrifice of the intellect) in an attempt to keep the faith. Is that a credible position? Is it a necessary one? The second view sees the miracle stories as either "misunderstandings" or "myths." This seems to capitulate to a materialist interpretation of reality and to disallow God acting in the world—at all. Some contemporary Christians live in the tension between these two options and seek to preserve both the biblical account of miracles and the scientific account of the way the world works by believing one thing on Sunday and something else the rest of the week. Are these really our only options? Might there be a way forward that is both more credible and more faithful?

This dilemma invites us to think more deeply, both about the parameters of science and about our theological understanding of miracles. The current religion and science dialogue has been very helpful (from both directions) on the particular question we are considering.

Two insights in particular are to the point in understanding contemporary science. The first concerns whether the "naturalism" (materialism) of science must automatically exclude God from the picture. Naturalism as a *methodology* for science is unavoidably reductionist; it functions from within the limits of what can be observed about the natural world. This is an appropriate and productive way of proceeding. Methodological naturalism, however, does not require *metaphysical* reductionism—the conclusion that "nature is all there is" or "there is no God." While methodological naturalism only says, "This is all we may know *from our observations*;" metaphysical naturalism adds, "and this is all there is to know." As John Haught has observed, to claim to know—one way or the other—about whether God exists is to go beyond science.

Another observation concerning contemporary science may help us by correcting our original question. We asked how God can act in a world that is a closed system of natural law and cause-and-effect relations. This question assumes a Newtonian (mechanistic) world-view, but contemporary science has gone in some new directions and well beyond this understanding. What were once thought of as "inviolable laws" are now seen as "probabilistic descriptions." They work, more or less reliably, at the macro level. Scientists working at the quantum level, however, need a different framework of understanding. They talk about uncertainty, unpredictability, nonlinear relations, and entanglement. "Cause-and-effect" proves inadequate for a number of fields of inquiry. For example, it does not cover the complexities of chaos theory, systems thinking, information theory, psychobiology, or ecology. In light of the new science, some scientists are asking the question, "How closed is this system really?" How constraining are "probabilistic descriptions"? This fuller picture of the scientific accounting of how the world works may open new possibilities for thinking about how God works with and within the natural world. It may be that our questions have been misdirected when theologians have been "tilting with the windmills" of Newtonian science[34]—offering a valiant challenge to a non-opponent.

We do well to think more deeply on the theological considerations of the present discussion as well. Perhaps the first question to ask is, "What do we mean by *miracle*?" Theologians differ in their meanings here. For some, it is precisely God's external intervention to overturn natural processes that makes a miracle *miraculous*. However, this way of thinking is only one of several available meanings for "miracle." In fact, it is only in the Middle Ages that miracles come to be seen primarily as supernatural acts to attest to supernatural truth. Both Augustine and Calvin offer alternatives to this way of thinking. In *The City of God*, Augustine argues that miracles are deeds of power that are *not* contrary to nature—though they may be contrary to what we *know* of nature. Calvin understood "laws of nature" to be God's own self-consistent activity. What we think of as "laws of nature" are, in themselves, already God acting. What is "miraculous" is that God is working (everywhere and always) within world process. To multiply loaves and fishes is not qualitatively different than providing daily bread; it is just more calculated to strike the eye.

---

34. Daniel Wolpert, "Theology and 'Natural Laws' in Relation to God's Action," final paper for *Theology and Biological Evolution*, Pittsburgh Theological Seminary, August 2010.

These views drawn from the tradition are already countering the external interventionist patterns of thought that have proven problematic in relation to scientific understandings of the way the world works. Much hinges on how we understand divine action and miracle. Can we think of them in ways that are more attentive to how the world actually works? What if we followed the lead of Augustine and Calvin and thought of miracle as God acting in the world with and within natural process? In this sense, "all of it" is miracle. God is at work in all things for good. From a human standpoint, it may be that it is only in rare moments (now and then) that we see through world process to "God acting." What we designate as "miracles" may be those "thin places;" places where divine activity becomes more transparent to us. In those places, "the light shines through," and we see what God is in fact already doing everywhere and always.

The traditional doctrine of providence has affirmed that God acts in the world. This is central for Christian faith. How we think about God's action is theologically important, however. There are *theological* (as well as scientific) problems with thinking about God's action as occasional intervention. Such a view brings in its wake the unwonted assertion of the ordinary absence of God. Furthermore, if we think that God sometimes overturns natural processes we may want to ask why God does not intervene more often—in the face of natural disasters and human evils. Much suffering and evil could presumably be prevented by divine intervention. The problem of theodicy is exacerbated by this external-interventionist understanding of divine action. Both the scientific and the theological problems invite us to reconsider such notions of God's activity. Is there any reason not to allow that God may act with and within natural processes? There are some very interesting proposals from scientists/theologians who are working on ways of understanding and articulating this perspective.

Arthur Peacocke (biochemist, theologian, and Anglican priest) suggests that divine activity might be thought of on the model of biochemical processes in which larger wholes are said to "influence" the parts that compose them. Higher levels constrain and shape the patterns of constituent units in a lower level in what is termed "whole-part influence." The world is a system-of-systems organized in levels of increasing complexity. God, who encompasses all, can act in a way that influences all the parts "without abrogating the laws and regularities that specifically apply to them."[35] This provides a way of understanding God's activity in the world without recourse to external interventionist models.

John Polkinghorne (theoretical physicist, theologian, and Anglican priest) offers another such proposal. Where Peacocke envisions a kind of "top down" model for divine working, Polkinghorne's model is more of a "bottom up" approach. He works from the unpredictability/uncertainty science finds at the quantum level (Heisenberg's uncertainty principle). Polkinghorne also points to the "exquisite sensitivity" of chaotic systems to small triggers (chaos theory). This dynamic of unpredictability/indeterminacy in physical reality, he conjectures, signals an "openness" in the system. If we thought of God's activity as a kind of "active information" working at this level, he says, we might have "the scientific equivalent of the immanent working of the Spirit on the inside of creation."[36]

These interesting proposals are representative of some very creative work on how God may act in the world in ways that do not amount to occasional external intervention that violates natural processes. Such proposals go a long way toward thinking about miracle (meaning simply "God acting in the world") in ways that take seriously what we are learning from science about the way the world works. They also envision God acting continuously rather than just occasionally (entailing the ordinary absence of God). The God-given freedom of the creation is upheld in a way that addresses the problem of suffering and evil. Such reflections as these take us a step further toward an account of divine activity in world process that is both more credible and more faithful.

35. Arthur Peacocke, *Paths from Science Towards God: The End of All Our Exploring* (Oxford: One World, 2001), 51.
36. John Polkinghorne, *Science and Theology: An Introduction* (Philadelphia: Fortress, 1998), 89.

10:1–11:1

Teaching: In Mission Together

This chapter is sometimes referred to as the "missionary discourse." For first world readers in mainline denominations this chapter seems a world away "with its talk of witness, persecution, poverty, and martyrdom. To the extent that it seems alien, it is a call to reexamine our own version of Christianity"[1] Such a reexamination is in order, I think. I wonder whether we in fact have a form of "culture Christianity;" an ecclesial existence that has become so "well-adapted" to our culture that it is indistinguishable from it? In our situation of ease, have we lost our prophetic edge and with it a sense of the distance between the reign of God and the status quo? Is it possible that the very things that, in our context, have made it easy to be a Christian have made it harder to follow Jesus?

> When not beleaguered by outside pressure, the church tends to slip into a comfortable religiosity that takes all too lightly its commitment to God and God's purposes.
>
> Douglas R. A. Hare, *Matthew, Interpretation Series, A Bible Commentary for Teaching and Preaching* (Louisville, KY: Westminster/John Knox Press, 1992), 115.

If we take a wider global view we see some churches in other contexts that live very much on the edge. They know the meaning of giving courageous and faithful witness in the face of opposition. They do not have the luxury of a peaceful and prosperous existence. It may be that secularization occurring in Europe and North America may disestablish the church from its place of easy acceptance

1. Eugene Boring, *The New Interpreter's Bible: New Testament Articles, Matthew, Mark* (Nashville: Abingdon Press, 1995), 8:263.

and privilege. We may come to know the harder realities that are the experience of Churches in some parts of Asia and Africa. The changes that are coming may lend a new relevance to this chapter in Matthew's Gospel which reacquaints its readers with the "cost of discipleship."

10:1–4

Summoning and Sending the Disciples

Chapter 9 closes with Jesus' expression of compassion for the people. They are "helpless and harassed." Oppressed and exploited by political and religious authorities—the very persons who should lead and care for them—they are like "sheep without a shepherd." Their need is great but the workers are few. In the final verse of chapter 9 Jesus charges the disciples to pray for God to send workers as the need is great and the workers are few. The first verse of chapter 10 finds them summoned. They are to become the answer to their own prayer's petition.

Here for the first time twelve disciples are listed by name. All are male. Much is made of the gender of the disciples in the resistance to women serving in ordained ministry. Less attention is drawn to the fact that all twelve were Jewish. Warren Carter questions whether the new community is really based upon restrictive gender (male) and ethnicity (Jewish). He notes that from this more circumscribed beginning the circle opens steadily outward. Even though this list of twelve includes no women and no Gentiles, the final chapter will find women to be first in proclaiming the resurrection and the mission will extend explicitly to Gentiles.[2]

The number twelve is important symbolically for Matthew. It hints at the reconstitution of the twelve tribes of Israel, which was part of the eschatological expectation. Apparently beginning with "twelve" was more important than which persons were actually among the twelve, since the names differ from one Gospel to another. This is the first place (v. 2) where the twelve are called

---

2. Warren Carter, *Matthew and the Margins: A Socio-Political and Religious Reading* (Sheffield, England: Sheffield Academic Press, 2000), 233.

"apostles" (Greek *apostoloi*, "sent"). Later the term applies to a much larger group[3] and generally means those who were witnesses to the resurrection or those commissioned to go and "make disciples" (28:20) of all nations.

> The church will change when we begin to look at people as Jesus did . . . when we look more closely at their suffering than at their sin, when we see them with the eyes of mercy rather than fear.
>
> José A. Pagola, *The Way Opened Up by Jesus*, 101.

They are to do what Jesus did. The "one having authority" now gives them "authority" and commissions them to cast out unclean spirits and to cure every disease and sickness. Here we see authority in the service of compassion (9:36). These "harassed and helpless" people are victims more than sinners. They need help and healing, not condemnation.[4] Compassion is the watchword.

10:5–15

Following Jesus in Mission

The disciples are summoned and sent out to engage the mission Jesus engaged. They will teach what he taught: "The kingdom of heaven has come near" (10:7). This is the message preached by Jesus and by John the Baptist before him. Preaching this word proved dangerous to them and so it will be for the disciples. The prevailing regime will take umbrage at the word that a new reign is coming. The reign of

> The announcement of the reign of God coming near is the "good news" that is "bad news" for demons and for demagogues.

God makes "a claim on human allegiance that challenges all other reigns including Roman imperial power and the religious elite's control."[5]

3. Boring, *The New Interpreter's Bible*, 8:254.
4. José A. Pagola, *The Way Opened Up by Jesus: A Commentary on the Gospel of Matthew* (Miami, FL: Convivium Press, 2012), 101.
5. Carter, *Matthew and the Margins*, 234.

Not only are the disciples called to teach what Jesus taught, they are called to do what Jesus did. "Cure the sick, raise the dead, cleanse the lepers, cast out demons" (10:8). The pattern Jesus set for the mission of his disciples (then and now) is attentiveness to suffering. Theologian Johann Baptist Metz has proposed that the suffering of others should be the heart and center of our work. "The dangerous memory of Jesus Christ," he says, is "the dangerous memory of suffering."[6] It is by attentiveness to the suffering of others that we discover our mission. José Pagola declares that if the church "turns its back on those who suffer . . . , it turns away from the Crucified One."[7]

To attend to the suffering of others in our day and time reconnects us with the original charge to the disciples which perhaps admits of a broader reading. The charge to cure the sick may include all kinds of healing—addressing the full range of things that hurt them or diminish their lives. Raising the dead could include challenging the death-dealing systems and structures and things that crush people and suck the life right out of them. Cleansing lepers would surely include not only physical healing but also the social restoration of those who are outcast, the "untouchables" of our own time and place. To cast out demons expands to include setting people free from whatever holds them in bondage—everything from addiction to political oppression.

> [To cast out demons is to] liberate people from the idols that enslave us, possess us, and pervert our life together.
>
> Pagola, *The Way Opened Up by Jesus*, 101.

To be disciples today is to get mixed up in the mission of Jesus as people summoned and sent to teach what he taught and do what he did.

After the calling of the disciples Jesus instructs them. That first injunction "go nowhere among the Gentiles and enter no town of the Samaritans" (v. 5) puzzles us, since we know something of the end of the story and how the universal reach of God's grace comes to

---

6. Johann Baptist Metz, "The Dangerous Memory of the Freedom of Jesus Christ: The Presence of Church in Society" in *Love's Strategy: The Political Theology of Johann Baptist Metz,* ed. John K. Downey (Harrisburg, PA: Trinity, 1999), 95.

7. Pagola, *The Way Opened Up by Jesus*, 102.

be revealed there. In fact it took a while for the early church to come to a full realization of the universality of its mission. Mission to the Gentiles was fraught with controversy as other NT texts make clear (Acts 1–15; Gal. 1–2). Jesus' instruction here seems to be a matter of what to do first. For now, they should go to the "lost sheep of the house of Israel" (v. 6). These would be the "sheep without a shepherd" alluded to in the preceding chapter (9:36). "The lost sheep are not a group within Israel but all Israel misruled and abused by false shepherds" (9:36; Ezek. 34). The mission of Jesus and the disciples begins here because Israel has "salvation-history priority in God's purposes."[8]

Nevertheless, from the very beginning of the story, there have been hints of a greater breadth to this mission. Gentiles have been presenting themselves (the three wise men, the Roman centurion, the Canaanite woman), and they have not been turned away. On the contrary, they have shown themselves to be examples of the faith to which all are being called. Another hint lies in the disciples' designation early as "salt of the earth" and "light of the world" (5:13, 16). After the resurrection the mission will be extended explicitly to Gentiles as they are sent "into all the world" (28:16–20).

More instructions follow as to how the disciples should equip— or not equip themselves—along the way. "Take no gold, or silver, or copper in your belts, no bag for your journey, or two tunics or sandals or a staff" (10:9). "Traveling light" is an apt description of the disciples on their journey. Why are their provisions to be so spare? Commentators offer many theories.

Boring suggests that going about without even the most basic traveling accoutrements may have demonstrated trust in God's faithful provision. A staff, for example, was for protection—they go defenseless—relying on divine protection. To travel with no means of "sustenance or self-defense"[9] might offer a visible sign like unto the symbolic actions performed by the prophets. The prophet Isaiah, for example, went about naked and barefoot (Isaiah 20:2).

Another theory is that carrying these things would mark them as travelers. A bag (which was just an ordinary knapsack for travelers)

8. Carter, *Matthew and the Margins*, 234.
9. Boring, *The New Interpreter's Bible*, 8:256.

and sandals were certainly basic traveling gear. Carter speculates that going without allowed them to move more freely in a situation of opposition and persecution. Perhaps not carrying a bag or a staff helped to make them inconspicuous.

Another possible reason for these rigorous rules is the way it might help to distinguish between authentic witnesses and entrepreneurs.[10] Jesus reminds the disciples that the grace they were given came freely; they must offer it freely. To carry coins or a money belt might give the appearance of preaching for hire. This is Wright's view of the matter. "They are to be scrupulous about avoiding any suggestion that they are on the make, out for money. They mustn't even take cash or provisions with them, or carry the sort of bag that beggars would normally have."[11] This is an issue more familiar to our experience where commercialized ministries of televangelists may be very profitable, and the profiteers discredit the proclamation. Living simply and free of material excess better serves the credibility of public witness.

Crosby proposes that "traveling light" has much deeper implications of a whole new economic expectation. It was not so much that they are called to poverty as that the community is called to a mutual sharing of resources between those who are sent and those who receive them. Those who are welcomed share their preaching, teaching, and healing. Those who welcome them share food, clothing, and shelter as needed. It is simple economics in the new community; "laborers deserve their food" (v. 10). Therefore, those who are sent out do not need to burden themselves with provisions.[12]

Whatever the reason, traveling light left the disciples dependent upon the hospitality of those they encountered. Hospitality was a "sacred obligation" emphasized in biblical stories (e.g., Gen. 18:1–8). Judgment against any who did not show hospitality (10:14–15) is symbolized in the instruction to "shake off the dust from your feet" upon leaving. This too was a traditional symbolic act signaling

10. Ibid., 264.

11. N. T. Wright, *Matthew for Everyone, Part 1* (Louisville, KY: Westminster John Knox Press, 2004), 113.

12. Michael Crosby, *House of Disciples: Church Economics and Justice in Matthew* (Maryknoll, NY: Orbis, 1988), 65.

rejection (Neh. 5:13). These words would have been heard by Matthew's community as a stern reminder to receive and support traveling missionaries.

When the disciples meet with hostility instead of hospitality, they are to move on from that house or town. They are not to retaliate. Instead they are to withdraw and continue the mission (10:14–15, 23). This action is at one and the same time both escape and opportunity to further the mission.[13] Non-retaliation is what Jesus taught (5:38–41) and this is what he did (12:14–15).

10:16–25

Expect Opposition: "A Disciple is not above the teacher."

"See, I am sending you out like sheep into the midst of wolves." This repeated metaphor signals the disciples' solidarity with the "lost sheep" of Israel (10:6). The religious and political leaders are cast as "wolves." The metaphor does not overstate the dangers of the mission. As Jesus faced opposition, so will those who follow in his way. As their mission aligns them with his mission, they will occupy the same liminal space he occupies (neither fleeing from society nor accommodating to the status quo). Because "a disciple is not above the teacher," they should not expect any better conditions or any better reception than Jesus experienced.

> Occupying a liminal societal location, prophets conflict with the center and challenge its commitments and priorities with a vision of life in relation to God.
>
> Carter, *Matthew and the Margins*, 245.

It is not a question of whether they will be persecuted only "when" (v. 23). They will know the experience of being "handed over" (Greek *paradidomi*). That is what happened to Jesus (10:4; 20:18; 26:2) and to John before him (4:12). The predicted floggings they will suffer are not random mob violence but officially sanctioned acts by religious leaders to punish heretics, blasphemers, and

---

13. Carter, *Matthew and the Margins*, 238.

disturbers of the peace (Deut. 25:1–3).[14] They will even be under the threat of death. All of these threats were realized in the life of Jesus as he advanced toward the cross. At Matthew's writing, Jesus' execution is no distant memory. It was surely clear to them it would be dangerous to follow someone whose life ended as his life did.

"Itinerancy, poverty, defenselessness, and love"[15] characterized Jesus' mission, into which he now calls the disciples. They will form an alternative community whose mission "confronts Rome's world of injustice, power, greed, false commitments, and death with God's mercy and justice. The community will challenge (in)vested interests despite conflict, division, suffering, and rejection.[16]

After the disconcerting instructions to go about defenseless and unprovisioned, (vv. 5–15) followed by the dire predictions of opposition and persecution comes the odd counsel, "Do not worry" (v. 19). God's own Spirit will be with them and will testify through them.

10:26–11:1

Courage and Faithfulness: "Have no fear of them . . .
Those who lose their life for my sake will find it."

This steadying byword is regularly repeated; "have no fear" (vv. 26, 28, 31). No matter what happens, God's care will sustain them. God knows and cares what happens to them and will see them through to the other side of it all. Once again we have an allusion to sparrows as a sign of God's care. Sparrows have little value; they are hunted and sold in the market place in bundles of ten; they are cheap food.[17] Yet God knows when each one falls,

> [The people to whom Jesus came lived with many fears:] living in terror of the power of Rome, intimidated by threats from the teachers of the law, separated from God by fear of God's anger. [Into this fearful context Jesus speaks the words, "Do not be afraid."]
>
> Pagola, *The Way Opened Up by Jesus,* 104.

14. Boring, *The New Interpreter's Bible,* 8:258.
15. Carter, *Matthew and the Margins,* 233 (quoting Luz).
16. Ibid., 232.
17. Boring, *The New Interpreter's Bible,* 8:264.

and it does not happen outside God's care. Clearly the passage does not promise that no harm will come, but it affirms God's presence and care *whatever happens*. In a sense this is a deeper security. It secures against the need to be secure. This deeper security is what gives us courage in a broken and fearful world.

The deep security founded in faith in God gives a boldness to our lives; it gives us courage "to make decisions and take responsibility. It leads us to take risks and make sacrifices . . . Believing the gospel does not lead to cowardice and resignation, but to audacity and creativity."[18]

Now is the time for bold proclamation. It was the custom for the Matthean community to gather in the evening to share in the remembered sayings of Jesus. Matthew's readers would have heard an invitation in verse 27, "What I say to you in the dark, tell in the light; and what you hear whispered, proclaim for the housetops." They may live in anticipation of a time when "the truth will out;" for "nothing is covered up that will not be uncovered"

> **The arc of the universe is long, but it bends toward justice.**
>
> Martin Luther King Jr., baccalaureate Address, Wesleyan College, Hartford, Connecticut, June 8, 1964.

(v. 26). Those who have been bold and faced up to the consequences will be vindicated when God's reign of justice comes.

Bold proclamation is risky. Matthew's community had martyrs in its memory and in its current consciousness. They could look back to the crucifixion of Jesus and before that to the beheading of John the Baptist. The threat is ongoing. "By Matthew's time . . . it was well known that Christians—including Simon Peter, who was so important to Matthean Christianity—had been crucified in Rome under Nero."[19]

The costs of discipleship are apparent to them. This chapter on mission spells it out in no uncertain terms (vv. 17–21, 28, 39). They testify under threat of being handed over to councils, dragged before governors and kings, flogged, and even put to death. Those who would seek a peaceful and prosperous existence should turn back

18. Pagola, *The Way Opened Up by Jesus,* 106.
19. Boring, *The New Interpreter's Bible,* 8:262.

now. There will be no peace for the present. Although God's reign inaugurates a true *shalom* (Hebrew peace, wholeness, well-being, safety), the announcement of God's reign comes as a genuine threat to those who reign now, and they will respond with violence.[20] There will be no peace but rather a conflict so fierce that it will even divide families. This is what some in Matthew's own church very likely faced as they were forced to choose between family and faith. Reminiscent of Micah 7:6, this disruption of families is yet another sign. "In some apocalyptic views the breakdown of family structures is part of the terrors preceding the eschaton."[21] Faithfulness to the coming reign of God takes priority over all else—even family ties. The phrase "the Spirit of your Father" used in verse 20 serves as a reminder that disciples are part of a new family, the family of God, "where the ties are closer and more demanding than natural family ties"[22] (v. 37).

A paradoxical outcome waits at the end of these conflicts. "Those who find their life will lose it, and those who lose their life for my sake will find it" (v. 39). To preserve one's life in safety from the opposition and persecution that comes with confronting the status quo is to lose one's life. To follow the way of the cross and lose one's life by resisting the reign of the empire and identifying with the reign of God is to find life. "To find life in the subversive way of the cross is to find it in an act that refuses to give the elite the power of intimidation and conformity which it craves. To find life is to enter into the fullness of God's purposes in the new age."[23]

As the chapter closes, Jesus comes back around to its beginning and underscores the disciples' identity with him. They now participate in his mission, with his authority, under the same conditions that attended his ministry. In this mission they are so identified with him that he could say, "Whoever welcomes you welcomes me" (v. 40). Jesus is so identified with God's mission that he could say, "Whoever welcomes me welcomes the one who sent me" (v. 40).

The mission of the disciples will imitate Jesus' own mission. Like him, they are sent first to the lost sheep of Israel, and they are

---

20. Carter, *Matthew and the Margins*, 242.
21. Boring, *The New Interpreter's Bible*, 8:262.
22. Ibid.
23. Carter, *Matthew and the Margins*, 244.

preaching the same message, doing the same deeds of power, wandering about unprotected and dependent, facing opposition without retaliation. This is what Jesus did; this is what disciples are now called to do.

FURTHER REFLECTIONS
The Church in the World Today

Having just read the "mission discourse" chapter in Matthew's Gospel, it is a good time to stop and reflect upon the mission of the church in the world today. New realities face the contemporary church and necessarily shape its mission. This reflection will pause to consider four of those realities. More could be named, but these four will give a sense of some of the challenges (opportunities?) that the church encounters. What does it mean for the church to be faithful in its calling amid these new realities? Vignettes from the author's experience in the wider church's work will set the stage for theological reflection on the church in the world today.

The Changing Ecumenical Landscape:
Post-denominational Christianity

The ecumenical landscape has shifted in recent years. There is a new sense of unity in mission across denominational divides. In part this is the fruit of years of ecumenical dialogue. We seem to be "leaving controversies behind."[24] Not only are we moving beyond confrontations of the past, but our ecumenical interchanges are moving beyond our more recent comparative analysis of our differing histories and beliefs. The comparative work has been productive in showing how much common ground we already occupy and clarifying the points of difference that remain. Comparative work, however, is reaching a point of diminishing returns. The focus of attention has shifted from doctrine to mission. There are an increasing number of shared mission endeavors that are not dependent upon agreements in doctrine and practice. A case in point is the shared projects for combating HIV/AIDS in Africa. The denominations joining

24. Pope John Paul, II, *Ut Unum Sint.*

in rightly ask, "Why should we divide our efforts by having several parallel agencies? We can be more effective if we pool our energies and resources."

Another change is a new recognition of the global church. Early ecumenical efforts were organized from Europe and North America. Leaders there decided what issues were important and who would have a place at the table of dialogue. Today leadership is in transition. The former "mission churches" in Asia, Africa, and South America are vital and growing, whereas there has been something of a decline in mainline denominations in Europe and North America. Leadership and energy are shifting accordingly.

These shifts portend larger changes on the global ecumenical landscape. The younger churches around the world do not always conform to the habits and prescriptions of their parent denominations. As evangelist D. T. Niles observed, when you transplant a growing thing to a new place, you must first break the pot in which you transported it. Only then can it take root in the native soil. The wide diversity of forms and practices of church life in its wider global expressions confirms that the "pot" has been successfully broken. New forms arise that are thoroughly enculturated. The old denominational distinctions brought by the missionaries do not apply in the new location. There is, for example, a growing impatience in the younger churches around the world with the sixteenth-century controversies of the Reformation era in Europe. A case in point is the response to the *Joint Declaration on the Doctrine of Justification* agreed by the Roman Catholic Church and the Lutheran World Federation. It is a landmark agreement, as justification was the church-dividing issue of the Reformation. South African theologian Russel Botman, while appreciating the significance of this agreement, has asked the provocative question, "What does justification have to do with justice?"[25] The landscape is shifting.

Perhaps the most significant shift in the global ecumenical landscape is the emergence of what might be termed "post-denominational" Christianity. The old denominational distinctions seem not to apply in many contexts. There is a decided loss of interest

25. Russel Botman, "Should the Reformed Join in?" *Reformed World* 52, no.1:12–17, 15.

in the differences that have historically divided the churches. People today move easily from one denomination to another. Some observe that today there seem to be more differences within denominations than among them. What seems to matter more is location on the theological spectrum. Liberals talk with liberals and conservatives talk with conservatives across denominations; but the conversations between liberals and conservatives within the same denomination are difficult. Are we entering a post-denomination era? What does that mean for the mission of the church?

At the very least these changes signal a new day in which new possibilities are rising. A positive outcome of these changes may be the prospect of a more visible unity. The church has affirmed that unity is the gift and calling of God, yet divisions have obscured the church's unity and hampered its mission. It may be possible now to adopt the "Lund Principle"—to do together whatever can be done together and only work separately where there is a compelling reason to do so. It may be possible to engage in more effective collaboration on issues of international consequence (e.g., hunger, water rights, ecojustice, HIV/AIDS). It may be possible to share in "pulpit and table fellowship" and have a mutual recognition of ministry. As we share in mission together, it may be possible to reconsider the historical differences that have separated us and engage in a "healing of memory" together.

Religious Pluralism

Another of the challenges/opportunities before the church in the world today is religious pluralism. How do we maintain the conviction that "Jesus is Lord" and at the same time "honor the integrity and value of other religions"?[26] This is a question not easily answered. Some of the central convictions of our faith tradition, however, may give helpful guidance. The conviction of human frailty and fallibility—the sense that we are "not God"—may nurture a fitting humility. It cautions against presumption that we know the mind of God or how God is at work among other peoples. The conviction that we are all in the image of God may ground a respect for others that

26. Daniel Migliore, *Faith Seeking Understanding: An Introduction to Christian Theology* (Grand Rapids: Eerdmans, 2004), 301.

honors them in their difference, neither seeking to overcome or to ignore the difference. The calling to bear witness to the good news that we have received in Jesus Christ includes the news that God loves *the world*. God's own presence and grace are limitless. These central Christian convictions open a space in the life of Christian faith for interreligious engagement.

Interreligious engagement was never more urgent for the church than it is today. In many places around the world believers from different religious traditions live and work alongside one another every day. This new closeness carries an opportunity for mutual witness, occasions for sharing the good news we have received and hearing the good news God has entrusted to others. There is the prospect of gaining mutual understanding and respect that will take us to new levels of toleration and cooperation. It becomes possible to make common cause around shared values such as religious liberty, economic justice, and the well-being of creation. Probably the most urgent concern of all, however, is the need to put an end to religiously sanctioned violence.

The press is not good on religion in general today. A representative from the World Bank, addressing a seminary class on globalization, shared a conversation that makes this point. She was trying to get religious leaders included in the World Bank Dialogue on Ethics and Values. What her colleagues told her was that this would not be helpful. They gave their reasons. Religion is defunct—this is a fully secular society. Where religion does still exist it is divisive and even dangerous. Religion is a purveyor of violence in our world today. Unfortunately, these charges are not without foundation. Religious discord has indeed been a source of conflict and violence. Jonathan Swift's acid observation is to the point: we have "just enough religion to make us hate one another—but not enough to make us love one another"[27]

Can religious people do better than this? How might we make common cause with other religious traditions to put an end to violence in the name of religion? How might we together resist the

27. Jonathan Swift, *Thoughts on Various Subjects from the Miscellanies* (1711–1726), quoted in Jonathan Sacks, *The Dignity of Difference: How to Avoid the Clash of Civilizations* (London: Continuum Press, 2002), 4.

cooptation of religion in national agendas of aggression, where aggression is mystified with religious language (i.e., "good and evil")? Religious leaders across faith traditions and nationalities could conspire together to, in the words of Rabbi Jonathan Sacks, "withhold the robe of sanctity when it is sought as a cloak for violence and bloodshed. If faith is enlisted in the cause of war, there must be an equal and opposite counter-voice in the name of peace."[28]

The potential and the urgency of interreligious engagement are apparent. This will be important for the mission of the church in the world today.

The "Prosperity Gospel"

There is contention today concerning the content of the "gospel" that the church is charged with preaching in its mission. The "prosperity gospel" seems to be gaining in popularity. One encounter will illustrate. The World Communion of Reformed Churches and the Lutheran World Federation held a meeting of its Joint Commission for Lutheran-Reformed relations in Windhoek, Namibia. Part of its work included visitations to see the many different ways Lutheran and Reformed churches are sharing in witness and mission. Local immersion experiences and conversations with church leaders in the region inquired into the distinctive challenges of the context and the church's creative response. In one such conversation a church leader from the region said there was a serious problem they were facing. He went on to say, "The problem is that one of our churches is growing." Several in the group confessed later to having thought to themselves, "I wish we had that problem where I come from!"

As it turned out, the speaker was describing a church where the pastor was preaching a "prosperity gospel" which promises "health and wealth" to anyone who prays with enough faith and contributes enough money to the church. The promise has a broad appeal that is easily exploited. Believers are told that giving to the church works something like the principle of financial investments: the more one gives the more one will receive material benefit.

One of the practices in the particular church that is a "problem"

28. Sacks, *The Dignity of Difference*, 9.

is its practice around the offering. The pastor invites people to put envelopes into the offering plates filled with evidence of sacrificial giving and to include with their gifts a list of their debts and to whom the debts were owed. After the service, the deacons go through the offering, select a few of these lists and secretly pay the debts. The next Sunday the pastor asks, "Who among you that contributed generously last week has had accounts miraculously settled this week?" Their testimonials are powerful. People and money flow to this church. The pastor lives luxuriously and drives a big car. This is taken as evidence of God's blessing on him and his ministry—a visible confirmation of what he is preaching.

The commission was astonished to hear this story. It was generally agreed that this is not the gospel; this is deception and exploitation of people by corrupt and greedy leaders. Yet the question hung in the air: What does the church offer instead of this that will bring authentic hope to people who live on less than a dollar a day? What is the "good news" to the poor that the church has to offer?

The Problem of Poverty: The Cries from Below

One of the most complex and troubling issues in the world today is the global economic crisis. An increasing proportion of the world's population lives in grinding poverty. This is all the more troubling by its contrast to the affluence of an elite minority. Evidence indicates that the gap between rich and poor nations is even widening. In 1980, the richest 20 percent of the world's people earned 45 times more than the poorest 20 percent, in 1990, 60 times more, and in 2000, 80 times more.[29] An alarmingly high number of people live below the poverty line; 1.4 billion live on less than $1.25 a day.

Global gatherings of church leaders have observed that it is not a matter of a few people "falling through the cracks" of an otherwise workable system. When so many suffer so much, the global economic system is not working. There was a time when it was plausible to argue that economic growth and production of wealth would, over time, make conditions better for everyone; wealth would "trickle down." Church leaders from the global South are

---

29. Radhika Sarin, "Rich-Poor Gap Widening," in *Vision for a Sustainable World: Vital Signs* (Washington, DC: Worldwatch Institute, 2003), 88–89.

rather pointed in their observation that there is a whole lot more wealth "trickling up" than trickling down.

World Communion of Reformed Churches at its General Council meeting in Accra (2004) lifted global economics to heightened awareness in what became the Accra Confession. The confession goes so far as to say that the integrity of the church's proclamation of the gospel is in jeopardy if we fail to address the issue of poverty in our global mission today. If we do not address this issue, in what sense is the church preaching good news to the poor (Matt. 11:4)?

The strong statements made by that gathered body were fueled by an experience we shared in Ghana. The host churches took the delegates to see what they call "the slave castles." These fortresses date back to the days of trading rum and sugar and spices. Under the castle were cargo holds where cargo would be stored until the ships came to transport it. In later years, Dutch traders found a more profitable trade—human beings. West Africans of the area were hunted down and captured, imprisoned in the cargo holds like so much cargo. The great doors of the hold were closed upon them and chained and padlocked. The doors did not open again until the slave ships arrived. This could be a period of up to three months. Food was sent down a chute from a window above. People got sick, but the doors did not open. Women gave birth, but the doors did not open. People died, but the doors did not open. It was unimaginable. The delegates were stunned to see the cargo hold and hear what had happened there.

The tour continued. The delegates found themselves in a large airy room with big windows, a lovely room just above the cargo hold. "What was in this place?" someone asked. The guide answered, "This room was the sanctuary where people worshiped." We were undone. One in the group said, "Blasphemy." Another quoted the prophet Amos, "I hate, I despise your feasts; I take no delight in your solemn assemblies . . . but let justice roll down like waters and righteousness like an ever-flowing stream" (5:21–24). Righteous indignation was palpable in the group. How could people possibly worship here above the cargo holds? Clearly, they were not making the connections between faith and life. Could they not hear the cries from below? There was a long silence. Then the whole experience turned on us. Someone asked, "Where are we not making the connections between faith and life? Where are we not hearing the cries from below?"

It was this transformative experience that galvanized the delegates to make the Accra Confession and to covenant for justice. Much work remains as the church tries to move from statements to steps, from rhetoric to reality. One thing is clear: the church cannot engage in mission with integrity without hearing the cries from below.

11:2–12:50

Narrative: Facing Opposition

11:2–6

John's Question

It is an almost universal experience that the life of faith is beset by doubts and questioning. Sometimes we think, if only we could have been there—sitting at the feet of Jesus—faith would be much easier. Doubts and questions would dissolve. Apparently, even those closest to Jesus were troubled by doubts and questioning.

Here we have John the Baptist wavering in his convictions about who Jesus is—the "messenger" himself, the one who was so sure at Jesus' baptism (3:14). Now, in much altered circumstances, he is having second thoughts. From prison he queries, "Are you the one who is to come, or are we to wait for another?" (11:3). Opposition has John doubting; fear for his future has him questioning. The opposition has imprisoned him, and his fear is well-founded; by chapter 14 he will be dead at the hands of Herod Antipas (14:1–12).

It is not just John who is uncertain. The disciples are "fearful, hesitant, and often baffled."[1] A theology student once described them as the "duh"-sciples. Among Jesus' closest followers there are doubters, deniers, and betrayers.

Beyond this inner circle are the unresponsive cities (named in vv. 20–23) who have been witness to Jesus' deeds of power and have gone on with business as usual. Still further afield are the Pharisees, who Matthew presents as offering resolute resistance and conspiring to destroy him (12:14).

It seems that God's revelation (Greek *apocalypsis*, "unveiling") is a "veiled" unveiling—for the religious leaders around Jesus, for

---

1. Donald Senior, *Abingdon New Testament Commentaries: Matthew* (Nashville: Abingdon Press, 1998), 123.

the inner circle of his followers, and even for his own "messenger," John (11:10). In Matthew's account, the ambiguities remain even for those who know Jesus best. Faith was for the early followers of Jesus—much as it is for us now— more of a "leap" than a confident stroll.

> Faith is the courage that conquers doubt not by removing it, but by taking it as an element into itself.
>
> Paul Tillich, *Dynamics of Faith* (San-Francisco: Harper and Row, 1957), 61.

Jesus responds to John's question. He offers an answer that is not about his identity so much as it is about his action. It is what he "does" that matters, not claims about who he "is." "Tell John what you hear and see: the blind receive their sight, the lame walk, the lepers are cleansed, the deaf hear, the dead are raised, and the poor have good news brought to them" (11:4, 5). These are the very signs to expect from "the one who is to come." The words of Isaiah the prophet bear witness (29:19; 35:5–6).

Then follows the enigmatic saying, "Blessed is anyone who takes no offense at me" (v. 6). In fact, however, there are many who take "offense" (Greek *skandalisomē*, "offense, obstacle, scandal"). Many are looking for a different kind of messiah. The Pharisees clearly take offense. When Jesus visits Nazareth (13:57) even his hometown will take offense. By the time of the Last Supper Jesus predicts that the disciples themselves will join the company of those who take offense (26:31, 33).[2]

11:7–24

John and Jesus: Rejected by the Religious Leaders

Jesus offers a strong affirmation of John and his role as prophet. John is no "reed shaken in the wind" nor someone who goes about in "soft robes" in "royal places." This language may be a not so subtle rebuke of Herod Antipas, who holds John in prison. Reeds were used as an image on coins minted during the reign of Herod Antipas, and the

---

2. Ibid., 126.

"soft robes" allusion highlights the corruption and extravagance of Herod's court. "Even on their surface level the image of a reed easily shaken by the wind and the finery of royal garb contrast effectively with Matthew's portrayal of John as the sturdy prophet who dressed in camel hair and unflinchingly challenged the authorities who ventured into the wilderness to hear him (3:4, 7–10)."[3] The regime is rightly accused of violence (v. 12) in John's arrest and imprisonment, and by the time of this Gospel's writing Matthew's community knows that John was beheaded.

Both the Messiah and his messenger (11:10) are rejected outright. The unresponsiveness of "this generation" to them is likened to child's play where playmates who do not respond appropriately to prompts. They do not dance to the sound of the flute or mourn to the sound of wailing. There follows a bit of humor implying that they are hard to please. When the ascetic prophet John comes neither eating nor drinking they say "he has a demon" (v. 18). When Jesus the bridegroom (9:15) comes eating and drinking they say "he is a glutton and a drunkard" (v. 19).[4] They seem set on rejection regardless of who God sends them.

"Yet wisdom is vindicated by her deeds" (v. 19). Here Jesus identifies with Wisdom (Greek *sophia*; Hebrew *hokmah*), a traditional feminine image of the divine. Wisdom founded the earth, walks in justice, guides into truth, and is beloved of God (Job 28; Prov. 8). Later verses in this chapter (vv. 25–30) continue the themes of the traditional role of Wisdom including divine revelation and life-giving refreshment and comfort.[5] "Wisdom" also has a history of mixed reception—accepted by the few and rejected by the many. This is Jesus' experience as well.

Rejection has its consequences, however. In Chorazin, Bethsaida, and Capernaum Jesus has done deeds of power so great that even Tyre and Sidon would have responded and repented. If Sodom had seen such deeds of power it would have "remained until this day" (v. 23). These latter three cities were notorious. Tyre and Sidon were frequent objects of prophetic invective for their idolatry and their

---

3. Ibid., 127.
4. Ibid., 128.
5. Elizabeth Johnson, *She Who Is* (New York: Crossroad, 1992), 86–100.

destruction is predicted (Isa. 23:1–12). Sodom was the paradigmatic instance of divine judgment on a wicked city. Its sin (popular views notwithstanding) is identified in Scripture as covenant unfaithfulness (Deut. 29:15–29) and social injustice (Isa. 1:9-10; Amos 4:1, 11).[6] The point is that people with the advantage of the Messiah and his messenger and the deeds of power they have witnessed have no excuse for their failure to repent.

11:25–27
John and Jesus: "Accepted by the Little Ones"

By contrast to these cities and to those designated "the wise and intelligent" (perhaps the Pharisees), the "infants" get it. This is a dramatic reversal of expectations. Wisdom was God's gift to the wise. God "gives wisdom to the wise and knowledge to those who have understanding" (Dan. 2:20–21). Now the wise ones are being passed over in preference for infants. This continues a theme begun with the crowds (7:28; 9:8, 33) and continued with the "little ones" (10:42;18:6, 10, 14). There is a privileging of the powerless—the least and the lost. The simple people are the ones who respond to Jesus.[7]

11:28–30
"Come unto me . . ."

This inviting text continues the tradition of divine Wisdom; "Wisdom is a fountain of life to one who has it" (16:22); it is life-giving, refreshing, renewing, a "rest" for souls" (v. 29). Jesus issues this welcome invitation to weary, burdened people. Who exhausts and oppresses them? It is precisely the religious leaders. "They tie up heavy burdens hard to bear, and lay them on the shoulders of others; but they themselves are unwilling to lift a finger to move them"

6. Warren Carter, *Matthew and the Margins: A Socio-Political and Religious Reading* (Sheffield, England: Sheffield Academic Press, 2000), 236.
7. Senior, *Abingdon New Testament Commentaries*, 132.

(23:4). The leaders have not learned that God desires "mercy and not sacrifice" (12:7). In place of their teaching, Jesus invites the people to take on his "yoke" (a traditional metaphor for teaching and wisdom).[8] Here again Jesus has "compassion" on "harassed and helpless" people (9:36).

12:1–21

Opposition from the Pharisees at Every Turn

At the beginning of chapter 12 Jesus comes into direct conflict with the Pharisees on the matter of Sabbath observance. Jesus is doing things that are "not lawful" to be done on the Sabbath. His "crimes" are feeding hungry people (his disciples) and healing a man with a withered hand.

Jesus answers in terms of his role and his authority. He first recounts the story of David feeding his hungry companions with the "bread of the presence" from the Temple. This was not lawful since they were not priests. In making this argument, Jesus identifies himself with David and claims his kingly authority as "Son of David."

Next Jesus reminds them that priests, in the performance of their duties, are allowed to break the Sabbath without incurring guilt. The implication is that he likens himself to a priest in performing his duties. Then Jesus goes so far as to say that "something greater than the Temple is here" (v. 6). It is an audacious claim given the import of the Temple. What could be greater than the Temple? The longed for "reign of God" coming in their midst would be greater. Jesus identifies himself with the "Son of Man" who was expected at the last. The Son of Man is surely "Lord of the sabbath" (v. 8).

Jesus also responds in terms of his role as the authoritative interpreter of the law. The Pharisees have misunderstood the law's deepest requirements. "I desire mercy and not sacrifice." What Jesus has done in feeding his hungry companions displays a compassion that

8. Ibid., 133.

is at the heart of the law. The law is not being laid aside; it is being rightly interpreted.

The Pharisees are rigorists in their teaching, going well beyond the guidance of the law. For them it is "not enough to keep the Sabbath 'in a general way'; it was necessary to define carefully which weekday activities constituted work and were therefore prohibited on the Sabbath."[9] Their further specifications, even if intended as ensuring faithfulness to the Torah, are burdening the people. The Torah should not be burdensome (11:28–30). "Jews traditionally look upon Torah as a blessing, not a burden."[10] Jesus' conflict with the Pharisees over healing on the Sabbath is a case emblematic of the point of difference between him and the Pharisees in the interpretation of the law (12:1–12). Jesus keeps Sabbath but gives priority to the works of mercy.

> In giving precedence to human need over cultic commands Jesus did not destroy, but fulfilled the law.
>
> Donald Senior, *Abingdon New Testament Commentaries*, 137.

When Jesus enters the Temple the Pharisees seek to entrap him. There is a man there with a withered hand and they ask him, "Is it lawful to cure on the sabbath?" (12:10). Apparently, his teaching about mercy (v. 7) has not registered with the Pharisees. Jesus (of course) heals the man with the withered hand right there in the synagogue and on the Sabbath. He tries again to teach them using the traditional argument from the lesser to the greater. They would surely help a sheep that fell in a pit on the Sabbath, why not help this man?

The opposition only intensifies. At this point it says, "The Pharisees went out and conspired against him, how to destroy him." Jesus knows well their intent. He simply withdraws and continues his ministry. This is his pattern (in all four instances of hostility). Jesus does not incite his enemies but withdraws instead. It is the way of

9. Douglas R. A. Hare, *Matthew*, Interpretation: A Bible Commentary for Teaching and Preaching (Louisville, KY: Westminster/John Knox Press, 1992), 266.
10. *The Jewish Annotated New Testament*, ed. Amy-Jill Levine and Marc Zvi Brettler (Oxford: Oxford University Press, 2011), 42.

nonretaliation and nonviolence. Jesus does proceed with greater caution, asking those whom he is healing not to "make him known" (v. 15). He is not, after all, healing for show or in order to provoke the Pharisees. Withdrawing is not so much a strategy to survive as it is an expression of his "gentle and humble" heart (11:29). Jesus does not "wrangle" with the Pharisees or "cry aloud" in the streets to draw attention to himself (v. 19). Matthew declares that his way of being is like the servant of God in Isaiah 12:17–21. The text announces, "Here is my servant, whom I have chosen, my beloved, with whom my soul is well pleased" (v. 18). Jesus is the fulfillment of this text, another confirmation that this is "the one who is to come" (11:2). They need not wait for another.

12:22–37
The Pharisees Charge That Jesus' Power Is Demonic

In sharp contrast to the increasing opposition of the Pharisees, the crowds to him are enthusiastic, amazed. When he heals a man who was blind and mute and demon possessed, the crowds hail him as the Son of David. The Pharisees denounce him as demonic; "It is only by Beelzebul, the ruler of the demons, that this fellow casts out the demons" (v. 24). "Beelzebul" probably means "Lord of the Flies," which is a "contemptuous designation that ridiculed the Philistine god "Baal-zebub" (2 Kgs. 1:2).[11]

To the charges of the Pharisees, Jesus offers two different kinds of responses. First he gives a reasoned response that what they are charging makes no sense. Why would Satan cast out Satan, working against himself? Next Jesus gives a warning. If his work is from the Spirit of God and they say it is from Satan, then they speak blasphemy against the Spirit. Their evil accusations reflect back on them, "For out of the abundance of the heart the mouth speaks" (12:34). The accusations are vicious, as befits the "brood of vipers" they are. Jesus warns that there will be an accounting for these slanders. Words have weight.

---

11. Senior, *Abingdon New Testament Commentaries*, 141.

12:38–45

The Pharisees Come Clamoring for a Sign

When the Pharisees come clamoring for a sign, Jesus will not "perform" for them. What he does is not for public spectacle; he does not do these things to prove himself. He will not put on a show for them. Have they not seen enough already in his many deeds of power? What more do they need? Why do they persist in their disbelief?

They ask for a sign, not because this would do it for them, but because they are an "evil" and "adulterous" generation. "Adultery" is often used as a metaphor for covenant infidelity and unfaithfulness to God (as in the story of Hosea and Gomer in Hos. 1–3). They have all the signs they need already, but their faithless hearts turn away from God's messenger, God's Messiah, and from God.

Nevertheless, there is a great sign of cosmic proportions on the horizon that will authenticate Jesus' messianic identity— Jesus' death and resurrection. It is presaged by the "sign of the prophet Jonah." Jonah, like Jesus, was a prophet who came preaching repentance. As Jonah came forth after three days in the belly of the sea monster, so also for three days Jesus will be "in the heart of the earth" (v. 40). The people of Nineveh, to whom God sent Jonah, repented, and the Pharisees should too. Something "greater than Jonah" is here, and if they do not repent the Ninevites themselves can by all rights rise up and accuse them on the day of judgment.

Joining the Ninevites in the condemnation of their unbelief will be the "queen of the South." The allusion here is to the Queen of Sheba who "came from the ends of the earth to listen to the wisdom of Solomon" (v. 42). It is somewhat surprising in the patriarchal culture to present a woman as judging in this divine court, and a foreign woman at that.[12] Once again, those at the margins come to the center. This is also a further demonstration of Gentile God-fearers of the nations flowing to Israel, as promised by Isaiah the prophet (2:2). In this way she is like the wise men who came from the east. She too is humble.

---

12. *The Jewish New Testament*, ed. Amy-Jill Levine and Marc Zvi Brettler (Oxford: Oxford University Press, 2011), 24.

Even though "she is herself a royal figure, she acknowledges greater Wisdom" in Solomon.[13]

12:46–50

Finding True Relations

The section closes with an encounter with Jesus' own biological family. He clarifies that his "true relations" are with those who do God's will. "Whoever does the will of my Father in heaven is my brother and sister and mother" (v. 50). This new shared commitment to God's will goes deeper than any kinship. What was anticipated in 10:34–37 in the way of family disruption and conflict has an answer here. There is a new family being constituted.

Conclusion

In these chapters, as Jesus interacts with people, we see his authority and his humility, his power and his compassion. Matthew, in the way he presents these encounters, underscores Jesus' identity as Messiah (Hebrew *mashiah*, "anointed"). In the Old Testament, the offices of prophet, priest, and king each involved a special consecration and anointing with oil. Matthew signals that Jesus is not just *an* anointed one but *the* anointed one. He has excelled all who went before and has fulfilled each of these offices. He is a prophet greater than Jonah (12:41) and a teacher of the law more authoritative than the Pharisees (12:7). He is the "Son of David," (12:3, 23) greater (and wiser) than King Solomon; he is the paragon of Wisdom (12:42). He is the priestly "Lord of the Sabbath," greater than the Temple itself (12:5, 6, 8). Beyond all this, he is God's chosen and beloved Servant, the Son with whom God is well pleased (3:17; 12:18).

13. Ibid.

FURTHER REFLECTIONS
The Threefold Work of Prophet, Priest, and King

Reformed theology emphasizes the threefold work (*triplex munus*) of Christ as prophet, priest, and king. All three are Old Testament offices that traditionally entailed anointing with oil. Jesus fulfills all three as Messiah (Hebrew *mashiah* and Greek *christos*, "anointed"). Reformed theology teaches that the anointing he received is not for himself alone but for his body, the church. Calvin draws out the implications of each office for the life and ministry of the church. It is not a matter of Christ's work being incomplete so that the church must complete it (*Christus prolongus*); his work is complete and sufficient. Rather, when we are joined to him we are joined to his work. To follow him is to take up the work he has shown us to do. His ministry is the pattern for our own.

Of Jesus' prophetic ministry Calvin says, "He received anointing, not only for himself that he might carry out the office of teaching, but for his whole body that the power of the Spirit might be present in the continuing preaching of the gospel."[14] As this anointing is diffused "from the Head to the members," the prophecy of Joel is fulfilled, "Your sons and your daughters shall prophesy."[15] The prophetic role is carried on in the proclamation of the gospel in the world and in the preaching and teaching ministry of the word in the church.

The priestly role we usually think of primarily in terms of sacramental ministry, and it includes this aspect. However, its meaning is much broader in Reformed theology. Priestly ministry is the work of the whole church in intercession, mediation, and reconciliation on behalf of the world. We commend the world to God in our intercession and God to the world in our ministry of reconciliation. The associations with the sacrificial system go forward transposed in our calling to be a "living sacrifice" offered for the glory of God—transformed and discerning the will of God (Rom. 12:1–2).

---

14. John Calvin, *Institutes of the Christian Religion* 2.15.2; ed. John T. McNeill, trans. Ford Lewis Battles, LCC (Philadelphia: Westminster Press, 1960), 1:496.
15. Ibid.

The kingly office, according to Calvin, is best understood in terms of Christ's rule within us. Other associations for Calvin are Christ's ruling and judging the world and his defending the church. In later Reformed theology another application emerges that is more like what Calvin does in the other two offices. The kingly office is to be lived out in terms of "wise rule" in the public arena as well as in administration and discipline within the church as we order our life together.

The church's ministry of Word, Sacrament, and Order reflect the pattern of the three offices of prophet, priest, and king as Christ fulfilled them. It is important to remember that these have a trajectory to the wider world and not only the inner life of the church.

13:1–58

Teaching: Parables of God's Reign

Chapter 13 is the third major teaching block in the Gospel of Matthew. As the third of five, it stands in the center. Jesus tells seven parables that illustrate what the reign of God is "like." This chapter is sometimes called the "parables of the kingdom" chapter. The phrase "kingdom of heaven," used in Matthew, or "kingdom of God," used in the other Gospels, refer to the "reign of God." The Greek word usually translated as "kingdom," *basileia*, is actually a verbal noun derived from the verb *basileuo*, which means "to rule or reign." Because the English words "rule" or "reign" are also verbal nouns, they are actually closer renderings of the original Greek. "Reign of God" will be used here throughout.

Parables seem to have been Jesus' preferred teaching method. Though concentrated in this one chapter, they are sprinkled throughout the Gospel of Matthew. In fact, fully one third of Jesus' teachings as recorded in the Gospels are in parable form. The parables of Jesus are widely known, even by those with little familiarity with the Bible. As a method of teaching, parables are powerful, memorable, and effective. Parables are simple stories about everyday things that anyone can understand, but they have profound meanings. C. H. Dodd suggested that a parable has the power of "arresting the hearer by its vividness or strangeness, and leaving the mind in sufficient doubt about its precise application to tease it into active thought."[1] Parables are sometimes enigmatic, concealing even as they reveal.[2] They are

---

1. C. H. Dodd, *The Parables of the Kingdom* (New York: Charles Scribner's Sons, 1961), 5.
2. Douglas R. A. Hare, *Matthew*, Interpretation: A Bible Commentary for Teaching and Preaching (Louisville, KY: Westminster/John Knox Press, 1992), 147.

multivalent. When "explained" they are sometimes reduced to allegories and lose some of their flexibility in the interest of clarity. In the text at hand, for example, Jesus, when pressed by the disciples (vv. 10, 36), explains the two parables about sowing by converting them to allegories.

Why teach in parables? This is what the disciples want to know (v. 10). Part of the answer, in Matthew's accounting, is that this is to fulfill what was spoken by the prophet: "I will open my mouth to speak parables" (v. 35). Mark (4:11–12) and Luke (8:10) imply that Jesus teaches in parables in order that some people will not understand, but Matthew's Gospel treats this differently. Here Jesus uses parables because people have not understood. Their incapacity to understand fulfills the words of the prophet Isaiah: "Seeing they do not perceive, and hearing they do not listen, nor do they understand" (Matt. 13:13). Jesus is teaching in parables so that "anyone with ears" (v. 9) can hear and understand. Unfortunately, this method does not work with the Pharisees. The more parables they hear, the more they reject his message and plot to destroy him (22:15). If the intent was to help people to hear and understand, parables backfire in the case of the Pharisees. Or maybe the better they understood what he was saying, the less they liked it.

The crowds are lacking in perception. The opponents manifest "obstinate disbelief and dullness of heart."[3] Matthew contrasts both the crowds and the opposition with the disciples and puts the disciples in a good light. The crowds are unable to understand and Jesus' opponents refuse to understand, but Jesus says to the disciples, "Blessed are your eyes for they see, and your ears for they hear" (v. 13). The disciples, who have made their commitment to follow, are capable of comprehending the "secrets of the kingdom" (v. 11).

13:1–30

"A sower went out to sow . . ."

The sower in this parable is sowing anywhere and everywhere, regardless of reception and regardless of risk. To the hearer of the

3. Donald Senior, *Abingdon New Testament Commentaries: Matthew* (Nashville: Abingdon Press, 1998), 159.

parable this may seem extravagant, even wasteful. Allan Boesak suggests that the reader is immediately struck by the "reckless abandon, the unchecked generosity, the undisciplined abundance of this sower."[4] God's initiating grace operates along these lines. The sower does not wait for "receptivity." Isaiah 65:1 expresses the divine initiative:

> I was ready to be sought out by those who did not ask,
>   to be found by those who did not seek me.
> I said, "here I am, here I am"
>   to a nation that did not call on my name.

Offense at the reckless sower is misplaced. Perhaps it is a "scarcity mentality" that creates the offense—as if there is not enough grace to go around. More grace for one means less for another. Grace should not be wasted on those who are not receptive. Our manner is miserly by contrast to this sower's. In Jesus' explanation, the seed corresponds to the "word of the kingdom." There is no "scarcity" here and no need to hold back. The extravagance of the sower manifests the "wideness of God's mercy, the boundlessness of God's love."[5]

> That's what the kingdom is like. Like a sower scattering seeds everywhere and a dragnet capturing everything.
>
> Wayne Myers, "The Kingdom of Heaven Is Like . . . Matthew 13:47–52" (sermon, Fair Oaks Presbyterian Church, Oak Park, IL, March 18, 2012).

The reality is that word/seed so graciously and generously scattered does not always fall on receptive ground. Even when it does there is always plenty to put the plant at risk. Those who first hear with enthusiasm but then fall away in the face of trouble and persecution are compared with seed that fell on rocky ground and did not really take root. Other seeds "fall among thorns" that choke the life from them as the "cares of the world" and the "lure of wealth" can do. In "good soil" the word is heard and understood and bears fruit. The final harvest is worth the sower's extravagance. It exceeds all

---

4. Allan Boesak, "Undisciplined Abundance," a sermon on Matthew 13:1–9, in *The Fire Within: Sermons from the Edge of Exile* (Capetown: New World Foundation, 2004), 113.
5. Ibid.

expectation with an increase of thirty, sixty, or a hundredfold (v. 23). The unchecked generosity of the sower is vindicated by the result.

The second parable about sowing (weeds among the wheat) is found only in Matthew. It serves as a metaphor to account for the mixed reception of Jesus' message and to forestall exclusion of those who are not responsive or who even stand opposed. The Pharisees, for example, have shown themselves in the preceding two chapters to be locked in opposition to Jesus. The lesson of the story is to let them be. This response is in accord with the principle of nonretaliation laid out in the sermon on the mount. Jesus' teachings about not judging (7:1), seeking reconciliation (5:23–26), and loving the enemy (5:44) require this approach. The parable urges trust that God is the one who is best able to judge between weeds and wheat and will do so at the time of the harvest. Harvest is a "stock metaphor for eschatological judgment"[6] and already appearing three times in Matthew's Gospel (3:10, 12; 9:37).

The mixed response that Jesus and the disciples witness also characterizes Matthew's community of faith and the wider world beyond that community as well. The parable does not equate the weeds with the world and the wheat with the church.[7] The mixture is both within and without the community of faith.

It is possible that Matthew's faith community (like our own faith communities) is at risk of trying to do the "sorting out" prematurely—confident of its capacity to distinguish between "weeds" and "wheat." Pagola suggests that there is a "mixture" not only in the wider world and the community of faith but also in the lives of the faithful: "Belief and unbelief, like the wheat and the weeds in the parable, are mixed together in each one of us."[8]

It is best to let the mixture grow together until the harvest rather than making premature judgments. That way we do not mistakenly exclude any of God's beloved. Nor do we give up on ourselves in the face of our own mixed response. Read in this way, the parable is a parable of grace—make no exclusions. This is God's harvest. God

---

6. Senior, *Abingdon New Testament Commentaries*, 149.
7. Ulrich Luz, *The Theology of the Gospel of Matthew* (Cambridge, UK: Cambridge University Press, 1995), 89.
8. José A. Pagola, *The Way Opened Up by Jesus: A Commentary on the Gospel of Matthew* (Miami, FL: Convivium Press, 2012), 132.

alone will judge. The theme of judgment runs through this chapter on the reign of God. For more discussion see "Further Reflections: Jesus and Judgment," pp. 281–85.

13:31–35
The Reign of God Is Growing in Our Midst: From Imperceptible to Undeniable

There follow two parables that assure the hearer that the reign of God—though imperceptible now— is very real. These parables are in sharp contrast to visions of the reign of God as coming in a cataclysmic event, revealed all at once in a blaze of glory. The parables of the mustard seed and the leaven together convey the inconsequential and inconspicuous character of the reign of God in its approach. What is now small, like the tiny mustard seed, and what is now hidden, like yeast in the dough, will become visible and great. A process has begun that will achieve God's purposes gradually, "like the slow growth of a plant or the steady leavening of a loaf."[9] A patient, expectant waiting is called for. Followers of Jesus are not to become discouraged because they do not yet see the fullness of God's reign. They are assured by these parables that it is growing in their midst even now and will surely come in a fullness that is great beyond all expectations.

The mustard seed was "proverbial among the Jews as the most minute of quantities."[10]

Smaller than the head of a pin, it grows to a height of eight to ten feet. It is still a bush, but its remarkable size justifies the hyperbole of calling it a "tree."[11] The addition of how the "birds of the air come and make nests in its branches" (v. 32) may resonate with Matthew's theme of the inclusion of the Gentiles. "Birds of heaven" was a frequent metaphor standing for Gentiles.[12]

9. N. T. Wright, *Matthew for Everyone, Part 1* (Louisville, KY: Westminster John Knox Press, 2004), 170.

10. Dean Kingsbury, *Proclamation Series: Jesus Christ in Matthew, Mark, and Luke* (Philadelphia: Fortress Press, 1977), 67.

11. Wright, *Matthew for Everyone, Part 1*, 157.

12. Ibid.

The parable of the yeast, like the parable of the mustard seed, moves from the small and hidden to the great and visible. This parable features a female figure as the main actor. Jesus often includes in his teachings images from the daily working life of women, and he presents them positively. It is interesting that many commentators and interpreters who work with these parables frequently draw an analogy between God and the male sowers in two of the parables (vv. 3 and 24) but do not draw an analogy between God and the female baker (v. 33). By her endeavor the dough is leavened. The "three measures" referenced would make quite a lot of bread. It is approximately a bushel of flour and probably the largest amount one person could knead.[13] It would feed a hundred people. This also calls to mind the three measures Sarah prepared for the divine messengers (Gen. 18:6). In both cases the huge amount of bread suggests preparation for a feast. The baker "hid" (RSV) the yeast in the flour. The Revised Standard Version translation of the Greek word *enekrypsen* as "hid" has the advantage of conveying more clearly the hiddenness of the reign of God. The NRSV translation "mixed in with" loses the connection with what follows; hiddenness is key to the prophetic text quoted next (v. 35). What has been "hidden from the foundation of the world" is now being revealed.

13:36–43

"Explain to us the parable . . ."

Verse 36 is a kind of turning point. The first half of the chapter (vv. 1–33) has a public setting,[14] but now Jesus leaves the crowds and goes into a house where he instructs the disciples privately. From this point forward the focus of Jesus' teaching will be their instruction. The disciples—notably with a little extra instruction (vv. 36–50)—do understand (v. 51) and follow. Already in the previous chapter Jesus has begun to set the disciples apart. "Pointing to the disciples, he says, 'Here are my mother and my brothers! For whoever does

13. Amy-Jill Levine, "Matthew," in *The Women's Bible Commentary*, ed. Carol Newsom and Sharon Ringe (Louisville, KY: Westminster/John Knox Press, 1992), 258.
14. Hare, *Matthew*, 148.

the will of my Father in heaven is my brother and sister and mother'"
(vv. 49–50).

All others offer disappointing responses. Pharisees aggressively
oppose; hometown folks reject him outright; and the crowds,
though interested, are dull of heart. Even with the help of parables
they are as the prophet Isaiah in his own day found the crowds to be,

> "You will indeed listen, but never understand,
>   and you will indeed look, but never perceive.
> For this people's heart has grown dull,
>   and their ears are hard of hearing,
>   and they have shut their eyes;
>   so that they might not look with their eyes,
>   and listen with their ears,
> and understand with their heart and turn—
> and I would heal them."
>
> (vv. 14–15)

The disciples who have committed themselves to following Jesus
are blessed with understanding. Jesus will turn his attention to the disciples and begin a more intensive instruction that will continue in the
chapters that follow. They have gained the capacity to comprehend
the "secrets of the kingdom." They will "shine like the sun" (v. 43).

The language and images of this passage have apocalyptic overtones. It describes "the end of the age" and the eschatological sorting
that is coming (v. 39–43). As with apocalyptic writing generally, this
is a faith interpretation of what is to come and not a straightforward
or literal logbook of events. The text resonates at several points with
the apocalyptic writings in the book of Daniel, which was a favorite
of Jesus' contemporaries.[15] Reference to "the Son of Man" in connection with the coming judgment (v. 41) harks back to Daniel's vision
of one "like the son of man" descending and judging the beasts that
have afflicted God's people (Dan. 7:13 RSV). Even the mention
of the "furnace of fire" (v. 42) recalls the "fiery furnace" of Daniel
chapter 3. The announcement that "the righteous will shine like the
sun" echoes Daniel's "prediction of the resurrected glory of God's

15. Wright, *Matthew for Everyone, Part 1*, 174.

people"[16] (Dan. 12:3). These resonances enhance the interpretive framework of this passage. From this apocalyptic interlude, the text returns to more parables that illumine what the reign of God is like.

13:44–46
The Reign of God Is Worth Everything You Have

The parables of the hidden treasure and the pearl of great value are found only in Matthew. Both serve to point to the unsurpassable value of the reign of God and the whole-hearted commitment that it ought to have. As the divine initiative of grace is emphasized in other parables, the human response comes to the forefront here. One has to dig to uncover a treasure; one has to seek in order to find a pearl of great value. Then, upon finding the treasure/the pearl, the reaction is wholehearted. Both parables involve a "sell all" response. "Finding the treasure disrupts normal daily life and promises a new way of life. The treasure is so valuable that it is worth doing new, joyful, risky, and costly things to possess it."[17] So it is with the reign of God.

13:47-50
God's Dragnet

The parable of the dragnet is found only in Matthew. It is not as familiar as the others in this chapter, yet by placing it as the seventh of the seven parables, Matthew is giving it a prominence of place.[18] Wayne Myers makes an interesting observation about fishing methods in Jesus' day that makes the point of the parable clearer. There were in that day two different kinds of nets for different kinds of fishing. One was a casting net. It would have been small and circular with weights tied to the edges. The fisherman would watch for a school of fish he wanted and cast the net among the school. It would sink down and

16. Ibid.
17. Warren Carter, *Matthew and the Margins: A Socio-Political and Religious Reading* (Sheffield, England: Sheffield Academic Press, 2000), 295.
18. Wayne Myers, "The Kingdom of Heaven Is Like . . . ," March 18, 2012.

trap the fish in the net. This method was for targeted fishing. The net Jesus describes here is very different. It was a large net pulled behind a boat or between boats, and it gathered everything in its path. A dragnet did not discriminate but gathered all together.[19] In this way the indiscriminate dragnet corresponds to the indiscriminate sower of the first parable. Gracious, generous sowing in the one parable and gracious, generous fishing in the other.

The NRSV says the net "caught fish of every kind" (v. 47). The Greek does not actually say "fish" at all.[20] A closer rendering would be "every kind gathering together" (*pantos genous synagagousē*). God's dragnet gathers all kinds. The diversity of the in-gathering is borne out in the unlikely swirl of people around Jesus:[21] sinners and tax collectors, a Roman centurion, people with leprosy and all kinds of diseases, a Gentile woman, people possessed by demons, a little child, a disciple who betrays Jesus, a disciple who denies him, Pharisees who plot his death. All are drawn in.

Matthew's community, with its mix of Jews and Gentiles, needed this message of God's indiscriminate gathering. The church through the centuries has needed this word as it has faced recurrent issues around diversity. Matthew's community was probably somewhat like church folks today in wanting to pluck up the weeds and pitch out the bad fish. We are pretty certain we know which is which. There is a "sorting out" coming, as the parables anticipate, but it is God's sorting out—not ours.[22] (See "Further Reflections: Jesus and Judgment," pp. 281–85.)

The insight that the "sorting out" belongs to God is central to theological discussions around the "visible" and "invisible" church. The "true" church is not necessarily identical to visible church. The true church is known only to God (and thus "invisible" to us). This in no way diminishes the importance of the visible church, which tradition terms "the mother of all believers." The point is that it is God who draws the boundaries. This insight is ancient and deep in Christian theology. Augustine said of the church, "How many sheep

19. Ibid.
20. Ibid.
21. Ibid.
22. Ibid.

are without, how many wolves within!"[23] (Augustine's sentiments may resonate with people who have worked in the church for very long.) It is well to remember who is Lord of the "harvest." The Second Helvetic Confession cautions, "We must not judge rashly or prematurely . . . nor undertake to exclude, reject or cut off those whom the Lord does not want to have excluded."[24] Elsewhere it says . . . we should "have a good hope for all."[25]

13:51–53
"Treasure what is new and what is old."

Some commentators say these verses constitute yet another parable. They tell what the scribe of the reign of God is "like" using the image of a master of a household who brings out both what is new and what is old from his treasure (v. 52). They propose that the old is the Torah and the new is Jesus' authoritative teaching of Torah. This would be in keeping with Jesus' affirmation in 5:17, "Do not think that I have come to abolish the law or the prophets; I have come not to abolish but to fulfill." The Torah stands, yet its fulfillment is something very "new." Now is the in-breaking of the reign of God, and now Gentiles are included in the promises of God's reign.[26] It is possible that the leadership in Matthew's community of faith was styled upon the role of scribe in knowing the Scripture and tradition of the faith community. The scribe of the reign of God "was one who could mediate both dimensions for a community stretched across a turning point in history."[27]

Verse 53 signals the end of this third of five teaching segments in the Gospel of Matthew. The transition formula "when Jesus had finished" appears at the end of each one (7:28; 11:1; 13:53; 19:1; 26:1). The narrative will be rejoined at this point with an account of Jesus in his own hometown.

23. Augustine, *Homilies on John,* Tractate 45, John 10:1–10, in *Nicene and Post-Nicene Fathers, First Series,* vol. 7, ed. Philip Schaff, trans. John Gibb (Buffalo, NY: Christian Literature Publishing Co., 1888).
24. *The Constitution of the Presbyterian Church (U.S.A.),* Part 1, *Book of Confessions,* (Louisville, KY: Office of the General Assembly, Presbyterian Church (U.S.A.), 2004), 5.140.
25. Ibid., 5.055.
26. Senior, *Abingdon New Testament Commentaries,*159.
27. Ibid.

13:54–58

Domesticating Jesus: "Where did this man get all this?"

The parables of the reign of God are bookended by texts about family and hometown (12:46–50 and 13:54–57). For the people in his home town, there is no question of Jesus' embodiment of wisdom and his deeds of power. They acknowledge and are astounded (v. 54). All the same, they reject him and his teachings. They must find a way to "put him in his place" so they can write him off along with the challenges he brings. What they say among themselves seems designed to domesticate: Where does he get all this? (v. 54). Who does he think he is? We know who he is. He is just a son of a carpenter. We know his mother Mary and all his brothers and sisters. He is just a home town boy, nothing special.

The people of Jesus' hometown take "offense" at him (v. 57). The word translated "offense" is the Greek word *skandalisomē*, which carries the sense of finding him an "obstacle." Perhaps his humanity and familiarity is an obstacle or stumbling block to them. His deeds of power and his embodiment of wisdom may be too great a contrast with the Jesus they think they know. Perhaps it is his unsettling message they are determined reject. Jesus' rejection at Nazareth foreshadows the wider rejection of his teaching and ministry that will culminate in the cross. Yet Jesus will go from stumbling block to corner stone. As he will say in 21:42, "Have you never read in the scriptures:

> 'The stone that the builders rejected
>   has become the cornerstone;
> this was the Lord's doing,
>   and it is amazing in our eyes?'

In response to their rejection Jesus' observes that "Prophets are not without honor except in their own country and in their own house" (v. 57). This verse is widely quoted and frequently misapplied. Not all who are rejected are prophets. It is well to remember that in our work of proclamation the fact that people "take offense" at us is not in itself a proof that we have been prophetic. If we do present a "stumbling block" in our preaching, may it be the stumbling block of the gospel and not some other of our own devising.

FURTHER REFLECTIONS
Jesus and the Reign of God

The reign of God is the heart and center of Jesus' message. He tells parable after parable that expresses what the reign of God "is like." There are seven such parables in Matthew 13 alone, and more are sprinkled throughout his teachings. They are stories of transformation, redemption, and judgment. Each one shines an illuminating cross beam over the new reality that "has come near" (Matt. 4:17). The Greek word (*ēngiken*) translated "has come near" can also mean "is soon to arrive" or "is already here." There is a sense in which the reign of God is both a future hope and a present reality. It is here even now, and it is in the process of becoming fully realized. The proximity of the reign of God adds urgency to Jesus' call to "repent" (Greek *metanoia*, a turning around).

A complete reordering of life and relationships is commensurate with the coming of God's reign. The prophets envisioned broad sweeping changes: the establishing peace and justice on earth, the renewal of nature, the inclusion of the nations. Jesus' teaching in the Sermon on the Mount traces the contours of life in accord with the reign of God. It is manifest in love without limits or exclusions—even love of the enemy. Mercy and justice/righteousness (Hebrew *tsedaqah*; Greek *dikaiosynē*) are its orienting center. Jesus' deeds of power announce the reign of God by casting out the powers of evil, healing diseases, bringing good news to the poor, and restoring life in the face of death (Matt. 11:5). His ministry overturns expectations and embraces those at the margins—the poor, the outcast, the powerless, the sick, and the sinful. Radical reorientation toward God's reign is not only about personal/individual lives but also about reordering religious, social, economic, and political life. The reign of God, as Jesus taught and lived it, proved such a threat to the status quo that religious and political powers conspired together to have him crucified.

Proclamation of the reign of God was at the center of Jesus' ministry. It is essential for the church to keep this message at the center of its ministry as well. While that may be obvious, it is in no way guaranteed. Krister Stendahl observed that Jesus preached the reign of

God, but the church preached Jesus. "We are faced with a danger: we may so preach Jesus that we lose vision of the reign of God."[28]

C. S. Song has taken this caution to heart and argued that when the church preaches Jesus without attending to the message Jesus preached, it devolves into a "cult of Jesus."[29] As a "cult object" Jesus is adored but not really *followed*. Jesus may become the focus of a popular (me-and-Jesus) piety; "the savior of individual souls and the guarantor of personal peace and prosperity."[30] Jesus may become the focus of detached theoretical speculation (about his nature and person) that diverts attention from his message.

> [Jesus, divorced from his message about the reign of God] is rendered innocuous and plays no role in the struggle of women and men or justice and freedom. This Jesus is a name without the substance, a word without the reality.
>
> C. S. Song, *Jesus and the Reign of God*, 17.

Jesus' life and ministry focused on the reign of God; he did not actually say too much about himself. More than once in the Gospel of Matthew Jesus redirects the listeners from a focus on him to a focus on obedience to God. "Not everyone who says to me, 'Lord, Lord,' will enter the kingdom of heaven, but only one who does the will of my Father in heaven" (Matt. 7:21). Jesus' orientation is theocentric. As Joseph Sittler has pointed out, "There is no future in Christians trying to be more christocentric than Jesus was."[31]

"This vision of God's reign is the *hermeneutical* principle of the life and ministry of Jesus. It is the *ethical* standard of his lifeview and worldview. It is the *theological* foundation of his relation to God and to his fellow human beings. And it is the *eschatological* vantage-point from which he relates the present time and the end of time."[32]

What was central for Jesus must be central for people who would follow in his way.

---

28. Krister Stendahl, "Notes for Three Bible Studies," in *Christ's Lordship and Religious Pluralism*, ed. Gerald H. Anderson and Thomas F. Stransky, 10 (Maryknoll, NY: Orbis, 1981).
29. C. S. Song, *Jesus and the Reign of God* (Minneapolis: Fortress Press, 1993), 16.
30. Ibid., 18.
31. Joseph Sittler, *Gravity and Grace: Reflections and Provocations* (Minneapolis: Augsburg, 1986), 106.
32. Song, *Jesus and the Reign of God*, 2.

14:1–17:27

Narrative: Preparing the Disciples for Ministry

In these three chapters, Jesus continues his ministry and along the way shows the disciples what they are meant to do. He is preparing them for their own ministry. He proclaims the reign of God and shows compassion by healing and feeding the people (14:13–21; 15:29–39). He faces and answers those who oppose him (15:1–20; 16:1–12). He signals to the disciples that this work will not be "safe;" to follow in this way will put them at risk (16:21–23). In fact, at this point in the Gospel account the disciples stand at a point between the execution of John (14:1–12) and the execution of Jesus (as foretold in 17:22–23). Nevertheless, the disciples receive assurance that in the storms ahead Jesus is there and can be relied on (14:22–33). They are called to respond in faith (14:31; 17:20–21).

Another feature of these chapters is the continuing evidence of a very mixed response to Jesus. The full range of responses is in fact played out in the persons and groups encountered in these chapters. Jesus has just moved on from Nazareth where his hometown folks—even though they are astounded by his wisdom and deeds of power— seek to "domesticate" him and reject him outright (13:54–58). Herod (Antipas) shows himself to be clueless about Jesus by thinking he is John the Baptist raised from the dead. Pharisees and Sadducees reappear with more accusations (15:1–20) and more demands for signs (16:1–12). The crowds offer an ambiguous affirmation; Jesus' popularity with them is a dubious popularity. They are indeed "followers," and there is the sense that they are always at Jesus' heels and will not give him a moment's peace (14:13). It appears, however, that they are there for the bread and the healings.

It is true that they recognize his authority, call him Son of David, and praise the God of Israel in response. Yet the reader knows how quickly they will turn against him. Their "cheers turn into jeers"[1] a few chapters further on (26:20–23). Among these groups and their mixed responses, the disciples stand out as people on the way to understanding and following. Though they have "little faith" and falter all along the way (17:14–17) they recognize Jesus as the Messiah—the Son of God (14:28–33; 16:13–23). The brightest light among those who acknowledge him in these chapters is the Canaanite woman whose faith is "great" (15:21–28).

14:1–12

The Death of John the Baptist

These verses tell of John's execution at the hands of Herod. Herod represents the empire's response to the proclamation of the reign of God. This is Herod Antipas, son of Herod the Great. He has already arrested John, bound him, and imprisoned him, but this is not enough. John is still a threat to Herod. Even though he wanted to execute John, he did not take action because "he feared the crowd, because they regarded him as a prophet." Now rather than be embarrassed before his guests, taking back his oath to the daughter of Herodias, he has him executed. Herod appears cowardly on all counts: afraid of John, afraid of the crowds, afraid of what his guests will think.

In contrast to Herod, John is portrayed throughout the Gospel of Matthew as a "fearless prophet, one not afraid to confront the powerful . . . and now he dies a prophet's death."[2] John's death is a sobering reminder to Jesus and the disciples "that God's prophets are not immune to death, that if anything they are more likely to die violently than quietly and sooner than later."[3] John's role has been as

---

1. Wayne Myers, "Call to Confession" (sermon, Palm Sunday, Fair Oaks Presbyterian Church, Oak Park, IL, April 1, 2012).
2. Donald Senior, *Abingdon New Testament Commentaries: Matthew* (Nashville: Abingdon Press, 1998), 164.
3. Barbara Brown Taylor, *The Seeds of Heaven: Sermons on the Gospel of Matthew* (Louisville, KY: Westminster John Knox Press, 2004), 49.

"forerunner" of the Messiah. He went before him into the wilderness. He went before him in proclaiming, "Repent for the kingdom of heaven has come near" (2:2). Now John goes before Jesus to his death. Theologically this passage anticipates Jesus' own death.

Upon hearing about Jesus, Herod is afraid that this is John come back to life. Here he reveals not only that he is clueless about who Jesus is but also his apprehension that God might indeed raise John from the dead and vindicate him. The reader will hear the irony in all this, knowing the truth of it; a violent death will not still the voice of John or of Jesus. The promise of resurrection lies at the horizon—Herod's fear and the disciples' hope.

14:13–21
"You give them something to eat."

When Jesus hears that John has been killed, he withdraws. This is the fifth time in the Gospel of Matthew that Jesus withdraws after an act of imperial aggression or religious opposition. (2:14–15, 21–22; 4:12–13; 12:15–21). The text notes that upon hearing from his disciples what had happened, Jesus withdrew to "a deserted place by himself." Readers can only speculate how he might have been affected by the beheading of this man who had been his forerunner and messenger. This was a portentous moment prefiguring Jesus' own destiny. In the narrative he is given little time to reflect on these things—if that is what he had hoped to do—the crowds follow him even to this deserted place. All the same, when he sees the crowds he is moved by compassion (v.14). Even in the face of John's death, Jesus carries on, engaging life-giving practices of healing and feeding He urges his disciples to get engaged as well.

The feeding of the five thousand is the only miracle story that

> [Jesus'] experience of God leads him to live by alleviating the suffering and hunger of those poor people. That is how the church must live if it wants to make Jesus present in today's world.
>
> José A. Pagola, *The Way Opened Up by Jesus: A Commentary on the Gospel of Matthew* (Miami, FL: Convivium Press, 2012), 140

appears in all four Gospels. It stands out as a central event of Jesus ministry and of the churches remembrance and proclamation of him. What is the nature of this miracle? Commentators treat it differently. (See "Further Reflection: Miracles in an Age of Science," pp. 139–45.)

Some understand it as a multiplication of loaves and fishes. It is a miracle of divine providence for people in need. Among these some point out that to multiply loaves and fishes is not qualitatively different than providing daily bread, though it is more calculated to strike the eye. It is a remarkable instance of God's gracious and abundant provision. In God's providence there is always "something more . . ." coming out of "nothing but . . ."[4]

Others read this as a miracle of sharing in which people were inspired to offer up what they had brought along with them and had kept hidden in their travel bags. Jesus' generosity evoked their generosity. Barbara Brown Taylor has proposed that when a whole crowd of people move from a sense of scarcity to a sense of plenty, "overcoming their fear of going hungry, giving up their need to protect themselves . . . refusing to play what-is-mine-is-mine-and-what-is-yours-is-yours, turning their pockets inside out for one another," this is truly miraculous.

> There is no such thing as "your" bread and "my" bread; there is only "our" bread, as in "give us this day our daily bread."
>
> Taylor, *Seeds of Heaven*, 53.

However we may understand the nature of the miracle, it is important not to get lost in the "miracle" of it and lose sight of the message. As the oriental proverb reminds us, "When the prophet points his finger at the moon, the fool keeps looking at the prophet's finger."[5] What is the message in the miracle?

Remembering that the context in Matthew is the chapters in which Jesus prepares the disciples for their ministry, what is he

---

4. Phrases drawn from discussions of "emergence" in theology and science dialogue. For example, the phenomenon we call mind emerges out of "nothing but" the physical realities of our neurobiology. Higher order realities emerge that seem to be more than the sum of their parts.

5. Pagola, *The Way Opened Up by Jesus*, 142.

teaching them here? They are to have compassion on the people, healing and feeding them—not sending them away. Faced with the hunger of the multitudes, the disciples had suggested a simple solution that was far less demanding. It is their hunger; it is their problem—everyone for him or herself. Jesus counters, "You give them something to eat." He would not let the disciples abandon hungry people to their fate.[6] The role and responsibility of the disciples in the feeding of the people is lifted up by Matthew. It is they who distribute the bread that Jesus has blessed and broken (14:19).

Followers of Jesus must learn the compassion of Jesus. Jesus manifests a freedom from self-concern that exposes our bondage to self-protection and the many forms of servitude to which self-regard holds us captive. Jesus' compassion unmasks our selfishness. It is becoming clear to the disciples in this chapter, and hopefully clear to readers of this Gospel, that it is not possible to follow Jesus and our own self-interest at the same time.

The feeding of the five thousand begins with Jesus' blessing. God, who creates and sustains all life, is acknowledged with thankfulness. The bread is broken and shared. People are giving and receiving nourishment from the hands of others. The image in this text is one of people seated in groups, sharing a meal together, perhaps in convivial conversation. Such a practice links us to God in blessing and to one another in a community of sharing. It has the potential of nourishing deeply and even of reorienting our lives.

On a very mundane level, this picturesque scene challenges some of our contemporary practices around eating by offering a sharp contrast. It is increasingly uncommon for people to pause to give thanks to God before eating—to remember with thankfulness the gift that we are receiving. Not only do we not pause to give thanks, often we do not pause at all—rather we eat on the run. By way of illustration one thinks of airport food appetizingly advertised as "Grab and Go." Many of us only rarely sit down and share food with others. Fast food is prepared for individual servings, forgoing community. For Americans age 18–50, approximately 20 percent of their eating is done in cars.[7] It is also served in throw away plastic/paper contain-

6. Ibid., 141.
7. Michael Pollan, *In Defense of Food: An Eater's Manifesto* (New York: Penguin Press, 2008), 188–89.

ers, disregarding ecology. Experts have thoughtfully criticized these current patterns as destructive to health, community, and the environment. Michael Pollan, for example, would have us reconsider what counts as "real food." In his food rules, Rule #20 quips, "It's not food if it arrived through the window of your car."[8]

This text is rich in its associations. It has trajectories that touch upon past, present, and future. The setting of the story in a "deserted place" (Greek *eremos,* "desert" or "wilderness") evokes remembrance of the story of Moses and God's provision of manna in the wilderness. A bit later in the story, Jesus will ascend the mountain as Moses did, and his face will shine as Moses' face shone (Exod. 34:29). The text also calls to mind the stories of Elijah and Elisha, where God's gift of sufficiency came out of what was "not enough" to share (1 Kgs. 17:16; 2 Kgs. 4:6–7). In both cases there was not only sufficiency but even surplus, like the twelve baskets of leftovers in this story. God is more than able to meet the needs of the people.

As the text looks back to manna in the wilderness and the provision to the prophets, it looks also to the present practice of the Lord's Supper in Matthew's community (26:26–29). In fact the same gestures and the same four verbs are used here that are used in 26:26–29: Jesus "took," "blessed," "broke," and "gave" the bread to the disciples.

In some aspects the text looks forward in anticipation to the messianic banquet. The hunger of the people, the presence of the Messiah who provides, and the abundance of the provision call to mind the eschatological feast in Isaiah 25:6–9. That text, however, envisions a sumptuous feast of rich food (meat and "mature wine"). The bread and fish of this story are more typical of a Galilean peasant's meal. In this way it points even more clearly to divine providence in the day-to-day living (daily bread). The message to Matthew's community, then, is that God can be counted on to provide what is needed.

> **Jesus enacts an alternative system marked by compassion, sufficiency and shared resources.**
>
> Warren Carter, *Matthew and the Margins: A Socio-Political and Religious Reading* (Sheffield, England: Sheffield Academic Press, 2000), 305.

8. Michael Pollan, *Food Rules: An Eater's Manual* (New York: Penguin Group, 2009), 55.

Jesus is the host at this meal. Perhaps we are meant to see the contrast between this simple and life-giving meal and the luxury of Herod's court with his death-dealing banquet (14:6–11). These are back-to-back in the chapter. Elsewhere Matthew has presented a picture of wealth and indulgence (11:8). Some of us have and consume more than enough while others suffer hunger and malnutrition. Mahatma Gandhi considered taking more than one needed to be a kind of stealing. He promoted the virtue of *asteya* (not stealing) and believed that he did not have a right to anything more until all the masses were fed and clothed.[9]

14:22–33
"Take heart, it is I; do not be afraid."

This story is the second stormy crossing for the disciples (8:23–27). The sea, as noted before (8:23–27) was understood to be wild and untamable, a symbol of chaos, darkness, and evil that threatened. The few references to the sea in Hebrew Scriptures were accounts where God's power over it were displayed such as the creation story or the exodus story. Here again is a story of its overcoming.

In the midst of the storm Jesus comes to them across the water, treading over the threatening sea. His word addresses them, "Take heart, it is I; do not be afraid." This is the fourth of seven significant texts in Matthew with the message "do not be afraid" (1:20; 8:26; 10:31; 14:27; 17:7; 28:5; 28:10). Apparently this was a much needed message. Surely the times of the early church were perilous.

Are the times any less perilous for the church today? Is the church any less fearful? Some would insist that, if anything, we are even more insecure and anxious. There is some evidence for that claim if we pay attention to the ink spilt over the decline in mainline denominations and ongoing threats of division on the horizon. There is so much anxiety about the future of the church. Patricia Brown, moderator of the General Assembly of the Presbyterian Church (U.S.A.), observed that it is as if church leaders are driving into the

---

9. Unto Tahtinen, *The Core of Gandhi's Philosophy* (New Delhi, India: Abhinov Publications, 1979), 53.

future "with hands clenched on the steering wheel and eyes firmly planted in the rearview mirror." Leaders may cling to an illusion that there was a Golden Age in the past when all was well in the church; whereas now there is only gloom and doom ahead. We are wrong on both counts. It was never so—not for mainline denominations in the United States and certainly not for the church in Matthew's day. Conflicts and divisions are ever with us in the church, then and now. The changes ahead may worry us as the storm worried the disciples. The church today needs as much as ever to hear Jesus' words of assurance, "Take heart, it is I; do not be afraid." There have been so many ways of being church through the centuries; we do not need to cling anxiously to our particular forms. We need rather to remember that this is God's church.

The fear-allaying message is "It is I" (Greek *ego eimi*). His English phrase resonates with the divine name given in God's revelation to Moses in Exodus 3:14—"YHWH" (translated "I am"). The prophet Isaiah, whom Matthew quotes more often than any other prophet, frequently uses this formulation (Isa. 41:4; 43:1–13; 47:8–10).[10] These text are full of assurance of divine presence and salvation, "Do not fear, for I have redeemed you; I have called you by name, you are mine. When you pass through the waters, I will be with you; and through the rivers, they shall not overwhelm you . . . For I am the LORD your God, the Holy One of Israel, your Savior" (Isa. 43:1–3).

These passages would speak meaningfully to Matthew's community, and they would easily associate the "it is I" (*ego eimi*) used to announce Jesus' presence with announcement of God's own presence and saving work in their midst. Their situation is not unlike that of the disciples' in the storm at sea. Matthew's faith community is "storm-tossed," beset by hostilities and persecutions from without and fears and doubts from within. They too are in need of assurance that the Lord is with them even in the storm and can be relied upon to save. Like the disciples, and like the church in our own day, they need to overcome their fear, hesitation, and "little faith" (Matt. 14:31). The incapacitating fear under which the church sinks is a

10. Senior, *Abingdon New Testament Commentaries*, 171.

failure to believe God's presence and power to save conveyed in the words, "It is I."

Although the story of the stilling of the storm appears in all the synoptic Gospels, only Matthew tells about Peter's experience. Peter is the first disciple called, the first named in the listings of the disciples, and generally is the main actor among the disciples in much of the narrative. In his mix of faith and doubt, Peter exemplifies the experience of most followers of Jesus. The "archetypal disciple,"[11] his experience is our experience. Peter seeks out and receives Jesus' teaching (15:15; 18:21; 19:27–30; 26:33–34). He draws close to Jesus even while exhibiting a frailty in his faith and following. It is Peter who affirms faith that Jesus is the "Messiah, the Son of the living God," yet he does not seem to understand what it means to be the Messiah (16:16, 22). When called upon to watch with Jesus, Peter falls asleep (26:37, 40). When Jesus stands arrested and accused, Peter bravely waits nearby in the courtyard, but to all who question him he denies ever knowing or being with Jesus (26:69–75). It is this same Peter who steps out in faith to walk on water but finds himself frightened and sinking until Jesus takes his hand.

Jesus asks, "Why did you doubt?" The verb translated as "doubt" is the Greek word *distazo,* which can mean "hesitate" and signifies the kind of "personal confusion or uncertainty that prevents action or commitment."[12] It is a term that characterizes Jesus' faltering followers both then and now. Nevertheless, there are signs of promise and progress among the doubting disciples in this second story of a storm at sea. When Jesus calms the storm in the first story (8:23–27) the disciples respond with wonder and ask "Who is this?" Now they respond with worship and confess, "Truly you are the Son of God" (14:33).

> In worshiping him, they align themselves with the marginal and subversive wise men (2:2).
>
> Carter, *Matthew and the Margins,* 312.

There are rudimentary elements of early Christian worship reflected in this chapter, all of which carry forward to the worship

---

11. Ulrich Luz, *The Theology of the Gospel of Matthew* (Cambridge, UK: Cambridge University Press, 1995), 94.

12. Senior, *Abingdon New Testament Commentaries,* 173.

life of the church today: eucharistic sharing, prayers of supplication (Lord, save me!"), and affirmations of faith ("Truly you are the Son of God.")

14:34–36
The Fringe of His Cloak

There follow two verses that provide a brief summation and transition. In these we find for a second time the reference to "the fringe of his cloak." This would refer to the tassels worn by observant Jews as decreed in Numbers 15:37–41 as a symbol of their obedience to Torah. Matthew's mention of these marks Jesus as an observant Jew.

15:1–20
Conflict with the Pharisees: "Why do your disciples break the tradition of the elders?"

The Pharisees are back on the scene in chapter 15 with one more in their growing list of complaints against Jesus. Why do your disciples not fast (9:14)? Why would you let them pluck grain on the Sabbath, even if they are hungry (12:2)? Do you dare to forgive sins (9:2–3)? Why are you healing on the Sabbath (12:10)? Why do you eat with tax collectors and sinners (9:11)? Why do your disciples not wash their hands before they eat (15:2)? There are more grievances yet to come about the Temple tax (17:24) and taxes to the emperor (22:17). The complaints are mounting as the conflict with the religious authorities intensifies.

This particular complaint is about breaking the "tradition of the elders." The disciples neglected to wash their hands. In fact there was no biblical instruction that required washing of hands before eating. Priests were required to wash before entering the tent of meeting (Exod. 30:19–21). By the tradition of the Pharisees, there came to be an extension of priestly ritual purity requirements into everyday life. This signified that Israel was a "nation of priests" and that every aspect of life is to be lived in service to God. The "tradition of the elders" referred to a whole set of "regulations and customs that had developed in interpretation of the law in order to apply it to everyday life."[13]

Jesus does not argue that there is anything wrong with the practice of washing hands before eating. Nor does he suggest that the "tradition of the elders" simply be laid aside. Rather he puts tradition in its place behind weightier matters of the law. He takes their complaint as an opportunity to criticize the Pharisees for places where they have allowed their traditions to nullify the clear demands of Torah. One such place was in their practice of "Corban" in which one declared all one's possessions to be dedicated to God. Again, there was nothing wrong with such a generous offering. However, the Pharisees allowed people to use it as a way of avoiding material care of one's parents. Corban was being allowed to trump the commandment to "honor your father and your mother" (Exod. 20:12; Deut. 5:16).

Not washing ones hands might be a violation of the traditional purity code, but "washing ones hands" of one's parents was a violation of the law of God. "The Pharisees' practices meant to implement and supplement Torah in fact nullify it."[14] Hand washing and Corban are not God's command. Jesus charges them, "So, for the sake of your tradition you make void the word of God" (Matt. 15:6).

"Tradition" is a word fraught with ambiguities. Our English word comes from the Latin root *tradere*, which simply means "to hand over." It is the root not only for "tradition" but also for "traitor." There is a similar ambiguity in the Greek term used here, *paradosis*. It is sometimes used positively, as in the passing on of the gospel message ("I received from the Lord what I also handed on to you" [1 Cor. 11:23]). It is sometimes used negatively, in the sense of betrayal ("the Son of Man will be *handed over* to be crucified" [Matt. 17:22]). When is "tradition" a faithful handing on, and when is it a betrayal? Reformed theology has counseled a certain carefulness with tradition in its motto "*ecclesia reformata, semper reformanda secundum verbum Dei*" ("reformed and always to be reformed according to

---

13. Ibid., 176.
14. Frederick Murphy, *An Introduction to Jesus and the Gospels* (Nashville: Abingdon Press, 2005), 159.

the word of God").[15] Traditions are always subordinated and judged according to the word of God.

Jesus' sharpens the contrast; "For God said . . . But you say . . ." (15:4–5) and he warns them to keep "tradition" in its place behind the law of God. His aphorism that it is what comes out of the mouth that defiles and not what goes into it is a call to give moral purity priority over ritual purity.[16] This is a message consistent with the prophets; purity of the heart is the touchstone of authentic worship.[17] "Lip service" is not enough. Very much to the point is the reference (15:7–9) from Isaiah,

> "This people honors me with their lips,
>   but their hearts are far from me;
> in vain do they worship me,
>   teaching human precepts as doctrines."

The Pharisees, not surprisingly, take "offense" (*skandalisomē*) at Jesus' criticism (15:12). Like Jesus' hometown folks (13:57), though perhaps for different reasons, the Pharisees are "scandalized" and find that Jesus is for them an obstacle, a stumbling block. Jesus drives the point home in 15:13 with a metaphor of judgment as the uprooting of a plant. In Jewish literature the symbol of the "righteous plant" was a way of claiming God's favor on a particular group. Perhaps the Pharisees see themselves as a righteous plant. Jesus counters this with the threat that they may well be uprooted. Changing metaphors, they are like blind guides leading blind people. Both will fall in a pit. They are on a path that will lead to destruction. Jesus then reiterates his point about

> **Exalting the merely legal over the truly moral is sheer hypocrisy, Jesus claims, because it professes allegiance to God's law while disregarding God's will.**
>
> Douglas R. A. Hare, *Matthew, Interpretation Series, A Bible Commentary for Teaching and Preaching* (Louisville, KY: Westminster/John Knox Press, 1992), 175.

15. Anna Case-Winters, "Our Misused Motto," in *Presbyterians Being Reformed: Reflections on What the Church Needs Today,* ed. Robert H. Bullock Jr. (Louisville, KY: Geneva Press, 2006).
16. Senior, *Abingdon New Testament Commentaries,* 178.
17. Ibid.

what truly defiles. "Authentic purity begins in the heart, not on the hands."[18]

15:21–28

Jesus' Ministry on the Borderline: "Woman, great is your faith!"

After the altercation with the Pharisees, Jesus withdraws. The text says "he left that place and went away to the district of Tyre and Sidon" (15:21). This would be Gentile territory; in fact Tyre and Sidon "were proverbially wicked Gentile cities attacked by the prophets."[19] Commentators disagree as to whether the word *eis* "to" in this verse means he went "toward" or "into" the region. Entering the territory would be against his own instructions to the disciples to "go nowhere among the Gentiles" (10:5). At the very least he is at the border within access of the Canaanite woman in the story. Either he is crossing the line or she is.

Matthew takes care to identify the woman in this story not simply as Syrophoenician (and therefore a Gentile) but as "Canaanite." Of all the Gentiles, the greatest animosity would be reserved for the Canaanites. From the perspective of Israel, Canaanites are the ones who had to be driven out for Israel to take possession of the promised land. They are a rival people, even "the enemy," in Israel's conquest of the land. They are accursed and destined for slavery (Gen. 9:25). Israel's victory over the Canaanites is, from the perspective of the victors, a gift of God and evidence of Israel's elect status. It was a conquest celebrated in Israel's traditions.[20]

Given these hostile relations, it is a bit audacious for this Canaanite woman to approach Jesus at all. Her gender as well as her ethnicity is a hindrance. According to Sharon Ringe, in first-century Palestinian society women were supposed to be invisible. "No Jewish man, especially one with a religious task or vocation, expected to be approached by a woman (Jew or Gentile)" unless she was a

---

18. Ibid., 179.
19. Carter, *Matthew and the Margins*, 321.
20. Ibid.

prostitute.[21] By her society's standards, she has transgressed the boundaries. She might be called an "uppity" woman. Unlike the woman in 9:21, who snuck up on Jesus from behind (appropriately invisible) and did not dare to speak to him, this Canaanite woman "came out" and "started shouting" (15:22). She is the first woman in the Gospel to speak. When she does, she dares to "demand her share in God's blessing," challenging the whole ideology of chosenness.[22]

At first, Jesus simply ignores her and does not deign to answer her (15:23). The disciples are on board with this and suggest that Jesus should "send her away." This was their advice in the previous chapter when faced with a multitude to feed (14:15). When she is not deterred he refuses her twice. The first time he simply reiterates what he has been saying all along: "I was sent only to the lost sheep of the house of Israel" (10:6; 15:24). He has clarity concerning the limits on the parameters of his mission.

When she persists, his second refusal is deeply disturbing. "It is not fair to take the children's food and throw it to the dogs" (15:26). It is amusing to watch how many commentaries tap dance around this difficult text. Some say the word for dogs is diminutive (more like "puppies") and probably refers to dogs who are house pets and held in affection by the family. Others say Jesus really did not mean this; he was just testing the woman's faith. Maybe he was even making a show for the disciples so they could see her great faith. Others go so far as to say this just cannot have been an authentic saying of Jesus.[23] Each of these maneuvers has been countered by the current scholarship. Perhaps it is better to face the text head on.

At the very least Jesus has employed a metaphor that is insulting as it identifies her and her ethnic group with "dogs" and the "lost sheep of Israel" with the children of the household. At worst he is employing a common racial slur. "Gentile dogs" was a common appellation. The words reinforce the boundary between Jew and Gentile. When Jesus puts off this woman begging healing for her daughter in this way it seems cruel; it seems that Jesus has been, as

---

21. Sharon Ringe, "Gentile Woman's Story" in *Feminist Interpretations of the Bible*, ed. Letty Russell, 70 (Louisville, KY: Westminster John Knox Press, 1985).

22. Carter, *Matthew and the Margins*, 323.

23. Hare, *Matthew*, 177.

Sharon Ringe puts it, "caught with his compassion down."[24] It seems a text that confirms what we have affirmed in principle theologically: that Jesus was not only fully divine but also fully human. In spite of this theological affirmation, readers and interpreters often resist the textual evidences of humanity and limitation. Could it be that Jesus was actually still learning about the fullness of the divine embrace and the scope of his own calling? Is it so hard to imagine that Jesus might actually have learned something in the encounter with the Canaanite woman?

As the story unfolds the Canaanite woman exemplifies the great faith that Jesus does not find among his hometown folks, or the religious leaders, or the crowds, or even the disciples. She addresses Jesus with christological titles of "Lord" and "Son of David." She "kneels" before him. The Greek word used is *proskynein*. It is a word that expresses an attitude of reverent faith. When the same word is used in reference to the disciples it is translated as "worship (14:33)."[25] She does not deny the distinctive place and priority of the "lost sheep of Israel," but she claims a place at the table of God's blessing as well. Her "great faith" stands in stark contrast to the "little faith" demonstrated by Peter (14:31). She is in fact an exemplar of faith for the disciples—though she is a woman, a Gentile, and even a despised Canaanite.

Her boldness, persistence, and remarkable faith empower the Canaanite woman to cross the boundaries that circumscribe her. In a sense, she empowers Jesus to do the same. Who can doubt that the love and compassion of God extends to one such as this? It seems that this Gentile woman from among the despised Canaanites teaches Jesus about a wider divine embrace. She is "crossing the line" in approaching Jesus and inviting him to do the same. Is it possible that Jesus learned from his

> Mission to the Gentiles was part of God's plan and not incompatible with reverence for Israel's historic privilege, a divine plan that would burst into reality in the post-resurrection experience of the community.
>
> Senior, *Abingdon New Testament Commentaries*, 183.

24. Ringe,"Gentile Woman's Story," 69.
25. Senior, *Abingdon New Testament Commentaries*, 173.

encounter with this remarkable woman and gained a larger vision of his calling? This story—offense and all—has been preserved and told and retold. The effect is an enlarged understanding of the parameters of God's purposes. The circle Jesus drew around the lost sheep of Israel is now expanding as he crosses the line into Gentile territory and encounters this Canaanite woman whose faith is so great.

Matthew's community would have heard in this story an affirmation of the mission to the Gentiles. The story of the Canaanite woman continues and extends the theme that was begun with the homage of the wise men from the East (2:1–2) and will culminate in the final chapter (28:16–20) where the mission bursts its boundaries and extends into "all the world."

15:29–39
Jesus' Compassion for the Crowds: Healing and Feeding

Verses 29–31 provide another summative interlude reminding the reader of the magnitude of Jesus' healing ministry. Great crowds flock to him, and all are amazed to see "the mute speaking, the maimed whole, the lame walking and the blind seeing." The image presented here evokes Isaiah 35:5–6:

> Then the eyes of the blind shall be opened,
>   and the ears of the deaf unstopped;
> then the lame shall leap like a deer,
>   and the tongue of the speechless sing for joy.

Other connections reinforce these associations with the messianic age. The Isaiah text is connected with Mt. Zion, and here Jesus has gone "up the mountain" (v. 29). He sits down. This may be a sign of authority as kings and judges in the culture generally sit to govern and judge. Those in need are put "at his feet" (v. 30). Jesus "sat" for the sermon on the mount where he showed himself to be the authoritative teacher. Now he sits on another mount and demonstrates authority through his ministry of healing. The crowds in this passage in Matthew stream up the mountain after him and praise "the God of Israel," as Isaiah prophesied all the nations would do one day (Isa. 2:1–3). Senior observes that "the entire scene becomes a verbal icon proclaiming Jesus' messianic authority expressed in his mission of healing."[26]

Jesus authority is the authority of compassion. It is his "compassion for the crowds" (v. 32) that moves him to heal and to feed them. Matthew, more than any other Gospel, speaks of Jesus' compassion (9:36; 14:14; 15:32; 20:34). Matthew may understand Jesus' compassion as a "manifestation of God's loving concern."[27]

This is the second miracle of feeding. It has much in common with the first feeding. It has all the rich associations: manna in the wilderness (Moses), feeding miracles by the prophets (Elijah and Elisha), eucharistic celebration in Matthew's community, and the coming messianic banquet. For a fuller discussion of each of these themes see comments on 14:15–21.

Just as in the first feeding story, the four verb forms that appear are the same as those found in 26:26 at Jesus' "last supper" with his disciples. Jesus took and blessed (Greek *eucharistēsas,* "giving thanks") and broke and gave the bread (and fish) to the disciples. These acts and these verb forms would evoke associations with the practice of eucharist in Matthew's church community.

There are some interesting differences from the first story as well. The extraordinariness is intensified with the note that the people had been there three days and thus would have consumed whatever they had brought with them. The text does not lend itself to the same "miracle of sharing" interpretations. Because this feeding miracle takes place on the mountain; it is even more readily associated with the messianic banquet pictured in Isaiah 25:6–9. Isaiah announces that God will "wipe away the tears form all faces" and "make for all people a feast"; Jesus' ministry of healing and feeding has this effect.

In this second story, the disciples seem to be further along in their understanding than they were in the first feeding story. In the first story they wanted Jesus to send the crowd away, but he responded, "You give them something to eat" (Matt. 14:16). Now

26. Ibid., 185.
27. Hare, *Matthew,* 182.

they seem to understand that they are to feed the crowds; they only ask where they should get sufficient food to do so (15:33). Perhaps this represents progress. Similarly the disciples demonstrate a kind of progress in the second calming of the storm as compared to the first. When Jesus calms the storm in the first story (8:23–27) the disciples respond with wonder and ask "Who is this?" In the second story they respond with worship and confess, "Truly you are the Son of God." (14:33). The reader may see in the disciples a growing understanding as Jesus continues to prepare them for their ministry.

16:1–12
Conflict with the Pharisees and Sadducees:
"Show us a sign from heaven."

The pairing of the Pharisees and Sadducees occurs only in Matthew. In a way it is an unlikely pairing, as the two groups were rivals. The Pharisees were a lay led group focused on the study and teaching of Torah (the law). The Sadducees were from aristocratic priestly families centered around Jerusalem and the Temple. The Pharisees generally favored a separatist nationalism and some even supported armed revolt against Rome. The Sadducees opposed revolutionary movements and generally got along better with Roman authorities, even colluding at times. Different as these two groups were, one thing they agreed upon in the book of Matthew was their opposition to Jesus. In this they form a companionable coalition.

At the beginning of chapter 16, they come together demanding signs from Jesus—to "test" him. The verb used here is the Greek verb *peirazo*, which means "to test" or even "to tempt." This is not a test that seeks to prove him but a test that seeks to fail him. It has the strong connotation of temptation. It hints at a parallel between the testing of Jesus by the Pharisees and Sadducees and Satan's testing of him in the wilderness (4:1–11). Satan tempts Jesus to show people a sign that he is the Son of God by throwing himself from the pinnacle of the Temple and demonstrating his divine protection (4:5–7). The Pharisees and Sadducees, in their demand for a sign, provide what is almost a mirror image.

This is not the first time religious leaders in the Gospel of Matthew have urged Jesus to make a spectacle to prove himself. He had a similar request from the scribes and Pharisees in chapter 12. He refused them as he now refuses the Pharisees and Sadducees. It is doubtful that a "sign" would have made any difference. Jesus has already given many signs in his healing and feeding ministry; yet these religious leaders persist in their opposition and disbelief. He charges that they are an "evil and adulterous" generation. The reader of the Gospel already knows from 12:14 that they are plotting "evil" against Jesus. The charge of "adultery" is likely to be linked with covenant infidelity and their "unfaithfulness" to God (as in Hos. 1–3). The religious leaders have all the signs they need, but their faithless hearts turn away from God's Messiah and from God. Jesus alludes to "the sign of Jonah," which they will yet receive. As Jonah came forth after three days in the belly of the sea monster, so also will Jesus come forth after three days in the tomb.

The second scene in this chapter (16:5–12) is a strange one. Jesus is warning about the "leaven" of the Pharisees and Sadducees. ("Leaven" commonly serves as a metaphor for corruption.) The disciples, however, respond with thoughts of the bread they have failed to bring. Either not paying much attention or being obtuse. Jesus expresses frustration that once again they do not get it. They do not understand his warning about the Pharisees and Sadducees, and in obsessing about the bread they seem to have completely forgotten how Jesus fed the multitudes—not once but twice already. Jesus charges them to "remember" (vv. 9–10). If they will only remember that God provides daily bread, they will not need to spend themselves in this anxious fretfulness symptomatic of their "little faith."

16:13–20
"Who do you say that I am?"

Jesus first inquires as to who other people think he is. All the answers the disciples offer (John the Baptist, Elijah, Jeremiah, one of the prophets) rightly identify Jesus with the great prophets. Only Matthew mentions Jeremiah in this line up. Jeremiah was a prophet who railed against Israel's infidelities, preached repentance, and was rejected by the people. He is an appropriate choice both in terms of message and in terms of reception.

The mention of the prophet Jeremiah is significant for Matthew. There are two earlier texts that draw upon Jeremiah. They are fulfillment formulas. Matthew 2:17–18 concerns the slaughter of the innocents drawing upon Jeremiah 31:15 ("Rachel weeping for her children). Matthew 27:9–10 tells of the purchase of the potter's field (the Field of Blood) with the thirty pieces of silver Judas returned to the chief priests just before his suicide. This connects with a "call to repentance" passage in Jeremiah 18:1–11. The association with Jeremiah befits the description of Jesus' destiny (16:21). Jeremiah was a prophet of "woe, persecution, and desolation."[28] Jeremiah was also the prophet who predicted both the fall and the restoration of Jerusalem as it occurred in his own day. This would have been an especially apt association for Matthew's audience, who were coping with how to understand and survive the fall of Jerusalem (70 CE) in their own time. Divine judgment for rejection of the prophetic message (Jeremiah's and Jesus') served as a kind of explanatory theodicy in both cases. If the parallel holds, then Matthew's faith community may also hope for the kind of restoration Jeremiah's community experienced if they likewise repent and respond to the message of the prophet.[29]

Then Jesus asks a more penetrating question, "But who do you say that I am?" Peter's answer goes to the heart of the matter: "You are the Messiah, the Son of the Living God." The disciples had affirmed this in part already. After the second calming of a storm at sea, they declared, "Truly you are the Son of God" (14:33). Peter's affirmation, however, is the first time a disciple has used the term "Messiah" (Greek *ho Christos*, "the Christ"). Peter gets it. Jesus makes a resounding affirmation of Peter's perception. This is when Simon becomes "Peter." Jesus makes a play on words, "You are Peter (Greek *petros*), and on this rock (Greek *petra*) I will build my church."

---

28. Michael Knowles, "Jeremiah in Matthew's Gospel: The Rejected-Prophet Motif in Matthean Redaction," *Journal for the Study of the New Testament*: Supplemental Series 68, (Sheffield, England: Sheffield Press, 1993), 308.
29. Ibid., 308–11.

This is the first mention of the church in the New Testament. In fact, among the Gospels it is only in Matthew that there is direct reference to the church. He uses the Greek term *ekklesia*, "called out." This is the same term used in the Septuagint (the Greek translation of the Hebrew Scriptures) to designate the assembled or called congregation of God's people. Matthew makes a clear identification between his community of faith and the congregation of God's people in the Hebrew Scriptures, even as it differentiates from both the institutions of Temple and the synagogue. There will follow, in Matthew chapter 18, a fuller discourse on the church. This new community is to be "marked by humility, forgiveness and service."[30] Jesus declares that the "gates of Hades" will not prevail against the church. Scholars generally agreed that "the gates of Hades" is a metaphor for the powers of death and the saying assures that the church will endure to the new age and never be overcome by this power. An alternative reading pictures the gates of Hades as imprisoning the dead. The *Christus Victor* theory of the atonement (also called the "ransom theory") builds upon Christ's triumph over the power of death through his own death and resurrection, by which he brings release to all whom death held captive. Death is destroyed and captivity taken captive. This understanding was the predominant one until the eleventh century. It sees the work of Christ as, first and foremost, a victory over what holds human beings in bondage: sin and death and the devil.[31] There is some support for this second interpretation of 16:18 in its parallel to 12:29. There the reference is to "the plundering of a strong man's property (Satan's victims)."[32]

When Jesus confers on Peter the power to "bind" and to "loose" this corresponds with the rabbinical terms meaning authority to declare what is permitted and what is forbidden and the authority to determine membership in the community.[33] Jesus grants this same authority to "bind" and "loose" to all the disciples later in the Gospel (18:18). There is much debate concerning Jesus' declaration to

30. Amy-Jill Levine, "Matthew," in *The Women's Bible Commentary*, ed. Carol Newsome and Sharon Ringe (Louisville, KY: Westminster/John Knox Press, 1992), 259.

31. Gustav Aulén, *Christus Victor: An Historical Study of the Main Three Types of Ideas of the Atonement* (New York: Macmillan, 1969).

32. Hare, *Matthew*, 191.

33. Michael G. Reddish, *An Introduction to the Gospels* (Nashville: Abingdon Press, 1997), 134.

Peter. Roman Catholic tradition has read this declaration in terms of personal office. Peter is the "rock" on which the church is founded, and there is a permanent legal primacy for Peter and his successors. This view has received more emphasis since the Reformation and has become the official exegesis of the text. Protestants have countered that it is not Peter himself but rather the confession of faith that Peter made that is the "rock" on which the church is founded. More recently, there is new recognition that the text probably does refer to Peter as the rock, but there is no textual indication that this is something repeatable, or an institution of a particular church office with a line of successors to Peter. Protestants also point out that the authority conferred upon Peter here to "bind" and "loose" is conferred upon all the disciples later (18:18). The discussion continues.[34] Whatever one's perspective on the role of Peter, it is clear that Matthew's presentation does not idealize him but presents him with faith and failings in clear view—the "archetypal disciple." The high praise he receives in 16:18 is soon followed by a sharp rebuke in 16:23.

16:21–28
What Does It Mean to Be the Christ?

The affirmation that Jesus is the Messiah is the turning point of the Gospel. A transition is signaled by the words "from that time on . . ."(16:21), and Jesus begins to make his way toward Jerusalem. Although he does not arrive there for several chapters, the journey begins in principle with his teaching about the passion.[35] He now teaches the disciples about what it means to be the Messiah and what lies ahead for him in Jerusalem. This is the first of three teachings on the passion ahead (17:22–23; 20:17–19). Jesus is on a collision course with the powers represented in Jerusalem—political, economic, and religious. The "elders" he mentions here would be the lay members of the Jerusalem Sanhedrin, supporters of the

34. Anna Case-Winters and Lewis S. Mudge, "The Successor to Peter," *The Journal of Presbyterian History,* special edition "Excerpts from the Ecumenical Revolution," 80, no. 2 (2002): 107–43.
35. Hare, *Matthew,* 187.

Sadducees (including the "chief priests"). The "scribes" would be the authoritative interpreters of the law. All these hold power and all stand in opposition to Jesus.

Jesus will suffer just as the prophets before him who challenged the powers in their day. Yet he is more than a prophet, and by his suffering and death he will "expose the limits of the elite's power to punish and control. God will raise him to show that while the political and religious elite trade in death, God's sovereignty asserts life over death."[36] The powers will do their worst, but their death-dealing powers do not have the last word. God's life-giving power prevails.

Peter balks at the mention of suffering ahead. "God forbid it Lord! This must never happen to you" (16:22). Peter may understand that Jesus is the Messiah, but he does not yet understand what it means to be the Messiah. He seems to have his own ideas about that. Perhaps Peter still holds an unreconstructed hope for a powerful king or mighty warrior that will reign in triumph and put down Israel's enemies. The disciples were unprepared for "the notion that Israel's eschatological champion should suffer a shameful death . . . The Christian message of a crucified Messiah, while merely foolishness to Greeks was a real stumbling block to Jews"[37] (1 Cor. 23–24). Whatever Peter's vision of the Messiah, it did not include suffering and dying.

> From its very beginning, the Church has taken offense at the suffering Christ.
>
> Dietrich Bonhoeffer, *Discipleship* (1949)
> Dietrich Bonhoeffer's Works, Vol. 4, English Edition, ed. Geffrey B. Kelly and John D. Godsey, trans. Barbara Green and Reinhard Krauss (Minneapolis: Augsburg Fortress, 2000), 85.

Jesus corrects Peter with a sharp rebuke. "Get behind me Satan! You are a stumbling block to me. How quickly Peter has gone from "rock" to "stumbling block."[38] The command to "get" or "depart" is the same word Jesus addressed to Satan in the temptation account (4:10). Satan tempted Jesus to take his special relationship to God as a position of privilege, using it to meet his own needs (avoid

---

36. Carter, *Matthew and the Margins*, 341.
37. Hare, *Matthew*, 194.
38. Wayne Myers,"From Rock to Stumbling Block" (sermon on Matthew 16:13–23, Fair Oaks Presbyterian Church, Oak Park, IL, Spring 2012).

suffering), receive protection from vulnerability, and exercise power over all the "kingdoms of the world." Peter presents that temptation all over again; surely there is an easier path than the way of the cross. Jesus commands him "get behind me." This could be heard as "get out of the way" if you mean to be a stumbling block in the path. Or it could be heard as a command to "fall in" behind me or even "follow" me. The very next verse pulls the meaning in the latter direction. "If any want to become my followers, let them deny themselves and take up their cross and follow me" (16:24). Jesus' "scandalous call"[39] is to "take up the cross" and follow (4:18–22). "Evasion of suffering is . . . incompatible with discipleship and contradicts the profession of faith in the Son of God."[40]

> Suffering, Matthew tells us, cannot be avoided when one chooses to travel the way of Christ and to take his radical commands at their full value.
>
> Luz, *The Theology of the Gospel of Matthew*, 102.

It is not only Peter who has trouble with this calling. Theologian and martyr Dietrich Bonhoeffer, who wrote about *the cost of discipleship*, saw in Peter's reaction evidence that "from its very beginning, the Church has taken offense at the suffering Christ."[41] This is certainly true for disciples in the present context as well. Philosopher Leszek Kołakowsky speaks of our modern culture as "a culture of analgesics" in which suffering is avoided at all costs, denied, and covered over. Our "analgesics" are not only drugs but myriad forms of distraction such as "entertaining ourselves to death."[42]

It is not that Jesus seeks out suffering or that his disciples are expected to seek it. On the contrary, in his ministry Jesus devoted himself to alleviating suffering. This is not a glorification of suffering as such, but a realistic assessment that suffering tends to accompany those who follow on this path.

Jesus reminds his followers again (as in 10:39) that those who "save" their life lose it. There is a sense in which the self-protective impulse, a life controlled by fear of suffering and death, is a life

---

39. Carter, *Matthew and the Margins*, 344.
40. Luz, *The Theology of the Gospel of Matthew*, 103.
41. Bonhoeffer, *Discipleship*, 85.
42. Leszek Kołakowski, *The Presence of Myth*, trans. Adam Czerniawski (Chicago: University of Chicago Press, 2001), 83–85.

> The deep secret of Jesus' hard words is that the way to have abundant life is not to save it but to spend it, to give it away.
>
> Taylor, *Seeds of Heaven*, 79.

already lost. Fear of death translates into a kind of "fear of life"—a constrained and "cautious way of living that is not living at all."[43] To lose one's life in following Jesus in the "subversive way of the cross"[44] is, ironically, to find life.

17:1–13

Transfiguration: "This is my Son, the Beloved; with him I am well pleased."

The vision (v. 9) we call the transfiguration takes place on the "high mountain" which has traditionally been associated with revelation and profound religions experience. Symbolically, it is a place where heaven touches earth. In the vision Moses and Elijah are present alongside Jesus. Their presence reminds the reader that the law and the prophets come together and are fulfilled in Jesus. Each of these figures has special prominence in this text.

As in other narrative portions of the Gospel, Matthew draws out parallels between Moses and Jesus. This association is made even more prominent in chapter 17 where there are at least seven points of parallel between Jesus in the transfiguration and Moses at Sinai. Both the transfiguration and the giving of the law on Mt. Sinai were "mountaintop experiences." Jesus takes three companions with him (Peter, James, and John) just as Moses took Aaron, Nadab, and Abihu (Exod. 24:2). The reference to six days in Mathew 17:1 recalls Exodus 24:16, where a cloud covered Mt. Sinai for six days before God spoke to Moses on the seventh day. In 17:2 it says that Jesus' "face shone like the sun." Similarly, Exodus 34:29–35 says of Moses, "the skin of his face was shining." The bright cloud overshadowing at the transfiguration (Matt. 17:5) reminds the reader of the cloud overshadowing Sinai and the manifestation of "the glory of

43. Taylor, *Seeds of Heaven*, 79.
44. Carter, *Matthew and the Margins*, 345.

the Lord" (Exod. 24:16). In both cases, the others who are present react to their transformed state (17:6; Exod. 34:30) with fear that Moses and Jesus seek to calm. These multiple associations reinforce the identity of Jesus with Moses and affirm Jesus' role as the authoritative interpreter of the law.

Elijah's presence has other associations. There was an expectation in the tradition that Elijah would come before the new age was issued in. The encounter with Elijah on the mountaintop provokes them to pose a question: What of this expectation? Jesus affirms this expectation but makes the bold claim that Elijah has already come. John the Baptist was "Elijah." Making this forthright association supports the expectation that the eschaton has in fact arrived and that Jesus is the promised Messiah. There is more that follows, however. It was not part of the expectation that Elijah would be so poorly received. Of John's reception Jesus recalls, "they did not recognize him and they did to him whatever they pleased" (17:9).

Jesus takes the occasion to warn that as they did to John the Baptist (Elijah) so they will do to the Son of Man. He will not be recognized but rejected. The theme of the "rejected prophet" that emerges in several places in the Gospel comes to the foreground here. Jesus, like the messenger who was his forerunner, will be rejected, arrested, and put to death (17:22–23).

Peter receives the vision with apparent eagerness and offers to build three "dwellings." The Greek term used is *skenas* and would call to mind the Hebrew *shekinah* used in many texts to indicate the "dwelling" or "presence" of God. "The shekinah is manifest in the symbols of cloud, fire, or radiant light that descend, overshadow, or lead the people."[45] There is an association with the tents or tabernacles that housed the ark of the covenant in the wilderness wanderings. God's presence in the Holy of Holies in the Temple was also identified as the shekinah.

In offering to build three dwellings, there is a sense in which Peter "gets it." He discerns that the presence of God is there and seems to be making an attempt to rise to the occasion. It is apparent that he is much more enthusiastic about the transfiguration than he was

---

45. Elizabeth Johnson, *She Who Is* (New York: Crossroad, 1992), 85.

about Jesus' earlier discussion of the passion. This is more like it—glory, not suffering! Peter's proposal, however, is wrong-footed on several counts, as what follows his offer will make clear. There will be no dwelling upon the mountain top in "spiritual retreat" from the world. Jesus and the disciples are very soon thereafter called to come down from the high places and minister in the valley where great need awaits them. Also, Peter is misunderstanding the meaning of the moment if he thinks of Jesus as simply one among three to be placed alongside Moses and Elijah. Perhaps he does not yet fully grasp what he earlier affirmed—that Jesus is the Messiah, "the Son of the Living God" (16:16). Lastly, Peter's disposition needs an alteration. He is disposed to talk, but this is not a time for talking; it is a time for listening. His words are interrupted by a voice from the bright cloud, "This is my son the Beloved; with him I am well pleased; listen to him" (17:5). These are exactly the words that appear in 3:17 at Jesus' baptism with the addendum "listen to him."

What is the theological weight affirming Jesus as the "Son of God"? (See fuller discussion in "Further Reflections: God Is with Us," pp. 32–38.) The term has rich associations in a Jewish context and is used variously for Israel (Exod. 4:22), for the King (Ps. 2:7), and for the coming Messiah (Ps. 2:7). For Matthew, the royal and messianic associations are most prominent. However, Matthew does affirm the "supernatural origin and status of Jesus"[46] and, in a Greek context (where Matthew's community is likely located), "Son of God" would connote divine or semi-divine being.[47]

Christology that works "from below" generally emphasizes humanity, and Christology that works "from above" generally emphasizes divinity. Matthew's Gospel has a strong emphasis on Jesus as teacher and exemplar. It is a Christology "from below." Now and then (3:16; 14:33; 16:16; 17:5; 27:40), however, this affirmation of Jesus as "Son of God" emerges and invites further reflection. Matthew in fact uses this title with more frequency and variety than the other Gospels.

In working out the meaning of Jesus as "Son of God" and "Son

---

46. Eugene Boring, *The New Interpreter's Bible: New Testament Articles, Matthew, Mark* (Nashville: Abingdon Press, 1995), 8:358.
47. Ibid., 357.

of Man," theologian Karl Barth insists on working from both directions; above and below, divine and human. In his doctrine of reconciliation he speaks of "the Lord who became Servant" and "the Servant who became Lord."[48] The divine condescension for the sake of human "uplifting" inextricably joins descent to ascent in the person of Jesus, the Christ. Incarnation means that God shares Jesus' human destiny of disparagement, rejection, isolation, and hiddenness. Thus the cross is no "alien element" in the divine life. The descent of God in Christ transvalues all values by favoring the weak and humble, not the high and mighty. Jesus' approach to established orders (family, Temple, political, economic) is genuinely revolutionary. He lives for humanity as Savior, not against humanity as Judge.[49]

In this story the ascent to the heights of the mountain and "peak" experiences of encounter with God is followed by descent into suffering and service in the valley of need where God's calling beckons. Ascent and descent are inextricably bound for the followers of Jesus, just as they were for him.

In response to the announcement, "This is my Son, the Beloved, listen to him," the disciples fall to the ground overcome by fear. Again do not be afraid. See 14:22–23. In the face of their fears Jesus comes to them and touches them. He says, as he has said before (14:22–23) and will say again (28:5), "do not be afraid." With this assuring word, they are called to "get up," and they follow Jesus into the valley below.

17:14–23
"If you have faith the size of a mustard seed . . ."

As Jesus and the disciples come down from the mountain, they are met at its foot by the crowds and their needs. The father of a boy with epilepsy presents himself and reports that the disciples, presumably the ones whom Jesus had left in the valley, could not heal him. It would appear that even as the time of the disciple's preparation for

---

48. Karl Barth, *Church Dogmatics*, IV/4, *The Christian Life*, ed. G. W. Bromiley and T. F. Torrance (Edinburgh: T. & T. Clark, 1936–1962), chap. 14.
49. Geoffrey Bromiley, *Introduction to the Theology of Karl Barth* (Grand Rapids: Eerdmans, 1979) 201.

ministry is drawing to a close, they are still not ready for the work to which they are called. Jesus' rebuke is stern, "You faithless and perverse generation, how much longer must I be with you? How much longer must I put up with you?" (17:17).

This outburst may provide yet another parallel to the Moses story. In the Exodus story, while Moses was away receiving the law on Mt. Sinai, the people left behind had grown impatient with this God of wilderness wandering—this amorphous, fire by night and cloud by day God. They decided on a more organized and tangible program of spirituality; so they constructed an idol. When Moses came down from the mountain that is what met him at its base. His response was similar: "Moses' anger burned hot, and he threw the tablets from his hands and broke them at the foot of the mountain" (Exod. 32:19–20).

When the disciples wonder about their inability to heal, there comes once again the honest appraisal: that they have "little faith" (6:30; 8:26; 14:31; 16:8). The encouraging word that follows is that it only takes a "little" faith—the size of a grain of mustard seed. The time for preparation is almost over. This time Jesus healed the boy himself. What about the next time? Will they be ready for what lies ahead?

This event is followed by the second of three passion predictions (16:21; 20:17–19). Again the term *paradidomi* is used. Jesus is going to be "handed over," "delivered up." The response of the disciples is not unlike Peter's response to the first passion prediction: "they were greatly distressed" (17:23).

17:24–27
Paying Taxes without Paying Tribute

The incident following the descent from the mountain is yet another clash with authorities, this time over the "Temple tax." This is a story that only Matthew tells. The matter is more complex than is apparent in these few verses due to the double setting of the story in two circumstances that were decidedly different as to the matter of the Temple tax. On the one hand, it is set in the story line during the life of Jesus, which places it before the destruction of the Temple in 70 CE. On the other hand, there is the setting of Matthew's writing. He is addressing a community that stands on the other side of the destruction of the Temple. Taking each setting in turn may illumine the story.

In Jesus' own time it was customary to pay the diadrachma (Greek the two-drachma coin) equivalent to a half shekel for support of the Temple as prescribed in Exodus 30:11–16. It was an expression of solidarity; even Jews in the diaspora paid the Temple tax. There was, however, a controversy over who should pay and how often. Pharisees were the most vigilant on the matter and would likely have been the ones to raise the challenge for Jesus and his disciples. The Pharisees believed that every male over nineteen should pay this Temple tax every year. Sadducees believed it should be voluntary and that priests should be exempt. The Qumran community understood it as a onetime only contribution.[50] In this setting, Jesus' response seems to signify that, just as earthly kings do not tax their own children, the "children of God" owe no "tax." All the same, in order not to give offense to others in the community who see this as an obligation (*skandalisomēn*, "cause to stumble"), they will pay the tax. Even though "the children are free," the exercise of freedom is within the frame of care for others inside and outside the community. This message has the effect of leading into the next chapter, which will discuss life together in the new community.

The passage might be heard altogether differently by Matthew's own community in their situation after the destruction of the Temple. It was no longer a question of a "Temple" tax or of Jewish solidarity. The Romans had formed an imperial treasury (the *fiscus Judaicus*) to oversee a continued appropriation of what had been the Temple tax for a new purpose. These funds were "co-opted to rebuild and sustain" the Temple of Jupiter in Rome.[51] The continuing imposition of this tax defined Jews and their God as defeated and "reminded Jews of Roman political, military, economic and religious sovereignty and superiority sanctioned by Jupiter."[52] Living

---

50. Boring, *The New Interpreter's Bible*, 8:371.
51. Carter, *Matthew and the Margins*, 357.
52. Ibid.

under Roman rule as they did, paying the tax was not really optional for Jews—including Matthew's Jewish-Christian community. Not to pay would be a punishable act of rebellion. The next moment in the story will significantly reframe the meaning of paying this tax, however.

The episode with the fish that delivers the coin for the tax proclaims God's sovereignty instead. All the fish stories in Matthew's Gospel (7:10; 14:13–21; 15:32–39) are stories of God's unexpected provision. This is in contradiction to the common wisdom that the emperor ruled over not only peoples and nations but also the fish and the sea. "Every rare and beautiful thing in the wide ocean—belongs to the imperial treasury."[53] In Matthew's Gospel, however, the sea obeys Jesus' command (8:23–27; 14:22–33) and the fish are "subject to God's sovereignty not Rome's."[54] Whereas Rome imposed the tax to subjugate and humiliate the people, the story of the fish that delivered the coin asserts that even the tax is "subject to God's power and sovereignty."[55] Paying the tax is no "tribute" to Rome's sovereignty but a subversion of it. The practice does not concede Rome's sovereignty.

Here again Matthew's Gospel shows Jesus teaching an alternative approach for dealing with oppressive powers; a path that is neither violent resistance nor complicity. This is the pattern he taught in the Sermon on the Mount (5:38–42). For Matthew's community, set in the time after the destruction of the Temple, this story is a reassuring reminder. This "taxing" Roman power, "which crucified Jesus and which must be taken seriously as a daily reality, is not the final or determinative reality. God's sovereignty will triumph."[56]

53. Ibid., 359.
54. Ibid.
55. Ibid., 360.
56. Ibid.

18:1–35

Teaching: The New Community

Chapter 18 begins the fourth teaching block in Matthew. This discourse is about the new community that is being formed. In chapters 14–17, Jesus has been preparing his disciples for ministry, gathering and instructing them. Others have rejected, opposed, or sought to domesticate Jesus. Still others have followed along in hopes of healing or feeding. The disciples stand out, not because they are perfect but because—frail and fallible though they be—they follow and are "on the way" to understanding. This discourse is directed to them (v. 1) as Jesus begins to form them into the new community that Matthew calls "the church." Of all the Gospels, Matthew alone speaks explicitly of the church (16:18; 17:18; 18:15, 17, 21). This teaching block is about how to be the church and makes it clear that discipleship is not worked out in splendid isolation but in life together. What kind of community is the church? How are they to conduct their life together? Chapter 18 unfolds a distinctive vision. This new community is to be a place where the least are the greatest and the "little ones" come first and the lost get found. It will never be a perfect community; even in this first reference to the church the reader discerns that it has "issues." Nevertheless, the church is to be a community where both accountability and forgiveness are practiced. These are not mutually exclusive but in fact require one another, as the teaching in this passage will make clear.

18:1–14

A Community That Cares for the Least, the Little, and the Lost

In the cultural context of Matthew's writing, "greatness" was a function of things like wealth, education, social status, lineage, and power exercised over others. Apparently the disciples have an inkling that these are not to be the measures of greatness in the new community. They want to know "who is the greatest" under the reign of God. Jesus' response makes clear that indeed there is a fundamental opposition between greatness as defined under the reign of the empire and greatness under the reign of God. In an inversion of the empire's values, the least are the greatest, the "little ones" come first, and the lost get found.

A dramatic reversal is conveyed by what Jesus does. In answer to the question "who is the greatest?" Jesus draws a child into their midst. Contemporary readers, working out of a context where children are viewed differently, forget how shocking Jesus' response would be. In Mediterranean culture of his day, however, children were without status or power, treated more like property and never held up as examples of anything.[1] Their social location was one of "insignificance, marked by powerlessness and marginality,"[2] and now the disciples are being invited to become like them. Surely this comes as an unwelcome invitation; this is anything but greatness as their culture defines it.

Jesus' response upsets things for the disciples in yet another way. They are assuming they are "in" and it is just a question of what their status will be. Jesus challenges all that when he says, to "get in" they need to "change" and become like children. The Greek term *straphete* implies conversion, turning around.[3] They are invited to cast their lot with the least and the lowliest. Solidarity with them means letting go of the concern for status and greatness they have raised.

---

1. Eugene Boring, *The New Interpreter's Bible: New Testament Articles, Matthew, Mark* (Nashville: Abingdon Press, 1995), 8:374.
2. Warren Carter, *Matthew and the Margins: A Socio-Political and Religious Reading* (Sheffield, England: Sheffield Academic Press, 2000), 366.
3. Donald Senior, *Abingdon New Testament Commentaries: Matthew* (Nashville: Abingdon Press, 1998), 206.

This will mean letting go altogether the concern for status they have just articulated.

Nevertheless, it is the humble place that Jesus occupies (11:29) and the one that he commends as blessed (5:5). He so identifies with the least and the lowly that he can say, "Whoever welcomes one such child in my name welcomes me." Jesus' identity with the weak and the vulnerable is a continuing theme in Matthew and in chapter 25 becomes the test by which all are judged (25:31–46).

Cultural assumptions about greatness are being overturned for those who would live in the reign of God. In this upside-down reorientation, "All who exalt themselves will be humbled, and all who humble themselves will be exalted" (23:12) as the high and mighty are brought down and those of low degree are lifted up.

Verse six shifts a bit to talk about careful treatment of the "little ones [Greek *mikrōn*, 18:6, 10, 14] who believe in me." This turns the attention more explicitly to the conduct of life within the community of faith. Who are the "little ones" in the community of faith? The text allows different meanings depending on whether it is read in terms of what precedes or in terms of what follows.

What precedes is the discussion regarding "greatness" and may indicate that these verses are about the problem of differentiated status in the community of faith. The disciples, as leaders in the church, are not to "look down on" (v. 10 NIV) the "little ones." All are brothers and sisters together in the new community. Jesus elsewhere makes objection to the apparent eagerness of religious leaders among the scribes and Pharisees for the "place of honor" (23:1–11). He takes care to convey that members of the new community are on equal footing. As he says, "You are not to be called rabbi, for you have one teacher and you are all students." The designation "rabbi," in fact, is sometimes translated "my great one," and the disciples have been asking "who is the greatest." Such a concern takes on the cast of an "appetite for prominence"[4] that Jesus has rejected. The caution amounts to a renunciation of hierarchy in the life of the church.

Another angle of vision is achieved when we read the segment in terms of what follows and the risk that "little ones" may stray (v.

---

4. Douglas R. A. Hare, *Matthew*, Interpretation: A Bible Commentary for Teaching and Preaching (Louisville, KY: Westminster/John Knox Press, 1992), 208.

12–14). Perhaps the reference is to those members of the church who are weaker in faith and more easily scandalized (*skandal-izo*, "made to stumble"). The disciples as church leaders must take care not to put any obstacle in their path. Furthermore, these leaders should not be so sure that they themselves cannot get tripped up. They must remove whatever causes them to stumble. Verses 6 and 8–9 caution rather graphically about stumbling blocks. While these cautions may be read as rhetorical hyperbole, they convey the urgency of the matter.

Whether these persons are "little ones" in terms of their marginal place in society or in terms of their weaker faith, the disciples are not to "look down on" them (v. 10 NIV). They in fact receive God's particular care. God's highest angels watch over them (v. 10). According to tradition there were angels who watched over people and nations and through them God's care and purview were exercised.[5] The most exalted angels were the ones who beheld God's face. These angels are the ones assigned to the "little ones." Pride of place is thereby given to those who "have no place" in terms of status.

The church is to be a community where the least are greatest and the little ones come first. It is also a place where the "lost" get found. Jesus tells a story of an extraordinary shepherd who goes to extremes to seek out one lost sheep. The shepherd/sheep image has real prominence in Matthew (2:6; 7:15; 9:36;10:6, 16; 12:11–12; 15:24; 18:12; 25:32–33; 26:31). It is an interesting choice in some ways. It derives from Israel's nomadic period, but by the first century Jews in Palestine were settled and shepherds were marginal members of the lower class.[6] This image, which is a humble one in the context, becomes the metaphor conveying how God is with God's people. The choice makes a powerful statement in its own right. In this passage of instruction to the disciples who will be leaders in the church as to how they should be in relation to the "little ones," church leaders are to manifest humility and care, readiness to seek out any who stray.

They are not to be like the shepherds lambasted in Ezekiel 34:2–4:

---

5. Carter, *Matthew and the Margins*, 365.
6. Boring, *The New Interpreter's Bible*, 8:377.

Ah, you shepherds of Israel who have been feeding yourselves! Should not shepherds feed the sheep? You eat the fat, you clothe yourselves with the wool, you slaughter the fatlings; but you do not feed the sheep. You have not strengthened the weak, you have not healed the sick, you have not bound up the injured, you have not brought back the strayed, you have not sought the lost, but with force and harshness you have ruled them. So they were scattered, because there was no shepherd; and scattered, they became food for all the wild animals.

This chapter as a whole instructs church leaders to care for the vulnerable, preserve each and all from stumbling blocks, seek out those who stray, and exercise discipline in ways that show accountability and forgiveness. Their shepherding should be more like God's shepherding. "I myself will be the shepherd of my sheep, and I will make them lie down, says the Lord GOD. I will seek the lost, and I will bring back the strayed, and I will bind up the injured, and I will strengthen the weak, but the fat and the strong I will destroy. I will feed them with justice" (Ezek. 34:15–16).

18:15–35
A Community of Accountability and Forgiveness

Now the chapter turns to matters of church discipline and calls, within the space of a few verses, for both accountability and forgiveness. On the face of it, these seem to be in opposition to one another, with accountability making demands and forgiveness issuing grace. It will become increasingly clear, however, that in the new community they require one another, and each has unexpected aspects of the other. Accountability (vv. 15–20) may entail gracious acts of truth-telling correction that aim to set things right, restoring both individuals and the community. Forgiveness places a claim on our lives, demanding that we extend to others the grace that we ourselves have received (vv. 16–35).

Accountability is essential to the new community. Life in community is not easy. Neither the church as a whole nor the individuals within it are perfect. There is sometimes a great distance between what we profess and how we live. Alfred North Whitehead once remarked that the only problem with Christians is that they do not follow Jesus. Jesus lived a life of "higher righteousness" (5:21–48) based upon the principle of love and calls his followers to do the same. It behooves the church to hold itself accountable to this calling and put some energy into closing the distance between the gospel we preach and the lives we live.

Chapter 18 proposes a pattern aimed at personal and communal accountability. The pattern has precedent in Jewish law and practice. The private rebuke is advocated by Leviticus 19:17. The calling in of witnesses is exemplified in Deuteronomy 19:15. Holding a hearing before the entire assembly is a practice from the Qumran community.[7] The graduated approach of this sequence of conversations holds some safeguards for the offender and for the community. The community is safeguarded by having a process for addressing serious breaches. The offender is guarded against unnecessary humiliation before others by the initial private conversation and opportunity for reconciliation. Opportunity for restoration is offered again in the calling of witnesses before the matter becomes public. Furthermore, the offender is protected from any hasty action taken by one person or by the two or three witnesses by provision for a hearing before the full assembly.

Even though the process advocated here is reasonable and holds safeguards, this is still a difficult passage. Who is to judge? No one wants to be a "meddling busy body." In an individualistic society, one's life is entirely one's own business. Being the church changes things. We become one family, brothers and sisters together. The image of being "one body" in Christ (1 Cor. 12) may make it even clearer that what happens with one affects all. We belong to one another irrevocably—even when we do not want to. In the new community our lives are no longer our own, as we belong to God and to one another.

In the new community, members have to find an alternative to each one going their own way. Life together requires accountability

7. Senior, *Abingdon New Testament Commentaries,* 209.

for the good of each and the good of all. There are occasions for speaking the truth in love—one forgiven sinner to another—in an attitude of humility and expectation of mutuality. Correction can be a gracious act that seeks the restoration of the brother or sister and the integrity of the community. Sometimes we talk one another back from the edge of self-destruction, down from the ledge in times of despair, back to the path in times of disorientation. This happens where people love one another. And the new community is to be a place where the love of God is taught and lived.

> Nothing can be more cruel than the leniency which abandons others to their sin. Nothing can be more compassionate than the severe reprimand which calls another Christian in one's community back from the path of sin.
>
> Dietrich Bonhoeffer, *Life Together* (1938), Dietrich Bonhoeffer's Works, English Edition, Vol. 5, (Minneapolis: Augsburg Fortress, 2000), 105.

Sometimes the matter is so serious that persons are being hurt and the health and well-being of the community is at stake. It is possible that the text has such situations in view. The "against you" in verse 15 does not appear in the most reliable manuscripts and is thought to be a later addition. It seems that the reference is not to a personal affront but to something more damaging to the community. The church must care enough to declare some things out of bounds. One thinks, for example, of sexual misconduct of church leaders and how damaging that is to the victims and to the community as a whole. There must be processes that protect. One thinks also of the excommunication of some churches in South Africa that were providing a theological justification of apartheid declaration with a declaration of statis confessionis (that the integrity of the church's proclamation of the gospel was at stake in this matter).

In these moments it is especially clear how important it is for the church to be a community of accountability. The responsibility for "binding and loosing" that is earlier given to Peter is now given to the church as a whole (18:18). In this context it is about church discipline as the church is assembled (19–20) in a process of discernment and deliberation. The new community takes responsibility for the well-being of the community as a whole and for all of its members. The promise of Jesus' presence (18:20) is given for the church in its difficult processes of deliberation over binding and loosing.

The verse admits of a wider interpretation as well. "For where two or three are gathered in my name, I am there among them" (18:20) calls to mind the rabbinic sayings about the shekinah (divine presence) in the midst of the community. "If two sit together and the words of the law [are spoken] between them, the Divine Presence rests between them."[8] The promise of presence that appears here is central also to the beginning and ending of the book of Matthew. In the birth narrative the name "Emmanuel" means "God with us" (1:23). The promise appears again after the resurrection in the final verse of the Gospel, "I am with you always" (28:20).

As the reader's attention transitions from a discussion of accountability to a discussion of forgiveness, a mediating note needs sounding. Commentators puzzle over the instruction that the offender who will not even listen to the whole church should "be to you as a Gentile and a tax collector." This seems an odd saying given Jesus' known association with tax collectors and his ministry to Gentiles along the way. In other places in Matthew these terms are code words for nonbelievers and outsiders (5:47; 6:7; 9:10; 10:18; 11:19; 20:19). Perhaps the best understanding is that the ostracized one is now like one who is on the outside and in need of conversion and incorporation into the community. The exclusion is not the last word or the end of care for this one. While the community must protect its members and its integrity, it may still extend care and hope for restoration—just as the extraordinary shepherd seeks after the one who strays. The goal of this discipline is reorientation, reconciliation, and restoration to the community. Judgment is ordered toward redemption because it is not God's will that even one be lost.

Peter poses the question of "how often" he should forgive a member of the church who sins against him and he makes a generous proposal of forgiving seven times. This is already magnanimous, but Jesus takes the matter over the top, suggesting "seventy-seven times." Seventy-seven times may allude to Genesis 4:24 as a reversal

8. Ibid., 210.

of Lamech's threat of avenging himself seventy-seven times. It signaled extreme and unlimited vengeance-taking. Jesus' saying turns Lamech's vengeance on its head, and, by contrast, advocates unlimited forgiveness.

It is, *de facto*, a complete renunciation of vengeance.

Jesus' response may imply that if Peter is counting, he has not yet understood about forgiveness. Jesus tells a parable to illustrate the absurdity of one who has been forgiven so much failing to forgive in turn. This parable of the "forgiven but unforgiving"[9] slave, found only in Matthew, brings home the point. The slave owes the astronomical sum of ten thousand talents. A single talent represented the wages of a manual laborer for fifteen years,[10] and ten thousand was in fact the highest denomination in ancient accounting.[11] It was a sum that the slave could not possibly repay—whatever he may have promised in his desperation. This slave with the astronomical, unrepayable debt receives astonishingly gracious forgiveness from the king. Yet, when the tables are turned, and the slave has a chance to be gracious, he seems to know nothing of grace. A fellow slave owes him one hundred denarii, approximately one hundred days' wages. Compared with ten thousand talents it is a small and fully repayable sum. When his debtor makes the very same plea he made to the king, the response is not forgiveness but imprisonment and torture. The hearer's likely response is outrage: "That's just wrong!" The implication is that no one should be like this ungrateful debtor.

> Our actions are irreversible . . . and the urge for vengeance seems irrepressible . . . The only way out . . . is through forgiveness . . . A genuinely free act which does not merely react, forgiveness breaks the power of the remembered past . . . and so makes the spiral of vengeance grind to a halt.
>
> Miroslav Volf, *Exclusion and Embrace: A Theological Exploration of Identity, Otherness, and Reconciliation* (Nashville: Abingdon Press, 1996), 121.

The parable itself makes its point and should probably not be reduced to a simple allegory where the king equals God in a point by

9. Carter, *Matthew and the Margins*, 370.
10. Boring, *The New Interpreter's Bible*, 8:382.
11. Senior, *Abingdon New Testament Commentaries*, 211.

point comparison with this king who starts with grace but finishes with torture. Jesus is telling a story about a Gentile tyrant and several features mark it as such: (1) the slave manages a vast sum of money (which indicates tax revenue and its management); (2) the king is worshiped by the servant (v. 26), which would not have been the practice for a Jew; (3) Jewish law would have prohibited selling the family into slavery; (4) a person could be imprisoned for debt but not tortured. The point is not that God is like this tyrant but that people who have received grace should extend it to others. By contrast with this tyrant, God desires that none should perish (18:14).

> God's forgiveness . . . is a transforming power which mandates a forgiving way of life.
>
> Carter, *Matthew and the Margins*, 375.

It is only possible to be unforgiving if one is either forgetful or ungrateful. Awareness of the grace we have received allows us to be gracious and to lay aside the compulsion to seek vengeance. It is common knowledge that people who are hurt are prone to respond in kind. Psychologists describe a "mysterious mimesis," in which victims of aggression imitate their aggressors. It is unconscious and perhaps instinctive.[12] One thinks of all the occasions where hurt gets turned to hate. While injustice and injury must be addressed—not simply ignored or passively endured—forgiveness transforms all concerned. Forgiveness is rather part of the effort to stop the spiral of reprisals, rehabilitate the other, and empower change in the other.[13] A new way is opened up when we return no one evil for evil (Rom. 12:17).

Conclusion

Jesus has been instructing the disciples concerning the new community that he has been gathering and preparing for ministry. This new community, the church, is genuinely different, even countercultural

---

12. José A. Pagola, *The Way Opened Up by Jesus: A Commentary on the Gospel of Matthew* (Miami, FL: Convivium Press, 2012), 177.
13. Ibid., 178.

to the prevailing norms. It is a place where the least is the greatest, the little ones come first, and the lost get found. It is a place that does not choose between accountability and forgiveness, but practices both together for the good of each and the good of all and in all under the sheltering horizon of the astonishing grace they have received.

FURTHER REFLECTIONS
On Being the Church

In the Gospel of Matthew a vision of a new community is unfolding. Matthew calls it "the church." It is to be a community that follows in the way of Jesus Christ, living into the reign of God and the "higher righteousness" that Jesus teaches through love of God and neighbor (22:37–39). On this basis relationships are reordered and resources are reallocated. This is a community of dramatic reversals where the least are the greatest, the "little ones" come first, and the lost get found. The followers of Jesus are in ministry with those at the margins—the sick, the ritually "unclean," Gentiles and foreigners, women and children, sinners and tax collectors. People who are usually excluded are all included. The whole system of "insiders" and "outsiders" is disregarded.

Choosing the reign of God over imperial reign leads to very different power arrangements. While it would be anachronistic to read the Gospel of Matthew as if it were a text of twenty-first-century liberation theology, there is much here that resonates with those impulses. Power relations are radically reconstructed in the new community. Patriarchal structures in the human community are subverted when there is but one "father" (who is God). Human hierarchies are undercut when there is but one "Lord" (who is Jesus the Christ). All other authorities are relativized when "all authority in heaven and on earth" is given to him (28:18). Love of God and neighbor calls forth a new way of being in the world that breaks the logic of the old order. The "great ones" serve.

Contemporary theologians use a variety of approaches to envision the church in its distinctiveness. A sampling must suffice.

Peter Hodgson speaks of the church as a "transfigured mode of human community." It is a sign and foretaste of the reign of God in our midst. As such, it will be "a community in which privatistic, provincial, and hierarchical modes of existence are challenged and are being overcome and in which is fragmentarily actualized a universal reconciling love that liberates from sin and death, alienation and oppression."[14] Letty Russell reflects upon the sense in which the church may be a "household of freedom" providing a "clearing for freedom within the domain of oppression."[15] Walter Brueggemann speaks of how the church should be a community of "alterative consciousness." "The task of prophetic ministry is to nurture, nourish, and evoke a consciousness and perception alternative to the consciousness and perception of the dominant culture around us."[16] Each of these voices illumines the distinctiveness of the new community that is the church.

Another approach to understanding the nature and calling of the church is to revisit the traditional four marks of the church as expressed in the Nicene Creed. The church is "one, holy, catholic and apostolic." What do these marks of the church signify in our day? How are they a living out of the distinctive vision expressed in the Gospel of Matthew? A few brief notes may hint at the possibilities.

The unity of the church is sometimes difficult to articulate in our day, given the many divisions in the church. Theologically, we affirm that we are one in Christ. "Our unity is a gift of God that we did not create and cannot destroy. Divisions in our life together obscure our unity and hamper our witness. The truth of our history is that realizations of the unity that is ours in Christ have been partial and fragmentary. Unity is not only God's gift but also God's calling."[17] We work in ecumenical endeavors to make more visible the God-given unity that is ours in Christ. Unity, when it is achieved, is not uniformity. It is a "pluriform richness" lived out in reconciled diversity.

---

14. Peter Hodgson, *Revisioning the Church: Ecclesial Freedom in the New Paradigm* (Philadelphia: Fortress, 1988), 102–4.
15. Letty Russell, *Authority in Feminist Theology: Household of Freedom* (Philadelphia: Westminster Press, 1987), 26.
16. Walter Brueggemann, *Prophetic Imagination* (Minneapolis: Fortress, 1983), 13.
17. "Communion: On Being the Church," final report of the World Communion of Reformed Churches and the Lutheran World Federation, Joint Lutheran-Reformed Commission.

In the Gospel of Matthew we see a reconsideration of the patterns of insiders and outsiders. Inclusion and diversity characterize the new community as the old boundary lines drawn on the basis of ritual purity, culture, status, race, and nationality are crossed over. In the new community divisions and exclusions on these grounds are delegitimized. Leonardo Boff has suggested that today our unity might be expressed in terms of "solidarity."

Like church unity, the "holiness" of the church also seems contradicted in church practice. It is apparent to all that the church does not fully exemplify the "higher righteousness" to which Jesus calls his followers. It does not possess holiness as sinlessness. If the church may be said to be "holy" then it is holy on some other basis. Perhaps "holiness" is best understood in terms of the presence and activity of the Spirit of Christ in the church's life and ministry. The promise of Christ's presence is not conditional upon the righteousness of the church. "For where two or three are gathered in my name, I am among them" (18:20). His Spirit is with us and acts on us and in us and through us and *in spite of us*. Holiness is grounded in the holiness of the Spirit in our midst. This kind of holiness is a gift and not a given. In Matthew's Gospel the injunction to "be perfect" (5:48; 19:21) carries the connotation of "wholeness." It can be said that—by the grace of God—the work of "making whole" does continue to happen in the church.

The catholicity of the church simply means its "universality." The church includes churches all around the world and down the years. Hans Küng has suggested that if we return to the original signification of the term (Greek *halos,* "whole"; "entire") we could identify catholicity with ecumenicity. "Ecumenical" carries the meaning of "the whole inhabited earth."[18] Jürgen Moltmann adds to this perspective by including "catholicity" in terms of the church's identity and integrity.[19]

Apostolicity has to do with the church's faithfulness to the apostolic witness. In some churches the sign of apostolicity is located in the "apostolic succession." This sign is given in the practice of ordination where, with prayer and invocation of the Spirit, there is a

---

18. Hans Küng, *The Church* (New York: Image Books, 1976), 391.
19. Jürgen Moltmann, *The Church in the Power of the Spirit* (Philadelphia: Fortress, 1977).

laying on of hands. Churches differ as to the import of there being an unbroken line of succession from the apostles forward. For most Protestants, this is not emphasized. Most agree that apostolicity is not something guaranteed or magically conferred by this practice of ordination in the laying on of hands. These practices are signs, but the thing signified is a matter of faith and life. Furthermore, apostolicity is not limited to our orders of ministry. As Roman Catholic theologian Hans Küng has pointed out, it is the whole church (and not just those in ordained ministries) who stand in the apostolic succession and have the responsibility of carrying forward the apostolic witness.

To these four classical "marks of the church" (unity, holiness, catholicity, and apostolicity) the Reformers added two "notes." As Calvin expressed them, "Wherever we see the Word of God purely preached and heard, and the sacraments administered according to Christ's institution, there, it is not to be doubted, a church of God exists."[20] In this way, even if the "marks" of the church are not expressed in their fullness, one may recognize a "church" by these practices that, among other things, nurture a greater fullness of these marks that are of the essence of the church.

In considering the classical marks of the church it becomes obvious that the church's "existence" as lived is often in tension with its calling or "essence." Even this brief review makes clear that we "have this treasure in earthen vessels" (2 Cor. 4:7). There is an "in spite of" quality to our affirmations here: the church is united in spite of its divisions; holy in spite of its sinfulness; universal in spite of its particularity and parochialism; and apostolic in spite of failure in its faithfulness to the apostolic witness. The mixed character of the church—its "wheat and weeds" growing together quality—is apparent at every turn (Matt. 13:24–30). Calvin warned that we cannot simply equate the "visible church" with the "true church" and that we also should not presume to judge who is "in" and who is "out." God alone judges. Following Augustine, Calvin put it this way, "there are many sheep without, and many wolves are within."[21]

---

20. John Calvin, *Institutes of the Christian Religion* 4.1.9; ed. John T. McNeill, trans. Ford Lewis Battles, LCC (Philadelphia: Westminster Press, 1960), 2:1023..
21. Ibid., 4.1.8.

This "mixed" quality of "wheat and weeds together" or "sheep and wolves" is something that runs not so much between us as within each one of us.

Although the church is not perfect, it is not optional for Christian faith and life. As Calvin put it, "the church is the mother of all believers" and "there is no other way to enter into life unless this mother conceive us in her womb, give us birth, nourish us at her breast, and lastly, unless she keep us under her care and guidance."[22] Theologically, the church is not a "voluntary organization." Christian faith is not something we think up on our own and afterwards opt to associate with like-minded individuals. Faith comes to us already mediated in community—a community of word and sacrament with texts and practices that form faith in us and us in faith. It is a place where the presence of Christ is encountered, "For where two or three are gathered in my name, I am there among them" (18:20). It is a community of belonging. In being joined to Christ we are joined to one another. This is our reality even when we are not "like-minded" or are not at all like one another or may not even like one another.

In the Gospel of Matthew the followers of Jesus become a "new family" of shared commitment that goes deeper than even biological kinship (12:48–50). "Family" has been one way of understanding what the church is for its members. There is a person-forming work of the church that is very much like what happens by nurturing in a family. A family is a "humanizing school" where we learn "how to share and how to work together and how to take care of one another. A healthy family has a way of smoothing out our rough edges by making us rub up against each other like tumbling pebbles in a jar ... We learn that we cannot have everything our own way."[23]

This kind of community is counter cultural in a context where individualism trumps community and concern for autonomy trumps concern for common good. As Larry Rasmussen[24] has pointed out, our context is almost anticommunity. The (centrifugal) forces that

---

22. Ibid., 4.1.4.
23. Barbara Brown Taylor, *The Seeds of Heaven: Sermons on the Gospel of Matthew* (Louisville, KY: Westminster John Knox Press, 2004), 84.
24. Larry Rasmussen, *Moral Fragments and Moral Community* (Minneapolis: Augsburg, 1993).

drive us apart seem to be stronger than the (centripetal) forces that might keep us all in motion around a common center (such as concern for the common good). In such a setting, the church, as a community of care and belonging, has a distinctive gift to offer. The church may be both a model and a force for community in a society characterized by fragmentation and alienation. The church may exemplify commitment to the common good and may provide a context for moral discourse and discernment.

The vision of "the beloved community" articulated by Martin Luther King Jr. holds promise as a contemporary image of what the church is called to be and what—at its best—it may offer to the wider society. He said of the nonviolent resistance in the civil rights movement that, "The end is redemption and reconciliation. The aftermath of non-violence is the creation of the beloved community . . . "[25] In a context of fragmentation and alienation, the church can be a force for community. In a place where difference leads to conflict, the church can be a sanctuary, a sacred space where issues can be deliberated in a community of moral discernment. In a context of violence and oppression, the church can be a community of peacemakers and justice seekers, a place of both forgiveness and accountability (Matt. 18:15–35).

In addition to the anti-community characteristic of our context, another reality that the church faces is its "disestablishment." The church is no longer at the center of power and influence. This is not necessarily a bad thing. In this way it is more like the church in Matthew's time, which lived at the margins as a community of the "little ones." Even without status or power the church may nevertheless dare to "cast our lot" with those who resist the forces of destruction and dehumanization in the world and who continue to affirm life in the midst of systematic denials of life. Our situation is something like that described by Adrienne Rich, who spoke of how her heart was moved by all that she could not save. In the face of all the destruction she nevertheless commits herself,

> I have to cast my lot with those
> who age after age, perversely,

25. Martin Luther King Jr., *Stride toward Freedom* (San Francisco: Harper and Row, 1958), 102.

> and with no extraordinary power
> reconstitute the world.[26]

The church is a community of memory. As Michael Welker has pointed out, there is a culture shaping power to memory. Not only does it offer a shared past, but it also shapes present experience and the expected future. This has both a stabilizing and dynamizing effect. The canon of Scripture, for example, is a vehicle of memory that is in some sense fixed but is also alive to ongoing interpretation in the lived experience of the community as it gathers around the word.[27] The church is a community shaped by memory of the Gospel message and the Christ event to which it bears witness. This memory places a calling on the church's "life together" and its mission in the world. The church remembers, represents, and reenacts. In doing so it becomes a place where the "dangerous memory of Jesus Christ" is kept alive.

---

26. Adrienne Rich, "Natural Resources," in *The Dream of a Common Language: Poems 1974–1977* (London: Norton, 1993), 67.
27. Michael Welker, "Resurrection and Eternal Life," in *The End of the World and the Ends of God,* ed. John Polkinghorne and Michael Welker, 285 (Harrisburg, PA: Trinity Press, 2000).

19:1–22:46

Narrative: On the Way to Jerusalem Where the Conflict Intensifies

This is the fifth narrative section in the Gospel of Matthew. It continues the themes of chapter 18 as it explores further what it is to be the new community under the reign of God. The outlines traced stand in stark contrast to ordinary practices. Chapter 19 explores what life as the "family of God" entails, considering family matters like marriage and divorce, children, and celibacy. The disciples continue to follow and they struggle to understand. They still get hung up on the dramatic reversals the reign of God ushers in, especially the parts about the first being last and the last first. Jesus explains and re-explains with many stories and parables along the way to Jerusalem. With chapter 21, Jesus and the disciples enter Jerusalem. Jesus enters with humility but arrives with authority. The conflict that has been smoldering between Jesus and the scribes, Pharisees, chief priests, and Sadducees erupts in Jerusalem. The conflict intensifies with the cleansing of the Temple. Jesus deftly defeats the challenges of his opponents as they try to trip him up with trick questions. He relates a number of stories with not so subtle unfavorable representations of the religious leadership.

Thematically the Gospel turned toward Jerusalem already in 16:21 as Jesus, "from that time on," began to show the disciples that he must go to Jerusalem. Now in 19:1 Jesus begins actual travel in that direction. Matthew's Gospel has a geographical progression in three decisive movements: (1) from Judea where Jesus is born and baptized to "Galilee of the Gentiles" where he calls the disciples, conducts his ministry, and begins forming the new community; (2) from Galilee to Judea where he will be betrayed, arrested, mocked, flogged, and crucified; and (3) from Judea to Galilee once again when he is raised on the third day.

19:1–22

Family Matters Reconsidered in the New Community

Jesus continues instructing his disciples as they make progress toward Jerusalem. Jesus' teaching suggests a reordering of relationships and a reallocation of resources in the new community of his followers. Elements included in chapter 19 include "an emphasis upon more egalitarian relationships and the use of marginal identities as images of disciples (eunuchs, children, the poor, slaves)."[1] This new community is clearly countercultural to the hierarchical, patriarchal patterns of the dominant culture.

Earlier in the Gospel, the prospect of disruption of families and the possibility that one might have to choose between family and faith arises (10:32–42). Faithfulness to the reign of God takes priority over all else—even family ties. Chapter 12 even suggests that followers of Jesus are part of a new family "where the ties are closer and more demanding than natural family ties."[2] He points to his disciples and says, "Here are my mother and my brothers. For whoever does the will of my Father in heaven is my brother and sister and mother." Jesus' response to Peter suggests that many of his followers have left their homes and families and fields (19:20). The present chapter continues reconsideration of family relations with more particular questions in view. Jesus will speak to the matter of marriage, divorce, celibacy, and the place of children in the new community. In every case his teaching entails a reordering of relationships.

It is the Pharisees who pose the question to Jesus, "Is it lawful for a man to divorce his wife for any cause?" Regarding the expectations behind the question, Warren Carter notes that "the Pharisees posit a husband's 'natural right' to exercise unrestricted male power

---

1. Warren Carter, *Matthew and the Margins: A Socio-Political and Religious Reading* (Sheffield, England: Sheffield Academic Press, 2000), 407.
2. Eugene Boring, *The New Interpreter's Bible: New Testament Articles, Matthew, Mark* (Nashville: Abingdon Press, 1995), 8:262.

over his inferior, submissive, obedient, children-producing, home-focused wife in a patriarchal household."[3] The question itself is a male-centered question regarding what a man can do. In the wider Greco-Roman world of the time, divorce for any reason was seen as legitimate. Some of the reasons recorded from that time include (but are not limited to) a woman's stealing, loss of looks, drunkenness, unpleasant temperament, arguments with her mother-in-law, sickness, and adultery.[4] The practice in Judaism was not this loose. If Jesus follows the stricter reading within his tradition, it will be an unpopular position. The hostile intent of the Pharisees is evident in this test question.

Jesus will in fact follow the stricter reading from his own Jewish heritage and will take it in a new direction. Interpretation of this text and similar ones has been important in feminist scholarship. Kathleen Corley claims that Matthew is both the "most Jewish" and the "most egalitarian" Gospel.[5] Her work has helped to correct the practice of interpreting everything about the Gospel that reflects patriarchal and hierarchical patterns as an inheritance from Judaism and everything that moves in an egalitarian direction as unique to Jesus. This is not a fair reading. Jesus is working within his own tradition, and as the authoritative interpreter of the law, here as elsewhere, he will go to the heart of the matter.

Jesus does not answer in terms of what is legally allowable, but rather in terms of the divine intention for men and women in marriage to become as one flesh. The legal allowance for divorce for anything other than unchastity is not divinely intended but a result of a culpable hard-heartedness (19:8).

There has been much discussion concerning what the term translated "unchastity" (Greek *porneia*) implies. It could refer to some form of sexual misconduct (most likely adultery). Or it might refer to "marriage within the forbidden lines of blood relationship."[6] If it is the former, Jesus is simply following the strictest of rabbinical

---

3. Carter, *Matthew and the Margins*, 378.
4. Ibid., 379.
5. Kathleen Corley, *Private Women, Public Meals: Social Conflict in the Synoptic Tradition* (Peabody, MA: Hendrickson, 1993), 185–86.
6. Donald Senior, *Abingdon New Testament Commentaries: Matthew* (Nashville: Abingdon Press, 1998), 215.

teachings. If it is the latter, then Jesus is not really admitting an allowance for divorce since such marriages were understood to be invalid already.

The implication of Jesus' ruling on the question posed is that divorce on other grounds might be legal, but it is not right. The divine intention for permanence and mutuality conveyed in Jesus' answer subverts the ordinary patriarchal arrangements. Phillip Sigal notes three important implications for the status of women that come out of Jesus' response: By insisting that divorcing a faithful wife and marrying another constitutes adultery, Jesus rules out polygamy. In a context where women were the ones subject to charges of adultery, Jesus' ruling that the man would be committing adultery (against his first wife) challenges the double standard. Lastly, Jesus' invocation of Deuteronomy 24:1, if taken seriously, would protect women against arbitrary and frivolous divorce.[7] In fact, the Greek words of Matthew's text—using the masculine *anthrōpos* in verse 3 and in verse 6 again—make it clear that it is precisely the husband who is being instructed not to separate. The NRSV, in translating it with the generic, "let no one separate," misses the specificity of this instruction to husbands.[8] Jesus' answer to the Pharisees' hostile question constitutes a significant reordering of relationships.

The disciples are so unsettled by Jesus' stricter standards on the matter that they propose that it might be better not to marry at all (v. 10). They make a truly countercultural proposal here in a context where it was universally expected that one should marry and have children. That Jesus concurs with the disciples' conclusion is remarkable. Even more shocking is his employment of the startling image of eunuchs to speak of those who forgo marriage to better serve the reign of God. Jewish law forbade castration (Lev. 22:24; Deut. 23:1).[9] Eunuchs were excluded from worship (Deut. 23:1) and from the priesthood (Lev. 21:20). They were thought of by some as being "neither male nor female." Thus they stood outside the boundaries of all the "carefully defined and separated roles of

---

7. Phillip Sigal, *The Halakah of Jesus of Nazareth according to the Gospel of Matthew* (Lanham, MD: University Press of American, 1986), 83–118.

8. Boring, *The New Interpreter's Bible,* 8:386.

9. Senior, *Abingdon New Testament Commentaries,* 215.

male and female in patriarchal households." They were "permanent outsiders, dishonored, marginal figures often despised and socially alienated."[10] Jesus observes that this sort of existence (voluntary celibacy) is not "given" to everyone. Peter's question pertained to voluntary celibacy. Jesus' answer seems an affirmation of this lifestyle as a possible model for dedicated discipleship. Jesus thereby lays aside prevailing cultural expectations for marriage and children and allows an alternative identity for the disciples—one that is at the margins in their culture. Disciples, as the reader has already seen in earlier passages, are called to solidarity and ministry with those "at the margins."

This orientation is carried further in the next verses as disciples are urged to welcome children (19:13–15). The disciples demonstrate that they still need instruction in this regard. They are speaking "sternly" to those bringing their children to Jesus. He charges them, "Let the children come to me, and do not stop them; for it is to such as these that the kingdom of heaven belongs." Jesus welcomes the children and blesses them. In first century Mediterranean culture children were without status or power and very much at the margins of social and religious life. In fact, children did not participate in religious observances before the age of twelve, when they were thought to achieve adulthood. Even then, it was only males that were fully admitted. By contrast, in the new community forming around Jesus, the reign of God "belongs" to the children (v. 4).[11] It may be that in Matthew's faith community new practices are allowing more inclusive participation in corporate life. That women and children are mentioned explicitly in the stories of Jesus feeding the crowds may give evidence of more inclusive community practices.

Marriage and divorce, celibacy and children, are being reconsidered in a new light. Jesus illumines these socially prescribed and delimited arrangements in the light of the law of love and the reign of God that has come near. There is a breaking down of hierarchical, patriarchal arrangements as relationships are being reconsidered and those who were "at the margins" are given a new place in the community. In the next section of this chapter, issues of economics

10. Carter, *Matthew and the Margins*, 383.
11. Senior, *Abingdon New Testament Commentaries*, 217.

are reconsidered as well. There is an intimation that living in the reign of God may entail a reallocation of resources.

19:23–30

The Risks of Riches

Luke is commonly regarded as "the evangelist of the poor," but this overlooks the renunciation of possessions that runs as a prominent theme throughout Matthew's Gospel.[12] A few illustrations will suffice. The Sermon on the Mount (chaps. 5–7) pursues this theme in several ways. In the Lord's Prayer, for example, forgiving debts owed to us by others is assumed in the petition "Forgive us our debts as we forgive our debtors" (6:12). Only a few verses later there is a caution against laying up "treasures on earth" (6:19) and a declaration that one must choose between serving God and serving wealth (6:24). In what follows, the birds and lilies are commended as foregoing anxious striving and relying completely upon God's reliable providence (6:25–34). In the Missionary Discourse in chapter 10, the renunciation of possessions is advocated once again. The disciples are invited to adopt a voluntary poverty (10:9–14). The parables of the reign of God that appear in chapter 13 include the observation that the "lure of wealth" can choke out the word (13:22) and two illustrations of "selling all" for the reign of God (13:44–46). In chapter 16, Jesus warns his disciples that following him is a "losing" proposition. Paradoxically, they must lose their lives to find life. What would be the profit of gaining the whole world while forfeiting life (16:26)?

These teachings from earlier chapters have already established the risks of riches. Possessions have a way of becoming the object of inordinate valuation, anxious striving, and the heart's devotion. These texts pave the way to the hard saying Jesus will deliver in response to the rich young man.

The young man is a good man. By his own report he has kept all the commandments that Jesus enumerates from the Decalogue and

---

12. Ulrich Luz, *The Theology of the Gospel of Matthew*, New Testament Theology (Cambridge, UK: Cambridge University Press, 1995), 109.

he has loved his neighbor as well. Jesus responds, "If you wish to be perfect, go sell your possessions, and give the money to the poor and you will have treasure in heaven, then come, follow me." The word translated "perfect" is the Greek word *teleios*, which has the connotation of being "complete" or "whole." It is the same term used where Jesus enjoins, "Be perfect, therefore, as your heavenly Father is perfect" (5:48). To be perfect in this way is to be "whole-hearted" in one's devotion. Loving God and loving others as God does is the essence of the "higher righteousness" that Jesus preaches and exemplifies (5:21–48).

Jesus has already puts his finger on the problem with wealth when he says, "You cannot serve God and wealth" (6:24). The rich young man faces a hard choice; he must decide between his possessions and whole-hearted devotion to God. It is too hard and he goes away "grieving" (19:22). He is a man who cannot become what he wants to be, dragged down as he is by the weight of all his stuff. Apparently his "many possessions" have taken possession of him. Jesus warned about the enslaving power of wealth and the anxious striving it generates (6:19–35).

> Earthly possessions dazzle our eyes and delude us into thinking that they can provide security and freedom from anxiety. Yet all the time they are the very source of anxiety.
>
> Dietrich Bonhoeffer, *The Cost of Discipleship*, vol. 4 of *Dietrich Bonhoeffer Works*, Eng. ed. Edited by Geffrey B. Kelly and John D. Godsey, trans. Barbara Green and Reinhard Krauss (Minneapolis: Augsburg Fortress, 2001), 40.

Jesus' authoritative interpretation goes to the heart of the law. He adds to the listing from the Decalogue the comprehensive command, "You shall love your neighbor as you love yourself" (19:21). Warren Carter challenges the rich young man's self-assessment in his claim to have kept this final commandment. How is it that the rich young man has accumulated and held on to all his wealth in the face of his neighbor's need? "Prophetic critiques . . . suggest that abundant wealth results from merciless oppression and deprivation of the poor (Isaiah 5:8–10; 10:1–3; Ezekiel 22:6–31; Amos 2:6–7; 5:10–12; 8:40)."[13] Jesus warns his

---

13. Carter, *Matthew and the Margins*, 388.

disciples, "It is easier for a camel to go through the eye of a needle than for someone who is rich to enter the kingdom of God" (19:24).

Many attempts to tame this provocative passage have been made by interpreters through the centuries. One approach concluded that "camel" was simply an error of translation. The word "rope" is only one letter different in the Greek language and sounds very much the same. This creates a more palatable reading; one only needs a very small rope and a very large needle to make this work. Another approach generated a medieval legend of a small gate in the wall of Jerusalem called "the Needle's Eye." A loaded camel could not pass through, but unloaded and walking on its knees, it might enter. The legend is actually very preachable; unfortunately, there never was such a gate. Another popular interpretation is that the standard Jesus applies here is only for those who would be "perfect;" it is not really meant for the average disciples. These approaches represent the resistance of the readers to a troubling text. Surely Jesus did not mean this; surely what he said here does not apply to us! When these machinations are seen for what they are, we are left with a text that "cannot be tamed."[14]

The disciples are as surprised at Jesus' saying about the rich as contemporary readers are. To them, the wealthy are seen as God's favorites, blessed as they are with so many possessions. If they cannot be saved, they ask with astonishment, "Then who can be saved?" (19:25). Jesus has overturned expectations yet again. It is only because "all things are possible" for God that even the rich might be saved. This invites speculation as to whether God might make it possible for the rich to unburden ourselves by giving to the poor? Then perhaps, no longer entrapped by riches, we may be free to follow Jesus and to enter into the reign of God.

When Peter overhears this conversation about "perfection" being connected with giving up possessions, he jumps in with both feet. "Look, we have left everything and followed you. What then will we have?" (v. 27) The question puts Peter in a bad light as greedy and ambitious, seeking reward and rank in return for his sacrifice. It is yet another indication that the disciples are not getting the point.

14. Ibid., 391.

Although Jesus assures Peter of a fitting reward "at the renewal of all
things," he also takes care to remind Peter that the "first will be last
and the last first" (v. 30). This reminder "bookends" another parable
of the reign of God that stands between the two forms of this same
aphorism (19:30 and 20:16). It is a parable that seems well-designed
to discourage the kind of ambition Peter has just demonstrated in
his eagerness for a reward commensurate with his sacrifice.

In the midst of his response to Peter, Jesus uses the title "Son of
Man" to refer to himself. This is a title of profound theological significance in Matthew. It appears fifty-eight times and with increasing
frequency as the story unfolds. It seems to be the preferred title in
Jesus' self-identification. He never speaks of himself as Son of God
or Son of David. Although these are titles that Matthew takes care
to lay out in the first chapter, they are given to Jesus by others in the
story;[15] he does not use them of himself. Son of Man is a title with
built in ambiguity. It can convey humility as in "just a human being"
and it can convey authority as in the "Son of Man" who would come
as judge in the eschaton as Daniel 7: 9–10; 13–14 (KJV) prophesied:

> As I watched, thrones were set in place, and an Ancient One
> took his throne. . . . The court sat in judgment, and the books
> were opened. . . . I saw in the night visions, and, behold, one
> like the Son of man came with the clouds of heaven, and came
> to the Ancient of days, and they brought him near before him.
> And there was given him dominion, and glory, and a kingdom,
> that all people, nations, and languages should serve him: his
> dominion is an everlasting dominion, which shall not pass
> away, and his kingdom that which shall not be destroyed.

This text illumines Jesus' response to Peter; "Truly I tell you, at the
renewal of all things, when the Son of Man is seated on the throne of
his glory, you who have followed me will also sit on twelve thrones
judging the twelve tribes of Israel" (19:28). Here the association of
the title "Son of Man" with the heaven descended judge in the book
of Daniel is clear. It is an association that will resurface in chapter 26:
46 during Jesus' interrogation before the Sanhedrin.

In Karl Barth's interpretation of the title Son of Man, he sees this

15. Luz, *Theology of the Gospel of Matthew*, 113.

as an "exaltation" of the human being. Barth affirms that God and the human being are united in the incarnation in such a way that God is humbled ("the Lord becomes servant") and human beings exalted ("the servant becomes Lord"). God does not cease to be God in this humiliation, but embraces "humanity in God." [16]

20:1–34

Concern for Reward and Rank: Ruled Out in the Reign of God

Although Jesus accommodates Peter's ambition with a vision of reward "at the renewal of all things," he finishes with a caution that "the first will be last and the last first" and proceeds to tell the parable of the generous employer by way of illustration. It is yet another instance of shocking reversals.

The parable of the laborers in the vineyard is found only in Matthew. The setting is one where the employer goes to the marketplace looking for laborers to hire for the day. Crossing the centuries, one might envision a setting not unlike what happens at the corner of Milwaukee and Belmont, a corner in Chicago where many men wait every day in hopes of a day's wage for a day's work. Nik Theodore, a University of Illinois at Chicago expert on day laborers, tells a grim tale of five hundred such street corners in the United States and more than half a million people afloat in the street-corner job market. Many are newly unemployed in the economic downturn and many are undocumented. In this "forgotten corner of the economy" workers are very vulnerable. The work is often difficult, strenuous, and dangerous. One in five reports being injured while working and having no medical care. Their biggest day-to-day worry is getting paid. Employers give them bad checks or hire them at one rate yet pay less when the work is done or vanish when it's time to pay up. [17]

What a contrast to the generous employer of this story. This landowner has made several return trips throughout the day, bringing

---

16. Karl Barth, *Church Dogmatics,* IV/2, *The Doctrine of Reconciliation* (Edinburgh: T. & T. Clark, 1958), 64.

17. Stephen Franklin, "Forgotten Corners of the Economy," *The American Prospect.* (September 9, 2009).

in more laborers to his vineyard each time. Those picked up in the morning were promised the usual daily wage (a denarius). Those picked up later were promised "what is right" (20:4). When it's time to pay up he pays the last ones to arrive first, and beyond all reasonable expectation, he pays everyone a full day's wage—even those who only worked one hour! When those employed from the early morning receive a day's wage, they grumble "you have made them equal to us" (v. 12). This equalizing is unacceptable. The latecomers do not deserve so much. Readers may sympathize with the grumbling of the all-day workers.

The employer responds, "Are you envious because I am generous?" A more literal translation would be, "Is your eye evil because I am good? The "evil eye" or the "unhealthy eye" (6:23) is associated in the context with covetousness or possessiveness.[18] "A greedy man's eye is not satisfied with a portion. A stingy man's eye begrudges bread" (Sir. 14:10). The grumblers seem to begrudge the full day's wage generously given to everyone—even to those who had not worked a full day to "earn" it.

One wonders how this parable of the reign of God was understood by the hearers. Who would they associate with the "latecomers"? Are they the "sinners and Gentiles" that are being included in the community? Are the grumbling workers the religious leaders who have all the usual objections to this inclusion? (9:9–13; 11:16–19) Or perhaps the grumblers are members of Matthew's community who—like Peter, James, and John—are expecting special advantages for their great sacrifice but find that God's grace is extended equally to all. However the characters in the parable are understood, this is a story of reversals and unexpected equalization. It presents a generosity that goes beyond calculation to grace. Hearers today may make theological connections. Our "calculating" ways are brought up short by God's incalculable grace.

Between the petitioning for rewards that Peter does and the petitioning for rank that the sons of Zebedee's mother brings comes the third passion prediction (20:17–19). Set off by the frame of self-seeking disciples, Jesus' words are all the more desolate. He tries

18. Senior, *Abingdon New Testament Commentaries,* 87.

to tell them one more time, in explicit terms, what will happen in Jerusalem. "See, we are going up to Jerusalem, and the Son of Man will be handed over to the chief priests and scribes, and they will condemn him to death; then they will hand him over to the Gentiles to be mocked and flogged and crucified; and on the third day he will be raised."

The disciples are clearly not on the same page with Jesus. The petition concerning the sons of Zebedee comes right upon the heels of Jesus' bleak announcement. Perhaps they are responding to what they overheard about the twelve thrones of judgment (v. 28). They (and their mother) want to be sure they have reserved seats on these thrones—preferably the best seats. Jesus inquires whether they are able to "drink of the cup" that he is about to drink. "Drinking from the cup" is often used in the Hebrew Scriptures as a metaphor for various forms of suffering endured by Israel (Is. 51:17; Jer. 25:15; 49:12; 51:7).[19] Perhaps oblivious to what he has just said in the passion prediction, they are undeterred. "We are able," they declare. The request to sit at Jesus' right and left hand carries with it a particular irony in connection with the cross. There two others were crucified with Jesus, "one on his right and one on his left" (27:38);[20] the places at Jesus' right and left are places of crucifixion.

Peter, James, and John in their preoccupation with ranks and rewards seem to be on an altogether different wavelength than the one whom they mean to follow. Jesus' way will be one of service and suffering, as the passion prediction signifies. Peter's petition provoked a story that concluded with "the last will be first and the first last" (20:16). This petition for James and John provides another teaching moment with a similar conclusion (20: 24–28).

Jesus makes a clear delineation between life in the new community and life in the communities they know about. "The rulers of the Gentiles lord it over them, and their great ones are tyrants over them" (v. 25). This oppressive exercise of power over others is to be renounced in the new community. "It will not be so among you: but whoever wishes to be great among you must be your servant (Greek

---

19. Ibid., 225.
20. Ibid.

diakonos), and whoever wishes to be first among you must be your slave" (v. 26).

Jesus' own example is the pattern: "just as the Son of Man came not to be served but to serve, and to give his life a ransom for many." This rich and often quoted verse drives the point home about greatness and service. It also evokes associations with the suffering servant role in Isaiah that has been a prominent way of understanding the salvific work of Jesus.

> The righteous one, my servant, shall make many righteous,
>   and he shall bear their iniquities.
> Therefore I will allot him a portion with the great,
>   and he shall divide the spoil with the strong;
> because he poured out himself to death,
>   and was numbered with the transgressors;
> yet he bore the sin of many,
>   and made intercession for the transgressors.
>
> (Isa. 53:11–12)

There is much discussion of the phrase "a ransom (Greek *lytron*) for many." The meaning of "ransom" in the context is "the redemption of someone captive or enslaved." "Many" is to be interpreted as an expansive expression signaling the broad impact of Jesus' redemptive mission.[21]

The disciples, even at this late juncture, seem not to understand the topsy-turvy nature of life under the reign of God, where the first come last and the last come first. Even less do they embrace the prospect of suffering and serving. Peter, James, and John have been engaged in negotiating rewards and "jockeying for the best seats."[22] It is an orientation in contradiction to what Jesus is saying and doing. Life in the new community under the reign of God is radically different. In chapters 19 and 20 some of the changes have been signaled in the reordered relationships of men and women in marriage, the welcoming of those who did not fit in well with the gender roles and expectations of the culture, the invitation to adults to become like

---

21. Ibid., 226.
22. Michael G. Reddish, *An Introduction to the Gospels* (Nashville: Abingdon Press, 1997), 136.

children, the requirement of the rich to become poor, and the expectations that the "great ones" will serve others instead of oppressing them. Relationships are reordered and resources reallocated in the reign of God.

All in all, it seems to be too much for the disciples to take in. They only understand in part; their vision is cloudy. The chapter closes with the healing of the blind men (20:29–33) who ask, "Lord, let our eyes be opened." It is "an apt prayer and a fitting conclusion for this section of the Gospel where discipleship instruction has been a strong motif."[23] The disciples need healing for their vision too. The blind men also speak words that reverberate in Christian liturgy to this day, "Lord, have mercy on us" (Kyrie Eleison). This is the last of the healing miracles before entry into Jerusalem. With it, key titles of "Lord" and "Son of David" are reiterated and the messianic expectation that the eyes of the blind will be opened (Isa. 35:5–6) is reinforced. In these verses, the Gospel "reasserts the messianic authority of Jesus on the eve of his Passion."[24]

21:1–22

"Who is this?" Jesus Enters Jerusalem with Humility and Acts with Authority

Jesus' entry into Jerusalem is powerful in its contrast—a humble entry followed by authoritative action. It is as full of fulfillment texts as are the chapters that tell of Jesus' birth and resonates with the sense of cataclysm surrounding the event of his birth. "The whole city" of Jerusalem is thrown into turmoil (v. 10). Reference to "the whole city" in this passage is reminiscent of the agitation of "all Jerusalem" with Herod over news of Jesus' birth (2:3). The Greek word translated here as "turmoil" more literally translated, calls up the image of an earthquake (*eseisthē,* "made to quake"; noun form *siesmon,* "earthquake"). The same word is used in 27:51 at the point when Jesus "breathed his last" and "the earth shook and the rocks were split" (27:51). Then again at the resurrection,

---

23. Senior, *Abingdon New Testament Commentaries,* 227.
24. Ibid., 228.

there is an "earthquake" (27:54). Jesus' entry into Jerusalem initiates disturbance—a seismic shift—that echoes from his birth and reverberates to his death and the resurrection. "Who is this?" indeed (v. 10).

Jesus enters the city with humility. He does not ride on a great warhorse in military/kingly style but enters on a humble donkey—or two in Matthew's account. Matthew takes a literal turn with the literary device of synonymous parallelism in Zechariah 9:9 and pictures Jesus as riding astride two donkeys (a donkey and the foal of a donkey). Many artistic renderings of Jesus' entry into Jerusalem depict his arrival just as Matthew describes it. Zechariah 9:9,

> Rejoice greatly, O daughter Zion!
>   Shout aloud, O daughter Jerusalem!
> Lo, your king comes to you;
>   triumphant and victorious is he,
> humble and riding on a donkey,
>   on a colt, the foal of a donkey.

Matthew has left out the "triumphant and victorious" reference, perhaps in his emphasis on humility. All the same, Jesus' authoritative action upon entry shows that humility and authority meet in him. Jesus' first act is an authoritative, prophetic act of cleansing the Temple. This event is recorded in all four Gospels. Jesus enters "turning over the tables of the money changers;" disrupting all the "buying and selling" that was going on in the Temple (v. 12). His decisive action and prophetic utterances align him with the great prophets Isaiah (56:7 "My house shall be called a house of prayer") and Jeremiah (7:11 "but you are making it a den of robbers.")

Jeremiah's text has a wider trajectory than what is quoted here. The fuller reference expresses divine outrage at the combination of worship and unrighteousness:

> Will you steal, murder, commit adultery, swear falsely, make offerings to Baal, and go after other gods that you have not known, and then come and stand before me in this house, which is called by my name, and say, "We are safe!"—only to go on doing all these abominations? Has this house, which is

called by my name, become a den of robbers in your sight? You know, I too am watching, says the Lord. (Jer. 7:9–11)

Matthew's community, at the time of his writing, has lived through the burning of Jerusalem and the destruction of the Temple in 70 CE. Jesus' prophetic act would take on additional significance as it becomes an anticipation of the Temple's destruction (24:1–2). The burning of Jerusalem is perhaps referenced in 22:7. The quotation from Jeremiah would further these associations. Jeremiah had prophesied the destruction of the Temple as punishment for covenant unfaithfulness.

How did Matthew's community come to terms with the horror of the burning of Jerusalem and the destruction of the Temple? The abuse of the holy places by profiteers and the unrighteousness of the worshippers and the failure of religious leaders may have become a way of understanding what had happened as a divine judgment. Whatever we may think of this reasoning, it is consistent with the retributive justice framework that runs throughout the Deuteronomic writings; the people sin and disaster follows. It is almost as if disaster can be born with, if it is in some way "justified." If it is punishment for wrongdoing, it may be terrible "but it reveals the ultimate goodness and justice of the cosmic order.[25] Countervailing voices in Scripture (i.e. Job, Lamentations, and the Psalms of lament) contradict that framework and allow for an alternative interpretation. After the destruction of Jerusalem in 587 BCE, there are voices that say God's people are being treated unjustly, "accounted as sheep for the slaughter."

> All this has come upon us,
>   yet we have not forgotten you,
>   or been false to your covenant.
> Our heart has not turned back,
>   nor have our steps departed from your way,
> yet you have broken us in the haunt of jackals,
>   and covered us with deep darkness.
>   (Ps. 44:17–19)

---

25. Wendy Farley, *Tragic Vision and Divine Compassion* (Louisville, KY: Westminster/John Knox Press, 1990), 20.

When this "tragic vision" breaks through the retributive justice framework, it opens a place for recognition of innocent/undeserved suffering. Innocent suffering is central to Jesus' passion. It is something we also see in his ministry among the many suffering people upon whom he had such compassion.

Having cleansed the Temple, Jesus' next act is to undertake a ministry of healing in the Temple. Instead of being a market place, the Temple becomes a healing place. Jesus receives the blind and the lame and heals them. This does not seem remarkable until we remember that the blind and the lame were exempt from obligation to attend festivals in the Temple. They were permitted to do so, but they were not allowed to "draw near" or to offer food offerings in the Temple. There were cultic restrictions against persons who were physically damaged or disabled serving in the role of priest (Lev. 21:16–17). Jesus is once again crossing boundaries. The "purity" of the Temple means its right use—not exclusion of persons who are disabled.

The children in the Temple were crying out, "Hosanna to the Son of David" (v. 15). All this proves to be too much for the chief priests and the scribes—cleansing the Temple, healing the lame and the blind right there in the Temple, and now the children are addressing Jesus as "the Son of David. "Do you hear what they are saying?" they ask, apparently expecting Jesus to correct the children. Instead he accepts their praise and the title they have given him, saying, "Yes; have you never read, 'Out of the mouths of infants and nursing babies you have prepared praise for yourself'" (v. 16).

Jesus' response is consistent with what he says elsewhere. In 11:25, he gives thanks to God who has "hidden these things from the wise and the intelligent and have revealed them to infants." The reader remembers also how Jesus brought a child into their midst in answer to the query as to "who is the greatest" in the reign of God (18:34). In 19:14 Jesus welcomes the children and goes so far as to say that the reign of God belongs to children (19:14). The least and the "little ones" are lifted up.

The conflict that has smoldered between Jesus and the religious leaders from the very beginning and all along the way is erupting now in Jerusalem. Jesus withdraws to Bethany for the night. The next morning there is the odd account of the withering of the unfruitful fig tree. Is this simply peevishness on Jesus' part? Perhaps the text in its context admits of a more meaningful interpretation. The focus on a harvest parable in 21:34 and judgment on those who do not produce the "fruits of the kingdom" in 21:41 provide a context for interpretation. The encounter with the fig tree may be a kind of enacted parable; a symbolic act of the one who is coming to judge those who do not bear fruit. If so, the disciples do not penetrate to the significance of the sign and are lost in amazement at the sign itself. They want to know Jesus did it, and Jesus responds with a lesson on faith.

21:23–27
"By what authority?"

The next day, as soon as Jesus enters the Temple and begins teaching, the chief priests and the elders come to him demanding to know, "By what authority are you doing these things and who gave you this authority?" Jesus says he will answer their question if they will first answer his question, "Did the baptism of John come from heaven or was it of human origin?" They dare not answer. They do not want to say it was "from heaven" (a traditional saying meaning "from God"). They really want to say that it was "of human origin," but they cannot because they are "afraid of the crowd," who regard John as a prophet from God (v. 26). They know which way the wind blows, so they simply say, "We do not know" (v. 27). This answer leaves open the possibility that John's authority *is* from God—since they do not deny it. The implication of the conversation is that Jesus' authority came from the same source as John's authority. The whole conversation has the unintended effect of "authorizing Jesus." Again the authority and the destiny of Jesus are being linked with John's.

21:28–22:14
Three Upsetting Parables

As with other parables, on the face of it they seem to be simple harmless stories. Each one of the next three has a father and a son among the characters. Those who have ears to hear, however, will know that the disobedient son, the evil tenants who kill the son, and the invited guests who do not come to the wedding banquet for the son all stand for the religious leaders. These three parables accuse them of hypocrisy and disobedience, rejecting/persecuting/executing God's prophets, and not responding to God's call. All the stories end in an "upset" and a judgment. Together the parables "inscribe a large historical arc from the biblical prophets and John the Baptist over Jesus and the community to the Day of Judgment."[26]

The first parable Jesus tells is the parable of two sons—one obedient and one disobedient. Like the earlier "laborers in the vineyard" parable (20:1–16), this one is unique to Matthew. It will be followed immediately by yet another "vineyard" parable, this one having evil tenants. In these (three in a row) vineyard parables, it is very possible that the "vineyard" is a symbolic reference to Israel as it is in Isaiah 5:1–7.

In the parable of two sons, both are asked by their father to go and work in the vineyard. One says he will not but later does; the other says he will but later does not. Jesus turns the question to the audience, "Which of the two did the will of his father?" Everyone (even the targets of the parable) knows which son did the will of the father. Just in case the chief priests and elders do not understand that they are being compared to the disobedient son, Jesus makes it plain for them. "Truly I tell you, the tax collectors and prostitutes are going into the kingdom ahead of you." These religious leaders have said yes to laboring in God's vineyard, but it is only lip service. Their hypocrisy and disobedience is now unveiled. This passage echoes the charges brought in Matthew 15:8 quoting the words of Isaiah the prophet, "This people honors me with their lips, but their hearts are far from me." Tax collectors and prostitutes (the designated unrighteous) are the ones who receive and believe the message proclaimed by John and Jesus. They have taken it to heart and will be ahead of the chief priests and elders in the entry line to the reign of God.

As if this is not enough, Jesus follows with another parable comparing the religious leaders unfavorably with tenants of a vineyard who refuse to turn over the produce of the harvest to the landowner. Instead they kill the servants whom the landowner sends them and,

26. Luz, *Theology of the Gospel of Matthew*, 118.

in the end, they even kill his son. This parable could not be more clear if it referred by name to John the Baptist and Jesus. The bottom line is this: what had been entrusted to them will be taken away and given to people that "produce the fruits" of the reign of God (v. 43).

There is a troubling (supersessionist) turn in some commentaries when they work out interpretations of these two parables. They take them to mean that the church now "supersedes" Israel in God's work of salvation. In the parable of the two sons they associate the disobedient son with Israel and the obedient son with the church. In the second parable, they associate the evil tenants with Israel and the "other" (new) tenants with the church. Quite apart from the way in which such interpretations could promote supersessionism and its attendant abuses, this is a distortion of the plain meaning of the parables. Jesus' "target" is the religious leaders, not Israel as such. It is unlikely that Matthew or his (predominantly Jewish) community would have promoted this idea, setting Jew against Gentile in their shared community of faith. Matthew maintains a privileged place for Israel in God's salvation history while opening God's blessing to all the nations. The inclusion of the nations was part of the traditional Jewish eschatological hope. There is much more reason to believe Matthew is associating Israel with the vineyard itself (as in Isa. 5:1–7). It is a change in the leaders that is needed; replacing the unfaithful with faithful leaders. The landowner in the parable seeks more obedient sons and better tenants for the care of his beloved vineyard. He does not go seeking a new vineyard.

These parables are not in the least subtle in their criticism of the religious leaders. The chief priests and the Pharisees realize he is "speaking about them." They would arrest him on the spot were it not for the crowds (21:45–46). Jesus does not ease off and let the matter rest but tells yet another excoriating parable along the same lines. This one is about a king whose invited guests will not come to the wedding banquet. Not only do they fail to respond to the invitation of the king, they even kill the messengers who deliver the invitation. They are destroyed and the king widens the invitation—taking it to the streets. The result is that the hall is filled with guests.

One guest does not wear the "wedding robe" and is cast out. Commentators puzzle over this step in the story. One interpretation proposes that the standard for the newcomers is the same as it was for those originally invited—repentance and living the higher righteousness that befits life under the reign of God are essential for entry into the banquet.

The extraordinary shift in the parable is its transition from an exclusive party of invited guests to a party of "invite everyone you find" (v. 9). This is consistent with the widening circle of inclusion that has been opening in the Gospel. "The banquet now taking place … is not a banquet for the selected few, not for the social elite, not for the politically powerful, not for the religious insiders. These people have boycotted it. And now it has become a banquet for the people—outcasts and strangers."[27] There is something quite shocking about the openness of the invitation, now yielding a hall "filled with guests."

> Can we worship a God who is so open, so ready to accept those to whom we have closed the gates of the kingdom? . . . Can we accept a God whose standards of admission are so much lower than ours? A God who is so . . . indiscriminately open-handed where we are so self-righteously close-fisted?
>
> Allan Boesak, "Undisciplined Abundance," a sermon on Matthew 13:1–9, in *The Fire Within: Sermons from the Edge of Exile* (Capetown: New World Foundation, 2004) 119.

The point of the story is not lost on the Pharisees. They see they are identified with the guests who made light of the invitation and even mistreated and killed the messengers sent to invite them. They stand accused of persecuting and killing the prophets. They have missed their chance for a place at the messianic banquet; others have been invited in their stead. Their reaction is swift. "Then the Pharisees went and plotted to entrap him in what he said" (v. 15). Jesus will be subjected to a set of "testy" questions designed to tempt him and trick him into springing the trap.

22:15–46
Four Difficult Questions: Cross-Examination

What follows is a kind of cross-examination. Jesus is tag-teamed with questions; first questions from the Pharisees and then from the

27. C.S. Song, *Jesus and the Reign of God* (Minneapolis: Fortress Press, 1993), 36.

Sadducees and then from the Pharisees again. The disciples of the Pharisees are up first. It is worth noting that the Pharisees do not come to Jesus themselves; instead they send their disciples (22:15). In doing so, "they avoid direct encounter; the indirect approach heightens the subterfuge."[28]

The disciples of the Pharisees have brought the Herodians with them. It is an unlikely coalition since the Herodians were clear supporters of Rome, serving at Rome's behest and furthering Roman interests. The Pharisees were of mixed mind on the matter of the Roman occupation. Some Pharisees advocated armed revolt (Shammai School). Others advocated a live and let live policy (Hillel School).[29] Here they are together, nevertheless, and asking a dangerous question about whether it is "lawful to pay taxes to the emperor" (v. 17). They sugar coat the question with flattery: "Teacher, we know that you are sincere, and teach the way of God in accordance with the truth and show deference to no one; for you do not regard people with partiality . . . " There is an irony in what they have said because they have spoken truthfully concerning Jesus—"more truthfully than they know"[30]—even in their attempt to entrap him. If they mean to disguise their intent through a flattering preface, they are unsuccessful. Jesus is not fooled by the flattery; he is "aware of their malice" (v. 18) and confronts them rather pointedly. "Why are you putting me to the test you hypocrites? (v. 18). The intent of the question is all too clear. If Jesus says "no" to paying the tax it will be "a dangerous repudiation of Roman authority."[31] By bringing the Herodians along with them, the Pharisees have raised the threat level (22:16).

"Whose head is this and whose title?" (v. 20) It is certainly not God's image that is on the coin; such a thing would be forbidden by the first commandment (Exod. 20:4). It was the Roman emperor's

---

28. Carter, *Matthew and the Margins*, 438.
29. N. T. Wright, *Matthew for Everyone, Part 1* (Louisville, KY: Westminster John Knox Press, 2004), 217. Shammai and Hillel were leading rabbis in the first century CE who established different schools of thought on matters of ethics and ritual practice. Another difference was that the Shammai School advocated resistance to Rome. They were in ascendency before 70 CE. The Hillel School opposed armed resistance. After the First Revolt, which resulted in the burning of Jerusalem and destruction of the Temple, the Hillel School predominated.
30. Carter, *Matthew and the Margins*, 458.
31. Senior, *Abingdon New Testament Commentaries*, 247.

image, and taxes to Rome must be paid with Roman coins. The Latin inscription that it likely bore at that time was "Tiberius, August son of the Divine High Priest Augustus." The coins functioned as "portable billboards, instruments of propaganda which reminded users of the emperor's political power and Rome's status as the favored of the gods"[32] It was also a symbol of defeat and humiliation for subjugated peoples. This would become all the more apparent after 70 CE, when the Emperor Vespasian issued newly minted coins commemorating the capture of Judea. In addition to his image, the coin had an image of a bound female and the inscription 'IVDAEA CAPTA' ("Judea prisoner").

When the people answer that it is the emperor's image on the coin, Jesus says, "Give therefore to the emperor the things that are the emperor's and to God the things that are God's." The answer is a skillful delimitation of the meaning of Roman taxation. To pay the tax is merely to give Caesar back his own. What is due to God is far more than this; wholehearted devotion and service belong to God (not to Caesar). With this aphorism Jesus "deftly permits the paying of taxes, even to a foreign power whose rule over Israel was illegitimate, while at the same time asserting the sovereignty of God."[33] It is a two-part answer where the second half trumps the first half. As in the earlier discussion around taxes (17:24–27), Jesus' followers may be paying taxes to the Roman authorities but they are not paying tribute. This is yet another instance of Jesus finding a "third way" that is neither the violence of revolt nor complicity of submission. It amounts to a nonviolent subversion of the oppressive power that does not concede Rome's sovereignty; only God is sovereign. Amazed at Jesus' answer, his questioners just leave him and go away (22:22).

Next come the Sadducees with a trick question about the resurrection (which they do not believe in in the first place). They mean to show the absurdity of the belief and misrepresent it in order to ridicule it. They import a predicament out of mundane experience, thereby painting a picture of resurrection that no one holds. Jesus accuses that they "know neither the scriptures nor the power of

32. Carter, *Matthew and the Margins,* 440.
33. Senior, *Abingdon New Testament Commentaries,* 249.

God." The scripture to which Jesus refers is Exod. 3:6 "I am the God of your father, the God of Abraham, the God of Isaac, and the God of Jacob." Jesus appends to this an affirmation that God is a "God of the living" (v. 32). It is not a claim that these forebears have already been raised from the dead. Rather, it is an affirmation that God's relationship with them and God's faithfulness to the covenant is not broken by death. The point at issue is not the particulars of "what happens when we die" but of the power and faithfulness of God. The Sadducees would have been familiar with both these affirmations, though perhaps not put them together in this way—"they were astounded at his teaching" (v. 33).

The Pharisees, upon hearing how he had "silenced the Sadducees" (v. 34), are back at him. They send in a lawyer who asks Jesus to select one of the commandments in the law and declare it the "most important." Latter rabbinic tradition counted 613 laws, all of which were to be respected and obeyed equally, though they recognized that some were "weightier than others."[34] Jesus' answer refuses to choose only one law and instead goes to the heart and center of the law as such. "'You shall love the Lord your God with all your heart, and with all your soul, and with all your mind.' This is the greatest and first commandment. And a second is like it: 'You shall love your neighbor as yourself.' On these two commandments hang all the law and the prophets'" (vv. 37–40). Jesus has spoken what is most central to their shared faith tradition. He quotes Deuteronomy 6:5 and Leviticus 19:18. Jesus is not innovating here; these are fundamentals he would have learned at his mother's knee. What he says is something the Pharisees should already know; they are put to shame.

Before they can also walk away, Jesus turns the tables and asks them a question, "What do you think of the Messiah? Whose son is he?" The Pharisees give the expected answer, "The son of David" (v. 42). This is the title that the children bestowed on Jesus in the previous chapter—to the dismay of the chief priests (21:15–16). The crowds and many petitioners for healing have also addressed him with it. Jesus quotes a Psalm where the Messiah is addressed as David's "Lord." How then can he be only a "son of David?" The

---

34. Senior, *New Testament Commentaries,* 252.

reader knows that the Messiah is more than that; Matthew's Gospel has made clear that Jesus is not only "son of David" but also "Son of God" (3:17; 17:5). The Pharisees are stumped by Jesus' follow up question. The chapter closes with these words. "No one was able to give him an answer, nor from that day did anyone dare to ask him any more questions" (v. 46).

Jesus has stood the test of their questions and they have failed the test of his question. The broad sweep of confrontations in these four chapters has included chief priests, elders, Pharisees, and Sadducees in varying combinations. As varied as these groups are, they are almost interchangeable in their opposition and hostility. Even so, they have been unable to defeat the authoritative teacher or draw out of him answers that will discredit and condemn him. They wanted to silence him, but it is they who are silenced. They are "amazed" and "leave" (v. 22) or "astounded" and "fall silent" (vv. 33–34). They "do not dare to ask him any more questions" (v. 46). In the next chapters, Jesus begins to teach the crowds and the disciples about the coming judgment in which these opponents will figure rather prominently.

23:1–25:46

Teaching: The Coming Judgment

The fifth and final teaching segment is delivered in three chapters unified around the theme of judgment. There is judgment rendered on the spot in chapter 23 as religious leaders are called into account for their hypocrisy, blindness, and corruption. They have misled the people and rejected prophets sent from God. Seven "woes" are delivered against them. An apocalyptic passage follows in chapters 24–25. It tells of tribulation ahead that is but the "birth pangs" of the new age. The "Son of Man" is coming in glory to judge. Parables warn those who are waiting to be faithful and be ready. The section closes with an accounting of the final judgment.

23:1–12

Religious Leaders Denounced for Hypocrisy:
"They do not practice what they teach."

While still in the Temple area, Jesus delivers a bitter diatribe against the scribes and Pharisees. Why are they so vilified, even demonized? What is going on that draws out such invective from one who is "gentle and lowly" and loves his enemies?

The Pharisees were part of a "lay reform movement" within Judaism, and the scribes were leaders among them. Their good intention was to breathe new life into the practice of Judaism by extending into the life of the ordinary Jew the laws of purity usually reserved to the priests."[1] They attended to issues of cultic purity, tithing, and Sabbath observance. Their reforms "were intended to renew Jewish piety and to provide a stronger sense of Jewish identity in the face of incursions by Hellenistic culture."[2] Jesus shared the concerns of the Pharisees. He was closer to their thinking than to that of the Sadducees or the Essenes. However, he differed from Pharisees in his understanding of the relative importance of such things as ritual purity, tithing, Sabbath, and what he considered to be the "weightier matters of the law" (23:23).

For Matthew's community these differences came to be intensified further by historical circumstances. The failed rebellion against Rome resulted in the burning of Jerusalem and the destruction of the Temple. There followed very turbulent times within Judaism. Jewish religious identity that had centered on the Temple was disrupted and was in process of being reconstructed with Torah as its center. It is probable that the Pharisees sought to consolidate their influence in the synagogues and were in an adversarial relation to minority groups, such as those who believed that Jesus was the Messiah. Jewish-Christian missionaries likely faced opposition from the Pharisees comparable to that described in 23:34. The "woes" that conclude chapter 23 climax in a bitter denunciation of their persecution. In this life-and death-struggle, Jerusalem's demise is cast as divine judgment on the religious elite who rejected Jesus. The Pharisee's leadership de-legitimated. The polemical language of these texts, which to our ears is quite extreme, is actually reflective of polemics of the day as employed by both Gentile and Jewish groups.

In some circles the attack rendered here on one group of Jewish leaders has been generalized to a "verdict on all Jews and Jewish religious leaders for all time."[3] This chapter, however, is no wholesale condemnation of Jews or Judaism. It is not even a wholesale condemnation of the Pharisees, as not all Pharisees were guilty of the abuses to which Jesus alludes in Matthew. In early rabbinic writings,

---

1. Donald Senior, *Abingdon New Testament Commentaries: Matthew* (Nashville: Abingdon Press, 1998), 258.
2. Ibid.
3. Warren Carter, *Matthew and the Margins: A Socio-Political and Religious Reading* (Sheffield, England: Sheffield Academic Press, 2000), 449.

in fact, Pharisees themselves engage in pointed criticism of those who manifest the flaws that Jesus notes here.

The Gospel of Matthew as a whole is not anti-Jewish or anti-Judaism. It does not tell a story of "God's rejection of Israel or Israel's rejection of God."[4] Matthew has been rightly termed "the Jewish Gospel." The five major discourses follow the five-fold form of the Pentateuch. Jesus is presented as an authoritative interpreter of the law. The Hebrew Scriptures are of central importance in Matthew, which is full of quotations and allusions to the prophets, especially Isaiah and Jeremiah. For Matthew, Jesus is the fulfillment of both the law and the prophets. The text also takes pains to show Jesus' parallels with Moses and his reception as "son of David." Jesus and Matthew speak as pious Jews.

As we read these sharp edged texts today we are tempted to let them rest in the past as a condemnation of a particular subset of the Pharisees. We locate ourselves among the righteous and know that Jesus is talking not about "us" but about "them." What if, instead, we took the texts as an occasion to examine our own religious life and practice to see if the things Jesus speaks so heatedly against are to be found there? Those who are religious leaders might look particularly closely at what is condemned here. These texts are surely a cautionary tale instructive for religious leaders and all "would-be" followers of Jesus.

Jesus' condemnation is directed at religious leaders who, charged with the role of leadership, fail miserably. The most frequent charge is that they are hypocrites because "they do not practice what they teach" (23:3). In their teaching they might be termed rigorists. They go further than what the law requires. For example, for them it is "not enough to keep the Sabbath 'in a general way'; it was necessary to define carefully which weekday activities constituted work and were therefore prohibited on the Sabbath."[5] Jesus observes here that they tie up heavy burdens, hard to bear. Torah should not be burdensome (11:28–30). "Jews traditionally look upon Torah as a blessing, not a

---

4. Ibid.
5. Douglas R. A. Hare, *Matthew,* Interpretation: A Bible Commentary for Teaching and Preaching (Louisville, KY: Westminster/John Knox Press, 1992), 265.

burden."[6] Another criticism of the Pharisees is that they make a show
of their religious practices. They make their "phylacteries broad and
their fringes long." Phylacteries are small leather boxes containing
scripture passages such as the *Shema* (Deut. 6:4–9). They are worn
on the arm and forehead during prayer. Fringes refer to the tassels
on the prayer shawl. Jesus did not object to either of these practices.
However, the exaggeration of them (broad phylacteries and long
fringes) accentuated outward signs and made a superficial display of
piety. Such ostentation is contrary to "true piety" (6:1–19).

Also objectionable was the Pharisees' predisposition to be self-
important (23:6–7). They are status seekers, loving the "place of
honor at banquets" the "best seats in the synagogue" and being
called "rabbi," which means "my great one." "Rabbi" was often used
as a term of respect for teachers, but it is forbidden in the new community (23:8–10). In the Gospel of Matthew, only Judas uses this
term of Jesus, and he does so when his treachery is most apparent
(26:25–29).[7]

In the new community, titles are eschewed, and egalitarian, non-
hierarchical patterns are advocated instead. There is a "leveling" in
relation to one another as all stand together before God. No one is
to be called "rabbi" for they are all "students" (23: 8, NRSV). "Students" offers an inclusive term in translation but does not convey the
same relationship as the Greek term given (*adelphoi*, "brothers"). To
translate as "brothers and sisters" would make clearer the relationship among the disciples themselves. They are all children of the one
"Father" who is in heaven. "Father" (Hebrew *ab*) was sometimes
used as a term of respect for a revered elder or teacher. This also is
forbidden as signaling a heighted status.

In a dramatic reversal of ordinary expectations, Jesus says, "The
greatest among you will be your servant" (v. 11). Members of the
new community should not seek heightened status reflected in titles
but rather humble themselves and seek to serve—aiming low instead
of aiming high (23:11). The use of titles is not conducive to the well-
being of the new community. Titles—whether "rabbi," or "father,"

---

6. *The Jewish New Testament*, ed. Amy-Jill Levine and Marc Zvi Brettler (Oxford: Oxford
University Press, 2011), 42.

7. Senior, *Abingdon New Testament Commentaries*, 259.

or "instructor" (or "Reverend")—have their dangers, both for those who hold them and for those who call others by these titles. Those who hold titles may be lured into a sense of self-importance and all the other pretensions and temptations of power. Titles are equally problematic for persons who bestow them on others. In doing so, they may be tempted to childlike dependence on designated leaders and authorities, abdicating their own responsibility and agency.

In this chapter, the Pharisees here become a bit of a foil. Jesus teaches what the new community is to be like (indirectly) by his delegitimation of the objectionable practices of the Pharisees. The passage is *parenesis* (exhortation) for the disciples and the implied reader of these texts. If the beatitudes teach what is desirable for the community of disciples, the "woes" teach what is to be rejected. The message is not to be hypocritical, rigorists, showy, or self-important. The scribes and Pharisees serve as an "anti-type": a negative stereotype. Jesus teaches by negative example what the new community should not be like.

Jesus begins this diatribe by counseling respect for the teaching authority of those who "sit on Moses' seat." "Moses' seat" is a symbol of authority for interpretation of the law as received from God and delivered to the people by Moses. In later synagogue architecture there was a literal "seat of Moses," and the rabbi would sit on it to give instruction. A question of consequence arises in Jesus' exhortation to do as the scribes and Pharisees say and not as they do. Are the scribes and Pharisees really the "true heirs" of Moses? Is it not rather Jesus who is the true heir? Early in the story the warning is given that those who want to be part of the reign of God must exceed the righteousness of the scribes and Pharisees (5:20). Jesus has a better claim, as the astonished people acknowledge: "He spoke as one with authority and not as the scribes and Pharisees" (7:29).

With the "woes" that follow, the Pharisees are in some sense "disinherited" from a claim to Moses' seat. They are presented as shallow, showy, self-important, concerned over minutiae while neglecting what is important, greedy, self-indulgent, a hindrance to those who would find their way to the reign of God, looking righteous on the surface but being lawless under that facade. It is not only their particular faults, as listed here, that discredit them as successors to Moses.

Their whole orientation is of a different character. In the stories of
Moses, we see one who is on pilgrimage. He is living an adventure in
the wilderness, following a cloud by day and a fire by night; scaling
the heights of Sinai to receive a new word from God. The Pharisees,
by contrast, have a settled existence and rely on inherited texts, of
which they are the masters. If Moses lived on the "frontiers of faithfulness" the Pharisees have become the "border patrol" and "immigration officers" of that frontier.[8] Readers may reflect once again,
where do we locate ourselves in this story?

23:13–36
Seven Woes

The use of "woes" is common in prophetic literature as a way of
announcing divine judgment. Isaiah 5:8–23 has a diatribe including
a series of six woes. The prophet addresses these to general hearing.
In this passage in Matthew, it is the crowds and the disciples who are
the audience, not necessarily the scribes and Pharisees themselves
(v. 1). There are seven woes in chapter 23. This being the "perfect"
number, it is a complete castigation of the Pharisees. The first six
are in pairs: two concerning their negative impact on others, two
about how they focus on lesser things and miss out on the greater
things, and two claiming a disparity between their outward appear-
ances and their inner realities. The final woe relates to their rejection
of God's messengers, now including Jesus.[9]

The Pharisees are addressed variously as "hypocrites," "blind
guides," "blind fools," "whitewashed tombs," and a "brood of vipers."
As persons who should be guiding the way into the reign of God
they lock people out instead (v. 13). This "locking out" draws a contrast with what is commended to leaders in the new community. In
granting their power to "bind" and to "loose" (18:18), Jesus charges
church leaders "to exercise great care in seeking out the stray,

---

8. Michael Winters "Giving Thanks for the Gifts of God" (sermon, Presbyterian Church of
   Berwyn, Berwyn, IL, All Saints Sunday, November 3, 1996).
9. Carter, *Matthew and the Margins*, 455.

expelling someone only after serious efforts to win over the erring member"[10]

As interpreters of what is the right thing to do, the Pharisees prove to be "blind guides." For example, they sort out practices of swearing oaths and entertain a casuistry as they argue the fine points about which oaths are binding and which ones are not. As they do, they demonstrate their misplaced values giving more value to gold than the sanctuary and more value to the gifts on the altar than the altar itself (v. 16–22). Jesus' own counsel has been "do not to swear at all" but simply answer yes or no.

Pharisees are further criticized for attending to trivial things. For example, their tithing of garden herbs (v. 23) goes well beyond the tithing requirements of Deuteronomy 14:22–23.[11] There is a play on words implied in the text since, in order to tithe these garden herbs, Pharisees must first weigh them. While they weigh out the herbs they are neglecting "the weightier matters of the law." This picture is followed by yet another contrast. It was the Pharisees' practice to strain liquids to avoid ingesting any tiny unclean insects.[12] Of this Jesus says that they, "strain out a gnat but swallow a camel" (v. 24). What really matters is "justice and mercy and faith" (23:23). Jesus has twice quoted a text from Hosea (6:6) that puts all their careful tithing into perspective, "I desire mercy, not sacrifice" (9:13; 12:7).

The next criticism accuses the Pharisees of cleaning the outside of the cup while the inside is (unclean) "full of greed and self-indulgence" (vv. 25–26). There was actually a scribal debate about the outside and the inside of a cup and whether the inside became ritually unclean if the outside was contaminated. This notation echoes the earlier debate with the Pharisees (15:1–20), which concludes that, when it comes to what is clean and what is unclean, right living is more important than hand-washing. What is on the "inside" of the cup in the case of the Pharisees is from (Greek *ek*, "on the basis of")[13] the proceeds of greed and self-indulgence. No amount of washing will make this cup clean.

---

10. Senior, *Abingdon New Testament Commentaries*, 261.
11. Hare, *Matthew*, 269.
12. Senior, *Abingdon New Testament Commentaries*, 263.
13. Hare, *Matthew*, 270.

The Pharisees are like "whitewashed tombs." Tombs were white-washed in order to clearly mark them so that people could avoid any accidental contamination by what they held inside. The contrast is sharp. White was a symbol of purity. As the psalmist prays, "Purge me with hyssop, and I shall be clean; wash me, and I shall be whiter than snow" (Ps. 51:7). Though "white" and clean on the outside, tombs are unclean by virtue of what is inside. Dead bodies were ritu-ally unclean. So it is with the Pharisees. The charge of "lawlessness" (Greek *anomia*) in 23:28 is especially damning because the Phari-sees see themselves as the authoritative interpreters of the law. While they have been attending to minutiae—debating the relative bind-ing power of different oaths, tithing of garden herbs, whether the outside of a cup can contaminates the inside—they have neglected the weightier matters of the law: justice and mercy and faith.

In the final "woe" the Pharisees receive the harshest judgment of all. They are not merely failed leaders; they are a "brood of vipers" (23:33; 3:7; 12:34). This is a very particular accusation. They are charged with being "predatory, poisonous."[14] In a way, it is their own judgment that condemns them. While making a show of building tombs and decorating graves for the prophets and the righteous dead, they pronounce judgment on the ancestors who killed them. Yet they go on to do the very same thing themselves. They will per-secute the followers of Jesus: flog them in the synagogues, pursue them from town to town, kill them and crucify them. Thus they prove to be just like the ancestors they have accused. They are true descendants of prophet slayers. Their hands are covered in righ-teous blood all the way from the innocent Abel (the first person in the biblical story to be murdered) to Zechariah, the last murder in the Hebrew Scriptures[15] (most likely the Zechariah referenced in 2 Chron. 24:20–27). Zechariah spoke a prophetic word that reso-nates with this passage in Matthew. "Thus says God: 'Why do you transgress the commandments of the LORD, so that you cannot prosper? Because you have forsaken the LORD, he has also forsaken you.' But they conspired against him, and by command of the king

14. Eugene Boring, *The New Interpreter's Bible: New Testament Articles, Matthew, Mark* (Nashville: Abingdon Press, 1995), 8:157.
15. Carter, *Matthew and the Margins*, 463.

they stoned him to death in the court of the house of the LORD." (2 Chron. 24:21–22)

23:37–24:2
"O Jerusalem . . ."

The prophetic message of Zechariah is especially poignant in this context. The God who has been forsaken will now "forsake." The next movements include the lament over Jerusalem and Jesus leaving the Temple. The story calls to mind for Matthew's readers the god-forsakeness of their experience of the burning of Jerusalem and the destruction of the Temple. These events resonate with the prophet Jeremiah's words on the divine judgment against Jerusalem in his own time, "I have forsaken my house, I have abandoned my heritage; I have given the beloved of my soul into the hands of her enemies" (Jer. 12:7).

Jesus' lament over Jerusalem paints a poignant picture of the care God extends to God's people. God is likened to a mother hen who would gather her brood under her wings. The feminine image conveys God's compassion; God's care for God's children is like this. Jesus laments the unresponsiveness of God's children. In offering this lament, Jesus takes on the "role of a public mourner, a role traditionally assigned to women"[16] (28:1). His lament echoes that of Rachel for her children (2:18). The image is one of loss and profound sorrow.

This segment could serve two purposes for Matthew's community as they hear it. It provides a rationale for the rejection of the Messiah—the people have been misled by their leaders. Also, living as they do on the other side of 70 CE, they have endured the destruction of Jerusalem and the Temple. This serves as a kind of theodicy: a justification for the suffering they have endured.

The closing announces, "You will not see me again until you say, 'Blessed is the one who comes in the name of the Lord'" (23:39). This reference leaves the matter of Jerusalem's final disposition open

---

16. Levine and Brettler, *Jewish Annotated New Testament,* 260.

ended. It seems to anticipate a day of returning again to Jerusalem and being received as Jesus was received in the triumphal entry (21:9). "There is no final rejection of Israel or its leaders. God remains faithful to the covenant promises."[17] As in the history of God with God's people, judgment is ordered toward redemption. For the time being, however, the Messiah "literally abandons the Temple and prophesies its destruction (24:1–2)."[18] He will not return to the Temple area until he is arrested and brought before the high priest Caiaphas.

24:3–44

The Apocalypse: "About that day and hour no one knows . . ."

From the Mount of Olives, Jesus and the disciples now look back upon Jerusalem. This moment draws to a close the momentous events in Jerusalem that have happened since they last stood there on the Mount of Olives (21:1) preparing for Jesus' entry into Jerusalem. In his "triumphal" entry the crowds had received him, greeting him with the words of Psalm 118:26, "Blessed is the one who comes in the name of the Lord" (21:9). It is the traditional greeting addressed to pilgrims coming into Jerusalem for Temple festivals. The children are the ones who offer extraordinary acclamation in the words, "Hosanna to the Son of David."

Upon entering the Temple, Jesus drives out those who are "buying and selling" there. He offers in the Temple a prophetic sign of the *eschaton* by healing people who were blind or lame (Isa. 35:5–6). All this has led to escalating conflict with religious leaders: chief priests and elders, Sadducees, scribes and Pharisees. At this juncture, Jesus is finished with his arguments with them. His words of judgment on them (23:1–36) and on Jerusalem (23:37–39) and even on the Temple itself (24:1–2) now hang in the air.

Only the disciples remain with him now, and his instruction concerning what is to come will be for their ears only. Jesus speaks from the Mount of Olives, a location that is associated with the final judgment (Zech. 14:4). From the vantage point of the Mount

17. Carter, *Matthew and the Margins,* 465.
18. Hare, *Matthew,* 272.

of Olives they can see the beautiful Herodian Temple across the Kidron Valley,[19] and they inquire concerning the devastation Jesus has announced, "when will this be?"

What follows is an apocalyptic deliverance. The Greek term *apocalypsis* means "to reveal or disclose" and signifies an "unveiling" of things that would otherwise remain hidden. "Apocalyptic" designates a genre of Jewish literature that flourished from 200 BCE to 135 CE.[20] The books of Daniel and Revelation are biblical texts of this genre. Generally this type of literature projects visions of the "end-times," including cataclysmic events of cosmic proportions and the rendering of judgment. Other texts of the New Testament that are apocalyptic in character include Mark 13 and 2 Thessalonians 2.

The vision of the end delivered here anticipates a time of tribulation leading up to the coming of the Son of Man in glory to judge all the nations. The cataclysmic events include signs in the heavens above (v. 29) and earthquakes and famines on the earth below (v. 7).

Sufferings will afflict the community of faith from without and from within. There will be "wars and rumors of wars" (24:6). Hatred and persecution from "all the nations" will put them at risk of torture and death. In their own faith communities there will be those who betray one another and fall away or are led astray by false prophets. Lawlessness will afflict them and "the love of many will grow cold (v. 12). This latter is perhaps the most serious threat for Matthew. Lawlessness (Greek *anomia*) is the ultimate crisis for a community that is centered around Torah. For love to "grow cold" signifies the loss of the very heart of the Torah, which is love of God and neighbor (22:34–40).

Some of the elements of the apocalypse echo the apocalyptic vision of Daniel that provides an analogy for these future signs,[21] including the Son of Man coming from the clouds of heaven in the time of judgment (Dan. 7). The "desolating sacrilege" (v. 15) in the context of the book of Daniel (9:27; 11:31; 12:11) referred to Antiochus IV (Epiphanes) setting up a statute of Zeus in the Temple in 168 or 167 BCE. This would have been "a searing memory

19. Senior, *Abingdon New Testament Commentaries*, 265.
20. Hare, *Matthew*, 273.
21. Senior, *Abingdon New Testament Commentaries*, 269.

for Israel and one that had spurred the Maccabean revolt (1 Macc. 1:54). In the language of the book of Daniel, Jesus warns of "great suffering" ahead (Dan. 12:1). Other aspects of the apocalypse are woven together from the writings of the prophets Isaiah, Jeremiah, Ezekiel, Joel, Amos, and Haggai.

It may be that Matthew's faith community receives this message of the apocalypse in terms of events of their own time. The Jewish-Roman War that began in 66 CE has indeed been a great tribulation. In the siege of Jerusalem, Josephus reports that 1,100,000 persons, most of them Jews, were killed. Ninety-seven thousand others were captured and enslaved. The city is devastated and the Temple destroyed. The headlong flight of those in Judea pictured in 24:15–20 would be a painfully imaginable picture. People may well be asking, "When will this end and why the delay?" Those who now lived at a distance from Jerusalem, as Matthew's community (which is possibly in Antioch) might well worry that the second coming could occur in Jerusalem and they would not know it. They need the assurance that comes in 24:26–27 that his coming will be apparent to everyone, everywhere.

The disciples explicitly ask, "When will this be and what will be the sign of your coming (Greek *parousia*) and of the end of the age?" (v. 3). They receive as answer the word that tribulations they are undergoing now and those that are ahead are but the "birth pangs" of the new age to come. The feminine image of birth pangs "graphically indicates the inevitability as well as the increasing intensity and pain associated with the end time."[22]

At the time of the writing of the Gospel of Matthew the faithful have been waiting for the "imminent return" for decades already. Some accounting is needed. Matthew offers a theological explanation for the delay. This time is a divine provision allowing the mission of the church to go forward. "This good news of the kingdom will be proclaimed throughout the world, as a testimony to all the nations and then the end will come" (v. 14). In a sense, Matthew's view is that the end will not come until the mission of the church is complete. The delay is in fact a time of grace in which many more

22. Levine and Brettler, *Jewish Annotated New Testament,* 260.

will have a chance to hear the good news. Jesus offers the assurance that no matter what happens—even though "heaven and earth will"—"my words will not pass away" (v. 35).

The focus of attention now shifts from "times and signs" to the matter of faithfulness. Jesus says that even he does not know the day or the hour (24:36) and he redirects the disciples' attention to the matter of what they should be doing in the meantime. An example and three parables will follow that encourage being vigilant, faithful, prepared, and diligent.

Before turning away from the apocalyptic to consider these, it is worth noting that our day seems to have a special fascination with the apocalyptic. Symptomatic is the popularity of the "left behind" series. This series constructs a story based upon what has been termed the "rapture." The stories build upon an imaginative account of texts like verses 40–41, "Two men will be in the field; one is taken and one is left. Two women will be grinding meal together, one is taken and one is left" (RSV). It seems to have captured the popular attention. There are even bumper stickers to the effect, "When the rapture comes this car will be without a driver." There are even responding bumper stickers such as one that says, "When the rapture comes can I have your car?"[23]

Throughout history there have been groups who sought to read the signs and calculate the times. Some have claimed to know the day and the hour and even the number of the saved. They build an elaborate edifice on the shaky foundation of apocalyptic literature that is visionary in nature and not a straightforward, simple description of historical events in the future. In a way these groups are claiming to know more than Jesus himself

> God calls us to hope for more than we have yet seen. The hope God gives us is ultimate confidence that supports us when lesser hopes fail us. In Christ God gives hope for a new heaven and earth, certainty of victory over death, assurance of mercy and judgment beyond death. This hope gives us courage for the present struggle.
>
> Presbyterian Church (U.S.A.), "A Declaration of Faith," https://www.pcusa.org/resource/declaration-faith/.

23. Barbara Brown Taylor, *The Seeds of Heaven: Sermons on the Gospel of Matthew* (Louisville, KY: Westminster John Knox Press, 2004), 110.

(24:36). Distracted by preoccupation with "when will this be and what will be the signs?" the church risks losing sight of what it is in fact being counseled to do as people who wait in hope for the coming of God's reign.

24:45–25:30

Vigilant Waiting, Faithfulness, Preparation, and Diligence

Jesus' next teachings serve to redirect the disciples' focus of attention. The important thing is not the signs and the times—as preoccupied as the disciples (and we ourselves) may become with such matters. It is far more important to know what to do between now and then. Such a focus of attention delivers the faithful from anxiety on the one hand yet can deliver them from apathy on the other. "While anxiety and apathy are very different dispositions, they both respond to focused attention."[24] The example and the three parables that follow all reflect the situation of "not knowing" and focus attention on vigilant waiting, faithfulness, preparation, and diligence.

The brief example of the householder reminds the hearers of the importance of wide-awake watchfulness. The householder would surely have "stayed awake" if he knew which night the thief was coming. The faithful who are waiting must remain vigilant. The church in the time between is enjoined to "wake up" and be ready; shaking off apathy, lethargy, and dissipation.

Three parables follow. Most of the parables in Matthew are gathered in chapter 13. There are two other sets of three: those addressed to Jesus' opponents announcing judgment (21:28–22:14) and those found here addressed to the disciples encouraging hopeful, faithful working and waiting.

The parable of the two servants (24:45–51)—one "faithful and wise" and the other "wicked"— is reminiscent of Jesus' teachings in the previous chapter and seems to continue counseling religious leaders in the community who have been "left in charge." In chapter 23, Jesus used the negative example of the Pharisees to teach what

---

24. Ibid., 111.

religious leaders should not be like in the new community. They are not to Lord it over the others (23:11–12) and they are not to be greedy or self-indulgent (23:25). The wicked slave in this parable is the anti-type Jesus condemns—mistreating "fellow slaves" and indulging himself in the master's absence. The threat issued is that people who abuse their power in this way will be put with the "hypocrites." In effect, the parable teaches that people who act like scribes and Pharisees will share their fate.[25] By contrast, the wise and faithful slave does what he is supposed to do and is put in charge of everything.

The parable of the ten bridesmaids is found only in Matthew. The term translated by the NRSV as "bridesmaids" is literally "virgins" (Greek *parthenoi*), but that term is used very generally to refer to any young women of marriageable age. In wedding customs of first century Palestine, it was common for the bridegroom to be escorted by such a company of bridesmaids/virgins to the home of the bride. They would then escort the couple to the house where the wedding and the wedding feast were to take place.[26] In this parable, five are wise and five are foolish. This contrasting of the "wise" and the "foolish" is an ancient conventional device used in wisdom literature. Jesus uses this device both here and in the Sermon on the Mount where a wise man builds on a rock and a foolish man builds on sand (7:24–27). Because the foolish bridesmaids are unprepared—having taken no flask of extra oil for their lamps—they miss the wedding banquet. The earlier motif of Jesus as the bridegroom (9:15) and the *eschaton* as a wedding banquet (22:2) is picked up once again here.

The foolish bridesmaids address the bridegroom: "Lord, Lord, open to us" (25:10), but the response is "Truly, I do not know you." (25:11–12). This accounting parallels the warning Jesus offers in 7:21–23, "Not everyone who says to me, ' Lord, Lord,' will enter the kingdom of heaven, but only the one who does the will of my Father in heaven ... I will declare to them, 'I never know you ... .'"[27] The text also anticipates the final judgment in 25:31–46, where the "goats" address the judge as "Lord" but have not done what God wills in the

---

25. Hare, *Matthew*, 284.
26. Levine and Brettler, *Jewish Annotated New Testament*, 46.
27. Senior, *Abingdon New Testament Commentaries*, 275.

way of showing compassion to "the least" Allegorizing in this light, the oil could signify the "higher righteousness" entailed in doing the will of God by loving the neighbor. This association calls to mind a text from Proverbs: "The light of the righteous rejoices, but the lamp of the wicked goes out" (Prov. 13:9).

Feminist interpreters have observed that much of the preaching on this text overplays the matter of the foolish bridesmaids, giving little notice of the wise bridesmaids who light the way for the bridegroom and join in the wedding feast. The wise bridesmaids may serve as examples of wisdom and anticipation of the advent of the Messiah. Such a reading is more consistent with the Gospel's direction and its overall positive portrayal of women. They are included and they are often made exemplars; as we see in the genealogy (1:1–17), the woman with a hemorrhage (9:20–22), the Canaanite woman (15:21–28), and the passion and resurrection accounts.[28]

This parable of the virgins makes clear yet again the Gospel's concern for women as reflected throughout the judgment discourse. Their responsibility to be faithful and vigilant is placed on par with that of the male slaves of the preceding parables. The assumption of agency and accountability is here apparent. There is also direct parallel in description of divine saving action in the judgment in 24:40–41 where a gendered pairs are presented. "Two men will be

---

We do not know when the final day will come. In our time we see only broken and scattered signs that the renewal of all things is under way. We do not yet see the end of cruelty and suffering in the world, the church, or our own lives. But we see Jesus as Lord. As he stands at the center of our history, we are confident he will stand at its end. He will judge all people and nations. Evil will be condemned and rooted out of God's good creation. There will be no more tears or pain. All things will be made new. The fellowship of human beings with God and each other will be perfected.

Presbyterian Church (U.S.A.), "A Declaration of Faith."

---

28. Marie-Eloise Rosenblatt, "Got into the Party After All: Women's Issues and the Five Foolish Virgins," in *A Feminist Companion to Matthew*, ed. Amy-Jill Levine, 171–95 (Sheffield England: Sheffield Academic Press, 2001).

> Here is your gospel, your project of the reign of God, your message of love for those who suffer. We have kept it faithfully. We haven't used it to transform our life or to introduce your kingdom in the world. We didn't want to take chances. But here it is, undamaged.
>
> José A. Pagola, *The Way Opened Up by Jesus: A Commentary on the Gospel of Matthew* (Miami, FL: Convivium Press, 2012), 39.

in the field; one is taken and one is left. Two women will be grinding meal together, one is taken and one is left" (RSV). The Revised Standard Version conveys gender here as is congruent with the gender assigned tasks common to the context. Further, the text conveys special concern for women in recognizing their special travail if they are pregnant or nursing (24:19) in the time of tribulation.

In distinction from the first parable that seems directed to leaders in the community of faith and the second that seems directed to all the members of the community, the parable of the talents seems to focus on those who have been entrusted with particular gifts.[29] The slaves are given charges that fit them; "to each according to his ability" (25:15). The parable urges diligence in making good use of whatever has been entrusted. The master in the parable entrusts money in varying amounts to three different servants. The sums given are significant; even one talent is about fifteen years of wages for a laborer. Two of the slaves work with the money and turn a profit while the master is away, but the third buries the talent in the ground. Although it was very customary to bury money to hide it from thieves, by comparison with the "good and trustworthy" slaves who put the money to work, this third one is unproductive, "wicked," and "lazy" (v. 26). The very least he could have done is put the money into the bank to earn interest. When called to give an account, the servant's rationale is "I was afraid." This fearful, protective, cautious disposition that proves so unproductive is not the disposition of a "good and faithful servant (KJV rendering; Greek *piste*, "faithful"). This serves as yet another negative example conveying what those who wait should not be like.

29. Hare, *Matthew*, 286.

25:31–46

The Last Judgment—A Surprise Ending:
"Lord when was it that we saw you . . . ?"

Following these parables that counsel vigilant waiting, faithfulness, preparation, and diligence, there comes an account of "the last judgment." Matthew's is the only such depiction in the New Testament. The "apocalyptic drama"[30] resonates with the vision in Daniel 7:13–14, which also speaks of the "Son of Man" coming in glory with his angels and sitting on a throne to judge.

"All the nations will be gathered before him." The word translated "nations" (Greek *ethnē*) is sometimes used to designate the Gentiles, but here it is simply "a synonym for 'the whole inhabited earth.'"[31] People from every race and nation, every culture and religion are gathered. All are included in this universal judgment, and the judge asks nothing about whether they are Jews or Gentiles or what they believe about Jesus. The issue at hand is whether they have showed compassion. Do they practice the love of neighbor, which is the heart of the law as Jesus has taught (5:17–48; 7:12; 22:34–40)?

> We are not truly following the steps of Jesus if we are more concerned about religion than about human suffering. Nothing will wake the Church out of its routine, its paralysis, and its mediocrity, until we learn compassion for the hunger, humiliation and suffering of people.
>
> Pagola, *The Way Opened Up by Jesus*, 219.

The judgment is likened to a shepherd separating sheep from goats. The metaphor pictures a "mixed flock of sheep and goats (a common sight in Middle Eastern herding) that are separated at the end of the day."[32] This would be ordinary practice since goats must be sheltered from cold whereas the sheep can be pastured through the night. This "final sorting" parallels passages in the parables of the reign of God given in chapter 13. There wheat and weeds are

---

30. Boring, *The New Interpreter's Bible*, 8:455.
31. Carter, *Matthew and the Margins*, 493.
32. Senior, *Abingdon New Testament Commentaries*, 281.

allowed to grow together until the harvest and God's dragnet takes in all kinds of fish, but there will come a time of sorting one from another. Similarly, in the three parables immediately preceding the last judgment there is a reckoning depicted in which good slaves, wise bridesmaids, and faithful stewards all receive their reward.

The theme of the Messiah as "shepherd" is reiterated throughout the Gospel of Matthew from the very beginning. In 2:6 it is announced that from Bethlehem there would come "a ruler who is to shepherd my people Israel." The theme is picked up again in 9:36 where Jesus had compassion on the crowds "because they were harassed and helpless, like sheep without a shepherd." In 18:10–14, God's care is likened to that of a shepherd who, having a hundred sheep, will leave the ninety-nine and go in search of the one who has gone astray.

Now the "Son of Man" coming in all his glory is likened to a shepherd. It is an image that reaches back to Ezekiel 34:

> For thus says the Lord GOD: I myself will search for my sheep, and will seek them out. As shepherds seek out their flocks when they are among their scattered sheep, so I will seek out my sheep. I will rescue them from all the places to which they have been scattered on a day of clouds and thick darkness. . . . I will seek the lost, and I will bring back the strayed, and I will bind up the injured, and I will strengthen the weak . . . but the fat and the strong I will destroy. I will feed them with justice. (Ezek. 34:11–16)

The judge knows the righteous from the unrighteous just as a shepherd knows the sheep from the goats. What marks these sheep as "righteous" (Matt. 25:37) is their particular attention to those in need (25:37). "I was hungry and you gave me food, I was thirsty and you gave me something to drink, I was a stranger and you welcomed me, I was naked and you gave me clothing, I was sick and you took care of me, I was in prison and you visited me" (vv. 35–36). The term translated "righteous" (Greek *dikaioi*) is one form of a favorite term in Matthew, *dikaiosynē* (righteousness). Its meaning joins justice and mercy in a way reminiscent of the Hebrew term *tsedaqah*. It is no more than simple "justice" for those who have the ability to care for those who have need through acts of mercy. This term appears with such frequency in Matthew that it is sometimes referred to as the "Gospel of Justice."[33] Here, in the accounting of the final judgment, this overriding concern comes to the fore decisively.

The "righteous" ones display "true piety" in that they do these works of mercy unselfconsciously, with no consideration for being seen or being rewarded (6:1–18). They seem surprised to have been discovered (25:37). Their compassion for "the least of these" (unnamed and perhaps unknown) is not a matter of garnering social approval or divine blessing. Nor is there any expectation of reciprocity from recipients who are in need. The categories of compassion in the list (25:35–36) are those that would be typical in any listing of acts of mercy in Judaism. Most things in the list are in fact aspects of Jesus' public ministry and commended to the disciples for their ministry. The only unusual entry regards visiting prisoners, but this may reflect needs particular to the early Christian community in times of persecution.[34]

> This is what it means to be contemplative in the heart of the world. Seeing and adoring the presence of Jesus, especially in the lowly appearance of bread, and in the distressing disguise of the poor.
>
> Mother Teresa, *In the Heart of the World: Thoughts, Stories, and Prayers* (Novato, CA: New World Library, 1997), 55.

The real surprise in the story is how the judge of all the nations identifies with the "least of these" (25:40). Jesus' solidarity with and advocacy for the least, the little, and the lost comes to its full realization in this text (18:1–14). Everyone is surprised. Both those on the right hand and those on the left hand respond, "When did we see you . . . ?"

In Matthew's community where the delay of the Parousia has become a troubling concern, the Gospel of Matthew puts the matter in its place. The real question is not, "When will the Son of Man come in all his glory?" The real question is, "How shall we live while

---

33. Michael Crosby, *House of Disciples: Church Economics and Justice in Matthew* (Maryknoll, NY: Orbis, 1988), 136.

34. Senior, *Abingdon New Testament Commentaries*, 282.

we wait?" To be among the "righteous" is to live out the love of the neighbor, demonstrating justice through acts of mercy for the most vulnerable. To live this way is to be always ready for the judgment and not in the position of saying, "I really was not expecting you— not here and not now—and certainly not in the 'distressing disguise' of this person in need."

Contemporary believers, centuries later, hear a similar message. We need not worry about the timing of the "second coming." Christ is already in our midst now and comes to us again and again—unexpectedly—in the form of the person in need. Our response to "the least of these" is our response to the judge of all the nations.

FURTHER REFLECTIONS
Jesus and Judgment

There is, among many contemporary Christians, a tendency to pass over the matter of judgment altogether. In common parlance today "judgmental" is a bad word, having only negative connotations. This reflection will offer words in praise of judgment and attempt a reclaiming of the concept.

Theologically, the meaning content of the judgment becomes desiccated when the concept is separated from redemption. Better insights arise when we are clear that *judgment is ordered toward redemption*. The response of passing over the concept of judgment altogether may in part be a reaction to accounts that—disconnected from God's redeeming work—are less than edifying and may even be offensive. Puritan preachers, for example, were known to dwell on the imaginative elaboration of the horrors of Hell in sermons designed to convert through the threat of everlasting torment. The Belgic Confession, written in a situation of persecution, promises that the elect "shall see the terrible vengeance which God shall execute on the wicked who most cruelly persecuted, oppressed and tormented them in this world." Part of the bliss of Heaven, then, is the opportunity to witness the suffering of those who persecuted the faithful in this life.

Marjorie Suchocki objects to this way of thinking and notes that, "Selfrighteousness and revenge are odd entryways into a vision of the kingdom of God."[35]

While we may have inherited some problematic visions of divine judgment, there are within the tradition some better alternatives that might help us in reclaiming a religiously viable understanding of judgment. Some notable theologians have rejected problematic readings without rejecting the concept of judgment altogether. Calvin, for example, interpreted biblical descriptions of the physical torments of Hell as metaphorical.[36] They convey the sinner's experience of separation from God, which is a kind of self-imposed spiritual torment. Hendrikus Berkhof proposed that Hell be thought of as a kind of refining fire purging away the dross and purifying the precious metal.[37] It is a vision consistent with the theological affirmation that judgment is ordered toward redemption. On a lighter note, popular writer and theologian C. S. Lewis proposed that what happens after we die is that through all eternity we become more and more who we are. For some this might be heavenly, for others, . . . not.[38]

Perhaps we do well to lay aside notions of judgment that would bifurcate judgment and redemption, but it will not do to simply cease to speak of the judgment. As many have insisted, if there is no judgment, there is no justice. Judgment is finally about setting things right: establishing justice. The coming of a just judge is something to be received with gladness—especially by those who have been oppressed or excluded by injustices. This sensibility is communicated well in Psalm 96 where the coming of the just judge who will "judge peoples with equity" is a cause for rejoicing in the whole of creation.

> Say among the nations, "The Lord is king!
> The world is firmly established; it shall never be moved.
> He will judge the peoples with equity.'"

35. Marjorie Hewett Suchocki, *God-Christ-Church: A Practical Guide to Process Theology* (New York: Crossroad, 1986), 178.
36. John Calvin, *Institutes of the Christian Religion* 3.25.12, ed. John T. McNeill, trans. Ford Lewis Battles, LCC (Philadelphia: Westminster Press, 1960), 2:1008.
37. Hendrikus Berkhof, *Christian Faith: An Introduction to the Study of the Faith,* trans. Sierd Woudstra, rev. ed. (Grand Rapids: Eerdmans, 1986), 536.
38. C.S. Lewis, *The Great Divorce* (New York: HarperCollins, 1946), chap. 9, par. 41.

Let the heavens be glad, and let the earth rejoice;
  let the sea roar, and all that fills it;
  let the field exult, and everything in it.
Then shall all the trees of the forest sing for joy
  before the Lord; for he is coming,
  for he is coming to judge the earth.
He will judge the world with righteousness,
  and the peoples with his truth.

(Ps. 96:10–13)

The Gospel of Matthew is often called "the Gospel of justice." It envisions the coming of a righteous judge for a judgment in which all are judged by the same standard. In the last judgment as pictured in 25:31–46, the standard universally applied is whether one shows compassion (Greek *dikaiosynē*, "justice"; "mercy") to those in need. The question is whether one practices the love of the neighbor that is the heart of the law.

If there is no resurrection and no judgment, then at the end of it all, evil will not have been seriously addressed. Nietzsche put it this way, "To redeem the past . . . that alone do I call redemption."[39] Miroslav Volf has come to a similar conclusion: "No fulfillment is possible if the past remains unredeemed; an unredeemed past will keep every present (and future) unredeemed. The eschatological transition cannot therefore be only about being giving a fresh beginning, but must also be about having all of one's failed beginnings, middles and ends redeemed."[40]

Evil in human history must be finally and unmistakably exposed and judged. Evildoers themselves must be transformed by God's grace so that they can be freed from evil and reconciled to one another. Such a vision requires both judgment and redemption— "a coming to terms with the reality of our lives and a purgation of what we are in order to become what God wills us to be."[41] In the

---

39. Friedrich Nietzsche, *Thus Spake Zarathustra*, trans. R. J. Hollingsdale (London: Penguin, 1969), 161.
40. Miroslav Volf, "Enter into Joy! Sin, Death, and the Life of the World to Come," in *The End of the Word and the Ends of God: Theology and Science on Eschatology*, ed. John Polkinghorne and Michael Welker (Harrisburg, PA: Trinity Press, 2000), 262.
41. John Polkinghorne and Michael Welker, "Introduction: Science and Theology on the End of the World and the Ends of God," in *The End of the Word and the Ends of God*, 13.

presence of God (the judgment) we confront the truth about ourselves and our brokenness and we receive God's mercy (redemption) and are made whole. Then, as Matthew proposed, "The pure
in heart shall see God" (5:8). Calvin spoke of a great "watching and
waking of the soul" after death, with which the soul "perceives" its
healing and its completion and experiences its rebirth for the life of
the world to come. Redemption is "always in progress" in the process of judgment.[42]

Miroslav Volf, who was a prisoner of war and lived under interrogation and threat throughout his imprisonment, has observed that
the judgment/redemption must surely be a social and not simply
an individual process. Those who are reconciled with God must also
be reconciled with one another so that "the final justification will
have to be accompanied by the final social reconciliation . . ."[43]

Judgment is part of the renewal of all things. The promise of
renewal is well described in A Declaration of Faith, a document
approved for study and liturgical use in the Presbyterian Church
(U.S.A.):

> **All things will be renewed in Christ.** In Christ God gave us
> a glimpse of the new creation he has already begun and will
> surely finish. We do not know when the final day will come.
> In our time we see only broken and scattered signs that the
> renewal of all things is under way. We do not yet see the end
> of cruelty and suffering in the world, the church, or our own
> lives. But we see Jesus as Lord. As he stands at the center of
> our history, we are confident he will stand at its end. He will
> judge all people and nations. Evil will be condemned and
> rooted out of God's good creation. There will be no more tears
> or pain. All things will be made new. The fellowship of human
> beings with God and each other will be perfected.[44]

The Gospel of Matthew is clear in its caution that God alone is
to judge. In the parable of the weeds and the wheat (13:24–30), the
laborers are warned not to try to sort things out for themselves.

---

42. John Calvin, "Psychopannychia," in *Tracts and Treatises in Defense of the Reformed Faith*, trans.
by H. Beveridge, vol. 3 (Grand Rapids: Eerdmans, 1958), 419–20.
43. Volf, "Enter into Joy!" 263.
44. Presbyterian Church (U.S.A.), "A Declaration of Faith."

They are to wait for the householder whose field this is and wait for the time of harvest. "Harvest" is a "stock metaphor for eschatological judgment"[45] and already appears three times in Matthew's Gospel before this point (3:10, 3:12; 9:37). The parable does not simply equate the weeds with the world and the wheat with the church.[46] The mixed nature of things is both inside and outside the community of faith. So also, "belief and unbelief, like the wheat and the weeds in the parable, are mixed together in each one of us."[47] It is best to let the mixture grow together. That way we do not mistakenly exclude any of God's beloved. Nor do we give up on ourselves in the face of our own mixed response. Read in this way, the parable is a parable of grace that urges "make no exclusions." This is God's harvest. God alone will judge.

Redemption (grace/mercy) and judgment are held together in this parable and other parables of judgment. A Declaration of Faith[48] offers a thoughtful summation on the matter of not bifurcating mercy and judgment:

> **God's mercy and judgment await us all.** In the life, death, and resurrection of Jesus God has already demonstrated his judging and saving work. We are warned that rejecting God's love and not caring for others whom God loves results in eternal separation from him and them. Yet we are also told that God loves the whole world and wills the salvation of all humankind in Christ. We live in tension between God's warnings and promises. Knowing the righteous judgment of God in Christ, we urge all people to be reconciled to God, not exempting ourselves from the warnings. Constrained by God's love in Christ, we have good hope for all people, not exempting the most unlikely from the promises. Judgment belongs to God and not to us. We are sure that God's future for every person will be both merciful and just.

---

45. Senior, *Abingdon New Testament Commentaries*, 149.
46. Ulrich Luz, *The Theology of the Gospel of Matthew* (Cambridge, UK: Cambridge University Press, 1995), 89.
47. Pagola, *The Way Opened Up by Jesus*, 132.
48. Presbyterian Church (U.S.A.), "A Declaration of Faith."

PART 3
THE CROSS OF CHRIST
26:1–27:61

Chapter 26 opens with a formulaic transition phrase, "When Jesus had finished saying all these things . . . " Each of the five blocks of narrative/teaching in Matthew closes with a similar saying (7:28; 11:1; 13:53; 19:11; 26:1). This final transition phrase adds the word "all" and signals an end to the narrative/teaching blocks as such. The phrase used here is not unlike Deuteronomy 32:45, "When Moses had finished reciting all these words . . . " The five blocks in Matthew have been compared to the "five books of Moses" (the Pentateuch). Throughout the Gospel of Matthew Jesus is presented as the authoritative interpreter of the law, the true heir to "Moses' seat."

Matthew here transitions to an accounting of the climactic events of Jesus' passion and resurrection. Themes and images that were present in the birth narrative now reappear in the passion and resurrection narrative. The ending of the Gospel in some ways reiterates the beginning.[1] Jerusalem is in an uproar (2:3; 27:24). The story of God's saving deliverance in Exodus gets recapitulated (2:13–15; 26:1, 17–29). Divine warnings come through dreams to the Wise Men and Joseph at the beginning (2:12–13, 19, 22) and now to Pilate's wife at the end (27:19). There are angels appearing (1:20, 24; 2:13, 19; 28:5). Some respond to the events with worship (2:2, 8, 11; 28:17) while others are troubled (2:3; 28:4). Jesus' authority/kingship gets emphasized through important titles and affirmations

---

1. Eugene Boring gives a complete listing of the elements that appear at the beginning and the end of the Gospel, *The New Interpreter's Bible: New Testament Articles, Matthew, Mark* (Nashville: Abingdon Press, 1995), 8:460.

(1:1; 2:2; 28:18). Emmanuel "God with Us" (1:23) now promises to be with us "always, to the end of the age" (28:20).

Running through Matthew's Gospel there has been a theme of crossing ethnic and religious divisions. Matters of faithfulness and falsity cross. In the beginning of the Gospel the Gentile wise men and the Jewish Holy Family are joined together as those who have faith in God and act upon that faith—worshiping and protecting the infant Jesus. They are contrasted now by a coalition of the Gentile governor Pilate and the Jewish high priest Caiaphas. Acting in bad faith, they will together condemn God's anointed to death.[2]

---

2. Amy-Jill Levine, *The Social and Ethnic Dimensions of Matthean Social History: Nowhere among the Gentiles* (Lewiston, NY: Edwin Mellen Press, 1988), 277.

26:1–27:31

On the Way to the Cross

26:1–5

"They conspire to arrest Jesus by stealth and kill him."

Who is in charge? In Matthew's accounting, Jesus knows what is ahead and proceeds nevertheless. In this passage (26:2) Jesus gives the fourth and final passion prediction (16:21; 17:22; 20:18). Matthew presents Jesus as fully cognizant of what is coming. Jesus knows Judas will betray him (26:25). Jesus knows the disciples will dessert him (26:31). Jesus knows Peter will deny him (26:34). He knows that crucifixion awaits him in Jerusalem.

As the action of the story now moves to Jerusalem, the main opposition shifts from scribes and Pharisees to the chief priests and the elders who were based in Jerusalem. The chief priests are from the priestly families who descended from the tribe of Levi. They are spread throughout the country and have local teaching authority. On rotation they travel to Jerusalem to perform the Temple liturgy and the sacrifices that can only be performed in Jerusalem in the Temple. The Gospel of Luke notes that John the Baptist's parents, Zechariah and Elizabeth, were of this priestly family and Zechariah was serving in the Temple when John's conception was announced to him by the angel Gabriel (Luke 1). Many of the chief priests from the surrounding countryside would gather in Jerusalem for the Passover. The "high priest" and his family would reside permanently in Jerusalem. The high priest—at this time Caiaphas—serves as "the nominal head of the people absent a king."[1] The elders are persons of social standing who represent the people on the Sanhedrin, a kind

---

1. *The Jewish Annotated New Testament,* ed. Amy-Jill Levine and Marc Zvi Brettler (Oxford: Oxford University Press, 2011), 48.

of deliberating/ruling council in Jerusalem. This is the cast of characters that are Jesus' main adversaries in Jerusalem

This is not Jesus' first encounter with chief priests and scribes. When he made his entry into Jerusalem—humble yet triumphant—they do not receive him well. The crowds welcome him as a prophet, spreading their cloaks on the road and cutting branches from the trees for his pathway (21:8). The children herald him as the "Son of David." Jesus goes directly to the Temple and disrupts all the buying and selling there. He gives signs of the end time (the eschaton) by healing the lame and blind there. He enacts a cleansing of the Temple—recalling its role as a house of prayer and healing for the people.

At that time the chief priests respond fairly aggressively challenging Jesus and asking him, "By what authority are you doing these things, and who gave you this authority? (21:23) Even in this first encounter the chief priests want to arrest him, but they do not because they fear the crowd who regard Jesus as a prophet (21:46).

In the final chapters of the Gospel, the chief priests are cast as formidable and even villainous antagonists. They plot and scheme against Jesus (26:3-4), paying Judas to betray him (26:15), seeking false witnesses against him (26:59), condemning him for blasphemy (26:65-66), mocking and abusing him (26:26-68) and then 'handing him over" to Pilate (27:2). When he is before Pilate they stir up the crowds to ask for Barabbas to be released and for Jesus to be crucified (27:20). They help the Pharisees securing soldiers to guard the tomb (27:62-66). They pay the soldiers "a large sum of money" (28:12) not to tell what really happened at the tomb but to lie and say that the disciples stole the body. No contemporary "follow the money" story of corruption and the abuse of power rivals this one.

What follows is the account of Jesus "passion" or suffering (from the Latin passi, "to suffer"). There is more to this than the cross itself. Jesus' suffering has many dimensions to it. Most obvious is the suffering that he undergoes at the hands of his enemies: arrest, trials before the high priest and before the Roman governor, slapping, spitting, flogging, the public humiliation of carrying the cross, mocking by the soldiers and the passers-by. What part do the disciples play in his suffering? Judas betrays him. The few he selects to watch with him through his agony of prayer in Gethsemane fall asleep. When he is arrested they all desert him. During his trial in the high priest's court Peter denies him three times. Where is God in all this? Jesus prays "deeply grieved, even to death" (26:38) that he may be spared this cup of suffering. Yet God does not deliver him, and the passion culminates in crucifixion—"the most cursed of deaths." From the cross Jesus' cry of dereliction reverberates, "My God, my God, why have you forsaken me?" (27:46). In these moments, no answer comes, and the full weight of god-forsakenness descends.

26:6–13

The Woman at Bethany and Her Extravagant Gift: "What she has done will be told in remembrance of her."

There is one bright interlude before the worst of it begins. Jesus is staying in the home of "Simon the leper," who lives in Bethany, just outside Jerusalem. As they sat at table, a woman came to Jesus with an alabaster jar of very costly ointment, and she poured it on his head (26:7). The immediate response of the disciples is anger at the waste. Why this extravagance? Their objection is not unfounded. Rabbinic tradition mandates the selling of luxury items to provide for the poor.[2] Almsgiving was an ongoing obligation but was especially emphasized during Passover week.[3]

When the disciples object, Jesus reframes what she has done. It is more than a "beautiful thing" (as the NRSV translates); it is a "good work." Rabbis in fact debated "the relative importance of two kinds of good works: giving money to the poor and burying the dead."[4] Some argued that burying the dead should be given higher priority because giving to the poor can be done at any time and involves an impersonal act of giving money whereas burial must be done at the right time and involves personal giving. She is attending to the

---

2. Levine and Brettler, *Jewish Annotated New Testament*, 48.
3. Douglas R. A. Hare, *Matthew*, Interpretation: A Bible Commentary for Teaching and Preaching (Louisville, KY: Westminster/John Knox Press, 1992), 294.
4. Ibid.

second "good work"—anointing him for burial. When Jesus says "you always have the poor with you," it is no callous remark but an agreement with the rabbis.

Jesus' commitments regarding care for the poor are already well established by this point in the Gospel. It is a centerpiece in his teachings in the Sermon on the Mount. He highlights it in commending responsiveness to beggars (5:42) and appropriate almsgiving (6:2–4) and serving God instead of wealth (6:24). This priority is clear in his invitation to the rich young man to sell his possessions and give to the poor (19:21). The final judgment is based upon care for the "least ones" (25:31–46).

Now is the time for a "good work" of another sort. The disciples do not seem attuned to the imminence of Jesus' death—despite the four passion predictions he has already delivered (16:21; 17:22; 20:18; 26:2)—it seems they still do not get it. Perhaps this woman was paying better attention. Perhaps she understood that Jesus was now a "dead man walking."[5]

The criticism she receives is reminiscent of the implied criticism that the disciples of John brought to the disciples of Jesus,[6] "Why do we and the Pharisees fast often but your disciples do not fast?" (9:14). Jesus' answer was that the wedding guests could not mourn in the presence of the bridegroom—a time for mourning and fasting would come later. The woman at Bethany, in her extravagance, seems to recognize the presence of the "bridegroom" and anticipate the time when he will be "taken away from them" (9:15).

That she anoints him "on his head" has another signification. Messiah means "anointed." In this way the woman at Bethany functions as a prophet—identifying and anointing the one whom God has chosen. Her role is not unlike the role of Samuel in identifying David as "the Lord's anointed" and carrying out David's anointing as king (1 Samuel 16:12–13). This act is in its own way a prophetic testimony. In the Hebrew Scriptures, prophets, priests, and kings are all "anointed." It is said of Jesus that, as the "Messiah" (the

5. Christine Vogel, "Jesus' Anointing at Bethany" (sermon on Matthew 26:6–12, McCormick Seminary, Chicago, IL, Maundy Thursday Service, March 27, 2013).

6. Donald Senior, *Abingdon New Testament Commentaries: Matthew* (Nashville: Abingdon Press, 1998), 293.

anointed), he embodies and fulfills each of these three anointed offices. (See "Further Reflections: The Threefold Work of Prophet, Priest, and King," pp. 173–74.)

This is the first of several places in the passion narrative where women will take the lead. This woman at Bethany anoints Jesus for burial; other women will be the last at the cross, the ones who accompany Jesus' body to the tomb, the ones who return to the tomb, and the ones who become the first witnesses of resurrection.

26:14–16
"What will you give me to betray him?"

The woman at Bethany is "a bright foil to the dark plotting of the enemies and Judas."[7] Her extravagant gift in preparation for Jesus' burial is in stark contrast to Judas' greedy grasping after a paltry sum to hand Jesus over to die. The disparity is made all the worse by her anonymity; Judas is "one of the twelve" (26:14).

The chief priests and the elders have already been conspiring to "arrest Jesus by stealth and kill him" (26:4). They are taking care, though, for fear of the crowds and not planning to arrest him in public (at the festival) lest "there may be a riot among the people" (26:3–5). This constraining "fear of the crowds" is reminiscent of Herod's fear that constrains him from killing John the Baptist outright (14:5).

Judas plays right in to their plans when he offers to "betray" Jesus. The chief priests pay him thirty pieces of silver. This would likely have been thirty shekels, worth four denarii each, for a total of approximately 120 days wages.[8] With this there begins a sequence in which Jesus is again and again "handed over" (Greek *paradidomi*, "to hand over; to deliver up, to betray"). Judas hands him over to the chief priests. The chief priests will hand him over to the high priest, Caiaphas. Caiaphas will hand him over to Pilate. Pilate will hand him over to be crucified.

---

7. Hare, *Matthew*, 293.
8. Levine and Brettler, *Jewish Annotated New Testament*, 48.

26:17-35
Sharing in the Passover Meal with the Disciples

Jesus speaks the words "My time is near" (26:17). There are two
kinds of time signified by different Greek terms. The one used here is
kairos, which signals an opportune time or a time of supreme importance. This meaning is in contrast to time as *chronos,* which is used
for the ordinary sequencing of chronological time. *Kairos* is a word
that has also been used of the end-time earlier in the Gospel (8:29;
13:30; 16:3; 21:34). Jesus' words give an eschatological aura to the
events that follow.[9] Signs of the end will become apparent to all at
the point of Jesus death (27:51-53).

The context of the Passover meal, which is the setting for the Last
Supper in Matthew's Gospel, looks not only backward to Israel's deliverance from slavery in Egypt but also forward to the messianic banquet at the end of time. Other Gospel accounts frame the last Supper
differently, but for Matthew and his community it is important that
this be a Passover meal, and his account makes it clear that this is the
setting (26:17-19). The Passover meal to be served (the seder) com-
memorates the flight from Egypt and God's deliverance of the people
from slavery (Exod. 12:1-20; Deut. 16:1-8). Special food is prepared
and served. Unleavened bread (matzah) recalls the haste of the flight
from Egypt—no time for the bread to rise. A paschal lamb recalls the
blood sacrifice marking the homes where the "angel of death" should
pass over. Bitter herbs recall the bitterness of the days in Egypt. Even as
the meal looks backward to this experience of deliverance it also looks
forward to the day when the fullness of God's reign will be established.

Often a prayer for the coming of the Messiah is lifted up at the
Passover meal. In the first century, it was believed that the Messiah
would come at Passover. A first-century rabbi put it this way, "On this
night they were saved; on this night they will be saved"[10] Readers are
meant to understand that the Messiah has indeed come. In Matthew,
the Last Supper, the prayer in Gethsemane, the betrayal and arrest,
and the trial before the Sanhedrin (chief priests and elders) all take
place on Thursday evening, which is the beginning of Passover. Jesus

---

9. Senior, *Abingdon New Testament Commentaries,* 295.
10. Hare, *Matthew,* 297.

is tried and crucified on Friday, which is the actual day of Passover. This setting evokes "the motif of deliverance from oppression associated with Passover as a back drop to Jesus own death."[11]

Now Jesus says, "Take, eat; this is my body." As he offers the cup he says, "Drink from it all of you; for this is my blood of the covenant, which is poured out for many for the forgiveness of sins" (26:26–27). These words convey the salvific import of Jesus' coming passion. God's covenant with God's people and God's saving work among them are what Jesus' life and ministry have been about from the beginning. This is what his coming passion and death will uphold. It has been so from the beginning of the Gospel and is even embedded in his name. "Jesus" means "God saves" (1:21). When Jesus got into trouble with the authorities early in his ministry it was for forgiving sins and healing on the Sabbath (9:2–8). God's saving work in Jesus is identified in Matthew with the innocent Suffering Servant of Isaiah 53 who brings forgiveness and healing to the people. His suffering is cast as redemptive suffering,

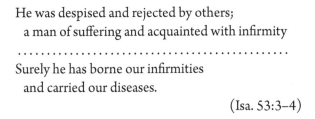

He was despised and rejected by others;
    a man of suffering and acquainted with infirmity
. . . .
Surely he has borne our infirmities
    and carried our diseases.

(Isa. 53:3–4)

Jesus' ministry is presented in servant terminology, "The Son of Man came not to be served but to serve and to give his life as a ransom for many" (20:28).[12]

In the Last Supper Jesus shares the meal of God's deliverance even as he is about to be "delivered up." The meal is set squarely between Judas's betrayal and Jesus' prediction that Peter will deny him and they all will desert him. In Matthew, Jesus is fully cognizant of the many ways in which they will all fail him, showing their frailty, foolishness, and "little faith." Nevertheless he sits down to share this holy meal with them, and none are excluded. The act is reminiscent of a practice emblematic to his ministry: he sits down with sinners and eats with

11. Senior, *Abingdon New Testament Commentaries*, 290.
12. Ibid., 299.

them. Again we find Jesus sits down with sinners as he was accustomed to do; it was one of the chief complaints against him (9:10–12).

Judas has already betrayed him (26:14–16). As he takes his seat with Jesus at the Passover meal the "blood money" is already in hand. When Jesus announces, "One of you will betray me," Judas makes a show of incredulity along with all the others, "Surely not I, Rabbi?" Does Judas not understand what he has done? Or is his question "as hypocritical as his kiss at Gethsemane"?[13] Jesus answers, "You have said so." It is a confirmation that is indirect but clear. It is the answer Jesus will give to Caiaphas when he asks whether Jesus is "the Messiah, the Son of God" and to Pilate when he asks, "Are you the King of the Jews?" (27:11).

Judas's choice of the word "rabbi" as the mode of address for Jesus is significant. Jesus has consistently taught the disciples that the title "rabbi" is not to be used in the new community and none of the other disciples address him in this way (23:8). Yet Judas employs the title here and will do so again in the act of betrayal at Gethsemane. There his address, "Greetings, Rabbi!" and his kiss will identify Jesus as the one to be arrested.

Peter sits at the meal making promises he cannot keep. "I will never desert you. . . . Even if I must die I will not deny you" (26:33–34). Despite his brave protestations, Peter cannot even stand by Jesus and keep awake with him during Jesus' agony of prayer (26:40). When the emissaries of the chief priests and elders come with their swords and clubs, Peter will flee with all the rest (v. 56). When put to the test in the courtyard of Caiaphas, Peter will deny Jesus with oaths and cursing (26:69–75).

Judas partakes, and Peter partakes, and all the disciples/deserters partake. Clearly this is a meal for sinners. It is to them that Jesus offers the cup "poured out . . . for the forgiveness of sins" (26:28).

26:36–46

Praying Alone: "Could you not stay awake with me one hour?"

After sharing the Passover meal, Jesus and the disciples go to a place called Gethsemane, which was at the base of the Mount of Olives;

---

13. Hare, *Matthew,* 296.

"Gethsemane" means "oil press" (Hebrew *gat shemen*). There Jesus takes aside Peter, James, and John—the same three disciples who shared in the vision of the transfiguration. He tells them, "I am deeply grieved, even to death; remain here, and stay awake with me" (26:37). Even this is beyond them, and they all fall asleep; the wakeful watchful stance Jesus counseled in chapters 24–25 has been lost on them. It is as if they have already deserted him as he warned they would, well before people from the chief priests and elders come after him with swords and clubs (26:47).

Jesus prays, "My Father, if this cannot pass unless I drink it, your will be done." He had taught his disciples in the Sermon on the Mount to pray, "Our Father" and "your will be done" (6:7–13). This is how he prays even now in the agonizing moments in Gethsemane. He petitions three times that God may "let this cup pass." "Cup" is a metaphor here and elsewhere for suffering or even death. The prayer for deliverance is more than earnest; it is "grieved and agitated." All the same, Jesus' response of faith and obedience to God is not contingent on an affirmative answer to this prayer. He prays, "Your will be done" (26:42).

26:47–56
"My betrayer is at hand."

Judas addresses Jesus as "rabbi"—the title Jesus instructed his disciples to eschew—and betrays him with a kiss. Jesus addresses Judas as "friend." (26:50). It is a "politely cool generic form of address to someone whose name one does not know."[14]

Accompanying Judas is a large crowd with swords and clubs. These are likely the Temple guard (v. 58) sent by the chief priests. When they lay hands on Jesus to arrest him one of the disciples responds with violence, drawing his sword to meet their swords. Jesus commands him to put away his sword.

Responding in kind to aggression and violence is not the way of the followers of Jesus. He has consistently taught love for enemies and regularly demonstrated nonviolent responses. When confronted

14. Boring, *The New Interpreter's Bible*, 8:477.

along the way Jesus has often withdrawn or simply absorbed the offence rather than responding in kind. As he taught in the Sermon on the Mount, "Do not resist an evil doer. But if anyone strikes you on the right check; turn the other also" (5:39). Reciprocal, retaliatory violence is ruled out. (See "Further Reflections: Blessed are the Peacemakers/Love Your Enemies," pp. 99–101.)

The effect of retaliation is only a spiraling of violence, and "all who take the sword will perish by the sword" (26:52). Not only is the way of the sword wrong, it is also futile. It is futile for both the ones arresting Jesus and the ones defending him. He has at his disposal twelve legions of angels. A "legion" in the Roman army was a company of "as many as six thousand men.[15] From this vantage point, the swords of those who arrest him are impotent and the swords of those who would defend him are unnecessary.

Yet Jesus does not call upon the angels to deliver him. In a sense, Jesus already made this decision at the time of his temptation in the wilderness. The tempter took him to the pinnacle of the Temple and said, "If you are the Son of God, throw yourself down; for it is written 'He will command his angels concerning you,' and 'On their hands they will bear you up'" (4:6). Jesus resolutely refused this self-serving path at that time, and he does so again now. His relationship with God is not to be used for self-protection or spectacle, as a point of power and privilege. Jesus has chosen the way of suffering and serving "to give his life as a ransom for many" (20:28).

In their manner of arrest they treat Jesus as some bandit (26:55–56). There have been ample opportunities to arrest him. He has, after all, been teaching in the Temple day after day— in broad daylight for all to see. Now they come by night and "by stealth" (26:4) to this private place to arrest him. Though they treat him as bandit there is more of the bandit in their manner than his.

The sad ending of this chapter tells the reader, "Then all the disciples deserted him and fled" (26:56). Jesus is taken away to the high priest's house, where officials are already gathering false testimony against him.

---

15. Michael G. Reddish, *An Introduction to the Gospels.* (Nashville: Abingdon Press, 1997), 171.

26:57–68

Jesus before Caiaphas

The chief priests are looking for an offense that is actionable. They want the death penalty, and "Jewish leaders may not have had the authority for capital punishment."[16] They must find something (even if false) that is serious enough to merit taking him to Pilate. So the high priests are reported here to be "looking for false testimony against Jesus so that they might put him to death" (26:59). The implication of seeking "false" testimony is that they know he is innocent and are acting in bad faith. Though they grant a hearing to many false witnesses they are unsuccessful. "At last" they find two witnesses (as Jewish law requires). These two report that Jesus said, "I am able to destroy the Temple of God and to build it in three days" (26:59–61). This is not what Jesus says in Matthew. He only predicts the destruction of the Temple (24:2); he does not threaten to destroy it himself.[17] Now they have something they can use for their purposes.

The question that Caiaphas puts to Jesus is itself a paradox of testimony. "Tell us if you are the Messiah, the Son of God" (26:63). The high priest himself speaks the words of Peter's confession. Though he intends this as an accusation, it becomes an unwitting confession. Jesus answers, "You have said so." This is the same indirect affirmation that he will soon offer to Pilate as well when asked whether he is the "King of the Jews" (27:11). Jesus follows his response to Caiaphas with an allusion to Daniel 7: "From now on you will see the Son of Man seated at the right hand of Power and coming on the clouds of heaven" (26:64). This is too much for the high priest, who tears his clothes and charges Jesus with blasphemy. The charge of blasphemy, in the strict sense, meant abuse of the divine name. However, it could be more widely applied to anything that constituted an insult to God.[18] In this case, the blasphemy was Jesus' claim—or failure to deny—that he was the Son of God (27:26). With Jesus'

---

16. Levine and Brettler, *Jewish Annotated New Testament,* 50.
17. Mark 14:58 has Jesus making this claim.
18. Senior, *Abingdon New Testament Commnetaries,* 313.

indirect acknowledgment, Caiaphas declares no further need of witnesses.

They begin to humiliate Jesus, spitting in his face and slapping him. They mock him, saying, "Prophesy to us, you Messiah! Who is it who struck you?" (26:68). Ironically, even in these acts of humiliation, they allude to his being a prophet and address him as "Messiah." In their hostility and derision, they speak more truly than they know.

26:69–75

Peter Denies Jesus in the High Priest's Courtyard: "I do not know the man."

Peter's denial is reported in all four Gospels with only minor variations. The contrast of his cowardice with Jesus' courage is dramatic. At the very time Jesus stands before Caiaphas and makes a bold confession, Peter caves in before a serving girl. Peter's three denials under pressure are the reverse image of Jesus in Gethsemane. Three times he petitions God to be spared the trials ahead; three times he stands fast in his faithfulness to God and God's will regardless of the outcome.

There is an increasing intensity[19] in Peter's denials. The first is a simple statement of ignorance. "I do not know what you are talking about" (26:70). The second denial adds an oath, and the third joins cursing to the oath. "I do not know the man!" (26:74). The sound of the cock crow recalls what Jesus had warned earlier in the evening. "Before the cock crows, you will deny me three times" (26:75). The chapter closes with Peter bitterly weeping.

Matthew's community, which faced resistance and persecution, could see a negative example in Peter and a contrasting positive example in Jesus. The mission discourse of chapter 10 already anticipates the trials ahead and the difficulty of standing firm in one's confession of faith: "Beware of them, for they will hand you over to councils and flog you in their synagogues; and you will be dragged

19. Ibid., 314.

before governors and kings because of me, as a testimony to them and the Gentiles" (10:17–18). This is the time for testimony—not denial. Jesus delivers a standing promise and its companion caution, "Everyone therefore who acknowledges me before others, I also will acknowledge before my Father in heaven; but whoever denies me before others, I also will deny before my Father in heaven" (10:32–33).

Peter's failure is all the more poignant for his prominence among the disciples as their leader and spokesperson—the first called (4:18), the one who spoke the confession at Caesarea Philippi (16:16), and a witness to the transfiguration (17:1–8).[20] It is significant that all four Gospels report his apostasy. Nevertheless, Peter is not rejected. He weeps here, but he is later restored to community. When the disciples meet the risen Lord on the mountain in Galilee he is right there with them (28:16). History has it that Peter goes on to become a leader in the new community.

27:3–10

Judas Confesses to the Chief Priests in the Temple: "I have sinned by betraying innocent blood."

Unlike Peter, Judas does not return to the community after he repents his betrayal. Both Peter and Judas know that they have been faithless. Peter returns to the other disciples and is restored; Judas goes off by himself and commits suicide (27:3).

Only Matthew, among the Gospels, gives an account of the suicide of Judas. This tragedy is yet another parallel with the story of David. Ahithophel, who was a counselor and friend to David and was known for his sagacity, deserted David for Absalom's opposition movement. When he saw the cause was lost he also hanged himself (2 Samuel 17:1–23).

When Judas sees that Jesus stands condemned, he repents what he did. Is the reader meant to believe that Judas anticipated a different outcome and is surprised at his condemnation? It is at the

20. Ibid., 315.

point of Jesus' condemnation that Judas makes an attempt to give back the money. The chief priests will not accept it. When he tells them, "I have sinned by betraying innocent blood," their response is, "What is that to us? See to it yourself" (27:4). In effect, "This is your problem—not our problem." In their response, the chief priests act very much like the Roman governor Pilate will act when he says, "I am innocent of this man's blood; see to it yourselves" (27:24).

When the chief priests will not take back the money, Judas throws the silver coins to the Temple floor (27:6). When Judas leaves, they pick up the silver coins but acknowledge that they are "blood money" and cannot be added to the treasury (27:6). It is a rule that "money related to death cannot be used for holy purposes."[21] They use the money to buy a field for the burial of foreigners. Matthew connects this with Jeremiah's buying land (Jer. 32:6–15) and the "potter" material in Jeremiah 17–18. The connections are not precise, but they provide an explanation as to how this particular field came to be called the "Field of Blood" (27:8).

Judas knows that Jesus is innocent. In fact most of the major players in the drama of destruction know that Jesus is innocent. The chief priests know it—that is why they must seek "false testimony." Pilate knows it, too.

27:11–23
"They bound him, led him away, and handed him over to Pilate."

Pilate was the Roman governor in Judea from 18–36 CE. It is likely that only he could decide a capital punishment case.[22] Pilate is "greatly amazed" that Jesus gives no answer to the "many accusations" that are brought against him. Again the image of the Suffering Servant in Isaiah 53 is evoked. "Like a lamb that is led to slaughter, like a sheep before his shearers is silent, so he did not open his mouth" (53:7).

Pilate asks Jesus a direct question, "Are you the King of the Jews? Jesus makes an indirect answer, implying affirmation, "You say so."

21. Levine and Brettler, *Jewish Annotated New Testament,* 51.
22. Senior, *Abingdon New Testament Commentaries,* 320.

These words on Pilate's lips form the first of several paradoxical testimonies applying the title "King of the Jews" to Jesus (27:11, 29, 37, 42). As it happens this paradoxical testimony comes from a Gentile/foreigner. Pilate's "anti-type" is the Gentile/foreigner wise men who, by contrast, asked in faith, "Where is the child who has been born King of the Jews?" (2:2). The title used at the beginning finds its full resonance in the ending.

Pilate can see plainly that Jesus is innocent, brought in on trumped up charges. He is not fooled by the ploys of the chief priest and the elders. "He realized that it was out of jealousy that they had handed him over" (27:18). Even Pilate's wife knows that Jesus is innocent. She has seen it in a dream. In the infancy narrative, dreams are a source of divine revelation and re-direction. The wise men are warned in a dream to go home by another way and not report the baby's whereabouts to Herod. Joseph receives a warning in a dream to flee to Egypt with Mary and the baby Jesus to escape Herod's slaughter of the innocents. Now this dream that comes to Pilate's wife would also serve to protect the innocent one, but Pilate does not heed the warning.

Pilate does not finally heed the dream. Pilate's wife is a bright foil for Pilate. Although both know Jesus is innocent, it is she who acts on her convictions while Pilate succumbs to the will of the crowd. Pilate relinquishes agency even as his wife exercises agency; his fearful accommodation is unmasked by her bold intervention. She "breaks with social convention and interrupts the governor while he is sitting on the judgment seat"[23] warning him to "have nothing to do with that innocent man" (27:19). The word here translated as "innocent" means much more than that. The Greek term is *dikaios* and could be translated as "righteous" or "just."[24] It is the root of the term used by Jesus as he calls the people to a "higher righteousness" marked by love of God and neighbor.

The Roman governor would sometimes release a prisoner at the time of the Jewish festivals. Pilate sees a way out and offers the people a choice between Jesus and "Jesus Barabbas" (27:17). Ironically,

23. Amy-Jill Levine, *The Social and Ethnic Dimensions of Matthean Social History: Nowhere among the Gentiles* (Lewiston, New York: Edwin Mellen Press, 1988), 264.
24. Senior, *Abingdon New Testament Commentaries,* 22.

Barabbas means "son of the father" (Hebrew *bar*, "son"; *abba*, "father"). In distinguishing between one Jesus and the other, Pilate offers unwitting testimony. He twice speaks of "Jesus who is called the Messiah" (27:17 and 27:22). When the crowds choose Barabbas, Pilate wants to know, "Why, what evil has he done?" (27:23). They have no answer, but only clamor all the more to have Jesus crucified.

This is a turning point for the crowds in Matthew's Gospel. Up to this point the crowds have been following Jesus with interest: recognizing his authority, astonished at his teachings, addressing him with christological titles, and eager for his healings and feedings. They are there for the words of wisdom and the deeds of power, but now their loyalty shifts with the winds of popularity. How quickly their "cheers turn into jeers."[25]

27:24–26

"I am innocent of his blood:" Roman justice is "all washed up."

Pilate washes his hands. It is an act which, for Matthew's community, would have signified a washing away of responsibility or cleansing from an evil act. In Deuteronomy 21:1–9, there was a ritual of sacrifice and hand washing in which the priests declare "our hands did not shed this blood nor were we witnesses to it." The intent is absolution from the guilt of "innocent blood."

After Pilate washes his hands, he seeks to transfer responsibility to the crowd with his "See to it yourselves" (27:24). In this way, Pilate "who is in charge of events, pretends that he is not. But a quick hand washing and a few words cannot remove the legal responsibility with

> Roman justice is all washed up. It is not exonerated but exposed as expedient, allied with and coopted by the religious elite who manipulate a crowd to accomplish its own ends.
>
> Warren Carter, *Matthew and the Margins: A Socio-Political and Religious Reading* (Sheffield, England: Sheffield Academic Press, 2000), 29.

25. Wayne Myers, "Call to Confession" Palm Sunday, Fair Oaks Presbyterian Church, Oak Park, IL, April 1, 2012.

which Pilate is charged as governor and agent of Roman power."[26] Nor can he transfer the guilt to the "faceless crowd."[27]

The crowd is very willing to be manipulated. Those who were cheering Jesus at his triumphal entry are now jeering him in Pilate's court. The crowds are both "fickle and dangerous."[28] What follows is the infamous "blood cry." "Then the people as a whole answered, 'His blood be on us and on our children, they say'" (27:25). This text has been used throughout history to assign blame for the crucifixion upon Jews of all times and places. Jews have been labeled "Christ killers," and "holy week" has been a time of terror for Jews in predominantly Christian lands. This text has become a "pretext" for prejudice and persecution and pogroms. The "preaching of contempt" for the Jews has contributed to a thought world that made the atrocities of the Holocaust thinkable.

> **Those who can make you believe absurdities can make you commit atrocities.**
>
> Voltaire, *Questions sur les miracles* (1765).

The misuse of this text is based on an unsupportable misinterpretation of it. Matthew means by "the people as a whole," all those who, under the influence of the chief priests in Jerusalem, call for Jesus' death. This is not even all the Jews in Jerusalem at the time, much less all Jews for all times and places. The Roman Catholic Church, in the encyclical Nostra Aetate (1965), declares that the crucifixion "cannot be charged against all the Jews, without distinction, then alive, nor against the Jews of today."

It is likely that this text (27:25) reflects Matthew's theological explanation of the tragic events of 70 CE.[29] It was not uncommon in biblical tradition to interpret disasters as punishments. In this case, the text is a polemic of one Jewish group against another Jewish group. It accuses the other group of being the cause of this tragedy and puts the words of responsibility in their own mouths

---

26. Carter, *Matthew and the Margins*, 527.
27. Ibid.
28. Ibid., 528.
29. Levine and Brettler, *Jewish Annotated New Testament*, 52.

as they say, "his blood be on us and on our children."[30] It is important to remember that this narrative is a religious work—not a complex analysis of the multiple causes (economic, political military, etc.) of the Fall of Jerusalem.

Even if Matthew's theological interpretation of those events were granted, it should be read, as Raymond Brown points out, in terms of God's "short-lived" wrath. The book of Lamentations affirms, even in the midst of distress of the earlier destruction of Jerusalem in 587 BCE, "the steadfast love of the LORD never ceases; [God's] mercies never come to an end; they are new every morning; great is your faithfulness" (Lam. 3:22–24). There is no "permanent rejection"—not even for whoever joined in the blood cry.[31]

27:27–31

Mocked at the Governor's House: "Hail, King of the Jews"

Pilate accedes to the demands of the crowd. Jesus is flogged and he is "handed over" yet again. He has been "handed over" multiple times by now: by Judas to the representatives of the chief priests, by them to Caiaphas, by Caiaphas to Pilate, by Pilate to the soldiers who will crucify him. The soldiers now take him to the governor's headquarters and gather the whole cohort (about six hundred men[32]) who will torment him further.

More is said of Jesus' humiliation here than of his flogging at the hands of Pilate. Jesus is twice stripped, first of his own clothes and then of the robe that they had dressed him in to mock his "kingship." This situation in the humiliation of nakedness recalls his self-identification with the "least ones" (including the naked) in the passage depicting the final judgment (25:36, 43).

Their mockery makes its own paradoxical obeisance to the one who is "King of the Jews." This title recurs with frequency in the passion narrative (27:11, 29, 37, 42). It is on the lips of Pilate in his questioning, the soldiers in their taunting, and the passers-by

---

30. Carter, *Matthew and the Margins,* 529.
31. Ibid.
32. Levine and Brettler, *Jewish Annotated New Testament,* 52.

in their derision. It even hangs over Jesus' head as a charge against him, "This is Jesus, King of the Jews." In these moments before the soldiers of the governor there is a mock recognition and obeisance as they give him a scarlet robe, a crown of thorns, and a reed to signify the royal scepter. For a moment they kneel before him saying, "Hail, King of the Jews" (27:29), but then they spit on him and strike him on the head with the reed.

The reader knows that this is indeed the King of the Jews, but his crown is a crown of thorns and his throne will be a cross.[33] Well before the actual crucifixion Jesus endured untold suffering.

> **Those who have turned their backs upon suffering have turned away from Jesus.**
>
> José A. Pagola, *The Way Opened Up by Jesus: A Commentary on the Gospel of Matthew* (Miami, FL: Convivium Press, 2012), 235.

---

33. N. T. Wright, *Matthew for Everyone, Part 2* (Louisville, KY: Westminster John Knox Press, 2004), 182.

27:32–61

The Crucified Savior

27:32–49

"This is Jesus, King of the Jews."

Warren Carter offers an extended passage on crucifixion, as such, which is briefly summarized here. Crucifixion was a cruel means of execution; Josephus referred to it as the "most pitiable of deaths." It was not used for Roman citizens but most often for "sociopolitical marginals such as 'rebellious' foreigners." The designation "bandits" for the two people crucified alongside Jesus likely identifies them as 'freedom fighters" who robbed for the cause. Robbery by itself would probably not be punished by crucifixion. Slaves and very violent criminals were subjected to crucifixion. Crucifixion divided the citizen from the noncitizen, the socially acceptable from the rejected. It was done in public places in hopes of deterring "noncompliant behavior." Carrying the crossbeam to the place of execution was part of the public humiliation. Commentators speculate that Simon of Cyrene was conscripted to carry the crossbeam for Jesus only because Jesus was so injured by flogging and abuse that he was unable to carry it himself. The cross was a political image of "shame, humiliation, pain, social rejection, marginalization and condemnation."[1]

The earlier invitation to the disciples to "take up your cross and follow me" (10:38) becomes all the more shocking from this vantage point, with Jesus' crucifixion in sight. It is a call to "identify with the nobodies like slaves . . . with those who resist the empire's control, who contest its version of reality, and who are vulnerable to its

---

1. Warren Carter, *Matthew and the Margins: A Socio-Political and Religious Reading* (Sheffield, England: Sheffield Academic Press, 2000), 243–44.

reprisals."[2] To "take up the cross" is "not to endorse the symbol but to reframe its violence." Ironically, the cross will reveal the empire's limits. Though it has done its worst in crucifying Jesus, God will raise him up and thwart the empire's presumed power.[3]

"Matthew does not present Jesus' death as something that must happen so that God could be forgiving . . ."[4] On the contrary, it is because God is forgiving that Jesus has come "to call sinners" (9:13). The taunters mock him, saying, "He saved others; he cannot save himself." The paradox is already in place in Jesus' own teaching. Those who save their lives, lose them; those who give up their lives—as Jesus did—save them. It is precisely in not saving himself but pouring himself out that Jesus' saving work is done (26:28).

Matthew is clear that to reject Jesus is to reject the one who sent him. All kinds of people join in this rejection. Religious leaders and the highest officials in government reject him—as the readers have just witnessed in Caiaphas and Pilate and their agents. The crowds turn on him, calling for his crucifixion. Even the disciples play a part when they betray, desert, and deny him.

Even in the face of rejection Jesus persists in calling people to repent as the reign of God comes near. He teaches love of God and neighbor and special care for the least, the last, and the lost. When he meets with violence he does not reciprocate and retaliate. He is ready to endure suffering rather than inflicting suffering on others.

Images from Psalm 22, one of the Psalms of Lament, are woven throughout Matthew's accounting of the crucifixion. Particulars of what Jesus undergoes readily evoke these associations: the soldiers at the foot of the cross look on as they divide his clothes among them by casting lots (27:35).

> They stare and gloat over me;
> they divide my clothes among themselves,
> and for my clothing they cast lots.
> (Ps. 22:17–18)

---

2. Ibid., 244.
3. Ibid.
4. Eugene Boring, *The New Interpreter's Bible: New Testament Articles, Matthew, Mark* (Nashville: Abingdon Press, 1995), 8:495.

Two bandits are crucified with Jesus, "one on his right and one on his left" (27:38). The reader recalls the irony of how James and John wanted the places at Jesus' right hand and left hand and how they declared that they could drink from the "cup" that he would drink. They did not know what they were asking. Jesus is once again in the company of sinners. Even the bandits being crucified with him taunt him (27:44).

> For dogs are all around me;
>   a company of evildoers encircles me.
> (Ps. 22:16)

Passers-by mock Jesus, shaking their heads. This is the third text in the passion story where Jesus is mocked (26:67–68; 27:27–31, 38–44). In the same words of the tempter used to tempt Jesus in the wilderness (4:6) they say, "If you are the Son of God . . . " come down from the cross (27:40). They imply that God would deliver him if God wanted to do so.

> All who see me mock at me;
>   they make mouths at me, they shake their heads;
> "Commit your cause to the LORD; let him deliver—
>   let him rescue the one in whom he delights!"
> (Ps. 22:7–8)

Most resonant with Psalm 22 and most poignant of all is the cry of dereliction, "My God, my God, why have you forsaken me?" (27:46). This is how the Psalm opens:

> My God, my God, why have you forsaken me?
>   Why are you so far from helping me, from the words of my
>   groaning?
> O my God, I cry by day, but you do not answer;
>   and by night, but find no rest.
> (Ps. 22:1–2)

Some question whether the cry of dereliction signifies a complete loss of faith. This is not the case in the Psalm of Lament that opens with this question. On the contrary, this Psalm is a prayer to God. The "why" question is often on the lips of the faithful. It is precisely faith that makes the question urgent and appropriate. If one does not believe in God who is good and sovereign, there is no reason to ask "why?" in the face of suffering. Suffering remains a stark reality, but it is not really a theological problem unless one is a person of faith. Scripture is full of faithful people questioning God in the face of apparent God forsakenness (e.g., the book of Job, the Psalms of Lament, and the book of Lamentations). Matthew's accounting of the crucifixion begins in this kind of experience and ends (nevertheless) with a faith affirmation that anticipates resurrection and the universal inclusion in the age to come.

> All the ends of the earth shall remember
> 　and turn to the LORD;
> and all the families of the nations
> 　shall worship before him.
> For dominion belongs to the LORD,
> 　and he rules over the nations.
> To him, indeed, shall all who sleep in the earth bow down;
> 　before him shall bow all who go down to the dust,
> 　and I shall live for him.
>
> 　　　　　　　　　　　　　　　　　(Ps. 22:27–29)

27:50–54
The Arrival of the Apocalypse

Jesus cries out with a loud voice and breathes his last (27:50). In this moment, the apocalypse arrives. Matthew, even more than the other Gospel writers, makes clear that this is an eschatological event. The curtain of the Temple is "torn in two from top to bottom" (27:51). Commentators differ as to the significance of this event. Some see it as a judgment on the religious leaders based at the Temple for their rejection of Jesus. Others note that the curtain is probably the curtain that sets off the Holy of Holies. Its being torn from top to bottom could have a theological meaning; it signifies the new, divinely given access to God opened up by Jesus. Only Mathew tells how the earth shook and the rocks were split and the tombs were opened (27:51–52). "It is possible that behind the earthquake at the cross is the rabbinic view . . . that the death of a righteous person could usher in tragic repercussions."[5]

Only Matthew gives the surprising account of tombs being opened and saints being raised from the dead (27:50–53). Matthew is placing Jesus' resurrection squarely in the context of the Jewish hope of a general resurrection in the end time. The opening of the tombs means that the end of the age is inaugurated and the resurrection has begun. The sequence of events is a little confusing given the historic affirmation that Jesus is the "firstborn" from the dead. Here tombs open and saints rise at the point of Jesus' death. Some commentaries try to right this order by noting that according to verse 53 these saints do not appear in the holy city until after his resurrection. It may not be imperative to impose an order there, if we recall that this is apocalyptic writing and a faith interpretation of events, not simply a straightforward literal logbook.

With all these signs, even the centurion and the soldiers who are keeping watch over Jesus are moved to announce, "Truly this man was God's Son!" (27:54). Once again the words that would constitute a faith affirmation come from an unexpected source. Their confession is unlike the paradoxical christological confessions of Caiaphas and Pilate; however, it is more like the confession the disciples themselves make when Jesus comes to them walking on the sea and calming the storm. They say, "Truly you are the son of God" (14:33). Now, just as in the moment Jesus calmed the sea, the forces of the natural world give testimony as the human beings stand by in terror.

27:55–61
"Many women . . . had followed Jesus from Galilee."

Also there at the cross are three women, "Mary Magdalene, Mary the mother of James and Joseph, and the mother of the sons of Zebedee"

5. *The Jewish Annotated New Testament*, ed. Amy-Jill Levine and Marc Zvi Brettler (Oxford: Oxford University Press, 2011), 51.

(27:55). Some commentators understand the mother of James and Joseph to be Mary the mother of Jesus (as in the Gospel of Mark), elsewhere referred to as the other Mary. These are women who had "followed him from Galilee and provided for him" (27:55).

This passage admits of more considered attention. Its meaning has been minimized in relation to the role of these women. Where it says these women had "followed" Jesus from Galilee, the term could be read reductively to mean that they tag along after him. However, it is more likely that this term indicates that they were "followers" in the way the disciples were "followers" of Jesus (4:20). The term implies the same "attachment and obedience in response to his disruptive call."[6] Also, where it says they "provided for him", this lends itself to a minimizing reading as in providing food and hospitality. However, the term used here is the Greek term *diakonousai* and might be translated as "served" or "ministered." At its root is the Greek term sometimes translated as "deacon" (Rom. 16:1, Phil. 1:1, and 1 Timothy 3:8–10). The office of deacon that emerged later in the church takes its orientation from this form of service and ministry.

"In the passion and resurrection story, it is in fact the women followers who are faithful, comprehending, and obedient."[7] They are bright lights among the followers of Jesus. In contrast to the disciples who "deserted him and fled" after Jesus' arrest (26:56), these women are "there" (27:55).

Another point in favor of the stronger reading of the discipleship for these women comes in the verse that immediately follows. There, Joseph of Arimathea is described as "also a disciple of Jesus" (27:57). The "also" could be referring to the women just discussed in the previous verse. Joseph of Arimathea is a rich man who also followed Jesus. He generously offers his own tomb for the burial and arranges with Pilate to be given the body. He prepares the body for burial, wrapping it in a clean linen cloth. His is a tomb such as the wealthy would possess, hewn into rock and having a great stone door. This reference to the luxury of Jesus' burial may be another reference in fulfillment of the Suffering Servant passage in Isaiah 53, "And they

6. Carter, *Matthew and the Margins,* 538.
7. Mary Rose D'Angelo, "(Re)Presentations of Women in the Gospel of Matthew and Luke–Acts," *Women in Christian Origins,* ed. Ross Shepard Kraemer and Mary Rose D'Angelo, 174 (Oxford: Oxford University Press, 1999).

made his grave with a rich man in his death" (53: 9). When Joseph closes up the tomb the women remain sitting opposite the rock. As they were there at the cross, so they are there at the tomb.

FURTHER REFLECTIONS
The Lord's Supper

Matthew 26:20-29 gives an accounting of Jesus' last supper with his disciples. This event in the final days of Jesus' life and ministry has taken on deep theological significance in the life of the church. It has formed the basis of our sacramental practice of celebrating the Lord's Supper. Matthew's Gospel offers points of particular illumination that bear further exploration. This reflection will center on the theological interpretation of the sacrament of the Lord's Supper and can only begin to trace the outline of its meaning in the life of the church. (For fuller elaboration of the distinctives of Matthew's account, see commentary on 26:20-29. For a discussion of sacramental theology more generally, see opening sections of "Further Reflections: Baptism as Calling to Ministry," pp. 59-66.)

The meaning of this sacrament is inexhaustible. Its pluriform richness is already signaled in liturgies with multiple ways of naming the sacrament as "the Lord's Supper" or "Holy Communion" or "the Eucharist." Each way of naming opens a different aspect of its meaning. This sacrament's meaning spans dimensions of time. It stretches toward the past as something we do "in remembrance." It manifests itself in the present as we experience "even now" Christ's real presence with us, joining us in communion with him and with one another. The sacrament leans into the future as this celebration prefigures the messianic banquet in the reign of God. Understandings of the way in which Christ is present to us in this sacrament differ across denominations (and within denominations). Each angle of vision contributes to fuller understanding; yet no one vision penetrates the mystery of these moments. Various dimensions of the meaning of this sacrament are outlined in what follows, noting contributions from Matthew's account along the way.

This is a "memorial meal." There is a sense in which this meal looks backward to the Christ event and remembers. Matthew's own presentation broadens this meaning by making clear—in a way that the other Gospels do not—that the Last Supper is framed in a Passover setting (26:17–19). The Passover meal in its own right looks backward to Israel's deliverance from slavery in Egypt. This remembrance of deliverance holds the promise of future deliverance. In this way the Passover meal looks not only backward but also forward, even to the messianic banquet at the end of time. Passover's reenactment is a "covenant sign." In Matthew's account, Jesus references the covenant, "This is *my blood of the covenant*, which is poured out for many for the forgiveness of sins" (26:27).

These aspects of the Lord's Supper as "memorial meal" and "covenant sign" are particularly well carried by Zwingli's theology of the Lord's Supper. For him, the centerpiece in this supper is the invitation to "Do this *in remembrance* of me" (1 Cor. 11:23).[8] This memorial meal is an exercise of our faith; it is a badge or emblem by which we identify ourselves with Christ and pledge ourselves to him anew. We remember Jesus and particularly his saving death. This memorial meal is one of those focal points where the church keeps alive "the dangerous memory of Jesus Christ."

This is a meal shared with sinners. For Matthew this dimension of meaning comes out with particular force as Jesus shares the last supper with Peter, who will deny him, and Judas, who has already betrayed him. This meal sits squarely between Judas's betrayal and Jesus' prediction of Peter's denial. All those present at this Last Supper will desert at the point of Jesus' arrest (Matt. 26:56). Yet he shares this meal with them. This is a place where sin is honestly confronted (26:21, 31, 34) and, nevertheless, sinners are not excluded. This meal with sinners calls to mind that one of the chief complaints against Jesus was his fellowship with "sinners and tax collectors" (9:10–12). Coming to this table is an opportunity for repentance and the renunciation of evil (1 Cor. 27–29). Here we remember that we are all deniers/betrayers/deserters. Yet God's grace is extended to us nevertheless. At this table we share not only bread and wine but also forgiveness.

8. Ulrich Zwingli "On the Lord's Supper" (1540), 176–238 in G. W. Bromiley, *Zwingli and Bullinger* 21, Library of Christian Classics (Philadelphia: Westminster Press, 1953).

This sacrament is a means of grace. In this connection, many theologians understand the sacrament of the Lord's Supper as in some sense not only a "memorial meal" but also a "means of grace." They are affirming that in this sacrament we receive the benefits of the grace that God extends to us in Christ. Calvin and Luther concur in this, insisting that the sacrament is not a *mere bare sign*. Though they treat the matter differently, both go beyond Zwingli's "symbolic" interpretation of the Lord's Supper. There is, for them, a real connection between the *sign* and *the thing signified.* [9]

The grace of God is here conveyed in the common elements of bread and wine. This forever changes how we view "common elements" as such. Greek Orthodox theology affirms that what one really sees in the sacrament is "an aspect of the cosmos that has been returned or redeemed to its essential significance and purpose. It is a foretaste of the redemption of the whole cosmos."[10] Incarnation and sacrament belong together. "Jesus identified the mode of his incarnation and reconciliation of God and humanity ("his body and his blood") with the very stuff of the universe when he took the bread blessed, broke and gave it to his disciples . . . "[11]

This is a place where Christ is really present. Beyond remembering and anticipating, there is "even now" a present experience that is an experience of Christ's presence. There are different ways of understanding Christ's presence in this sacrament even among those who affirm that it is a sharing in the body and blood of Christ. Roman Catholics see this in terms of "transubstantiation": the bread and the wine become (in "substance") the body and blood of Christ even as the visible characteristics ("accidents") are unchanged. Lutherans see Christ's real presence "in, with, and under" the

9. For further reading on Calvin and Luther on the Lord's Supper, see these good sources. John Calvin, "Short Treatise on the Lord's Supper" (1541), 140–66 in J. K. S. Reid, ed., *Calvin's Theological Treatises* 22, Library of Christian Classics (Philadelphia: Westminster Press 1954); Martin Luther, *The Sacrament of the Body and Blood of Christ: Against the Fanatics,* 1526, in *Word and Sacrament II* , ed. Abdel Ross Wentz and Helmut T. Lehmann, trans. Frederick C Ahrens.; vol. 36 of *Luther's Works,* American Edition, ed. Jaroslav Pelikan and Helmut T. Lehmann (Philadelphia: Fortress, 1955), 331–50.

10. Christopher Knight, "Theistic Naturalism and the Word Made Flesh," in *In Whom We Live and Move and Have Our Being,* eds. Arthur Peacocke and Philip Clayton, 55 (Grand Rapids: Eerdmans, 2004).

11. Arthur Peacocke, *Paths of Science toward God: The End of All Our Exploring* (Oxford: One World, 2001), 149.

bread and the wine. It is a local, physical presence likened to the way in which fire permeates a glowing ember.[12] The Reformed generally follow Calvin's emphasis on Christ's real presence as "spiritual presence" actualized by the work of the Spirit in word and sacrament. It is not so much that Christ comes down to be locally, physically present at each table, but rather—by the power of the Holy Spirit—we are "lifted up" to be with him.

The table is a place for faith. There are a variety of understandings of the place of "faith" in the reception of the sacrament. For Zwingli, the exercise of faith is the primary event in the sacrament. For Luther, by contrast, there is such a connection between the sign and the thing signified that faith is really not necessary in order for the sacrament to be the sacrament. Even the nonbeliever receives the sacrament (though unworthily and unto judgment). Calvin's view is somewhere between these two. The sacrament is truly the sacrament with or without faith, but faith is necessary for the sacrament to be efficacious. All receive the *sign,* believers and nonbelievers alike, but not all receive *the thing signified.* Without faith, it is as if water were poured over a stone. The water is truly water, but stone is not sufficiently porous to receive it. In this sense, it might be said that, "those who believe, receive." There is no question of whether Christ is really present in the sacrament; the question is whether *we* are really present.

This sacrament is a communion in Christ. "Communion" is a naming of the sacrament that recognizes our "participation" in Christ. In this sacrament we are joined to Christ and to one another. Jesus' words, "this is my body" (26:26) identify the broken bread with his own body. At another level, there are theological associations of Christ's body with the church in its unity. To "discern the body" is to know ourselves to be members of one another (1 Cor. 12).

In his discussions of the Lord's Supper, Calvin makes clear that we cannot separate communion with Christ from communion with one another:

> We shall benefit very much from the Sacrament if this thought
> is impressed and engraved upon our minds: that none of the
> brethren can be injured, despised, rejected, abused, or in

---

12. Daniel Migliore, *Faith Seeking Understanding: An Introduction to Christian Theology,* 2nd ed. (Grand Rapids: Eerdmans, 2004), 221.

any way offended by us, without at the same time, injuring, despising, and abusing Christ by the wrongs that we do; that we cannot disagree with our brethren without at the same time disagreeing with Christ; that we cannot love Christ without loving him in the brethren; that we ought to take the same care of our brethren's bodies as we take of our own; for they are members of our body; and that, as no part of our body is touched by any feeling of pain which is not spread among all the rest, so we ought not to allow a brother to be affected by any evil, without being touched with compassion for him.[13]

Our celebration of the sacrament of the Lord's Supper assumes this communion with one another in Christ.

This is a table of reconciliation. Here we remember God's reconciling work in Christ. We cannot come to this table and not commit ourselves to the work of reconciliation. This is somewhat parallel to the injunction concerning bringing a gift to the altar in Matthew 5:24 where Jesus counsels, "first be reconciled to your brother or sister . . . " It is a scandal that Christians are not even reconciled among themselves and do not welcome one another to the table. Here of all places there should be reconciliation and not division. It is a failure to "discern the body."

Calvin shared Luther's regret over the division of the church. He expressed his deep concern in a letter to the Archbishop of Canterbury (Thomas Cranmer), saying that the division of the church "is to be ranked among the chief evils of our time . . . Thus it is that the members of the Church being severed, the body lies bleeding. So much does this concern me, that, if I could be of any service, I would not grudge to cross even ten seas."[14] Calvin's depiction of Christ's "dismembered" body is a powerful and compelling image. How can we conduct the ministry of reconciliation to which we are called in the wider world if we cannot be reconciled among ourselves? The church around the world and across all differences is called to come together at the table. Unrestricted eucharistic sharing may be a way

---

13. John Calvin, *Institutes of the Christian Religion* 4.17.38; ed. John T. McNeill, trans. Ford Lewis Battles, LCC (Philadelphia: Westminster Press, 1960), 2:1415.
14. Letter to Cranmer (1552), *Selected Works of John Calvin: Tracts and Letters*, pt. 4.

of moving toward the deep reality of our unity in Christ. It need not wait until we agree on the theological details.

This is a eucharistic celebration (Greek *eucharisto*, "good gifts, thanksgiving"). Sometimes in this connection the celebration is spoken of as a "sacrifice of praise." The church offers its "sacrifice of praise" lifting up our hearts in thanksgiving to God for what God has done in Christ. For Protestants there is an insistence that Christ's sacrifice, while it may be represented at the table, is not *re*-presented. His is a once-and-for-all, fully sufficient sacrifice. The church does not need to repeat it or remind God of it. We offer up our praise and our very selves to God as a "living sacrifice," worshiping God with transformed lives (Rom. 12:1).

As we do this we are becoming new. One Anglican theologian has offered that in this act we become a new "species" of human being, *Homo eucharisticus.*[15] This new species of humanity is created and sustained by the eucharistic gathering.

> At this table is proclaimed the possibility of reconciled life and the imperative of living so as to nourish the humanity of others. . . . There is no transforming Eucharistic life if it is not fleshed out in justice and generosity, no proper veneration of the sacramental Body and Blood that it not correspondingly fleshed out in veneration for the neighbor.[16]

This is a meal shared in joyful anticipation of the coming reign of God that anticipates the messianic banquet. In Matthew, the Passover is the setting for this meal and "the motif of deliverance from oppression associated with Passover is a back drop to Jesus' own death."[17] This setting combines powerfully with the shared belief that the Messiah would come at Passover. The reader is meant to understand that in Jesus the Messiah has come, and the reign of God is inaugurated in him. This aspect is very clear in Matthew's accounting. Jesus declares, "I will never again drink of this fruit of the vine until that day when I drink it new with you *in*

15. Rowan Williams, keynote address to the Eleventh Assembly of the Lutheran World Federation, Stuttgart, Germany, July, 2010, paragraph 17.

16. Ibid.

17. Donald Senior, *Abingdon New Testament Commentaries: Matthew* (Nashville: Abingdon Press, 1998), 290.

my Father's kingdom" (26:29). The future dimension is drawn out also
in the classic communion text in 1 Corinthians, "As often as you eat
this bread and drink the cup you proclaim the Lord's death *until he
comes."* These texts strain toward the full realization of the reign of
God in the age to come. We "look eagerly for the consummation of
the liberating and reconciling activity of God in which (we) are even
now co-workers."[18]

An essential aspect of the vision of the new age as articulated
in Matthew is the prospect that "all the nations" (28:20) are to be
included. There is to be a universalizing of God's blessing to Israel.
This is anticipated from the beginning in the establishment of the
covenant (Gen. 22:18) and is carried forward in prophetic visions
such as that articulated in the prophet Isaiah (2:2–4; 60:1–6). We
convey this hope in Communion liturgies when we say, "This is the
joyful feast of the people of God. People will come from North and
South and East and West and sit at table in the kingdom of God."[19]
At this feast all are welcome.

At this feast, no one will go away hungry. The feeding miracles
in Matthew demonstrate Jesus' compassion for the hungry. When
his disciples would have sent the hungry multitudes away, Jesus
instructs them, "You give them something to eat" (14:16). Matthew's
accounting of the feeding miracles makes a vivid connection with
the Last Supper. He uses the same four verbs in both. In Matthew
14:19, Jesus feeds the multitudes, "Taking the five loaves and the
two fish, he looked up to heaven and blessed and broke the loaves
and gave them to his disciples." At the last supper, described in Matthew 26:26–29, Jesus also "takes," "blesses," "breaks," and "gives" the
bread to the disciples. It seems the reader is meant to make the connection between partaking of the Lord's Supper and feeding hungry people. Those who come to this table cannot turn people who
are hungry away.

Matthew also alludes to the messianic banquet in his response
to the question of why his disciples do not fast. Drawing upon the
image of a wedding banquet his answer is that "the wedding guests

---

18. Migliore, *Faith Seeking Understanding,* 220.
19. Presbyterian Church (U.S.A.), *Book of Common Worship* (Louisville, KY: Westminster/John
Knox Press, 1993).

cannot mourn while the bridegroom is with them" (9:15). The messianic banquet is pictured as a genuine feast. Isaiah 25:6–9 provides one model:

> On this mountain the LORD of hosts will make for all peoples
>   a feast of rich food, a feast of well-matured wines,
>   of rich food filled with marrow, of well-matured wines
>   strained clear.
> And he will destroy on this mountain
>   the shroud that is cast over all peoples,
>   the sheet that is spread over all nations;
>   he will swallow up death for ever.
> Then the Lord GOD will wipe away the tears from all faces,
>   and the disgrace of his people he will take away from all
>   the earth,
>   for the LORD has spoken.
> It will be said on that day,
>   Lo, this is our God; we have waited for him, so that he
>   might save us.
>   This is the LORD for whom we have waited;
>   let us be glad and rejoice in his salvation.

We can almost see it. Everyone is included; no one is sent away hungry. "There is plenty for all and more to share. . . . Everyone is gathered at God's table of plenty . . . all at that table are pushed back and satisfied and enjoying one another."[20] The messianic banquet offers a compelling vision that followers of Christ may not only anticipate but also live toward.

Conclusion

Matthew's Gospel accounting of Jesus' last supper with his disciples makes distinctive contributions to interpretation of the meaning of sacrament of the Lord's Supper in the life of the church. Memory, celebration, and anticipation attend our participation in the sacrament of the Lord's Supper. Visions of how Christ is present to us there abound. The multiple dimensions and visions and interpretations

---

20. Michael Winters, "The Food of Justice: Matthew 25:31–46" (sermon, Oak Lawn Community Church, Oak Lawn, IL, November 23, 2008).

enrich our understanding of the sacrament of the Lord's Supper: it is a memorial meal, a meal shared with sinners, a means of grace, a place of Christ's real presence, a place for faith, a participation in Christ, a reconciliation, and a feast anticipating the messianic banquet and the coming reign of God. Even with these multiple theological elaborations, this sacrament maintains its mystery.

FURTHER REFLECTIONS
On the Meaning of the Cross

When we think of God's saving work in our behalf, the cross is very much at the center theologically. It is the symbol without parallel in Christian tradition. Some contemporary challenges concerning the meaning of the cross have arisen in our context. They require a thoughtful response. A wider vision of the fullness of the Christ event may help us to reclaim the cross from misunderstandings. This reflection will look at major aspects of the Christ event and think about each in turn as an expression of God's saving work. In this effort, Matthew's Gospel will prove particularly helpful.

Joanne Carlson Brown and Carole Bohn charge that "Christianity is an abusive theology that glorifies suffering." Substitutionary atonement, they say, looks a lot like "divine child abuse, . . . God the Father demanding and carrying out the suffering and death of his own son so that God can forgive our sins."[21] This is a challenge that needs an answer.

Womanist theologian Delores Williams has pointed out that interpreting God's saving work in Christ primarily through the images of substitution and sacrificial suffering does not play itself out as "good news" for people accustomed to having roles of surrogacy and sacrifice and suffering forced upon them.[22] This challenge needs an answer as well.

What theological responses are available to us for addressing

---

21. Joanne Carlson Brown and Carole R. Bohn, *Christianity, Patriarchy, and Abuse: A Feminist Critique* (Cleveland: The Pilgrim Press, 1989), 26.
22. Delores Williams, *Sisters in the Wilderness: The Challenge of Womanist God Talk* (Maryknoll, NY: Orbis Books, 1995).

these challenges? If it is the case that the preaching of the cross has been heard as a glorification of suffering, then the meaning of the cross has been misrepresented or misunderstood. Perhaps it would be good to begin again at the beginning. Second Corinthians 5:18 says, "God was in Christ reconciling the world." This story is not about God punishing someone or requiring that someone pay or needing someone to suffer in order to love and forgive. On the contrary, it is about God's own suffering and sacrifice in Christ. God in Christ stands in solidarity with us in our sin and suffering, becoming one of us and one with us in a way that offers healing and emancipatory hope.

In the Gospel of Matthew, the crucifixion is primarily a social and political response to the challenge Jesus posed to principalities and powers of his day. Dorothee Soelle, in her book *Suffering*, has urged that we open our eyes to the suffering that is all around us and realize that, in a sense, people are crucified every day. What is distinctive about Jesus is not his crucifixion, but the life he led that led him to the cross. It was a life of love for God and neighbor. Part of the work of following him is to "stop the crucifixions."[23] It is time to reclaim the cross—not as a glorification of suffering but as a scene of "dangerous remembrance, empowering resistance, and emancipatory hope."[24]

Matthew would not have had on his radar the contemporary misinterpretations of the cross as "divine child abuse" or as a "glorification of suffering." Nevertheless, recovering his account may help us to avoid these pitfalls. Matthew "does not present Jesus' death as something that must happen so that God could be forgiving."[25] Furthermore, God's saving work pervades the whole of the Christ event in Matthew and does not begin only at the point of the passion and crucifixion. Also important is the fact that the story is not cast as already divinely decided in all its details. Why would Jesus pray his agonized prayer in the garden? The Jesus whom the reader meets in Gethsemane actually struggles with fear of the suffering and death

---

23. Dorothee Soelle, *Suffering* (Minneapolis: Fortress Press, 1984), 9ff.
24. Joy Ann McDougall, unpublished paper, American Academy of Religion conference, 1999.
25. Boring, *The New Interpreter's Bible*, 8:495.

that he sees ahead. He is not "an actor reciting the lines" of a divinely pre-scripted drama."[26]

Matthew's Gospel does not dwell upon the details of Jesus' suffering at all. This is not attributable to stoic, courageous endurance on the part of Jesus in Matthew's Gospel. Nor is it attributable to a Docetic Christology (a belief that Jesus only "appeared" to be human). The inattention to the details of Jesus' suffering and death is a function of the Gospel's focus on the theological meaning of the Christ event. Matthew presents God's saving work in the cross (20:28; 26:28, 31) and elsewhere but offers no theory of the atonement as such.

The cross is best understood—not in isolation—but in the context of the entire Christ event. This is how it is presented in the book of Matthew. What would happen if we framed the cross in this larger picture, taking into account all aspects—birth, life and ministry, cross, and resurrection—and seeing all of it in its redemptive power?

The Birth of the Messiah

For the Gospel of Matthew the redemptive meaning of the birth of the Messiah is very apparent. Matthew draws upon the prophetic text from Isaiah 7:14 to interpret the meaning of Jesus' birth, "and they shall name him Emmanuel," which means, "God is with us" (Matt. 1:23). The fundamental meaning of the incarnation is that God chooses to be and really is *with us*. Theologically this has been explored in the doctrine of incarnation and especially our contemplation of the sense in which Jesus, the Christ, is fully God and fully human.

Incarnation is the wonder of the word made flesh. There is a sense in which the incarnation all by itself could be redemptive. This line of thought, although it is not prominent in Western classical tradition, has significant voices through Christian history. It can be traced through the Gospel of John, Irenaeus (second century), Gregory of Nyssa (335–395), Bonaventure (1221–1274), and even into Schleiermacher (1768–1835) in the twentieth century. Today it is still the primary focus for Greek Orthodox Christians. If you ask

26. Ibid.

"how are we saved?" they will answer that it is by God's becoming one with us in Christ. The goal of our lives is union with God (*theosis*).

Irenaeus is an interesting instance of this perspective. He offers an alternative to Augustine's particular reading of salvation history. Irenaeus sees our perfection as being at our end rather than at our beginning. He pictures human beings as created immature and intended to grow toward fullness in God's image. Sin is a mark of immaturity and ignorance (rather than rebellion) and summons forth God's compassion (rather than punishment). In the incarnation God comes in the flesh to show us the way. Jesus is understood to be the "pioneer and perfecter of our faith." (Heb. 12:2) Irenaeus is intrigued by Jesus' passage through all the stages of human life and proposes that as he "recapitulates" our lives, he is redeeming as he goes. With each step, another aspect of our life is taken up into the divine life. He became as we are, that we might become as he is.[27] This divine embrace of our lives in the incarnation accomplishes our salvation. In this sense, the incarnation would be enough.

From this standpoint, the incarnation is no "emergency measure" on God's part due to the fall into sin. It lies, rather, in the primordial creative intent of God. The goal of all creation is union with God as we see it manifest in Jesus, the Christ. There is a sense in which the work of Christ is redemptive precisely because the union with God—that is intended for all—is manifest in him.

At the heart of created reality there is an openness to the God who "unfolds" and "enfolds" creation (Nicholas of Cusa). The vision of God offered in the birth of the Messiah is a vision of God's "real presence" in this world that God loves. The work of creation and the work of redemption are joined. In both there is the wonder that Matthew expresses in 1:23: God is with us.

The Life and Ministry of Jesus

For Matthew the life and ministry of Jesus provide another angle of vision on God's saving work in our midst. Jesus spends his time in the saving work of teaching, healing, and feeding. He proclaims

---

27. This insight was expressed by Irenaeus early in the second century. As he said, "Our Lord Jesus Christ ... through his transcendent love, became what we are, that He might bring us to be even what he is himself." *Against Heresies*, book 5, preface.

the coming reign of God and calls for repentance and transformation of life that befits those under God's reign. As the authoritative interpreter of the law, he teaches that its center was love of God and neighbor. He calls his followers to a "higher righteousness" (*dikaiosynē*) reflected in the exercise of justice and mercy for the least, the last, and the lost. Jesus demonstrated divine compassion in healing and feeding the people. In his life and ministry, Jesus is the "Exemplar" of God's love.

Christ the "Exemplar" is an understanding of God's saving work that focuses upon Christ's example and teaching. Peter Abelard (1079–1142) articulates this vision. In his view, the human problematic is not so much God's wrath evoked by human sin. It is more a problem of our sense of shame for sin. It is not a matter of God turning away from us in anger; rather we turn away from God in shame and hide from God.[28] This may be more central to the biblical witness concerning the human predicament than has been recognized. In the story of Adam and Eve in the garden, they hide from God and hide from one another with coverings of fig leaves (Gen. 3:8). God seeks them out.

Christ as the Exemplar manifests God's love, acceptance, and forgiveness—it is a revelation of what is already the case with God. Once we know of God's great love, we are drawn out of guilty hiding and inspired to live lives marked by love and acceptance and forgiveness. Jesus is the Exemplar in this second step of transformed life as well. What he does and what he teaches exemplify what we are called to be and do. As we grow in grace, our lives come to be, more and more, conformed to his pattern.

The Cross of Christ

The cross is the symbol that has been most to the forefront of our understanding of God's saving work in Christ. Can this symbol be reclaimed in ways that correct for its misunderstanding as a glorification of suffering? A good first step is to try to get to the biblical

---

28. Peter Abelard, *Commentary on the Epistle to the Romans*, book II, in *Fathers of the Church: Medieval Continuations*, trans. Stephen R. Cartwright (Washington, DC: Catholic University of America Press, 2011), 278–79; 281–84.

and theological roots of what later became the substitutionary theory of the atonement.

The book of Hebrews interprets the meaning of the cross through images from the Jewish sacrificial system. In this model Christ is pictured as both high priest and perfect sacrifice—the lamb without blemish (Heb. 7:23–27). Misunderstandings of this model treat it as a kind of transaction through which forgiveness is purchased. However, the Jewish sacrificial system did not entail this way of thinking. The priest stood as mediator between God and the people, offering sacrifices to atone for sin. However, the shedding of blood was understood to be done in expiation, not propitiation; that is, as a sign of sorrow for sin and not in order to curry favor or buy forgiveness. The model is sacrificial, but it is not transactional and, as noted, it is only one of several models for understanding God's saving work in Christ.

Paul uses a variety of metaphors to talk about the human predicament: enslavement in Galatians 4:8; imprisonment in Romans 7:23; hostility to God in Romans 8:7; a mind set on the flesh in Romans 8:5–6; and others. However, the metaphor that has received the most attention and further theological extension is his juridical metaphor. The question is, "How may human beings be justified?" They are unable to be justified by "works of the law" as they do not obey the law, and "Cursed is everyone who does not observe and obey all the things written in the book of the law" (Gal. 3:10). In the face of this predicament, "Christ redeemed us from the curse of the law by becoming a curse for us—for it is written, "Cursed is everyone who hangs on a tree . . . " (Gal. 3:13). This scenario developed into a full blown substitutionary theory of the atonement and came to be the predominant understanding of God's saving work in the cross of Christ.

Anselm (1033–1109) envisioned a courtroom scene in which human beings stand accused as those who have broken the law. Christ is both our advocate and the one who takes upon himself the consequences of our crimes. The metaphor was actually picked up by Anselm to answer a different kind of question. He was not asking, "Why the cross?" In *Cur Deus Homo* (literally "why God man") usually translated as, "Why God Became Man," Anselm is asking why the one who saves us *must be* both fully human and fully divine.

Anselm recasts the Pauline metaphor, redescribing it in the feudal setting of his own day. In that context, the seriousness of a crime depended upon the person against whom in the hierarchy it was committed. To steal a sheep from a serf was less serious and incurred a lesser guilt/penalty than stealing from the lord. Anselm reasoned that since our crimes are against God we incur an infinite guilt/penalty. Only an infinite restitution—which only God can provide—will satisfy the demands of justice. Of course, it is the offender who must make restitution—thus only a human being will do. The only possible resolution, then, entails action by one who is both *fully divine and fully human*. Nothing less would suffice for God's work of salvation. A "divinized" human nature would not suffice (God walking around giving an appearance of being human). If Jesus is not fully human, then the cross is just play-acting. If he is not fully divine, then the cross does not have saving power. For Anselm this is the logic of the incarnation. The cross is seen in the light of the incarnation.

Moltmann (following Luther's own insights into the theology of the cross) puts the matter rather provocatively: What we have in the cross is "the crucified God." "The Christ event on the cross is a God event."[29] This must reframe our whole understanding of the cross. Divine solidarity with us in our sin and suffering is powerfully portrayed.

From this standpoint, God can no longer be pictured as the great punisher of sin and inflictor of suffering. God is revealed to be "the fellow sufferer who understands."[30] This solidarity is God's saving work. The cross is not something God requires in order to love and forgive. It is rather because God loves and forgives that God enters into our world. In this way God enters into our situation of struggle and suffering, our cruciform natural reality with its dissolution and desolation in the whole long crucifixion that is life. A "crucified God" is one who really is "God *with* us." Joseph Sittler put it this way: "Unless you have a crucified God, you don't have a big enough God."[31]

The cross is no glorification of suffering but a calling on our own lives to manifest solidarity with the suffering as God has done

29. Jürgen Moltmann, *The Crucified God* (New York: Harper and Row, 1974), 205.
30. Alfred North Whitehead, *Process and Reality* (New York: Macmillan Co., 1978 [1929]), 351.
31. Joseph Sittler, *Grace Notes and Other Fragments* (Minneapolis: Augsburg, 1981), 228.

in Christ. This is to the invitation to "take up the cross and follow." We need this word of the cross. H. Richard Niebuhr warns about the risks of a Christianity without the cross, proclaiming that, "(A) God without wrath brought men (*sic*) without sin into a kingdom without judgment through the ministrations of a Christ without a cross."[32] Christianity, without the word of the cross, risks becoming, as Johann Baptist Metz warned, a "bourgeois religion" that invents a more "convenient God,"[33] one that better fits into our agendas and better serves our interests. The gospel is not a sedative.[34] It will be far better to find a deeper understanding of the cross and reclaim its meaning.

The Resurrection of the Lord

Western classical tradition has not paid as much attention to the place of resurrection in God's saving work as it has to the cross. However, this was not always the case. The early church developed a rather strong association of God's saving work with resurrection. The association is already there in Pauline writings. First Corinthians 15:17 teaches that, "If Christ has not been raised your faith is futile and you are still in your sins." To say this is to attach redemptive significance to the resurrection and to assume that the cross does not complete God's saving work. Matthew's own accounting of the resurrection treats it as a cataclysmic event of eschatological significance (Matt. 28:1–10).

There are many dimensions of meaning that convey God's saving work in resurrection. The principalities and powers have done their worst in the crucifixion—now in the resurrection their impotence is unveiled. Suffering and death do not have the last word; God has the last word. God is the one who restores the dead to life. Resurrection also signals divine validation of the way Jesus lived. His salvific role as Exemplar is confirmed. This is the life that God affirms and intends for human beings.

There are two models for understanding God's saving work that rely on resurrection in particular as the central symbol. In each of

---

32. H. Richard Niebuhr, *The Kingdom of God in America* (New York: Harper and Row, 1959 [1937]), 193.
33. José A. Pagola, *The Way Opened Up by Jesus: A Commentary on the Gospel of Matthew* (Miami, FL: Convivium Press, 2012), 109.
34. Ibid.

these our human situation is likened to imprisonment or slavery from which we cannot extricate ourselves. Our situation is utterly helpless and hopeless. The power of evil has a "death grip" on us. It is in the resurrection that we see the sign that God has in Christ broken the power of evil in our lives. With the resurrection, our captivity is taken captive; the devil is defeated, and death is done to death. The two models that keep resurrection as central are the *Christus Victor* theory and the ransom theory. They share these central themes but rely upon different metaphors to illumine how the resurrection breaks the power of evil and sets free those who are held in its bondage.

The *Christus Victor* theory uses military images. God and the devil are pictured as locked in combat over the destiny of humankind. Christ is seen as the warrior of God, who, after having been apparently defeated on the cross, by his death invades the realm of the evil one. In this descent into Hell he does battle with sin and death and the devil. When God raises Jesus from the dead, death is swallowed up in victory (1 Cor. 15:54). As he rises he leads out from captivity all those who had been carried off. Sin and death and the devil are put "under his feet" as God overcomes and becomes "all in all" (1 Cor. 15:24–28).

Matthew has a distinctive contribution to offer here in his presentation of the events that follow Jesus' crucifixion (27:50–54). For him, this event signals the arrival of the apocalypse. Only Mathew tells how the earth shook and the rocks were split and the tombs were opened (27:51–52). Only Matthew gives the surprising account of saints being raised from the dead (27:50–53). Matthew is placing Jesus' resurrection squarely in the context of the Jewish hope of a general resurrection in the end time. The opening of the tombs means that the end of the age is inaugurated and the resurrection has begun. The victory over death theologically articulated in the *Christus Victor* theory is well presented in Matthew's account.

The "ransom theory" draws upon financial metaphors and images of payment. "Redemption" is itself a financial image. In this model, the human condition is compared to slavery or imprisonment. Jesus gives his life as a "ransom" to "redeem" the enslaved/imprisoned. Matthew picks up this theme in the description of

Jesus' life-giving work. "[T]he Son of Man came not to be served but to serve, and to give his life a ransom for many" (20:28). The resurrection is the sign that the work is done; the transaction is complete. The slaves/prisoners are free.

Concluding Note

There are in Scripture and in traditional theology many illuminating visions and metaphors for understanding how God's saving work is accomplished in Christ. The Gospel of Matthew makes a distinctive contribution to these theological models. Each one offers a particular angle of vision on what is and remains a mystery beyond all comprehension. It may be that the misunderstandings of the cross in our context are a result of taking one particular metaphor, using it exclusively, literalizing it, and distorting it. This sometimes happens with the substitutionary theory of the atonement that is the most prominent understanding. A fuller range of the alternative perspectives within Scripture may help to correct distortions and misunderstandings. The contributions from Matthew's Gospel can be part of that broadening and correcting work as it treats the whole of the Christ event and interprets the cross within the wider frame of Jesus' birth, life and ministry, and resurrection.

PART 4

THE RESURRECTION OF THE LORD

27:62-28:20

27:62–28:10

At the Tomb

27:62–66
The Tomb That Must Be Guarded

Only Matthew tells of the guards at the tomb. This tomb must be kept under surveillance. At the point of Matthew's writing there is already an attempt to discredit the resurrection by a claim that the disciples stole the body and said Jesus was raised. This addition counters the claim.[1] The chief priests and the Pharisees are in collusion, appearing before Pilate together. It is not enough that they have gotten Jesus crucified; now they want to ensure that his tomb is well guarded—just in case. They are concerned because the Pharisees recall Jesus' response when they asked him for a sign—some evidence of authenticity. Jesus refused to perform for them; instead he alluded to the "sign of Jonah": "Just as Jonah was three days and three nights in the belly of the sea monster, so for three days and three nights the Son of Man will be in the heart of the earth" (12:38). They want the tomb secured through the third day. "Some Jews believed the soul departed from the body after three days."[2] So they ask for a three-day guard, "otherwise his disciples may go and steal him away, and tell the people, 'He has been raised from the dead'" (27:62–66).

For Pilate this is another "see to it yourself" situation (27:24, 65). "You have a guard of soldiers; go, make it as secure as you can" (27:65). Their efforts, though considerable, are futile. Make the tomb secure against the power of God who will bring life out of death.

1. Frederick J. Murphy, *An Introduction to Jesus and the Gospels* (Nashville: Abingdon Press, 2005), 142.
2. *The Jewish Annotated New Testament* , ed. Amy-Jill Levine and Marc Zvi Brettler (Oxford: Oxford University Press, 2011), 50.

28:1–10

"But the angel said to the women, 'Do not be afraid.'"

"Last at the cross, first at the tomb," the women have come to watch. It was not uncommon for friends to come and wait by a tomb in case an apparently dead person should revive. This might continue as far as the third day. The effect of these visits was to confirm death. The women who come to perform this sad task of confirming death instead find themselves running for joy, announcing life.[3] Waiting and watching in sadness, they have become the first witnesses to the resurrection. Once again the last are first. They are also first to worship the risen Lord.

The Gospel of Matthew ends as it begins with an angel saying, "Do not be afraid" and then guiding the faithful ones as to what they are to do. In the first chapter the angel said to Joseph, "Do not be afraid to take Mary as your wife for the child conceived in her is from the Holy Spirit. She will bear a son, and you are to name him Jesus, for he will save his people from their sins" (1:20–23). Now, in the final chapter of Matthew's Gospel, the angel says to the women, "Do not be afraid; I know that you are looking for Jesus who was crucified. He is not here; for he has been raised, as he said. Come, see the place where he lay. Then go and tell his disciples" (28:5–7). This is the sixth of seven important texts with the message "do not be afraid" (1:20; 8:26; 10:31; 14:27; 17:7; 28:5; 28:10). The women obey the angel, just as Joseph did in the beginning; "with fear and great joy they ran to tell his disciples" (28:8). Jesus meets them on the way and addresses them with the final "do not be afraid" (28:10).

They respond by worshiping him. The Greek term *prosekynēsan*, "worshiped," is a favorite in Matthew for signaling the appropriate attitude and approach to Jesus. The women "took hold of his feet." This latter establishes not only their posture of worship but that this resurrection appearance had "feet"—this is not a ghost.[4]

---

3. Thomas Longstaff, "What Are These Women Doing at the Tomb of Jesus: Perspectives on Matthew 28:1," in *A Feminist Companion to Matthew*, ed. Amy-Jill Levine, 198, 202 (Sheffield: Sheffield Academic Press, 2001).

4. Donald Senior, *Abingdon New Testament Commentaries: Matthew* (Nashville: Abingdon Press, 1998), 342.

28:11–20

The Risen Lord

28:11–15

The Story That Must Be Suppressed

The guards react rather differently than the women to the angel and his message. At first they "shook and became like dead men." They had been prepared to face down disciples coming to steal the body, but nothing prepared them for this. Later, while the women are proclaiming the good news of the resurrection, they are circulating a false story that they have been paid to tell in order to discredit that message (28:13).

The chief priests and the elders, upon hearing what happened at the tomb, take measures to suppress the story. They pay "a large sum of money" to the soldiers to lie to the people. In the account of the passion of Jesus there is a lot of money changing hands. The chief priests pay Judas to betray Jesus, and Judas tries to hand back the money to the chief priests. It ends up on the Temple floor and then invested in the "Field of Blood." Soldiers get paid to guard the tomb and then paid "a large sum of money" to lie about what really happened at the tomb. It is a "follow the money" intrigue from beginning to end.

28:16–19

"All authority in heaven and on earth has been given to me. Go therefore . . ."

The disciples go to Galilee. They are following the instructions given for them to the women from the angel and from Jesus himself. Apparently they believed these women. Though they have not seen the risen Lord, they see the effect of the risen Lord on these women.[1] They do as the women have told them, and as a consequence they meet the risen Lord. He has gone on ahead of them to Galilee, just as he had promised (28:7). Now the disciples worship him, though the text says that "some doubted" (28:17).

Here he gives what has been called The Great Commission. It begins, "All authority in heaven and on earth has been given to me" (28:18). From the first, Jesus has taught and acted with authority. After the Sermon on the Mount, "the crowds were astounded at his teaching, for he taught them as one having authority and not as their scribes" (7:29). The disciples are amazed at Jesus' authority when he calms the storm; "What sort of man is this, that even the winds and the sea obey him?' (8:22). The Pharisees are deeply offended that Jesus claims and demonstrates authority not only to heal but also to forgive sins (9:2-8). Forgiving sins is God's prerogative (as administered through them—the designated authoritative interpreters of the law). From that point on, the Pharisees hound Jesus with questions and challenges to the very end of his life and ministry. Jesus even authorizes others, sharing his authority with his disciples. He gives them authority over unclean spirits and to cure every disease (10:1). When Jesus enters Jerusalem and continues his teaching and healing, the chief priests and the elders are distressed enough to ask, "By what authority are you doing these things, and who gave you this authority?" (21:23). The implication in Jesus' answer is that his authority is from God (21:23-27). Now there is no doubt of Jesus' authority. God has raised him from the dead; it is a validation of his life and ministry. Now he announces "All authority in heaven and on earth have been given to me."

His command to the disciples is that they should "Go therefore and make disciples of all nations" (Greek *panda ta ethnē*). In much of Matthew *ethnē* means the Gentiles. The mission that was only for the "lost sheep of Israel" is now decisively opened to the Gentiles. Amy-Jill Levine has proposed that in Matthew's Gospel salvation history is "constructed along two axes: a temporal axis that incorporates ethnic categories and a social axis that transcends the divisions between Jew and Gentile." The mission to Israel is never abrogated, just as

---

1. Michael Winters, "The Aweful, Joyful Resurrection: Matthew 28:1–10," Easter, Morton Grove Presbyterian Church, 1999.

Jesus comes not to abolish the law but to fulfill it. "It is because the promises to Israel have been fulfilled in Jesus' mission that the message . . . can now be proclaimed to the Gentiles"[2] God's work with Israel is not abolished or abrogated, it is rather extended outward to others who will be included even as was the Jewish eschatological hope. All will be judged—not on the basis of their religious affiliation or ethnic origin but on the basis of their love of God and neighbor as demonstrated by what they actually do (25:31–46).

Jesus' followers are called to "make disciples." To "disciple" means "to teach;" a disciple is a learner. The outreach to the Gentiles must include the teaching of the law; teaching all nations to obey everything that Jesus, the authoritative interpreter of the law, has commanded them (28:20). They are to baptize in the name "of the Father and of the Son and of the Holy Spirit." By the time of Matthew's writing this threefold formula was in use in the practice of baptism that was in place. Even older texts show the threefold affirmation of faith associated with baptism. It should be noted that this passage is not about "church growth." It is about "discipling" (teaching) and baptizing (calling people into ministry).[3] (See "Further Reflections: Baptism as Calling to Ministry," pp. 59–66.)

28:20

"I am with you always."

The Gospel closes with a promise. "I am with you always, to the end of the age." "I am with you" has been a central theme for the Gospel. This theme also pervades the book of Isaiah, which is the Scripture Matthew relies upon more than any other. It offers an understanding of God's way with God's people. It offers a vision of the coming reign of God and the coming Messiah. Isaiah is a book full of assurances of God's presence and saving work. Emblematic is Isaiah 43, "Do not fear, for I have redeemed you; I have called you by name,

2. *The Jewish Annotated New Testament*, ed. Amy-Jill Levine and Marc Zvi Brettler (Oxford: Oxford University Press, 2011), 273.
3. Michael Winters, "Always Means Forever: Matthew 28:16–20," The Presbyterian Church of Berwyn, Illinois, June 6, 1993.

you are mine. When you pass through the waters, I will be with you; and through the rivers, they shall not overwhelm you . . . For I am the LORD your God, the Holy One of Israel, your Savior" (Isa. 43).

"I am with you" is the beginning, middle, and ending of Matthew's Gospel. Jesus is identified from the beginning as "Emmanuel" (1:21), which means "God with us." Midway in the Gospel Jesus comes to the disciples across the storm tossed sea and addresses them with his assuring presence: "'Take heart, it is I. Do not be afraid'" (14:27). Now the promise is given, "I will be with you always, to the end of the age." It is the final word of the Gospel, and perhaps the only word we really need.

FURTHER REFLECTIONS
On the Meaning of the Resurrection

Introduction

In the memorial acclamation the people gathered for Communion affirm:

> "Christ has died,
> Christ is risen,
> Christ will come again."

The resurrection is both the foundation of the church and the focus of its eschatological hope. Although the Eastern church has given more attention to incarnation than it has to resurrection and the Western church has given more attention to the cross than it has to the resurrection, the early church did not give resurrection second place. Resurrection was perhaps the central symbol and certainly a primary symbol for God's saving work in Christ. In 1 Corinthians 15:17, Paul insists, "If Christ has not been raised, your faith is futile and you are still in your sins." To say this is to attach redemptive significance to the resurrection and to assume that the cross does not in itself complete God's saving work.

Matthew's accounting of the resurrection treats it as a cataclysmic event of eschatological importance (Matt. 28:1–10). It is the beginning of the general resurrection anticipated at the end-time. It is anticipated in the Hebrew Scriptures (Isa. 26:19; Dan. 12:2). This hope is grounded in conviction that God, who is the giver of life, holds the power of life and death (Deut. 32:39; Job 1:21) and that even the dead are not lost to God. The psalmist asks,

> Where can I go from your spirit?
> Or where can I flee from your presence?
> If I ascend to heaven, you are there;
> if I make my bed in Sheol, you are there.
>   (Ps. 139:7–8)

It was understood that in our dying as in our daily living, we are in God's presence and in God's hands. It was customary in the Jewish evening prayer to use the words of Psalm 31:5:

> Into your hand I commit my spirit;
> you have redeemed me, O Lᴏʀᴅ, faithful God.

This was the text that shaped the last words of Jesus in Luke's account of the crucifixion (Luke 23:46).

Resurrection as such would not be a strange concept to Matthew's context given this understanding of belonging to God in death as in life and the eschatological hope of a general resurrection. However, for the firstborn from the dead to be someone who was rejected by the religious authorities and crucified by the political authorities as a common criminal was completely unexpected. Nevertheless, Jesus' resurrection was understood by the early church as divine validation of his person and work—confirmation that he was indeed the Messiah in spite of his rejection by the religious authorities and his crucifixion by the political authorities. Furthermore, his resurrection was seen to be the first installment on the general resurrection, the inauguration of the age to come.

The Reality of the Resurrection

Contemporary theology has confronted the difficulty of affirming the resurrection as a historical event. Some, as a result, have taken the turn of "demythologizing" the resurrection, speaking of it as, for example, "the rising of faith within the early church." While an event

of the proportions of resurrection is *more than* historical, the historical moorings should not be simply cut.

There are many considerations. There is the testimony of the
"empty tomb." This, in itself, does not give much to go on. Even the
guards and the chief priests know the tomb is empty. Testimony
that the tomb was empty has evoked alternative accountings. In
Matthew (28:11–15) the guards are paid to spread one of these
alternative accounts. They are to say that while they were asleep in
the night, the disciples came and stole the body. Other alternatives
are also proposed. Some say that Jesus was not really dead when
he was placed in the tomb or that he was resuscitated and walked
out. Matthew's notation concerning the great stone (27:60) and the
posted guard (27:62–66) seem to rule out this alternative account.
Most remarkable is the proposal that it was simply the wrong tomb,
and Jesus' remains are still there if we could but find the right tomb.

Wolfhart Pannenberg was theologically committed to the historicity of the resurrection. He insisted that one cannot judge what
is possible by the constraints of what has already happened in the
past. Nothing new can happen under those constraints. If something new in fact happens, it must be judged to be possible. Pannenberg suggested that the best approach in thinking about the
historicity of the resurrection is to shift attention from the empty
tomb to the experience of the risen Christ in the early church. He
takes note of the many witnesses and their accountings.[4]

Interestingly, the earliest texts do not hide the ambiguity inherent in the experience of the risen Lord. In the Gospel of Matthew,
even *when* Jesus meets the disciples in Galilee, "some doubted"
(28:17). In the shorter ending of Mark, upon finding the tomb
empty and hearing the news of resurrection, the women flee from
the tomb in terror and amazement and say nothing to anyone. In
the longer ending, Mary Magdalene does tell the disciples the news
of resurrection but the text notes that "they would not believe it"
(Mark 16:8, 11). In the Gospel of John, Thomas doubts the news of
resurrection. He says, "Unless I see . . . I will not believe" (20:25). In the

---

4. Wolfhart Pannenberg, "The History and Reality of the Resurrection," in *Resurrection Reconsidered*, ed. Gavin D'Costa (New York: Oxford University Press, 1990), 62–72.

Gospel of Luke it says the disciples are "disbelieving and still wondering" (24:41).

One of the most compelling evidences of the resurrection has been the transformation in the followers of Jesus after his death. In the midst of Jesus passion, the disciples desert him and flee (Matt. 26:56). However exemplary the life of Jesus had been and however much faith (or "little faith") he had evoked in the disciples, the passion and crucifixion posed a crisis. They abandoned him to it. This was the end of their hopes in him as Messiah. It was the end of *him*. He became one more martyr executed by Rome in occupied territory—this was nothing new. Yet something took hold of this sorrowing band of deniers and deserters and welded them together, more certain and committed than ever. They went forward in an unprecedented missionary movement. The disciples respond to the crisis of Jesus' death and the death of their hopes in him with strengthened faith and missionary zeal. How can this be? It is a completely inexplicable response and enigmatic apart from the explanation that the believers themselves offer.

It is one thing to affirm the resurrection but quite another to claim to know exactly *what resurrection is*. No one got this on video. The texts we have are remarkably silent on the "moment" of resurrection or its detailed description. The texts seem more intent on its reality and its meaning than painting a picture of the resurrection.

Believers today are in the position of those who "have not seen and yet have come to believe" (John 20:29). Like the early witnesses, even doubting and fearing as we do, many of us encounter the risen Lord along the way. When that happens, perhaps we do not even need to see the empty tomb to believe the Lord is risen.

Why Resurrection of the Body?

In Christian theology, the Greek philosophical doctrine of the "immortality of the soul" is laid aside in favor of "resurrection of the body." There is a significant difference between these alternatives. The philosophical dualism from Plato forward divides soul from body and presumes that the soul is "an inherently indestructible element of human life that is separable from the mortal, corruptible body that it temporarily inhabits."[5] For Plato, the body is, in fact, the "prison-house" of the soul. Death sets the soul free from the lifeless corpse at death.

In affirming "resurrection of the body" the dualistic understanding of the human being is in favor of a more holistic understanding of the human being as reflected in the account in Genesis 2:7 of the creation of the human as a "living being" (Hebrew *nepesh hayya*). This view sees the human being holistically and recognizes embodiment as part of who we essentially are. This perspective may in fact ring more truly to how we experience ourselves. As Whitehead observed, no one ever says, "Here *I* am, and I have brought my body with me."[6] In the resurrection of the body, the whole self receives the gift of life.

Another problem with immortality of the soul is its assumption that the soul's immortality is an inherent quality that the human being already possesses. Resurrection of the body is God's doing. It is a gift— not a given. Affirmation of resurrection of the body makes a profound difference theologically.

The New Testament accounts offer the depiction of a strange kind of body. There is a sense of both continuity and discontinuity in Christian eschatology generally. The language of hope for a "*new* creation" or "a *new* heaven and a *new* earth" signals the continuity and discontinuity that is the "strange logic of eschatology."[7] This continuity-discontinuity that characterizes Christian eschatology generally shows itself in resurrection of the body particularly.

There is reference to a "spiritual body" in Pauline writings (1 Cor. 15:44). In the Gospel of Matthew, Jesus' resurrected body walks and talks and travels (Matt. 28:8–28). Matthew gives the explicit detail of the women who met Jesus on the way taking "hold of his feet" (28:9)—this is a body that has feet. In the Gospel of John, Jesus cooks and eats breakfast (John 21:9–15); yet he also passes through walls (John 20:19). His scars are visible (John 20:24–28) yet he is not

---

5. Daniel Migliore, *Faith Seeking Understanding: An Introduction to Christian Theology,* 2nd ed. (Grand Rapids: Eerdmans, 2004), 243.

6. Alfred North Whitehead, *Modes of Thought* (1938; repr., New York: The Free Press, 1968), 114.

7. Michael Welker and John Polkinghorne, "Introduction" in *The End of the World and the Ends of God: Science and Theology on Eschatology,* ed. John Polkinghorne and Michael Welker (Harrisburg, PA: Trinity Press, 2000), 2.

always recognizable to those closest to him. In the story of Mary Magdalene at the tomb in the Gospel of John, Mary thinks Jesus is the gardener until he calls her by name (John 20:11–18). In Luke 24, two disciples on the road to Emmaus walk with Jesus all day but do not recognize him until their eyes are opened in the breaking of the bread (Luke 24:30–31). He shares a meal of bread and broiled fish (Luke 24:42–43) with them.

These accounts present a different kind of embodiment that is puzzling to the reader. It is an altogether strange accounting. Nevertheless, Migliore rightly observes that "Even if we cannot adequately conceive of a resurrection body, the symbol stands as a bold and even defiant affirmation of God's total, inclusive, holistic redemption."[8]

Where are the dead as they await the resurrection of the body? This is a question that evokes much theological reflection. "Death is the boundary of our lives, but not the boundary of God's relationship with us."[9] Process theology envisions two aspects of our ongoing relationship with God. First, there is something like an "objective" presence for us (objective immortality) in the trajectory of the effects of our lives in the world and consequently our effects upon the divine life. God experiences and receives the world in its process, moment by moment, event by event. This process goes on continuously. Beyond this there is also the prospect of "subjective" presence for us (subjective immortality). Just as we—even now— live life "in God," so also we will be "in God" when we die.[10] God is the one "in whom we live and move and have our being" (Acts 17:28). In a sense, we already participate in God's everlasting life.

Dimensions of the Meaning of Resurrection: Resistance and Solidarity

As the cross demonstrates the solidarity of "God with us" in the face of sin and evil, suffering and death, so now the resurrection signals divine resistance in the face of sin and evil, suffering and death. We do not see divine solidarity only, but also divine deliverance.

---

8. Migliore, *Faith Seeking Understanding*, 244.
9. Jürgen Moltmann, "Is There Life after Death?" in *The End of the Word and the Ends of God*, 246.
10. Alfred North Whitehead, *Process and Reality* (New York: Macmillan Co., 1978 [1929]), 351.

Christus Victor understandings of God's saving work in the resurrection convey this dimension in a striking way. (See "Further Reflections: On the Meaning of the Cross," pp. 322–31.)

Both solidarity and resistance actually pervade each aspect of the whole of the Christ event. Jesus' birth narrative in Matthew carries the affirmation of Emmanuel, "God is with us," (Matt. 1:23). At the same time it is clear that this one poses a threat to Herod and an alternative reign over against Roman imperial rule (Matt. 2). The life and ministry of Jesus demonstrates solidarity with those at the margins—the least, the last, and the lost. At the same time it instigates change in their situation—treatment of the "least of these" is what matters in the judgment; the last are first; the lost are found. There is resistance inherent in these dramatic reversals. Jesus engages in a ministry of healing and feeding that resists the disease and deprivation of the people. Those who were excluded now are included; outsiders become insiders. The cross, while perhaps more clearly a symbol of solidarity, is also a peculiar kind of resistance—exercising the paradoxical power of suffering love. Matthew conveys the dramatic effects of this power using apocalyptic symbols. The earth quakes and rocks are split and the Temple curtain is torn from top to bottom (27:51–52).

In the resurrection is resistance, where we see God overcoming all that hurts and destroys—even the last enemy, death. Karl Barth proposes that it is not death as such that is problematic. Mortality is only the "shadowside" of life and is not in itself genuinely evil. Death may even place a "salutary limit to life."[11] It is rather our lives as we live them that make a problem of death. "The sting of death is sin" (1 Cor. 15:56). Eberhard Jüngel, drawing out Barth's view, says that "the shadow cast by death (over human life) is no more than the haunting primordial shadow, now extended and magnified, which our life casts upon our ending."[12]

Miroslav Volf counters this point of view and insists that it is both "transience and transgression" that overshadow us in life and

11. Karl Barth, *Church Dogmatics,* III/2, *The Doctrine of Creation,* ed. G. W. Bromiley and T. F. Torrance (Edinburgh: T. & T. Clark, 1936–1962), 553–72.

12. Eberhard Jüngel, *Death: Riddle and Mystery,* trans. Iain and Ute Nicol (Philadelphia: Westminster, 1974), 74–75.

death.[13] Transience keeps us ever in a state of disruption. "Our present is not at peace with our past and future. We feel anxiety about what we expect and carry the burden of what we remember, and are thus robbed of an unattenuated joy in the present."[14] We need the assurance that in the resurrection of the body, death will be destroyed. A contemporary summation of this affirmation follows.

Death will be destroyed. In the death of Jesus Christ God's way in the world seemed finally defeated. But death was no match for God. The resurrection of Jesus was God's victory over death. Death often seems to prove that life is not worth living, that our best efforts and deepest affections go for nothing. We do not yet see the end of death. But Christ has been raised from the dead, transformed and yet the same person. In his resurrection is the promise of ours. We are convinced the life God wills for each of us is stronger than the death that destroys us. The glory of that life exceeds our imagination, but we know we shall be with Christ. So we treat death as a broken power. Its ultimate defeat is certain. In the face of death we grieve. Yet in hope we celebrate life. No life ends so tragically that its meaning and value are destroyed. Nothing, not even death, can separate us from the love of God in Jesus Christ our Lord.

> Jesus is Lord!
> He has been Lord from the beginning.
> He will be Lord at the end.
> Even now he is Lord.[15]

Not only does Jesus' resurrection begin the anticipated "resurrection of the dead," it also inaugurates the all-inclusive transformation envisioned in concepts of "new creation" or "a new heaven and a new earth." As this comes to fruition, all things are reconciled to God (Greek *apokatallasai*) and all things are reconstituted/restored (Greek *apokatastasis*).

Jesus' resurrection represents the first fruits of the hoped for

13. Miroslav Volf, "Enter into Joy! Sin, Death, and the Life of the World to Come," in *The End of the Word and the Ends of God: Theology and Science on Eschatology,* ed. John Polkinghorne and Michael Welker (Harrisburg, PA: Trinity Press, 2000), 274.

14. Ibid., 275.

15. Presbyterian Church (U.S.A.), "A Declaration of Faith," https://www.pcusa.org/resource/declaration=faith, 10.3.

restoration of all things. This fills his followers with hope that gives courage to join in God's work of resistance against all that would hurt or destroy. Resurrection hope overcomes all "hopelessness in the face of present trouble, complacent inactivity regarding suffering and injustice, and irresponsible self-concern."[16] In Jesus, the Christ, God's reign has come near; now the old order can no longer be tolerated. We are people called to transformed lives befitting the reign of God; we participate in God's work of resistance "with an urgency born of this hope."[17] To take up the cross and follow Jesus (Matt. 10:38) means "risking the consequences of faithful discipleship." It involves walking by faith and not by sight, hoping for "what we have not yet seen."[18]

If the first word about resurrection is resistance, the last word for Matthew returns to solidarity. The "real presence" of the Risen Lord is "with us." Jesus promises, "I am with you always, to the end of the age" (Matthew 28:20). With this promise, the Gospel of Matthew comes full circle. The good news with which the Gospel opens is the news of the fulfillment of the promise of "Emmanuel, which means 'God is with us'" (1:23). Now this final verse makes good on the promise. "I am with you always" is the good news that is the final word of the Gospel, and perhaps the only word we really need.

---

16. Kathryn Tanner, "Eschatology without a Future?" in *The End of the Word and the Ends of God*, 226.
17. The Confession of 1967, in *The Constitution of the Presbyterian Church (U.S.A.)*, Part I, *Book of Confessions* (Louisville, KY: Office of the General Assembly, Presbyterian Church (U.S.A.), 1999), 9.55.
18. Presbyterian Church (U.S.A.), "A Declaration of Faith," 9.5.

Final Thoughts

My prolonged immersion in the Gospel of Matthew while writing this commentary has had a profound impact on me. It does not overstate the matter to say that I have been "reoriented" professionally and personally.

As a theologian, I must confess to having had some reservations as I began this project. It is a little unusual these days for a theologian to write a Bible commentary. I had the feeling I was "coloring outside the lines." My decision to write a Bible commentary was met by some with puzzlement and by others with palpable alarm. What is a theologian doing writing a Bible commentary? One very suspicious response I received was, "Do theologians actually read the Bible?!"

In fact there was a time, not so long ago, when the church's theologians routinely wrote commentaries on Scripture and took as part of their calling careful scholarship and theological interpretation of these texts. In more recent history though, for several generations now, with increased specialization of professional disciplines there has been a sense that the Bible belongs to people trained for biblical studies. Commentaries have been very focused on matters of form, authorship, historical setting, social context, and philology. This is essential work if we would be responsible interpreters. However, I am convinced, as was Karl Barth, that this kind of work is a "first step toward a commentary." The step of theological reflection and interpretation is an essential second step. This is especially for those called to preach, who live day to day "between text and sermon." I was intrigued by the vision of this project, and when asked to write on Matthew I was honored and eager.

My reservations came later. I began to question my decision. My graduate training is in theology; do I really know what I need to know in order to do this work well? Is it really legitimate for a theologian to write a Bible commentary? What will the other theologians think as I transgress boundaries of the discipline and do something that is thought not to be the "proper" business of a theologian? Finding myself outside my area of expertise (and my comfort zone), I turned to colleagues in biblical studies. This turn is where my work as a theologian got reoriented.

I found colleagues in biblical studies to be quite interested in this project, receptive to my questions, and willing to help. They pointed me to resources that helped me get a good grounding. This experience has set me on a course of cross-disciplinary interaction that is now deeply enriching my work as a theologian. In theological education we often bemoan the "silo" approach—discreet disciplines fields that do not talk to one another. The pattern leaves students in a quandary as to how to integrate what they are learning. This project was an experience of the enrichment that stepping outside those constraints can offer. I am convinced that theology is best done in a framework of wider engagements and that it is more likely to be relevant and meaningful for the life of the church when such an engagement is maintained.

Rediscovering the Bible as a primary text for theology has been another kind of reorientation in my work as a theologian. Although the study of Scripture has always been important for my theology, there is an undertow in this work that tempts professional theologians to focus their work on interactions with other theologians. We do well to recover something of John Calvin's insight that the whole purpose of theology is nothing more than putting in systematic form what is already there in Scripture. It is a gift to receive this reorientation.

The Gospel of Matthew itself has its "reorienting" effect. It is an amazing book that continues to speak to people of faith today with eloquence, relevance, and power. There is good reason why this Gospel account is so beloved. Its meaning unfolds in multiple layers. At the base there is a portrait of Jesus—a compelling story of his life and ministry. Another layer is added as this story intersects with the world of

Matthew's faith community. Their issues and struggles give shape to Matthew's narrative and his distinctive interpretation of the story of Jesus. Then there is the layer of meaning that comes from the reception of this text by contemporary readers like us, who are seeking insight and inspiration for the life of faith amid the issues and struggles of our own day and time. The back and forth between the "then" of the story of Jesus and the "now" of our own stories is an interaction of great power.

At first I wondered, how can an ancient text like this be relevant to our very different context? Five points of resonance in particular took me by surprise:

1. *Matthew was written in a time when there was conflict and division in the community of faith.* We discover that the Jesus movement was a renewal movement *within* Judaism. It was at odds with the mainstream under the leadership of the Pharisees; tensions and conflicts come right to the surface in this text. As we know from experience, "There is no fight like a church fight."

2. *Matthew was written in a time when some were insiders and others were outsiders.* Jesus and the disciples minister from the margins to those who have been marginalized and over-turn all those assumptions about who is "in" and who is "out" in the reign of God.

3. *Matthew was written in a time when political and religious leaders were coopted, mistrusted, and discredited.* Would that this were not so relevant for us. The people were harassed and helpless, like sheep without a shepherd.

4. *Matthew was written in a time when the great majority of the common people were without power.* We find in Matthew an ongoing narrative of resistance to empire. It has "occupy wall street"—a movement contemporary to our own time—written all over it. The new community that Jesus is forming cares for the least, the last, and the lost.

5. *Matthew was written in a time when cultures clashed.* The questions about whether the Gentiles can be included among the people of God pushes the question, "How wide is the divine embrace?" This is a question that is very much still with is in our context of cultural and religious pluralism.

How very relevant is the Gospel of Matthew, and how very

powerful in its impact! Having my own life of faith reoriented was the biggest surprise of this immersion in the Gospel of Matthew. Many of the stories and teachings of Jesus touched me deeply. Even after hearing and reading these texts all my life, I found they still had the power to surprise me and to "seize" me.

The text that most disturbed my "scholarly quietude" was the Sermon on the Mount. I read it closely, and then I read a mountain of commentaries on it. I was interested to see the many and ingenious attempts to find what we might call a "work around." Three proposals stand out in this regard.

1. One approach argues that this passage offers an "interim ethic" for a time when Matthew's faith community thought the second coming was imminent. Maybe people could have lived as this Sermon commends for a short time, as an emergency measure, but now we are in a different situation. The delay of the second coming calls for a different kind of ethic, something a bit less demanding.
2. Some other commentators say that the Sermon commends a lifestyle for the inner circle—those who would be perfect—the folks who join religious orders. It is not for ordinary people who have to live in the real world of economics and politics and must compromise on the ethic of love.
3. Still others contend that the Sermon on the Mount offers an "impossible ethic." They say that its real function is just to show us that it is impossible to be righteous. It convicts us of sin and shows our need for grace.

These proposals strike me as designed to deliver the church from the demands of discipleship. The Sermon on the Mount, however, is a "text that cannot be tamed."

Right there in the middle of the Sermon on the Mount is the Lord's Prayer. You would not think this prayer could hold surprises for us. After all, this is a prayer on the lips of every Christian. It is one that crosses the theological spectrum, the divides of denomination, and the disagreements of our current debates. It has been prayed by Christians for two millennia. It is offered up most every Sunday in almost every church. But what are we really saying as we speak these words? What way of life is incumbent upon those who pray in this way? The more I really considered this, the more difficult it became to pray this prayer.

For example, we have a habit of privatizing the petitions of this prayer. But there are no first person pronouns in this prayer. It is not about "I and mine." It is about "us and our." I felt convicted to take the "our" to include the widest possible circle and consider the global dimensions. A petition for "our" daily bread lays upon us a calling to address the problem of world hunger. A petition that goes "forgive us our debts as we forgive our debtors" lays upon us a calling to address the global debt crisis. So it goes, petition by powerful petition.

Michael Crosby proposes that praying the Lord's Prayer is a "subversive" activity. When we pray "thy kingdom come"—remembering that kingdom is not a place but a new reality, namely the reign of God in our midst—we are actually praying for the overturning of the present order. We are aligning our hearts and lives with a new reality. We cannot pray for the coming of God's reign while contradicting it and even resisting it, all at the same time.

Christians pray this prayer by heart—what would it mean to pray it from the heart—to begin to live as we pray?

There is a reorientation implied. A deep engagement with the Lord's Prayer, the Sermon on the Mount, and indeed the whole of the Gospel of Matthew is a reorienting experience. I commend the Gospel of Matthew to your reading, but it is a powerful text that must come with a warning: read it at your own risk.

For Further Reading

Abelard, Peter. *Commentary on the Epistle to the Romans*, Book II, in *Fathers of the Church: Medieval Continuations*. Translated by Stephen R. Cartwright. Washington, DC: Catholic University of America Press, 2011.

Aulén, Gustav. *Christus Victor: An Historical Study of the Three Main Types of the Idea of Atonement*. Reprint. New York: Macmillan, 1969.

Barth, Karl. *Church Dogmatics*. Edited by G. W. Bromiley and T. F. Torrance. Translated by G. W. Bromiley. 4 volumes. Edinburgh: T. & T. Clark, 1936–1975.

Berkhof, Hendrikus. *Christian Faith: An Introduction to the Study of the Faith*. Translated by Sierd Woudstra. Rev. Ed. Grand Rapids: Eerdmans, 1986.

Boesak, Allan. "Undisciplined Abundance," sermon on Matthew 13:1–9. In *The Fire Within: Sermons from the Edge of Exile*. Capetown: New World Foundation, 2004.

Bonhoeffer, Dietrich. *Discipleship* (1949). Dietrich Bonhoeffer's Works, Vol. 4, English Edition. Edited by Geffrey B. Kelly and John D. Godsey. Translated by Barbara Green and Reinhard Krauss. Minneapolis: Augsburg Fortress, 2000.

———. *Life Together* (1938). Dietrich Bonhoeffer's Works, Vol. 5, English Edition. Edited by Geffrey B. Kelly. Translated by Daniel W. Bloesch and James H. Burtness. Minneapolis: Augsburg Fortress, 2000.

Boring, Eugene. "Matthew." In *The New Interpreter's Bible,* 8:87–506. Nashville: Abingdon, 1995.

Botman, Russel. "Should the Reformed Join in?" *Reformed World,*
      Vol 52, no.1:12–17.

Bromiley, Geoffrey. *Introduction to the Theology of Karl Barth.*
      Grand Rapids: Eerdmans, 1979.

Brown, Joanne Carlson and Carole R. Bohn. *Christianity, Patriarchy,
      and Abuse: A Feminist Critique.* Cleveland: The Pilgrim Press,
      1989.

Brown, Raymond E. *The Birth of the Messiah: A Commentary on
      the Infancy Narratives in Matthew and Luke.* Garden City, NY:
      Doubleday, 1977.

Brueggemann, Walter. *Praying the Psalms.* Winnona, MN: St.
      Mary's Press, 1982.

———. *Prophetic Imagination.* Minneapolis: Fortress, 1983.

Bruner, Frederick Dale. *The Christbook: Matthew 1–12.* Grand
      Rapids: Eerdmans, 2004.

Bultmann, Rudolf. "New Testament and Mythology." In *Kerygma and
      Myth.* Edited by H. W. Bartsch, 1–16. New York: Harper, 1961.

Cahill, Lisa Sowle. "The Ethical Implications of the Sermon on the
      Mount." *Interpretation* 41, no. 2 (1987):144–56

Calvin, John. *Institutes of the Christian Tradition.* Edited by John T.
      McNeill. Transated by Ford Lewis Battles. 2 vols. Library of
      Christian Classics. Philadelphia: Westminster Press, 1960.

———. "Psychopannychia." In *Tracts and Treatises in Defense of the
      Reformed Faith.* Translated by H. Beveridge. Grand Rapids:
      Eerdmans, 1958.

Carter, Warren. "Love Your Enemies." *Word and World* 28, no.
      1:13–21 (Winter 2008).

———. *Matthew and Empire: Initial Explorations.* Harrisburg:
      Trinity Press International, 2001.

———. *Matthew and the Margins: A Socio-Political and Religious
      Reading.* Sheffield, England: Sheffield Academic Press,
      2000.

———. *What Are They Saying about Matthew's Sermon on the Mount?*
      New York: Paulist Press, 1994.

Case-Winters, Anna. *God's Power: Traditional Understandings and
      Contemporary Challenges.* Louisville: Westminster/John Knox
      Press, 1990.

―――. "Joint Declaration on the Doctrine of Justification: Reformed Comments." In *Concord Makes Strength: Essays in Reformed Ecumenism.* Edited by John Coakley, 88–98. Grand Rapids: Eerdmans, 2002.

―――. "Our Misused Motto." In *Presbyterians Being Reformed: Reflections on What the Church Needs Today.* Edited by Robert H. Bullock Jr., xxix-xxxii. Louisville, KY: Geneva Press: 2006.

―――. *Reconstructing a Christian Theology of Nature: Down to Earth.* Hampshire, England: Ashgate, 2007.

―――and Lewis S. Mudge. "The Successor to Peter," *The Journal of Presbyterian History.* Special edition, "Excerpts from the Ecumenical Revolution." Vol. 80, no.2 (2002): 83–102.

Coffin, William Sloane. *Credo.* Louisville, KY: Westminster John Knox Press, 2004.

Corley, Kathleen. *Private Women, Public Meals: Social Conflict in the Synoptic Tradition.* Peabody, MA: Hendrickson, 1993.

Crosby, Michael. *House of Disciples: Church Economics and Justice in Matthew.* Maryknoll, NY: Orbis Books, 1988.

―――. *Thy Will Be Done: Praying the Our Father as Subversive Activity.* Maryknoll, NY: Orbis Books, 1973

Cyprian, "The Lord's Prayer" (Treatise IV). In *St. Cyprian: Treatises.* Edited by Roy Deferari. Washington, DC: Catholic University Press, 1958.

D'Angelo, Mary Rose. "(Re)Women in the Gospel of Matthew and Luke–Acts." Chap. 8 in *Women and Christian Origins.* Edited by Ross Shepard Kramer and Mary Rose D'Angelo. Oxford: Oxford University Press, 1999.

Davies, W. D. and D. C. Allison. "Matthew 1–7." In *The Gospel according to St. Matthew,* 1:1–693. International Critical Commentary. Edinburgh: T. & T. Clark, 1988–97.

Dodd, C. H. *The Parables of the Kingdom.* New York: Charles Scribner's Sons, 1961.

Farley, Wendy. *Tragic Vision and Divine Compassion.* Louisville, KY: Westminster/John Knox Press, 1990.

Farris, Patricia. "Be Happy (Micah 6:1–8; Matthew 5:1–12)." *Christian Century.* January 26, 2005.

Gale, Aaron M. "The Gospel according to Matthew." In *The Jewish Annotated New Testament.* Edited by Amy-Jill Levine and Marc Brettler, 1–54. Oxford, England: Oxford University Press, 2011.

Galloway, Allan. *The Cosmic Christ.* New York: Harper Bros., 1951.

Garland, David E. *Reading Matthew: A Literary and Theological Commentary on the First Gospel.* New York: Crossroad, 1993.

Gregersen, Niels Henrik. "Deep Incarnation: Why Evolutionary Continuity Matters in Christology." *Toronto Journal of Theology.* 26/2 (2010): 173–188.

Guthrie, Shirley. *Christian Doctrine.* Rev. ed. Louisville, KY: Westminster John Knox Press, 1994.

Hare, Douglas R. A. *Matthew.* Interpretation: A Bible Commentary for Teaching and Preaching. Louisville, KY: Westminster/ John Knox Press, 1993.

Hauerwas, Stanley. *The Peaceable Kingdom:A Primer in Christian Ethics.* Notre Dame, IN: University of Notre Dame Press, 1983.

Hodgson, Peter. *Revisioning the Church: Ecclesial Freedom in the New Paradigm.* Philadelphia: Fortress Press, 1988.

Irenaeus. *Against Heresies.* Book 5. Preface.

Jeremias, Joachim. *New Testament Theology: The Proclamation of Jesus.* New York: Charles Scribner's Sons, 1971.

Johnson, Elizabeth. *She Who Is.* New York: Crossroad, 1992.

Jüngel, Eberhard. *Death: The Riddle and the Mystery.* Translated by Iain and Ute Nicol. Philadelphia: Westminster Press, 1974.

Kingsbury, Dean. *Jesus Christ in Matthew, Mark, and Luke.* Proclamation Commentaries. Philadelphia: Fortress, 1977.

Knowles, Michael. *Jeremiah in Matthew's Gospel: The Rejected-Prophet Motif in Matthean Redaction. Journal for the Study of the New Testament.* Supplemental Series 6. Sheffield: Sheffield Academic Press, 1993.

Kołakowski, Leszek. *The Presence of Myth.* Translated by Adam Czerniawski. Chicago: University of Chicago Press, 2001.

Kraemer, Ross Shepard and Mary Rose D'Angelo, eds. *Women and Christian Origins.* New York: Oxford, 1999.

Küng, Hans. *The Church.* New York: Image Books, 1976.

Lamott, Anne. *Traveling Mercies: Some Thoughts on Faith.* New York: Anchor Books, 1999.

Lapide, Pinchas. *The Sermon on the Mount.* Maryknoll, NY: Orbis, 1986.

Levine, Amy-Jill. *A Feminist Companion to Matthew*. Sheffield: Sheffield Academic Press, 2001.

———. "Matthew." In *The Women's Bible Commentary*. Edited by Carol Newsom and Sharon Ringe, 252–62. Louisville, KY: Westminster/John Knox Press, 1992.

———. *The Social and Ethnic Dimensions of Matthean Social History: "Go Nowhere among the Gentiles"*. Lewiston, NY: Edwin Mellen Press, 1988.

———, and Marc Brettler, eds. *Jewish The New Testament*. Oxford: Oxford University Press, 2011.

Longstaff, Thomas. "What Are These Women Doing at the Tomb of Jesus: Perspectives on Matthew 28:1." In *A Feminist Companion to Matthew*. Edited by Amy-Jill Levine, 196–204. Sheffield: Sheffield Academic Press, 2001.

Luz, Ulrich. *The Theology of the Gospel of Matthew*. New Testament Theology. Cambridge, UK: Cambridge University Press, 1995.

McDougall, Joy Ann. Unpublished paper presented at the American Academy of Religion conference. Boston, Massachusetts, 1999.

McNutt, James E. "A Very Damning Truth: Walter Grundmann, Adolf Schlatter, and Susannah Heschel's *The Aryan Jesus*." *Harvard Review* 105:280–301.

Migliore, Daniel. *Faith Seeking Understanding: An Introduction to Christian Theology*. Second Edition. Grand Rapids: Eerdmans, 2004.

Mollenkott, Virginia Ramey. *The Divine Feminine: The Biblical Imagery of God as Female*. New York: Crossroad, 1983.

Moltmann, Jürgen. *The Church in the Power of the Spirit*. Philadelphia: Fortress Press, 1977.

———. *The Crucified God*. New York: Harper and Row, 1974.

———. "Is There Life After Death?" In *The End of the World and the Ends of God: Science and Theology on Eschatology*. Edited by John Polkinghorne and Michael Welker, 238–55. Harrisburg, PA: Trinity Press, 1990.

———. *The Way of Jesus Christ: Christology in Messianic Dimensions*. Minneapolis: Fortress Press, 1993.

Mother Teresa. *In the Heart of the World: Thoughts, Stories, and Prayers*. Novato, CA: New World Library, 1997.

Murphy, Frederick J. *An Introduction to Jesus and the Gospels.* Nashville: Abingdon, 2005.

Myers, Wayne. "'The Kingdom of Heaven Is Like . . .': Matthew 13:47–52." Sermon at Fair Oaks Presbyterian Church, Oak Park, IL. March 18, 2012.

Newsom, Carol, Sharon Ringe, and Jacqueline Lapsley, eds. *The Women's Bible Commentary: Revised and Updated.* Twentieth Anniversary ed. Louisville, KY: Westminster John Knox Press, 2012.

Niebuhr, H. Richard. *The Kingdom of God in America* (1937). New York: Harper and Row, 1959.

Nietzsche, Friedrich. *Thus Spake Zarathustra.* Translated by R. J. Hollingsdale. London: Penguin, 1969.

Ogletree, Thomas. *The Use of the Bible in Christian Ethics.* Philadelphia: Fortress, 1983.

Pagola, Jose A. *The Way Opened Up by Jesus: A Commentary on the Gospel of Matthew.* Miami: Covivium, 2012.

Pannenberg, Wolfhart. "The History and Reality of the Resurrection." 62–72 in *Resurrection Reconsidered,* ed. Gavin D'Costa. New York: Oxford University Press, 1990.

Peacocke, Arthur. *Paths from Science Towards God: The End of All Our Exploring.* Oxford: One World, 2001.

Polkinghore, John. *Science and Theology: An Introduction.* Philadelphia: Fortress, 1998.

———, and Michael Welker. "Introduction: Science and Theology on the End of the World and the Ends of God." In *The End of the World and the Ends of God: Science and Theology on Eschatology.* Edited by John Polkinghorne and Michael Welker, 1–16. Harrisburg, PA: Trinity Press International, 2000.

Pollan, Michael. *Food Rules.* New York: Penguin Group, 2009.

———. *In Defense of Food: An Eater's Manifesto.* New York: Penguin Press, 2008.

Pregeant, Russell. *Christology beyond Dogma: Matthew's Christ in Process Hermeneutic. Semia Studies* 7. Philadelphia: Fortress, 1978.

Presbyterian Church (U.S.A.). *The Constitution of the Presbyterian Church (U.S.A.),* Part I, *Book of Confessions.* Louisville,

KY: Office of the General Assembly, Presbyterian Church (U.S.A.), 2004.

Presbyterian Church (U.S.A.). "A Declaration of Faith." Document for study and liturgical use. PCUSA, https://www.pcusa.org/resource/declaration-faith.

Rasmussen, Larry. *Moral Fragments and Moral Community.* Minneapolis: Augsburg, 1993.

Reddish, Mitchell G. *An Introduction to the Gospels.* Nashville: Abingdon, 1997.

Rich, Adrienne. *The Dream of a Common Language: Poems 1974–1977.* New York: W.W. Norton and Company, 1993.

Ringe, Sharon. "A Gentile Woman's Story." In *Feminist Interpretation of the Bible.* Edited by Letty Russell, 65–72. Philadelphia: Westminster Press, 1985.

Rosenblatt, Marie-Eloise. "Got into the Party After All: Women's Issues and the Five Foolish Virgins." In *A Feminist Companion to Matthew.* Edited by Amy-Jill Levine, 171–95. Sheffield: Sheffield Academic Press, 2001.

Russell, Letty. *Authority in Feminist Theology: Household of Freedom.* Philadelphia: Westminster Press, 1987.

Sacks, Jonathan. *The Dignity of Difference: How to Avoid the Clash of Civilizations.* New York: Continuum, 2002.

Senior, Donald. *Abingdon New Testament Commentaries: Matthew.* Nashville: Abingdon Press, 1998.

———. *The Gospel of Matthew.* Interpreting Biblical Texts. Nashville: Abingdon, 1997.

Sigal, Phillip. *The Halakah of Jesus of Nazareth according to the Gospel of Matthew.* Lanham, MD: University Press of America, 1986.

Sittler, Joseph. *Grace Notes and Other Fragments.* Minneapolis: Augsburg, 1981.

———. *Gravity and Grace: Reflections and Provocations.* Minneapolis: Augsburg, 1986.

Soelle, Dorothee. *Suffering.* Minneapolis: Fortress Press, 1984

Song, C. S. *Jesus and the Reign of God.* Minneapolis: Fortress, 1993.

Stegemann, Ekkehard W., and Wolfgang Stegemann. *The Jesus Movement: A Social History of Its First Century.* Minneapolis: Fortress, 1999.

Stendahl, Krister. "Notes for Three Bible Studies." In *Christ's Lordship and Religious Pluralism*. Edited by Gerald H. Anderson and Thomas F. Stransky, 96–110. Maryknoll, NY: Orbis, 1981.

Suchocki, Marjorie. *God-Christ-Church: A Practical Guide to Process Theology*. New York: Crossroad, 1986.

———. *God's Presence: Theological Reflections on Prayer*. St. Louis: Chalice, 1996.

Talbert, C. H. *Reading the Sermon on the Mount: Character Formation and Decision Making in Matthew 5–7*. Grand Rapids: Baker Academic, 2008.

Tannehill, Robert. "The 'Focal Instance' as a Form of New Testament Speech: A Study of Matthew 5:39–42." *Journal of Religion* 50 (1970): 372–85.

Tanner, Kathryn. "Eschatology without a Future?" In *The End of the World and the Ends of God: Science and Theology on Eschatology*. Ed. John Polkinghorne and Michael Welker, 222–37. Harrisburg, PA: Trinity Press, 2000.

Taylor, Barbara Brown. *The Seeds of Heaven: Sermons on the Gospel of Matthew*. Louisville, KY: Westminster John Knox Press, 2004.

Tennis, Diane. *Is God the Only Reliable Father?* Louisville, KY: Westminster/John Knox Press, 1985.

Theissen, Gerd. *Sociology of Early Palestinian Christianity*. Philadelphia: Fortress, 1977.

Tillich, Paul. *Dynamics of Faith*. New York: Harper Bros., 1958.

Tutu, Desmond. *No Future Without Forgiveness*. New York: Doubleday, 1999.

Via, Dan O. *Self-deception and Wholeness in Paul and Matthew*. Philadelphia: Fortress, 1990.

Vogel, Christine. "Jesus' Anointing at Bethany: Matthew 26:6–12." Sermon for Maundy Thursday service, McCormick Seminary. March, 27, 2013.

Volf, Miroslav. "Enter into Joy! Sin, Death, and the Life of the World to Come." In *The End of the World and the Ends of God: Science and Theology on Eschatology*. Edited by John Polkinghorne and Michael Welker, 256–78. Harrisburg, PA: Trinity Press, 2000.

————. *Exclusion and Embrace: A Theological Exploration of Identity, Otherness, and Reconciliation*. Nashville: Abingdon, 1996.

Welker, Michael. "Resurrection and Eternal Life." In *The End of the World and the Ends of God: Science and Theology on Eschatology*. Edited by John Polkinghorne and Michael Welker, 279–90. Harrisburg, PA: Trinity Press, 2000.

Whitehead, Alfred North. *Modes of Thought*. 1938. Reprint, New York: The Free Press, 1968.

————. *Process and Reality*. New York: Macmillan Co., 1978 [1929].

Williams, Delores. *Sisters in the Wilderness: The Challenge of Womanist God Talk*. Maryknoll, NY: Orbis Books, 1995

Williams, Rowan. Keynote address to the Eleventh Assembly of the Lutheran World Federation, Stuttgart, Germany. July 2010.

Willimon, William and Stanley Hauerwas. *Lord Teach Us: The Lord's Prayer and the Christian Life*. Nashville, TN: Abingdon Press, 1996.

Winters, Michael. "Always Means Forever: Matthew 28:16–20." Sermon at The Presbyterian Church of Berwyn, Berwyn, IL. June 6, 1993.

————. "The Aweful, Joyful Resurrection: Matthew 28:1–10." Easter sermon, Morton Grove Presbyterian Church, Morton Grove, IL. 1999.

————. "Giving Thanks for the Gifts of God: Matthew 23:1–12," Sermon on All Saints Sunday at the Presbyterian Church of Berwyn, Berwyn, IL. November 3, 1996.

————. "The Food of Justice: Matthew 25:31–46." Sermon at Oak Lawn Community Church, Oak Lawn, IL. November 23, 2008.

Wolpert, Daniel. "Theology and 'Natural Laws' in Relation to God's Action." Final paper for Theology and Biological Evolution. Pittsburgh Theological Seminary. August 2010.

World Communion of Reformed Churches and the Lutheran World Federation, Joint Lutheran-Reformed Commission. "Communion: On Being the Church." Final Report. 2006–2012.

Wright, N. T. *Matthew for Everyone, Part 1*. Louisville, KY: Westminster John Knox Press, 2004.

————. *Matthew for Everyone, Part 2*. Louisville, KY: Westminster John Knox Press, 2004.

Index of Ancient Sources

Old Testament

Genesis

1	112
1:2	51
3:8	326
9:25	200
12:2	79
12:3	25
18:1–8	151
18:6	180
20:15–21:7	26
22:18	20, 24, 79, 320

Exodus

3:6	259
3:7–8	89
3:14	195
4:22	214
12:1–20	294
14:29	131
15:21	105
16	115
16:18	115
20:4	257
20:12	198
24:2	212
24:16	212, 213
30:11–16	217
30:19–21	197
32:19–20	216
34:6	100
34:29	193
34:29–35	212
34:30	213
40:15	23n1

Leviticus

11:22	43
13–14	127
15	136
19:17	224
19:18	82, 259
21:16–17	252
21:16–20	137
21:20	239
22:24	239
25:23ff	118

Numbers

15:37–41	197
27:17	138

Deuteronomy

5:16	198
6–8	53
6:4–5	54
6:4–9	264
6:5	259
6:6–8	54n21
6:16	54
8:2–3	53
14:22–23	267
16:1–8	294
19:15	224
21:1–9	304
23:1	239
24:1	239
25:1–3	153
29:15–29	167
32:39	341
32:45	287

1 Samuel

1:15–25	26
3:10	105
10:1	23n1

2 Samuel

17:1–23	301

1 Kings

17:16	193

2 Kings

1:2	170
1:8	43
4:6–7	193

2 Chronicles

24:20–27	268
24:21–22	268–69

Nehemiah

5:13	152

Job

251, 311

1–2	66
1:21	341
28	166

Psalms

105, 251, 259, 311

2	33, 51
2:7	33, 51, 214
8:2	11
19	75
22	309
22:1–2	310

Psalms (*continued*)
22:7–8   310
22:16   310
22:17–18   309
22:27–29   311
23:4   121
31:5   341
44:17–19   251
44:23–24   106
51:7   60, 268
72   45, 50
85:11   99
89:46   39
96   282
96:10–13   283
96:11–13   49
100:3   114
118:26   270
139:7–8   341

Proverbs
7–9   13
8   166
13:9   276
14:1   98
16:22   167

Isaiah   6, 17, 20, 181,
        263, 272,
        339–40
1:9–10   167
2   126
2:1–3   204
2:1–4   7
2:2   171
2:2–4   20, 31, 128, 320
2:2–5   79
5:1–7   254, 255
5:8–10   242
5:8–23   266
6:5   60
7   25
7:14   324
9:1   56
9:2   56
10:1–3   242
11:4–7   56
12:17–21   170
20:2   150
23:1–12   167
25:6   128

25:6–9   193, 204, 321
26:19   341
29:13   47
29:19   165
35:4–6   136
35:5–6   165, 203,
        249, 270
35:6   137
40–55   90
40:3   44
41:4   195
42:1   51
42:6   79
43   339
43:1–3   195
43:1–13   195
43:5–6   128
44:22   44
49:6   79
51:1–2   47
53   125, 129, 295,
        302, 313
53:3–4   295
53:7   302
53:9   313–14
53:11–12   248
56:7   250
58   90
58:3–5   90
58:6   136
58:6–7   90
60:1–6   20, 31, 320
61:1   23n1
61:1–2   136
65:1   177

Jeremiah   6, 206–7, 263,
        272
7:9–11   250–51
7:11   250
12:7   269
17–18   302
18:1–11   207
21:8   97
22:15–16   76
25:15   247
31:15   30, 207
31:33   81
32:6–15   302
49:12   247
51:7   247

Lamentations 251, 306,
        311
3:22–24   306

Ezekiel   272
18:31–32   45
22:6–31   242
34   125, 138, 150,
        279
34:2–4   222–23
34:11–16   279
34:15–16   223
36:22–36   110

Daniel   181, 244,
        271–72
2:20–21   167
3   181
7   271, 299
7:9–10   244
7:13   181
7:13–14   244, 278
9:27   271
11:31   271
12:1   272
12:2   341
12:3   181–82
12:11   271

Hosea
1–3   171, 206
6:6   125, 126, 134,
        267
11:8–9   117

Joel   173, 272
2:13   44

Amos   272
2:6–7   242
4:1   167
4:11   167
5:10–12   242
5:21–24   47, 162
8:40   242

Micah
6:8   110, 155

Haggai   272

Zechariah
9:9   250
14:4   270

Malachi
3:1   43
3:2–3   49
4:5   43n2
4:5–6   43

New Testament

Matthew
1   33
1.1   288
1:1–17   276
1:1–25   23–27
1:1–2:23   23–39
1:18   51
1:20   32, 194, 287, 336
1:20–23   336
1:20–25   26
1:21   25, 132, 295, 340
1:22–23   32, 129
1:23   26, 32, 226, 288, 324–25, 346, 348
1:24   287
2   23, 48, 346
2:1–2   203
2:1–23   20, 27–30
2:2   190, 196, 287–88, 303
2:3   28, 249, 287
2:5–6   32
2:6   30, 222, 279
2:8   28, 287
2:11   287
2:12   32
2:12–13   287
2:13   30, 32, 287
2:13–14   26
2:13–15   26, 287
2:14–15   190
2:15   32
2:17–18   32, 207
2:18   30, 269
2:19   287

2:19–21   26
2:20   32
2:21–22   190
2:22   287
2:23   30, 32
3:1–12   43–49
3:1–17   59, 63
3:1–4:25   43–69
3:4   166
3:7   28, 46, 268
3:7–10   166
3:8   46
3:9   26, 47
3:10   178, 285
3:11   48
3:12   48, 166, 178, 285
3:13   50–51
3:13–17   50–52
3:14   164
3:16   51, 214
3:17   52, 172, 214, 260
4:1–11   52–55, 59, 140, 205
4:3   53
4:4   53
4:5–7   205
4:6   298, 310
4:8   54–55
4:10   210
4:12   152
4:12–13   190
4:12–17   55–56
4:14–16   129
4:16   56
4:17   44, 59, 186
4:18   129, 301
4:18–22   56–58, 211
4:20   57, 313
4:21   129
4:23   138
4:23–25   58–59
4:24   58
4:25   14
4:40   14
5–7   123, 138
5–9   138
5:1   14
5:1–2   76
5:1–7:29   70–122

5:3–13   76–78
5:5   85, 221
5:7   72
5:8   284
5:9–11   101
5:10   85
5:13   20, 81, 150
5:13–16   78–79
5:16   20, 79, 150
5:17   97, 184
5:17–20   79–80, 129
5:17–48   278
5:18   80
5:20   85, 265
5:21–24   162
5:21–48   70, 80–84, 224, 242
5:23–24   81, 117
5:23–26   178
5:24   318
5:28   81
5:29–30   83
5:34–35   45, 110
5:38–41   152
5:38–42   218
5:39   298
5:42   292
5:43–48   9
5:44   101, 121, 178
5:44–45   72
5:45   83
5:47   226
5:48   83, 86, 231, 242
6   93, 95
6:1   85
6:1–18   70, 85, 280
6:1–19   86, 264
6:1–35   84–86
6:2   86
6:2–4   86–87, 292
6:5   86
6:5–7   103
6:5–15   88–89
6:7   88, 226
6:7–13   297
6:8   103, 111
6:12   72, 241
6:14–15   116
6:16   86, 90
6:16–18   89–91, 134

Matthew (*continued*)
6:19   91, 241
6:19–21   78
6:19–35   91–93, 242
6:20   91
6:21   91
6:23   246
6:24   92, 121, 241–42, 292
6:25   92
6:25–33   104
6:25–34   241
6:27   93
6:29–30   82
6:30   216
6:31   92
6:33   85, 93
6:34   92
7:1   178
7:1–5   94
7:1–6   94–95
7:1–27   70
7:2   94
7:2–4   83
7:3–5   95
7:6   95
7:7   95, 102
7:7–11   95–96
7:9–10   96
7:10   218
7:12   96–97, 278
7:15   98, 222
7:21   98, 187
7:21–23   275
7:22–23   98
7:24–26   98
7:24–27   275
7:25–33   89
7:28   14, 84, 167, 184, 287
7:29   99, 124, 265, 338
8–9   123, 126, 135, 138
8:1   14, 125
8:1–4   9, 126–27
8:1–17   126–29
8:1–9:38   123–45
8:3   124
8:5–13   127–29
8:5–18   20

8:8   128
8:8–9   128
8:10   47, 128
8:14–17   129–30
8:15   129, 135
8:16   129
8:17   129–30
8:18–22   130
8:20   130
8:22   338
8:23–27   130–31, 194, 196, 205, 218
8:23–9:17   130–34
8:26   14, 125, 128, 131, 136, 194, 216, 336
8:27   131
8:28–34   131–32
8:29   126, 131, 294
9   147–48
9:1–7   9
9:1–17   132–33
9:2–3   197
9:2–8   295, 338
9:3   133
9:5   135
9:6   124, 126
9:8   14, 133, 167
9:9   135
9:9–13   10, 246
9:9–17   133–34
9:10   226
9:10–12   296, 315
9:11   197
9:12–13   9, 133
9:13   87, 133, 267, 309
9:14   134, 197, 292
9:15   166, 275, 292
9:17   126, 134
9:18   136
9:18–26   134–36
9:18–38   134–45
9:20–22   12, 276
9:21   201
9:22   125, 129, 136
9:25   129
9:27   126
9:27–31   136–37
9:29   125

9:30   137
9:31   137
9:32–34   137
9:33   137, 167
9:34   124, 137
9:35   138
9:35–38   137–38
9:36   14, 124, 138, 148, 150, 168, 204, 222, 279
9:37   178, 285
9:37–38   138
10   138, 147, 241, 300
10:1   124, 338
10:1–4   147–48
10:1–11:1   146–63
10:2   147
10:4   152
10:5   20, 56, 149, 200
10:5–15   148–53
10:6   128, 150, 152, 201, 222
10:7   148
10:8   149
10:9   150
10:9–14   241
10:10   138, 151
10:14–15   151–52
10:16   222
10:16–25   152–53
10:17–18   301
10:17–21   154
10:18   226
10:19   153
10:20   155
10:23   152
10:26   153
10:26–11:1   153–56
10:27   154
10:28   153–54
10:29   92, 112
10:31   153, 194, 336
10:32–33   301
10:32–42   237
10:34–37   172
10:37   155
10:38   308, 348
10:39   154–55, 211
10:40   155

10:40–42	97	12:38–43	140	14:1–12	164, 188–90
10:42	167	12:38–45	171	14:1–17:27	188–218
11:1	184, 287	12:40	171	14:2	135
11:2	170	12:41	172	14:5	293
11:2–6	164–65	12:42	171–72	14:6–11	194
11:2–12:50	164–72	12:46–50	172, 185	14:13	188
11:3	164	12:48–50	233	14:13–21	188, 190–94,
11:4	162, 165	12:50	172		218
11:5	136, 165, 186	13	13, 241, 274,	14:14	87, 190, 204
11:6	165		278–79	14:15	201
11:7–24	165–67	13:1–30	176–79	14:15–21	53, 204
11:8	194	13:1–33	180	14:16	116, 204, 320
11:10	165–66	13:1–58	175–87	14:19	192, 320
11:12	166	13:3	180	14:21	10, 141
11:14	43	13:9	176	14:22–33	194–97, 215,
11:16–19	246	13:10	176		218
11:18	166	13:11	176	14:27	194, 336, 340
11:19	10, 166, 226	13:13	176	14:28–33	189
11:23	166	13:14-15	181	14:31	188, 195, 202,
11:25	252	13:19	68		216
11:25–26	11	13:22	241	14:33	33, 196, 202,
11:25–27	167	13:23	178		205, 207, 214,
11:25–30	166	13:24	180		312
11:28–30	17, 167–69,	13:24–30	232, 284	14:34–36	197
	263	13:30	294	15	128, 197
11:29	167, 170, 221	13:31–33	73	15:1–20	188, 197–200,
12	206, 237	13:31–35	179–80		267
12:1–12	169	13:32	179	15:2	197
12:1–14	7, 80	13:33	180	15:4–5	199
12:1–21	168–70	13:35	176, 180	15:6	198
12:2	197	13:36	176, 180	15:7–9	199
12:3	172	13:36–43	180–82	15:8	254
12:5	172	13:36–50	180	15:12	199
12:6	168, 172	13:39–43	181	15:13	124, 199
12:7	87, 168–69,	13:41	181	15:15	196
	172, 267	13:42	181	15:16	32
12:8	168, 172	13:43	181	15:21	200
12:10	169, 197	13:44–46	182, 241	15:21–28	12, 20, 189,
12:11–12	222	13:47	58, 183		200–203, 276
12:14	164, 206	13:47–50	97, 182–84	15:21–31	128
12:14–15	152	13:49–50	181	15:22	201
12:15	170	13:51	180	15:23	201
12:15–21	190	13:51–53	184	15:24	19, 128, 201,
12:18	170, 172	13:52	184		222
12:19	170	13:53	184, 287	15:26	201
12:22–37	170	13:54	185	15:29	203
12:23	172	13:54–57	185	15:29–30	55
12:24	170	13:54–58	185, 188	15:29–31	203
12:29	208	13:57	124, 165, 185,	15:29–39	188, 203–5
12:34	46, 170, 268		199	15:30	203
12:38	335	14–17	219	15:32	87, 204

Matthew (*continued*)
15:32–38   53
15:32–39   218
15:33   205
15:38   10
16   133, 241
16:1–4   140
16:1–12   188, 205–6
16:3   294
16:5–12   206
16:8   216
16:9–10   206
16:13–20   206–9
16:13–23   189
16:16   33, 196, 214,
            301
16:18   55, 208–9,
            219
16:21   207, 209, 216,
            236, 289, 292
16:21–23   188
16:21–28   209–12
16:22   196, 210
16:22–23   55
16:23   55, 209
16:24   211
16:26   241
17   212
17:1   212
17:1–2   55
17:1–8   301
17:1–13   212–15
17:2   212
17:5   212, 214, 260
17:6   213
17:7   194, 336
17:9   212–13
17:14–17   189
17:14–23   215–16
17:17   216
17:18   219
17:20–21   188
17:22   56, 198, 289,
            292
17:22–23   188, 209, 213
17:23   216
17:24   197
17:24–27   216–18, 258
18   208, 219, 236
18:1   219
18:1–4   9

18:1–14   220–23, 280
18:1–35   219–36
18:3–7   11
18:4   221–22
18:5   11
18:6   167, 221–22
18:8–9   222
18:10   167, 221–22
18:10–14   279
18:12   221–22
18:12–14   221–22
18:14   167, 228
18:15   219, 225
18:15–20   223
18:15–35   223–29, 234
18:16–35   223
18:17   219
18:18   208–9, 225,
            266
18:19–20   225
18:20   226, 231, 233
18:21   117, 196, 219
18:21–35   118
18:22   117
18:23–35   74, 97
18:26   228
18:34   252
19   236–37
19–20   248
19:1   184, 236
19:1–22   237–41
19:1–22:46 236–60
19:3   239
19:3–9   9, 81
19:4   240
19:6   239
19:8   238
19:10   239
19:11   287
19:13–15   11, 240
19:14   252
19:20   237
19:21   93, 119, 231,
            242, 292
19:22   242
19:23–30   241–45
19:24   243
19:25   243
19:27   243
19:27–30   196
19:28   244

19:30   244
20:1–16   254
20:1–34   245–49
20:4   246
20:12   246
20:16   244, 247
20:17–19   209, 216, 246
20:18   52, 56, 289,
            292
20:19   32, 226
20:20–28   9
20:24–28   247
20:25   247, 342
20:26   135, 248
20:26–28   129
20:28   247–48, 295,
            298, 331
20:29–33   249
20:34   204
21:1   270
21:1–22   249–53
21:8   97, 290
21:9   270
21:10   249–50
21:12   29, 250
21:15   11, 252
21:15–16   259
21:16   252
21:23   124, 290, 338
21:23–27   46, 253, 338
21:25   63
21:26   253
21:27   253
21:28–32   47
21:28–22:14 253–56, 274
21:34   253, 294
21:41   253
21:42   185
21:43   124, 255
21:45–46   255
21:46   290
22:2   275
22:7   251
22:9   256
22:15   176, 256–57
22:15–46   256–60
22:16   257
22:17   197, 257
22:18   257
22:20   257
22:22   258, 260

22:32	259	24:14	272	26:26	37, 204, 317
22:33	46, 259	24:15	271	26:26–27	295
22:33–34	260	24:15–20	272	26:26–29	193, 320
22:34	259	24:19	277	26:26–68	290
22:34–40	271, 278	24:26–27	272	26:27	315
22:37–39	229	24:29	271	26:28	37, 296, 309,
22:37–40	259	24:35	273		324
22:40	80, 97	24:36	273–74	26:29	320
22:42	259	24:40–41	273, 276	26:30–32	55
22:46	260	24:41	13, 343	26:31	165, 222, 289,
23	5, 94, 261–62,	24:45–51	274		315, 324
	266, 274–75	24:45–25:30	274–77	26:32	135
23:1	266	25	13, 221	26:33	165
23:1–11	221	25:10	275	26:33–34	196, 296
23:1–12	261–66	25:11–12	275	26:34	289, 315
23:1–36	270	25:15	277	26:36–46	296–97
23:1–25:46	261–85	25:26	277	26:37	196, 297
23:3	263	25:31–46	97, 221, 275,	26:38	291
23:4	168		278–81, 283,	26:40	196, 296
23:6–7	264		292, 339	26:42	297
23:8	264, 296	25:32–33	222	26:46	244
23:8–10	264	25:35–36	279–80	26:47	297
23:11	264	25:36	306	26:47–56	297–98
23:11–12	275	25:37	279–80	26:50	297
23:12	221	25:40	16, 280	26:52	298
23:13	266	25:43	306	26:53	53
23:13–36	266–69	25:45	29	26:53–56	140
23:16	94	26:1	184, 287	26:55–56	298
23:16–22	267	26:1–5	289–91	26:56	296, 298, 313,
23:17	94	26:1–27:31	289–307		315, 343
23:19	94	26:2	52, 56, 289,	26:57–68	299–300
23:23	262, 267		292	26:58	297
23:24	94, 267	26:3–4	290	26:59	290, 299
23:25	275	26:3–5	293	26:59–61	299
23:25–26	267	26:4	293, 298	26:63	299
23:26	94	26:6–13	291–93	26:64	299
23:28	268	26:7	291	26:65–66	290
23:33	268	26:13	20	26:67–68	310
23:34	5, 262	26:14	293	26:68	300
23:37–39	270	26:14–16	293, 296	26:69–75	196, 296,
23:37–24:2	269–70	26:15	290		300–301
23:39	269	26:17	294	26:70	300
24–25	261, 297	26:17–19	294, 315	26:74	300
24:1	20	26:17–29	287	26:75	300
24:1–2	251, 270	26:17–35	294–96	27:2	290
24:2	299	26:20–23	189	27:3	301
24:3	272	26:20–29	314	27:3–10	301–2
24:3–44	270–74	26:21	315	27:4	302
24:6	271	26:22	69	27:6	302
24:7	271	26:25	289	27:8	302
24:12	271	26:25–29	264	27:9–10	207

Matthew (*continued*)
27:11   23, 296, 299,
              303, 306
27:11–23   302–4
27:17   303
27:18   303
27:19   287, 303
27:20   290
27:22   304
27:23   304
27:24   287, 302, 304,
              335
27:24–26   304–6
27:25   305
27:26   299
27:27–31   306–7, 310
27:29   23, 303, 306–7
27:32–61   308–31
27:35   309
27:37   23, 303, 306
27:38   247, 310
27:38–44   310
27:39–44   140
27:40   33, 55, 214,
              310
27:42   23, 303, 306
27:43   33
27:44   310
27:46   291, 310
27:50   311
27:50–53   312, 330
27:50–54   311–12, 330
27:51   249, 311
27:51–52   312, 330, 346
27:51–53   294
27:53   312
27:54   250, 312
27:55   313
27:55–56   13
27:55–61   312–14
27:57   313
27:60   342
27:62–66   290, 335
27:62–28:10   335–48
27:65   335
28   15
28:1   13, 269
28:1–10   336, 340
28:4   287
28:5   194, 215, 287,
              336

28:5–7   336
28:6–7   135
28:7   338
28:8   336
28:8–28   344
28:9   344
28:10   194, 336
28:11–15   337, 342
28:11–20   337–40
28:12   290
28:13   337
28:16   301
28:16–19   337–39
28:16–20   55, 150, 203
28:17   287, 338, 342
28:18   229, 288, 338
28:19   20
28:20   27, 59, 65,
              148, 226, 288,
              320, 339–40,
              348

Mark   2, 32n22, 33,
              94, 313, 342
1:11   51
4:11–12   176
4:40   15
13   271
14:33   33
14:36   109
14:58   299n19
16:8   15, 342
16:11   342
16:16   33
27:40   33
27:43   33

Luke   2, 7, 24,
              32n22, 33, 77,
              94, 241, 289
1   289
1–2   26
8:10   176
23:46   341
24   345
24:30–31   345
24:41   343
24:42–43   345

John   32n22, 33, 324
1:1–14   36n28

1:46   30
9:2   137
20:11–18   345
20:19   344
20:24–28   344
20:25   343
20:29   343
21:9–15   344

Acts
1–15   18, 150
2:38   60
16:15   61
17:28   35, 104, 345

Romans
6:1–4   60
6:1ff   83n28
7:19   68
7:23   327
7:28   103
8:5–6   327
8:7   327
12:1   319
12:1–2   173
12:17   228
16:1   313

1 Corinthians   320
8:6   36n28
11:23   198, 315
12   224, 317
12:12–13   60
15:17   329, 340
15:24–28   330
15:28   37
15:44   344
15:54   330
15:56   346
23–24   210
27–29   315

2 Corinthians
4:7   232
5:18   323
5:19   100
15:17   60

Galatians
1–2   18, 150
2:16   74

3:10	327	1:19	35	**James**	74–75
3:13	327	2:15	120	2:17	75
3:27–28	60				
4:8	327	**2 Thessalonians**		**Revelation**	271
		2	271	1:5–6	60
Ephesians					
1:13–14	36n28	**1 Timothy**			
5:26	60	3:8–10	313	*Apocrypha*	
6:12	68				
		Titus		**Sirach**	
Philippians		3:5	60	14:9	92
1:1	313			14:10	92, 246
2	36	**Hebrews**	25n5, 327		
2:6–11	36n28	1:1–4	36n28	**1 Maccabees**	
		4:15	50	1:54	272
Colossians		7:23–27	327	6:10	93
1:15–20	36	12:2	325		

Index of Subjects

Abelard, Peter, 326
Abraham, 23–26, 32, 47, 128, 259
accountability, 223–35
Accra Confession, 16, 18, 119, 162–63
action
    of God, 144
    human, 74
adultery, 24, 81, 171, 206, 238–39, 250
Against Heresies (Irenaeus), 37, 324–25
almsgiving, 84–89, 93, 291–92
angels, 26, 32, 53–54, 222, 278, 287, 289, 298, 336
    of death, 294
    fallen, 66
anointing, 23n1, 291–93
Anselm of Canterbury, 34, 327–28
anxiety, 68, 93, 194, 242, 274,
apartheid, 118, 225
apocalypse, 181, 270–74, 311–12
apostasy, 309
apostles, 57, 148. *See also* disciples
Apostles' Creed, 65
apostolicity, 231–32
apostolic succession, 232, 240
Aramaic language, 109
asking, searching, and knocking, 95–96
Athenaeus, 57
atonement, 208, 322, 324, 327, 330, 331
Augustine, 62, 111, 132, 143, 183-84, 232, 235
authorities, elite, 11, 15–16, 25, 28–31, 90, 148, 155, 210, 256

opposition to Jesus from, 28–31
    today, 161
    See also religious leaders
authority, 123–25
    of ethical leadership, 1, 14–15
    of Jesus, 99, 123–45, 148, 168, 204, 249–53

banquet, messianic. *See* messianic banquet
baptism, 51, 59–66, 339
    of Jesus, 50–52, 63–64
barrenness/barren women, 26
Barth, Karl, 64, 215, 244–45, 346, 349
Bathsheba, 24–25
beatitudes, 76–78, 99–101
Beelzebul, 170
Belgic Confession, 281
Berkhof, Hendrikus, 68–69, 282
Bethany, woman's gift at, 291–93
Bethlehem, 27–28, 30, 279
bin Laden, Osama, 100
birth of Jesus/birth narrative, 21–39, 52, 226, 287, 324–25, 346
bleeding woman, Jesus as healing, 134–36
blessedness; blessing, 76–79, 99–101, 320
blindness; blind persons, 136–37, 141, 203
    hypocrisy as, 94
    Jesus as healing, 136–37, 290
    Pharisees as blind, 199, 266

body, resurrection of, 65, 343–45
Boesak, Allan, 177
Boff, Leonardo, 231
Bohn, Carole, 322
Bonaventure, 36n28, 324
Bonhoeffer, Dietrich, 210–11, 225, 242
Boring, Eugene, 23n1, 24, 33, 52, 54,
   103, 141, 150
Botman, Russel, 157
bread
   feeding miracles, 53, 190–94, 203–5
   "of presence," from the Temple, 168
   petition for, Lord's Prayer, 107, 113–15
   See also Lord's Supper
bridegroom, 134, 166, 275–76, 292, 321
bridesmaids, ten, parable of, 13, 274–77
Brown, Joanne Carlson, 322
Brown, Patricia, 194
Brown, Raymond, 12, 25n3, 306
Brueggemann, Walter, 106, 230
Bultmann, Rudolf, 141

Cahill, Lisa Sowle, 72, 83–84
Caiaphas, 270, 288–89, 293, 296,
   299–300, 306, 309, 312
calling, 43–69
calming of the storm, 130–31, 205, 207,
   312
Calvin, John, 7, 59–60, 74-75, 93, 96,
   102-3, 112, 114, 173-74, 232–33,
   282, 284, 316–18, 350
Canaanites, 200–203
cannibalism, 101
Carole Bohn, 322
Carter, Warren, 9, 16–17, 45, 50–51,
   57, 75, 84, 92, 95, 101, 105, 107,
   111, 147, 151–53, 193, 196, 228,
   237–38, 242, 304–6
   on crucifixion, 308
catechesis, 64
catholicity, 231–32
Catholic theology. See Roman Catholic
   theology
celibacy, 236–37, 240
centurion's servant, healing of, 10, 20, 47,
   126–29, 150

Chalcedon, Council at; Chalcedonian
   Formula (451), 33, 37
charity, 87, 91. See also almsgiving;
   generosity; love
chief priests, 11, 55, 207, 252–55, 259,
   293–306, 335, 337–38, 342
   descriptions of, 210, 289–90
   See also religious leaders
children, 10–14, 30–31, 220–23, 229,
   240, 269
   as accepting John and Jesus, 167
   of the covenant, 61
   of God, 99–100
Christ, 23. See also Jesus Christ
Christ event, 36–37, 235, 315, 322–24,
   328, 331, 346
Christianity, 6, 144, 224
   post-denominational, 156–59
   as rooted in Judaism, 3, 5–6, 351
   See also church
Christology, 33–38, 214, 324
Christus Victor (ransom) theory of
   atonement, 208, 330
church, 71, 208, 219–36
   conflict and division in, 3–8, 195
   Eastern and Western, 113, 340
   ecumenical landscape, changing,
      156–58
   marks of, classical, 232
   ministry of Word, Sacrament, and
      Order, 174
   "mother of all believers," 183
   and the "prosperity gospel," 160–61
   religious pluralism, 156–60
   today, 156–63
   true, 183, 232
   visible and invisible, 183, 232
   See also Christianity; specific topics,
      e.g., poverty: problem of
Cicero, 57
City of God, The (Augustine), 143
Clement of Alexandria, 36n28
Coffin, William Sloane, 78
commandments to love. See love:
   commandments to
common good, 233–34

common/ordinary people, 1, 14, 16–17, 24, 31, 68, 71, 351–52
communion, 63, 87-88, 10, 314, 317–18, 320. *See also* eucharist
community, Matthew's. *See* Matthew: community of
community, new, 124, 219–41
compassion, 80, 100, 148, 192–93, 225, 276, 278, 283, 318
    authority in service of, 148
    of God, 138, 139, 269, 325
    of Jesus, 14, 59, 138, 148, 168, 172, 188, 190, 192–93, 202–5, 252, 279, 320, 326
    mercy and, 87-88, 125, 135, 280, 283
confessions, Reformed, 19
conversion, 51, 63, 220, 226
Corban, practice of, 198
Corley, Kathleen, 238
cosmic Christology, 35–38
courage, 153–56
Cranmer, Thomas, 318
creation, 51, 131
    new, 51, 60, 73, 112, 284, 344, 347
    redemption and, 325
    as work of love, 36, 39
Crosby, Michael, 77n13, 85, 87, 90, 111, 124, 151, 353
cross, 39, 312–14, 322–31, 345–46
crowds, 167
    fickle and dangerous, 305
    following Jesus, 58–59
    miracles of Jesus feeding, 190–94, 203–5
crucifixion of Jesus, 154, 308–31
cup metaphor, 247, 267–68, 291, 296–97, 310
Cur Deus Homo (Anselm of Canterbury), 34, 327–28
Cyprian, 107-8

Daly, Mary, 108
David, 30, 51, 67, 168, 292, 301
    Son of, 6–7, 11, 14, 23–37, 126, 168, 170, 172, 189, 202, 244, 249, 252, 259–60, 263, 270, 290

deacon, office of, 129, 161, 313
death and dying, 62, 291–92, 347–48. *See also* resurrection of the body
debts and debtors, 34, 116–19
Declaration of Faith, A, 273, 276, 284–85, 347–48
deeds of power, 98–99, 126–38, 143, 156, 164, 166–67, 171, 185–86, 188, 194, 304
demons/demonic possession, 66–67, 124, 125, 141, 149, 183
    Canaanite woman's daughter, Jesus' healing of, 200–203
    men, Jesus' healing of, 131–32
    mute man, Jesus' healing of, 137
    Pharisees' charge that Jesus' power is demonic, 170
devil. *See* Satan
dikaiosynē, 76, 85, 87, 186, 279–80, 283, 326
disciples, 339
discipleship, 57–58, 62, 71, 78, 219, 240, 348, 352
    cost of, 130, 147, 154, 211
    teachings on, 125, 130, 133, 138, 249
    test of, 120
    "true," 13–14
    women and, 13–14, 313
disciples of Jesus, 57–58, 65–66, 130, 147–48, 152–53
    faith of, 215–16
    Great Commission, 55, 337–39
    Jesus' instruction to, 180–82, 237
    Matthew becoming a disciple, 133–34
    ministry, as preparing for, 188–218
    mission of, 148–53, 155
divorce, 81, 236–40
Docetism, 34, 324
Dodd, C. H., 175
dogs, 201–2
doubt, 120, 164–65, 195–96, 338, 342–43. *See also* unbelief
dragnet, parable of, 182–84
dreams, 25–26, 29, 31–32, 78, 287, 303
dying. *See* death and dying

earthquakes, 249–50, 271, 312
ecumenism/ecumenicity, 156–58, 230–31
Egypt, 25, 30, 45, 294, 315
    flight into, 29–31, 38, 303
ekklesia, 208
"elders," 4, 209–10, 253–54, 289,
    293–94, 296–97, 303, 337–38
    tradition of, 4, 197–99
    See also religious leaders
Elijah, 43, 193, 204, 206, 212–14
Elisha, 193, 204
elite authorities. *See* authorities, elite
emergence, 191n4
Emmanuel, 7, 23, 26, 29, 32, 226, 288,
    324, 340, 346, 348
empire, Gospel of Matthew as challenge
    to, 16–18
end times, 270–74, 311–12
enemies, love for, 99–101
eschatology, 43, 70, 72–73, 78, 99,
    112–13, 134, 136, 147, 178, 181,
    187, 193, 210, 283, 294, 311
    Christian, 344
    hope, eschatological, 7, 112, 131,
        255, 339–41, 344
    Jewish, 255, 338
    and resurrection, Matthew's
        accounting of, 329, 339–41
eschaton, 135, 155, 213, 244, 270, 275, 290
Essenes, 4, 262
ethnic and religious divisions, crossing,
    288
eucharist, 204, 314–22
eunuchs, 237, 239
evil, 39, 49, 60, 66–69, 104, 115, 131, 160,
    171, 206, 283–84, 298, 330, 345
    not returning evil for, 228
    temptation and, 54, 107-8, 113, 119–21
    See also sin; suffering
eyes
    healthy and unhealthy, 91-92, 246.
        See also blindness

faith
    belief and unbelief, mixture of, 178, 285
    of Canaanite woman, 200–203

confessions of, Reformed, 19
    of disciples, 215–16
    miracle and, 139
    Peter, faith and doubt of, 195–96
    sacraments and, 317
    the size of a mustard seed, 215–16
    and works, 74–75
faithfulness, 52, 237, 259, 266, 273–78,
    288, 300, 306
    courage and, 153–56
    of disciples, 105
    of the heart, 81
family, 172
    of God, 236–60
    of Jesus, 172
    new community and, 236–41
    reign of God and, 155
Farris, Patricia, 77–78
fasting, 52, 84–85, 89–91, 93, 134, 292
fear
    "do not be afraid," 153–56, 194–95,
        336, 340
    and facing opposition, 164–72
feeding miracles, 53, 190–94, 203–5, 320
fig tree, 252–53
five thousand, feeding of, 190–92
followers of Jesus. *See* disciples of Jesus
foolishness. *See* wisdom and foolishness
forgiveness, 9, 94, 120, 326–27
    church as community of, 133, 208,
        219, 223–35
    Lord's Prayer petition for, 107, 113,
        115–18
    seventy-seven times, 117, 226–27
    of sin, 60, 74, 132, 295–96, 315
    what it does and does not mean, 118
freedom, 39, 60, 68, 104, 131, 145, 217
    church and, 230
    justice and, 187
"fringe of his cloak," 136, 197

Galilee, 12–13, 30, 55–58, 236–37, 301,
    312–13, 337–38, 342
Galilee, Sea of. *See* Sea of Galilee
Galloway, Allan, 35
Gandhi, Mohandas, 194

Garland, David E., 28n15, 32n22
genealogy, 7, 12, 23–26, 24, 28, 276
generosity, 83, 91-92, 177–78, 183, 198,
    245–46, 313, 319
    divine, imitating, 93–96
    reciprocity vs., 83, 280
Gentiles, 24–25, 55–56, 179, 200–203
    inclusion of, 10, 31, 126, 179, 203
Gethsemane, 291, 294, 296–97, 300, 323
goats and sheep parable, 278–81
God, 108
    action of, 144
    children of, 99–100
    fatherhood of, 107–10
    image of, 158
    kingdom of, 111–12, 123
    knowing, 76
    masculine images and pronouns for,
        108-9
    mother, as likened to, 269
    name of, 110–11
    nature of, 38
    union with, 235
    as with us, 7, 26, 29–30, 32–38, 226,
        231, 288, 324–25, 328, 339–40,
        345–46, 348
    See also reign of God; will of God;
        word of God
Golden Rule, 96–97
grace, divine, 8, 20, 35, 45, 72, 74–75, 78,
    96, 120, 151, 283, 352
    forgiveness and, 223, 227–29, 315
    as free but not cheap, 116
    growth in, 326
    law and, 83n28
    as limitless, 159
    parables of, 177–78, 182, 227, 246,
        285
    Paul on, 83n28
    sacraments and, 59–61, 63, 66, 316,
        322
    universal reach of, 149
Great Commandment, 97
Great Commission, 55, 337–39
greatness, 220–23
    as service, 9, 229, 247, 264

greed, 68, 85, 90, 91-92, 114–15, 121,
    153, 161, 246, 265, 267, 275,
    293
Greek Orthodox Christians, 36n28, 316,
    324
Gregory of Nazianzus, 34
Gregory of Nyssa, 115, 324
Guthrie, Shirley, 68–69

Hans Küng, 231
Hare, Douglas R. A., 146, 199
harvest metaphor, 48–49, 138, 177–78,
    184, 253–54, 279, 285
Hauerwas, Stanley, 71
Haught, John, 142
healing miracles, 66, 127–38, 252, 290
heaven, 45. See also kingdom of heaven
Hebrew Scriptures, 2, 25, 30–32, 50,
    79, 87, 131, 194, 208, 247, 268,
    292, 341
    importance in Matthew, 6, 263
hell, 281–82, 330
Herod Antipas (son of Herod the Great),
    189–90, 194
    and John the Baptist, 44, 164–66,
        188–90, 213, 293
Herodians, 257, 271
Herod the Great, 14–15, 17, 23, 27–39,
    56, 249
    Jesus as threat to, 27–39
    slaughter of the innocents, 38–39,
        48, 303
Heschel, Susannah, 3n3
hidden treasure, parable of, 182
hierarchy, 9, 85, 123, 221, 229–30,
    237–38, 240, 264, 328
higher righteousness. See righteousness:
    higher, calling to
Hillel School, 257n29
Hippolytus, 65
Hodgson, Peter, 230
holiness, 107, 231–32
Holocaust, 8, 38, 305
Holy Spirit, 48, 51–52, 59–60, 63–65,
    78, 103, 119, 145, 153, 155, 170,
    173, 231, 317, 336, 339

"Home by Another Way" (James
    Taylor), 31n19
Homo eucharisticus, 319
hope
    eschatological, 7, 112, 131, 255,
        339–41, 344
    and present reality, 72
humanity
    human life, goal of, 235
    in image of God, 158
    Jesus as God and human, 32–35
    Jesus as living for, as Savior, 215
    See also Son of Man
human rights, 29, 125
hypocrisy, 86–90, 93–95, 199, 254,
    261–66

"I am with you," 339–40, 348
Ignatius of Antioch, 2
incarnation, 32–33, 35–38, 112, 215,
    245, 324–25, 328, 340
    sacrament and, 316
individualism, 107, 224, 233
inequality. *See* injustice; poverty
injustice, 48, 68, 90, 115, 153, 167, 228,
    282, 348
invitation ("Come unto me"), 167–68
Irenaeus, 36n28, 37, 324–25
Israel
    as blessed, 20, 320
    Galilee as heart of, 56
    God's covenant with, 7, 19–20, 24,
        50, 259, 270, 295, 315, 320
    as "nation of priests," 4, 197
    nations flowing to, 171
    suffering endured by, 247, 269

Jeremiah, 206–7, 207
Jeremias, Joachim, 71
Jerusalem, 2, 4–5, 12, 27–31, 207, 209,
    262, 272, 287, 289–91, 305–6
    Bethlehem, contrast with, 27–28
    conflict on the way to, 236–60
    Jesus' entry into, 11, 249–53, 338
    Jesus' lament over, 269–70
    Sadducees in, 46n10, 205

Jesus Christ, 6, 23
    central message of, 76
    as "Exemplar" of God's love, 326, 329
    as God and human, 32–35
    "I am with you always," 339–40
    identity of, 23–37, 171–74, 206–12,
        287, 327
    life and ministry of, 39, 41–285,
        325–26
    the name, 25, 295
    as prophet, priest, and king, 60,
        173–74, 293
    the risen Lord, 337–40
    as Son of Abraham, 23–25, 32
    as Son of David, 6–7, 11, 14, 23–37,
        126, 168, 170, 172, 189, 202, 244,
        249, 252, 259–60, 263, 270, 290
    teaching of, 70–122, 146–63
    See also Emmanuel; incarnation;
        King of the Jews; Messiah; Son of
        God; Son of Man; *specific events,*
        e.g., baptism; crucifixion; passion;
        resurrection; *specific topics,* e.g.,
        authority; compassion
Jewish-Roman War, 272
Jews/Judaism, 3–8, 12, 261–62
    anti-Judaism, 3, 5, 8, 263, 305
    the Holocaust, 8, 38, 305
    Jesus as observant Jew, 197
    Jesus movement as renewal
        movement within, 3, 5–6, 351
    Matthew as most Jewish Gospel, 5–7,
        238, 263
    See also King of the Jews
John (apostle), 57–58, 212, 246–48,
    297, 310
John the Baptist, 43–52, 55, 56, 72, 134,
    136–37, 148, 152, 254–55, 292
    authority of, 253
    children ("little ones") as accepting,
        167
    death of, 154, 188–90, 213, 293
    as "Elijah," 213
    Jesus' baptism, 50–52, 63–64
    Jesus thought to be, 206
    parents of, 289

question of, 164–65
religious leaders as rejecting, 165–67
Joint Declaration on the Doctrine of
Justification, 75, 157
Jonah, 171–72, 206, 335
Joseph, husband of Mary, 24–27, 29–32,
38, 56, 287, 303, 336
Joseph of Arimathea, 313–14
Josephus, 44, 272, 308
Joshua, 25, 138
jubilee year, 119
Judaism. *See* Jews
Judas Iscariot, 13, 207, 264, 289–90,
293–302, 306, 315, 337
judgment, 178–79, 199, 261–85
the coming, 38, 44, 51, 261–85
judging others, refraining from,
94–95
justice and, 48–49, 282–83
the last, 278–81
redemption, as ordered to, 226, 270,
281–85
"sorting out" as for God alone to do,
178, 181, 183, 278–79
Jüngel, Eberhard, 346
justice, 16–17, 47–51, 56, 72–73, 84–88,
90–91, 99, 153–54, 162–63
calling to, 51, 72, 110, 113
concern for, as central theme, 85,
93–95
economic, 159
freedom and, 187
and Jesus' central message, 76–77
judgment and, 48–49, 282–83
justification and, 157
and knowing God, 76
Matthew as Gospel of, 85, 279–83
mercy and, 76, 87–88, 95, 113, 125,
153, 326
peace and, 99, 186, 234
retributive, 39, 251–52
righteousness and, 76, 85–86, 90, 99,
113, 125, 129
Roman, as all washed up, 17, 304–6
Wisdom and, 166
See also dikaiosynē

justification, 74–75, 157, 225, 284, 327
Justin Martyr, 36n28
Juvenal, 58, 92

king, Jesus as, 173–74, 287
King, Martin Luther, Jr., 154, 234
kingdom of heaven, 7, 11, 43–49, 56,
148, 175, 177, 187, 190, 240, 275.
See also reign of God
King of the Jews, 14–15, 23–39, 296,
299, 302–3, 306–11
Kingsbury, Dean, 123
Kołakowsky, Leszek, 211
Küng, Hans, 231–32

Lamott, Anne, 105, 118
last judgment. *See* judgment: the last
last things. *See* eschatology
law
exulting the legal over the moral, 199
grace and, 83n28
Jesus as authoritative interpreter of,
168, 213
justification and, 327
righteousness and, 26
"third use of," 76n11
See also Torah
law and the prophets, 31, 79–80, 97–99,
263
lawlessness, 268, 271
leaders, religious. *See* religious leaders
leadership
ethical, authority of, 1, 14–15
in Matthew's community of faith, 184
as service, 9
leaven, 13, 73, 179–80, 206, 294
leprosy; lepers, 125–27, 136, 149, 165, 291
Levine, Amy-Jill, 129, 338
Lewis, C. S., 282
life, human, 235
light, salt and, 78–79
"little ones," 167. *See also* children;
powerless, the
loaves and fishes miracles, 190–94, 203–5
Lord's Prayer, 106–21, 352–53
Lord's Supper, 314–22

love, 98–99
  commandments to, 72, 81, 82–83,
    87, 96–97, 100, 229, 259, 271,
    276, 278, 281, 283, 303, 309, 323,
    326, 339
  creation as work of, 36, 39
  for enemies, 99–101
  God's great, 326
  and higher righteousness, 26, 80–85,
    242, 303
  of neighbor, 72, 80, 276
Luther, Martin, 60, 74–75, 316–17, 328
Lutherans, 74–75, 115, 157, 160, 316,
    319n15
Luz, Ulrich, 70, 83, 211

magi. *See* wise men
man. *See* humanity; Son of Man
marginality/marginal identity, 8–10, 12,
    81, 136–37, 196, 220, 222, 237,
    240, 308, 351
marriage, 10, 236–40, 248, 275
martyrs/martyrdom, 146, 154, 211, 343
Mary, 24, 26–27, 29–31, 38, 56, 185,
    303, 313, 336
Mary, mother of James and Joseph, 13, 312
Mary Magdalene, 13, 312, 342, 345
Matthew, 133–34
  community of, 2–9, 17–19, 26, 67,
    133, 152, 154, 166, 178, 183–84,
    193, 195, 203–4, 214, 218, 246,
    251, 262, 269, 272, 280, 300, 304
Matthew, Gospel of, 1–23
  central emphases of, 51
  as challenge to empire, 16–18
  as Gospel of Justice, 85, 279–83
  Hebrew Scriptures' importance in,
    6, 263
  as most egalitarian Gospel, 12, 238
  as most Jewish Gospel, 5–7, 238, 263
  relevance of, 1–23, 87, 147, 350–52
McDougall, Joy Ann, 323
McNutt, James E., 3n3
mercy, 68
  compassion and, 87–88, 125, 135,
    280, 283

divine, 140, 285
  instead of sacrifice, 68, 125, 134–35,
    168, 267
  righteousness and, 76
  works of, 169, 280
  See also justice: mercy and; *tsedaqah*
Message of the Psalms, The
    (Brueggemann), 106
Messiah, 279, 292
  birth of, 324–25
  Jesus as, 3–8, 23–29, 171–72, 206–12
messianic banquet, 113, 128, 193, 204,
    256, 294, 314–22
metanoia, 44, 186
metaphors, 83, 328, 330–31. *See also*
    specific metaphors, e.g., harvest
Metz, Johann Baptist, 149
Migliore, Daniel, 66, 158, 317, 320, 344–45
ministry
  baptism as calling to, 59–66
  of the Church, 174
  disciples, preparing for, 188–218
  of Jesus, 41–285, 325–26
miracles/miracle stories, 7, 125–45,
    194–97, 207, 312
  of feeding, 53, 190–94, 203–5, 320
  of healing, 66, 127–38, 252, 290
  See also specific miracle descriptions
mission
  of the church today, 160
  to the Gentiles, 203
  of God, Jesus, and disciples, 148–53,
    155
  to the world, 203
missionary discourse, 146–63
Mollenkott, Virginia Ramey, 108n79
Moltmann, Jürgen, 35–36, 231, 328
Moses, 19, 25, 216, 266
  Jesus' parallels with, 6–7, 30, 38, 53,
    125, 138, 193, 195, 204, 213, 216,
    263, 287
  the Pentateuch, 287
  seat of, 265, 287
  the transfiguration, 212–15
mountaintops, 54–55
mustard seed, 73

faith the size of, 215–16
  parable of, 179–80
Myers, Wayne, 177, 182
mystery, 38, 314, 322, 331

Nazareth, 30, 32, 165
  rejection of Jesus in, 185, 188
new community, 219–41
Nicene Creed, 230
Niebuhr, H. Richard, 329
Nietzsche, Friedrich, 283
nonbelievers, 226, 317
nonviolence/nonretaliation, 9, 56, 83,
  84, 170, 234, 238, 258, 297–98
Nostra Aetate (Roman Catholic
  encyclical, 1965), 305

Old Testament. See Hebrew Scriptures
opposition, facing, 153–56, 164–72
ordinary people. See common people
ordination, 64, 231–32

Pagola, José A., 148–49, 153–54, 178,
  190–91, 277–78, 307
Pannenberg, Wolfhart, 332
parables, 13, 175–87, 254
  the bridesmaids, 13, 274–77
  the dragnet, 182–84
  the hidden treasure, 182
  the mustard seed, 179–80
  the pearl of great price, 182
  the scribe of the reign of God, 184
  the sheep and the goats, 278–81
  the sower, 176–79
  the talents, 274–77
  the ten bridesmaids, 274–77
  the two servants, 274–77
  the two sons, 47, 253–56
  the vineyard's tenants, 253–56
  the wedding banquet, 253–56
  the wise and foolish bridesmaids, 13,
    274–77
  the yeast, 179–80
paradidomi (handed over), 56, 152, 216,
  293
paralysis, 9, 58, 128, 132, 135, 141
Parousia. See second coming of Christ

passion and resurrection narrative, 33, 287
passion of Jesus, 31, 210–12, 252, 289–307
Passover, 289, 291, 294–96, 315, 319
patriarchy/partiarchal culture, 9–12, 24,
  81, 85, 109-10, 123, 129, 171,
  229, 237–40
Paul, 25n5, 68, 74, 83n28, 328, 329,
  340, 344
peace; peacemakers, 56, 99, 186, 234
Peacocke, Arthur, 37, 144
pearl of great price, parable of, 182
Pentateuch, 5, 263, 287
persecution, 5, 8, 29, 62, 77n13, 78,
  98, 101, 151–55, 177, 195, 207,
  253, 256, 262, 268, 271, 280–81,
  300, 305
Peter, 55, 57–58, 210–12, 237, 243–44,
  246–48, 297
  as "archetypal disciple," 57–58, 209
  denying Jesus, 13, 196, 289, 291,
    295–97, 300–301, 309, 315
  faith and doubt of, 195–96, 202
  and forgiving seventy-seven times,
    117, 226–27
  as martyr, 154
  mother-in-law, Jesus as healing,
    129–30
  power to "bind" and to "loose," 133,
    208, 225
  recognizing Jesus' identity, 206–9
  as "rock," 209
  Simon becoming Peter, 107
  the transfiguration, 212–15
  walking on water, 2, 196
Pharisees, 17, 63, 74, 128, 140, 172,
  256–68, 292
  charge that Jesus' power is demonic,
    137, 170
  conflict with, 197–200, 205–6
  descriptions of, 4–6, 14–15, 46n9,
    48, 69, 80, 83, 94, 99, 134, 169,
    205, 257, 261–68
  disciples of, 256–57
  and Jesus eating with sinners and tax
    collectors, 133–34
  as negative example, 265, 274–75

Pharisees (*continued*)
 opposition from, 164–65, 168–70,
  176, 178, 181, 183, 290, 335, 338
 signs, clamoring for, 171, 188, 205–6
 and Temple tax, 217
 See also religious leaders
phylacteries, 264
piety, 4, 89, 187, 262
 and hypocrisy, 47, 86, 90, 264
 true, 84–86, 88–89, 91, 93–95, 96,
  264, 280
Pilate, Pontius, 65, 287–90, 293, 296,
  299, 302–6, 309, 312–13, 335
 Herod and, 14–15, 17, 28
 wife of, 287, 303
Plato, 343–44
pluralism, religious, 18–20, 158–60
Polkinghorne, John, 145
Pollan, Michael, 192–93
possessions, 78, 121
 putting in their place, 91–93, 119
 risks of riches, 241–45
 See also treasure
poverty/the poor, 16–18, 50, 76–78,
  113, 118–19, 280
 problem of, 161–63
 the risks of riches, 241–45
 See also almsgiving
power, 16–18, 78. *See also* authority;
  deeds of power; greatness;
  leadership
powerless, the, 30–31, 221. *See also*
  children
prayer, 88–89, 102–21, 353. *See also*
  Lord's Prayer
priests; priesthood, 168, 252
 of all believers, 64
 Israel as "nation of priests," 4, 197
 priestly ministry of Jesus, 173–74
 See also chief priests
process theology, 345
prophecies, 32, 173
prophet, priest, and king, 60, 173–74, 293
prophets, 263
 feeding miracles by, 204
 Jesus as prophet, 173–74, 206

rejected, theme of, 213
true and false, 98
See also law and the prophets;
 individual names, e.g., Elijah
prosekynēsan (worshiped), 336
"prosperity gospel," 160–61
prostitutes, 24, 69, 201, 254
Protestant Reformation. *See*
 Reformation, Protestant
providence, divine, 92, 112, 144, 191,
  193, 241
purity, 49, 126–29, 268
 authentic, 199–200
 ritual, 4, 46–47, 79, 134–36, 197–99,
  231, 261–62
 of the Temple, 252

questions, four difficult, 256–60
Qumran community, 5, 217, 224

rabbis; rabbi, the title, 57, 221, 264–65,
  296–97
Rahab, 24
rank, reward and, 245–49
ransom, 248
 ransom theory of atonement, 208, 330
reality
 divine and created, 35
 present, 70, 73, 74, 78, 186
real presence, divine, 37–38, 314,
  316–17, 322, 348
reciprocity, 85, 104
 generosity vs., 83, 280
reconciliation, 37, 44, 100, 116, 118, 173,
  178, 215, 224, 226, 234, 284, 316
 love and, 81–82
 sacraments and, 318–19, 322
redemption, 36, 73–74, 112, 186, 234,
  248, 316, 330, 345
 creation and, 325
 judgment as ordered to, 226, 270,
  281–85
Reformation, Protestant, 140, 157, 209
Reformed theology, 16, 18–19, 76n11,
  160, 162, 172–73, 198, 317
reign of God, 9, 18, 45, 49, 51, 55,

57, 72–78, 82–85, 92, 97–98,
111–12, 155
Jesus and, 186–87
parables illustrating, 13, 175–87
and reward/rank, concern for, 245–49
sacraments and, 319–21
religious and ethnic divisions, crossing, 288
religious leaders, 1, 5–6, 28, 51, 133–34,
138, 152, 159–60, 164–65, 202,
206, 221, 236, 246–47, 251–55,
260, 270, 304, 311
description of, 14–15
hypocrisy of, 88–89, 254, 261–66
Jesus as undermining authority of,
123–25
Matthew as cautionary tale for, 6
oppression by, 167–68
parables about, 254–56, 274–75
as rejecting Jesus, 164–67, 262, 309
as rejecting John the Baptist, 165–67
and titles, 264–65
today, 6, 351
See also authorities, elite; chief priests;
Pharisees; Sadducees; scribes
religious pluralism, 18–20, 158–60
renewal, 3, 73–74, 112, 186, 244–45,
284, 351
repentance, 43–51, 56, 60, 63–64, 72,
166–67, 171, 186, 190, 207, 256,
309, 315, 326
resistance, 16–17, 39, 120, 128, 234, 323,
348, 351
and solidarity, 345–47
rest, 167–68
resurrection, 135–36, 312
and God's saving work, 329–30, 340
what it is, 343
resurrection of Jesus, 287, 312, 329–31,
335–48
resurrection of the body, 65, 343–48
revelation, divine, 11, 37, 52–54, 112,
140, 164, 166, 195, 212, 303, 326
reward and rank, 245–49
Rich, Adrienne, 234–35
riches. See possessions; treasure
righteousness, 26, 50–52, 76, 85-86, 99

the "designated righteous," 69
higher, calling to, 26, 80–86, 242, 303
Ringe, Sharon, 200–202
risen Lord, 337–40
Roman Catholic theology, 59–60, 64,
74–75, 140, 157, 209, 232, 305, 316
Roman Empire, 16, 67, 90
Russell, Letty, 230
Ruth, 24–25

Sabbath, 7, 26, 80, 87, 124, 168–69, 172,
197, 262–63, 295
Sacks, Jonathan, 160
sacraments, 174, 314–22. See also
baptism; eucharist
sacrifice, 327
blood, 294, 304
Christ's perfect, 319, 322–23, 327
living, 173, 319
mercy vs., 68, 125, 134, 168, 267
of praise, 319
Sadducees, 4, 48, 140, 188, 217, 256–60
conflict with, 205–6
descriptions of, 4, 46n10, 205, 262
See also religious leaders
salt and light, 78–79
salvation, 12, 18, 34, 50, 136–37, 195,
255, 285, 325
faith and works, 74–75, 83n28
resurrection and God's saving work,
328–30, 340
salvation history, 19, 25, 150, 255, 325,
338
sanctification, 74
Sanhedrin, 28, 123, 209, 244, 289, 294
Satan, 55, 66–68, 170, 205, 208, 210–11
Schleiermacher, Friedrich, 114, 324
science, 142–45
scribes, 55, 69, 80, 99, 128, 132–33, 247,
261, 265–66, 275, 289–90, 338
as anti-type, 265
description of, 210
parable of the scribe of the reign of
God, 184
would-be follower of Jesus, 130
See also religious leaders

sea, 15, 131, 194–96, 207, 338
Sea of Galilee, 55, 194–97
second coming of Christ, 48, 71, 272, 280–81, 352
Second Helvetic Confession, 19, 75, 184
Seeds of Heaven, The: Sermons on the Gospel of Matthew (Taylor), 191, 212, 233, 273
Senior, Donald, 77, 91, 169–70, 202, 204
September 11, 2001, 100
Septuagint, 25, 83, 87, 118, 208
Sermon on the Mount, 55, 70–122, 186, 352–53
    central elements of, 98-99
servants/servanthood, 51, 105, 170, 172, 215, 228, 245, 277, 295
    greatness as service, 9, 229, 247, 264
    parable of, 274–77
    See also centurion's servant, healing of; suffering servant
seven, the number, 24
seven woes, 266–69
Shammai School, 257n29
sheep
    and goats, parable of, 278–81
    See also shepherd/sheep image
shekinah, 213, 226
shepherd/sheep image, 14–15, 138, 147, 150, 222–23, 226, 278–79, 351
Sigal, Phillip, 239
signs, 27, 253
    Pharisees as clamoring for, 140, 171, 205–6, 335
    and the things signified, 316–17
Simon Peter. *See* Peter
sin, 325–26, 345
    grace and, 83n28
    post-baptismal, 62
    suffering and, 132
    See also evil; forgiveness: of sin
sinners, 8, 10, 12, 50, 61, 63, 68, 120, 148, 183, 229, 246, 309–10
    Jesus eating with, 126, 133–34, 137, 197, 295–96, 315, 322
Sittler, Joseph, 187, 328
slaughter of the innocents, 38–39, 48, 207, 303

Soelle, Dorothee, 323
solidarity, 39, 50, 63, 113, 152, 217, 220, 240, 280, 323
    and God's saving work, 328,345-46
    as last word for Matthew, 348
    resistance and, 345–47
    unity as, 231
Song, C. S., 187
Son of David. *See* David: Son of
Son of God, 33–34, 52–53, 55, 65, 126, 131, 140, 189, 196–97, 205, 207, 211, 214, 244, 260, 296, 298–99, 310, 312
Son of Man, 126, 168, 181, 198, 213, 247–48, 261, 271, 278–80, 295, 299, 331, 335
    title, theological significance of, 244
"sonship," 33, 51
soteriology, 34
soul, 284–85, 343–44
sowing, parables about, 176–79
sparrow, God's care for, 112, 153
Spirit. *See* Holy Spirit
Stendahl, Krister, 186–87
storm, Jesus' calming of, 130–31, 205, 207, 312
substitutionary theory of atonement, 327, 331
Suchocki, Marjorie, 104, 111, 282
suffering, 38–39, 144, 145, 269, 272, 311
    of Christ, 210–12, 247–48, 309
    "drink of the cup," 247
    God as fellow sufferer, 328
    innocent/undeserved, 252
    of others, attentiveness to, 149, 278, 348
    sacrificial, 322
    sin and, 132, 148
    See also cross; passion of Jesus; *specific topics,* e.g., poverty
suffering servant, 129–30, 248, 302, 313
supersessionism, 7–8, 255
Swift, Jonathan, 159
synagogue leader's daughter, Jesus as healing, 134–36

Talbert, C. H., 97
talents, parable of, 274–77

Tamar, 24
Tannehill, Robert, 84
tax collectors, 8, 10, 69, 125–26, 133–34, 137, 183, 197, 226, 229, 254, 315
taxes, 17, 115, 197, 216–18, 257–58
Taylor, Barbara Brown, 191, 212, 233, 273
Taylor, James, 31n19
teaching of Jesus, 70–122, 146–63
    the coming judgment, 261–85
    the new community, 219–36
    parables of God's reign, 175–87
    in the Temple, 253, 298
    See also Sermon on the Mount
Temple in Jerusalem, 53, 88, 110, 132, 168–69, 172, 208, 272
    chief priests and, 289, 297, 301–2, 337
    the "desolating sacrilege," 271
    destruction of, 2–4, 46n10, 218, 251, 257n29, 262, 269, 299
    Jesus' cleansing of, 236, 250, 252, 270, 290
    Jesus healing in, 252, 270
    Jesus leaving, 269–70
    Jesus as reordering, 124, 215
    Jesus teaching in, 253, 298
    religious leaders denounced for hypocrisy, 261
    shekinah, 213
    tax, 197, 216–17
    tearing of curtain in, 311, 346
    See also temptation: of Jesus
temptation
    and evil, 119–21
    of Jesus, 52–55, 119–20, 205, 298
    petition for deliverance from, 107, 113, 115, 121
ten bridesmaids, parable of, 13, 274–77
Teresa, Mother, 280
Tillich, Paul, 165
tithing, 4, 80, 262, 267–68
titles, 264–65
tomb of Jesus, 14, 335–36
tombs, whitewashed, 266, 268
Torah, 3–4, 46n9, 80, 97, 124, 134, 169, 184, 197–98, 205, 262–63, 271.
    See also law
tradition, 198–99

transfiguration, the, 212–15
transubstantiation, 316
Traveling Mercies (Lamott), 105, 118
treasure, 91, 184, 232, 241–42
    hidden, parable of, 182
    See also possessions
trespasses. See debts and debtors
Trinitarian formula, 59, 65
tsedaqah, 50, 76, 87, 279
Tutu, Desmond, 118
twelve, the number, 147–48
two servants, parable of, 274–77
two sons, parable of, 47, 253–56
two ways, admonition of, 97–99

unbelief, 128, 171, 178, 226, 285. See also doubt
unity, 230–32

Vanstone, W. H., 39
vengeance, 82, 227–28, 281
Via, Dan, 86, 94, 98
vineyard parables, 253–56
violence, 38, 50, 78, 85, 100–101, 121, 125, 155
    of the cross, reframing, 309
    religiously sanctioned, 159–60
    responses to, 84, 234, 297–98, 309
    See also nonviolence
vipers, 15, 46, 170, 266, 268
virgins, parable of (ten bridesmaids), 13, 274–77
Vogel, Christine, 292
Volf, Miroslav, 121, 227, 283–84, 346–47
Voltaire, 305

walking on water, miracles, 2, 141, 194–97, 312, 340
warnings, 72, 97–98
"wars and rumors of wars," 271
washing of hands, 51, 198, 267, 304
water, 51, 104. See also baptism
wealth. See possessions; treasure
wedding banquet, 134, 253–56, 320–21
wheat, weeds and, 48–49, 178, 232–33, 278, 284–85

Whitehead, Alfred North, 49, 224, 344–45
Williams, Delores, 322
Williams, Rowan, 319n15
will of God, 47–48, 50, 74, 77, 98, 124, 172–73, 199, 276
    Lord's Prayer petition, 107, 110–13, 120
Wilshire, Bruce, 86
Winters, Michael, 266, 321, 338, 339
Wisdom/Wisdom teachings, 13, 166–67, 171–72
wisdom and foolishness, 13, 98, 274–77
wise men, three, 2, 15, 20, 27–32, 126, 150, 171, 196, 203, 287–88, 303
woes, seven, 266–69
women, 10–14, 24, 180, 229
    birth pangs, feminine image of, 272
    at the cross, 312–14
    and discipleship, 13–14, 313
    Gentile, 24–25
    God as likened to mother, 269

at Jesus' tomb, 14, 336
in Matthew's genealogy, 24–25
and ordination, 64
portrayal in Gospel of Matthew, 12, 238
    See also individual names/ descriptions
Word of God, 55, 120, 174, 198–99, 232
works
    faith and, 74–75
    rabbis debating two kinds of, 291
World Communion of Reformed Churches and the Lutheran World Federation, 160, 230n17
worship, 336
Wright, N. T., 46n9, 151, 257n29

yeast, parable of, 179–80
yoke, 17–18, 168

zimzum, 35–36
Zwingli, Huldrych, 59–60, 315–17

Lightning Source UK Ltd.
Milton Keynes UK
UKHW011920060120
356461UK00001B/90/P